INVISIBLE HANDS, RUSSIAN EXPERIENCE, AND SOCIAL SCIENCE

This book investigates cases in which national and international activities have gone massively wrong, entailing seriously negative consequences, and in which the sophisticated analytical models of social science have ceased to be helpful. Illustrations range from the global financial crisis to the failure to achieve speedy systemic change in the Former Soviet Union and the failure to achieve development in the Third World. The analysis uses as a backdrop long-term Russian history and short-term Russian encounters with unrestrained capitalism to develop a framework that is based in the so-called new institutionalism. Understanding the causes of systemic failure is shown to require an approach that spans the increasingly specialized subdisciplines of modern social science. Demonstrating that increasing theoretical sophistication has been bought at the price of a loss of perspective and the need for sensitivity to the role of cultural and historical specificity, the book pleads the case for a new departure in seeking to model the motives for human action.

Stefan Hedlund was appointed professor of Soviet and East European Studies at Uppsala University in 1990. Over the years since then, he has published extensively on the breakup of the Soviet order, on attempted Russian reforms, and on the importance of historical legacies. Professor Hedlund has been a frequent commentator in the media and has traveled and lectured widely; he has spent two sabbatical semesters at Harvard University as well as briefer stays at the Kennan Institute and George Washington University in Washington, D.C.; Stanford University; and Hokkaido University in Sapporo, Japan. His most recent publications include *Russian Path Dependence* (2005), *Russia since 1980* (Cambridge University Press, with Steven Rosefielde, 2009), and *Authoritarian Market Economy* (Chinese edition, 2011).

For Lilian, with love,
as always

Invisible Hands, Russian Experience, and Social Science

Approaches to Understanding Systemic Failure

STEFAN HEDLUND
Uppsala University

CAMBRIDGE
UNIVERSITY PRESS

CAMBRIDGE UNIVERSITY PRESS
Cambridge, New York, Melbourne, Madrid, Cape Town,
Singapore, São Paulo, Delhi, Tokyo, Mexico City

Cambridge University Press
32 Avenue of the Americas, New York, NY 10013-2473, USA

www.cambridge.org
Information on this title: www.cambridge.org/9780521768108

First published 2011

Printed in the United States of America

A catalog record for this publication is available from the British Library.

Library of Congress Cataloging in Publication data
Hedlund, Stefan, 1953–
Invisible hands, Russian experience, and social science: approaches
to understanding systemic failure / Stefan Hedlund.
p.   cm.
Includes bibliographical references and index.
ISBN 978-0-521-76810-8 (hbk.)
1. Economics.   2. Economic development – Russia (Federation)   3. Economic
history.   4. Financial crises.   I. Title.
HB171.H475   2011
330–dc22   2010054311

ISBN 978-0-521-76810-8 Hardback

Contents

Preface

Things will and do at times go wrong, and actions taken will at times have unintended consequences. As such there is nothing at all remarkable in any of this. Things that go wrong will most often work themselves out on their own, and unintended consequences will most often be compensated for by other action. What has prompted the writing of this book is a growing realization of the significance to social science theorizing of cases where none of this is true, that is, where things go wrong to the point that systemic mechanisms of self-correction break down and the analytical models of social science cease to be helpful.

The essence of the argument is that such extraordinary cases of systemic failure represent causal chains of events that may be fully understood only by taking into account a wide range of factors that are no longer possible to house in toto within any of the increasingly specialized subdisciplines of modern social science. The reasons for the latter are simple and essentially represent a trade-off. Increasing theoretical sophistication has been bought at the price of a loss of perspective and of sensitivity to the controversial roles of cultural and historical specificity. In routine situations of marginal change, the benefits of this development clearly outweigh the costs. In cases, however, of major societal transformations that result in systemic failure, an important part of the problem will be that impressions of theoretical sophistication have produced overconfidence in the powers of prediction and of political action to achieve anticipated goals.

To illustrate these rather bold claims we may recall the fall of the Berlin Wall, a momentous event that was widely perceived – at the time – as the dawn of a new era. The effective end of the Cold War was expected to bring in its wake a whole slew of good things, ranging from the "peace dividend" *it did* that would result from paring down military forces and the economic gains that would be derived from a transition from planned to market economy, to a new climate of fruitful international cooperation, and – especially – a new role for a Europe no longer divided by an Iron Curtain.

The high point on the latter count was marked in December 1991. Meeting in the small Dutch town of Maastricht, European leaders proudly agreed to launch their grand project of building a European Union (EU). Tacitly patterned as a United States of Europe, the EU would not only have its own parliament, its own government, and its own constitution. Most important, it would also have its own currency, to be supervised by a European Central Bank. The days when Henry Kissinger could quip about the absence of a phone number on which to contact Europe would be finally over.

Counting from the time of German unification in October 1990, the two decades that followed would bring home two essential and highly painful lessons. The first teaches what was hinted at earlier, namely, that things do not always take care of themselves, at least not with generally desirable outcomes. While deregulation, for example, may be essential for market economy, it carries no guarantee that the outcome will be good economic performance, and while holding elections may be essential to a democratic system, it carries no guarantee that the outcome will be democracy. The second lesson is that even if system managers do recognize that policy intervention may at times be critically needed, they will face serious limitations on what can be achieved, and they will run serious risks that actions taken will produce outcomes that differ greatly from those intended.

Both of these may at first appear to be rather trivial. Yet, as will be argued throughout this book, many of the bad things that happen in this world can be led back to a failure to consider the deeper message that is embedded here. As further illustration, we shall advance four cataclysmic events that were played out over the two decades from 1991 until 2010. All will serve to underline the need for a new departure not only in policy making but also, and perhaps more important, for a new departure in those social sciences that claim to underpin the making of good policy and the building of good society.

The first of these events was the sudden collapse of Soviet power, which in a stroke redrew the global security architecture. Entailing the end of three artificially created federations – in addition to the USSR also those of Yugoslavia and Czechoslovakia – it brought in its wake dissolution of the Warsaw Pact of military cooperation and of the COMECON association for economic cooperation among socialist states within the Soviet sphere of interest. Two dimensions of the ensuing process of adaptation are of particular importance.

An immediate consequence of the "democratic revolutions" that spread across Central Europe was loud calls for national self-determination. Once so proudly touted by Woodrow Wilson, in his fourteen-points speech to the U.S. Congress, such calls would now be associated with virulent nationalism that in some cases resulted in ethnic tension, ethnic cleansing, and bloody civil wars. Given the clearly instrumental way in which aspects of culture and history played into the process, with at times disastrous outcomes, the lesson was that state-building turned out not to be so easy after all, and clearly not something that could be simply left to its own devices.

In a less spectacular dimension, the ambitions to embark on a "transition," away from central planning and communist rule, would again illustrate that matters at hand were vastly more complex than had been anticipated. The end of Soviet power also marked the end of a distinctive social order, resting on institutions that were introduced to suppress democracy, market economy, and the rule of law. Early beliefs that post-Soviet reconstruction could proceed by simply rebooting the system failed to consider that over time those institutions had become associated with norms, beliefs, and expectations that by the time of dissolution were deeply embedded. They would in consequence not be easily amenable to deliberate change by simply rewriting the formal rules of the game.

The second of our four events was the U.S.-led invasion of Iraq in March 2003. Representing a breach of international law (probably), it also served to create deep ruptures within the alliance of Western powers (definitely). Ignoring all speculation about the role of oil as a motivating force, there can be little doubt that those who pleaded for the operation had wider ambitions than simply ridding the world of Saddam Hussein and the weapons of mass destruction that he was alleged to possess.

The grand ambition was that by introducing democracy in Iraq, a host of despotic regimes in the Arab world would come under intense pressure to follow suit. The world in consequence would come to witness a new wave of democratization, coupled with the emergence of successful market economies that promised tantalizing opportunities for new business. As we now know, it did not work out quite like that. The effective outcome instead was to strengthen Iran, to destabilize Pakistan, to aggravate even further the Arab-Israeli conflict, and to give Al Qaeda a greatly expanded role.

The message again has much to do with the role of culture and history, as determinants of the functioning of clan-based societies and as forces of motivation for deep-rooted antagonisms between Islam and the Western world. At stake here was the presumed universality of Western values. The vision in itself was very clear. If only given the opportunity, all the nations of this world would gladly opt for the type of social order that has evolved in Western Europe and North America and in a few outliers. From a social science perspective, this brought into question some truly fundamental issues. Following widely acclaimed approaches of agency and functionalism, the task was seen to be to simply create opportunity and good things would follow. Well, they did not and lessons are due to be learned.

The third event was the global financial crisis that erupted in September 2008, conveniently dated to and associated with the collapse of the venerable investment firm Lehman Brothers. The shock and awe produced by this event provided sordid insights into the myopic worldview of financial markets and of government agencies responsible for oversight and policy management. The valuable time that was lost debating whether it really *was* a crisis may be taken as a first indication of the price that would have to be paid for failing to understand how markets really work.

What produced the crisis was a combination of hard and soft factors. On the former count we may note a string of legislation designed to liberate markets and thus to allegedly improve their performance. While all of this represented necessary conditions for the crisis to occur, none was also sufficient. What really made the crisis possible was the long wave of neo-liberal ideology of privatization and deregulation that was inspired by Milton Friedman and implemented by politicians following the lead of Margaret Thatcher and Ronald Reagan.

Reflected here is a need to draw a line between legitimate self-interest, without which no market economy will be possible, and the presence of endemic human greed, which constitutes by far the most serious threat to the functioning of markets. While the outbreak of the crisis could in a technical sense be led back to actions such as the 1999 repeal of the (Glass-Steagall) Banking Act of 1933, the fundamental cause was the accelerating erosion of norms of self-restraint that went hand in hand with the emergence of a public culture of hard-nosed individualism. The question that emerges here is how the social sciences should model *homo economicus* and what the implications are for the pursuit of economic and other policies. Subsequent chapters will have much to say on these issues.

The fourth and final event is the renewed financial crisis that erupted in April 2010, when it suddenly dawned on European leaders just how close Greece was to state bankruptcy. Placing into focus the visions of European hubris that were expressed at Maastricht, the Greek crisis brought home two points. One was that critics had been right in pointing at the incompatibility between a common monetary policy and national fiscal policies, and the second that we live in a world where politics and vested interests will always trump ambitions to enforce formal rules that somehow get in the way.

In purely technical terms, it did look as though a solution had been found. The Stability and Growth Pact of 1997 was introduced to ensure that no member of the euro zone would be allowed to exceed set limits on public debt and on budget deficit as shares of gross domestic product (GDP). If all governments had abided by their commitments, all might have been well. The only problem was that governments look to their own interests first, and if those governments represent major powers then their breaches will go unpunished. Given that in the years preceding the crisis both Germany and France had been allowed to openly flaunt the Stability Pact with impunity, there seems to be some poetic justice in the fact that when Greece needed rescue they were the ones that would have to pay the highest price. What is reflected here is a serious problem of moral hazard, of leading governments into temptation to cheat and cook their books, and creditors to play along with obfuscation, all in the belief that in the end, when needed, help will be made available courtesy of the taxpayers.

Arriving on the heels of the global financial crisis, at a time when fragile recovery was seen to be on the way, the Greek crisis added renewed suffering to populations that again had no share in the blame. Recalling previous outbursts of anger about governments preferring to bail out bankers rather than households, it was revealing that the option of restructuring the credits so lavishly provided by bankers to Greece, while the going was good, was not even placed on the agenda. Protecting those who really were at fault remained a priority.

The notion of "systemic failure" will be used in the following to describe events of precisely these kinds and magnitudes. Looking back at what happened during the two decades under consideration, we will come away with impressions of outcomes that are widely different from the expectations that prevailed at the time when the new era dawned. The damage that has been done is substantial, and there is nothing to say that the books may at any time soon be closed on any of the four processes that have been outlined here.

This should certainly not be taken to imply that the world is coming to an end. In a long-run perspective there is nothing at all unique in any of this. History is replete with cases of financial crisis, of ethnic violence and civil wars, and of misguided government interventions aiming to implement change. What does make it all worth considering more closely is that the outcomes stand in such sharp contrast to initial expectations, and that we are still in a learning mode seeking to grasp what happened and why it happened.

As noted at the outset, our more specific understanding of "systemic failure" shall be set aside from the simple facts that things often do go wrong and that policies often do have unintended consequences. In most such cases, this is trivial and negative effects will somehow be ironed out by themselves. What we are concerned with here is different, namely, cases where things go massively wrong, and where systems and system managers fail to cope. The approach will be broad, in the sense of taking into consideration processes that are played out over the long run, over the medium term, and in the very short term.

Beginning with the long term, we shall be looking at cases of persistent failure to break out of suboptimal institutional solutions. This may be manifested in protracted historical processes of divergence between countries in economic development paths, as well as in more recent failures to escape poverty traps and infelicitous constellations of power that produce predatory regimes. The core challenge is that so many of these have proven so resistant to even determined ambitions to achieve change. The track record of foreign aid in the post–World War II era is, for example, not a happy one. Seeking to atone for colonialism, rich countries have put up massive amounts of aid but achieved little in the way of results. Structural adjustment programs and the like have been based on agency and functionalism, with little to show in terms of sustained reductions of deprivation. While some countries have succeeding in breaking out of poverty, notably China, they have as a rule not been the ones most heavily pampered by outside assistance.

In the medium term, we have two decades of ambitions by countries in the central and eastern parts of Europe to achieve a "transition" to democracy, market economy, and the rule of law. Given the wide variety of outcomes, we again have reason to question the assumption of universality. The agency approach of the "Washington Consensus" was limited to setting a few parameters, such as "getting the property rights right," and then to wait for the market to do the rest. The very fact that social science remains embroiled in debate over what went wrong and why, and indeed even over whether anything really *did* go wrong, shows that we are faced here with an issue of fundamental importance. Again it is also the case that those who have performed the best have as a rule not been those that were the most favored by outside advice and assistance – the case of Russia offering an outstanding illustration.

In the short term, we have the global financial crisis and the ensuing Greek turmoil. Both are stunning not only in the huge size of the losses and the political disruptions involved, but even more because both apparently arrived as total surprises to system managers. With the exception of a few whistleblowers, who were easily and conveniently ignored, nobody in positions of power saw it coming, on either occasion. Given the massive industry that has emerged to predict and forecast what markets will do, this is not a happy verdict. When push came to shove, when serious prediction and forecasting were most desperately needed, the systems failed. The fact that it has all happened so many times before, albeit perhaps not on the presently global scale, and that the same will likely happen many times again in the future illustrates that we are looking here at an endemic problem of quite some magnitude and significance.

Our approach to grappling with the issues laid out here is divided into three interwoven themes. One concerns the belief in notions of invisible hands that are assumed to guide action in socially desirable directions. The next holds up the role of Russian experience as a vital source of illustration, and the third will investigate what implications may be seen for social science theorizing.

Beginning with the belief in invisible hands that was famously introduced by Adam Smith, there has been a strong tendency in the liberal tradition to believe that things will indeed work themselves out – if only governments can be kept at bay. Quite in line with the agency approach, deregulating markets will generate good economic performance, holding elections will ensure democracy, and writing laws will produce the rule of law.

The problems that are encountered here move on two levels. One is that of individual actors, where reasonable assumptions about self-interest produce less obvious conclusions regarding the congruence between individual and collective good. While it has been recognized that such congruence may not always be at hand, deviations have often been regarded as aberrations that will iron themselves out. Little attention has in consequence been paid to such types of motivation for action that will determine the choice between rule-abiding and rule-evading behavior.

At the level of government we may find a similar belief in self-interest that drives governments to maximize the collective good, entailing ambitions to optimize taxation over time and to provide an optimal supply of public goods that may enhance the performance of markets. All will be consistent with ideals of accountability, transparency, and good governance. Again, however, we must take into account the presence of temptations to place narrow self-interest before the common good. The core question concerns what may cause governments to deviate from the good path and to proceed instead down a road that leads – in the extreme – toward predation and outright kleptocracy.

The challenge on both counts is to model the circumstances under which action will be taken that is consistent with or in contradiction to the collective good. If motivation for action is to be portrayed in terms of invisible hands, logic demands that such portrayal must include both options. In neither case may we talk of forces of nature, or of genetic predisposition, but merely of the presence of norms, beliefs, and expectations that are embedded in traditions, in collective memories, and in "culture" very broadly defined. While the wide attraction of presenting correlations between differences in economic performance and differences in soft variables such as religion may be taken as evidence that "culture matters," it still leaves open questions of causation and of remediability.

The second of our three themes is that of Russian historical experience, which will be used as a rich source of illustration. Four important reasons motivate this choice. One is that Russia has a long tradition of governance that has been distinctly market-contrary, serving to illustrate what may happen at the level of individual action when government interdicts freely negotiated horizontal contracting. Another is that there is an equally long tradition of change being implemented by intervention from above, with little or no participation from below, serving to illustrate limitations to the agency approach of undertaking political interventions. The third is that we have repeated cases both of state collapse (in 1598, 1917, and 1991) and of financial market collapse (in 1998), which may add to our understanding of the causes of systemic failure. The fourth and final reason to bring Russian experience into the account is that the presence of deep historical roots, going back to the fifteenth century and earlier, may help shed further light on theories of path dependence.

Our third overriding theme concerns the role of social science theorizing. It constitutes the mainstay of the account as a whole and is designed to blend lessons derived from the first two themes into a broad understanding of what causes systemic failure and what implications may be seen for how such causes should be understood. The core challenge rests in understanding motivation for action, which at the individual level may be viewed as a choice between work and shirk, or between value adding and purely redistributive activities. At the level of government, a distinction between rent *seeking* and rent *granting* may serve to illustrate how the provision of preferential treatment becomes embedded into personalized network relations, with negative implications for governance.

In general terms, it may be recognized that notions such as *homo economicus, homo politicus, homo sociologicus,* and indeed *homo sovieticus,* serve as convenient shorthand for sets of core assumptions that define the approaches of different social sciences. Building on what was said earlier about invisible hands, two theoretical challenges emerge. One is that these sets of core assumptions differ fundamentally on issues relating to individual action. Should action be modeled as instrumentally rational and forward looking, or as the result of individuals being captives of the past, mindless playthings with little or no latitude for deliberate choice? The other concerns the crucial importance of identifying what components of the institutional context of transactions will determine whether individuals will opt for rule-obedient or rule-evasive actions. Under what conditions may such choices cluster in the latter direction, to the extent that systemic failure results?

The argument will begin with an introductory *tour d'horison* that covers the global financial crisis, placed into the context of prior discussions on crises of capitalism, and the preceding Russian hyperdepression, viewed as illustration of what may happen when markets are suddenly liberated. The main purpose in providing this broad empirical background will be to set the tone for appreciating the full gravity of the problems that will be dealt with in the subsequent account.

Work on this book was begun in 2007, during a sabbatical semester at Harvard University's Davis Center for Russian and Eurasian Studies. I went there with the stated intention of writing a book about new institutionalism and the presence of reform-resistant institutions, as revealed by the complexities of post-Soviet transition. Although the scope of the book would subsequently be broadened and redefined, much of the essential groundwork was done during this stay. My gratitude to the Davis Center, and to friends and colleagues in residence there, is, as on previous occasions, deep and warmly felt. Special thanks must go to Tim Colton, Marshall Goldman, Loren Graham, Mark Kramer, Tom Owen, Richard Pipes, Tom Simons, and Lis Tarlow.

Time to rethink and refocus was provided by a generous grant from the Kennan Institute at the Woodrow Wilson Center, allowing me to spend a month in Washington, D.C., in the spring of 2008, at which time I also enjoyed the generous hospitality of the Institute for Russian, European and Eurasian Studies at George Washington University. Thanks go to Blair Ruble and especially to James Millar, an old and dear friend who is regrettably no longer among us. A final word of thanks must also go to Roland Hsui at Stanford University's Freeman Spogli Institute, where I enjoyed a brief but very productive stay as Anna Lindh scholar in December 2009.

Numerous colleagues have assisted in shepherding me along the path of rethinking and rewriting. Included here are four anonymous referees, tasked with reading the first book proposal submitted for review by Cambridge University Press and with commenting on my responses. Thanks in this context also go to Scott Parris, my editor at Cambridge, who has patiently maintained faith that my rewrites would in the end be worthwhile. Among those who have generously taken time to read the manuscript in full, and whose comments have been most valuable, special thanks must go to Archie Brown, Jukka Gronow, Philip Hanson, Eugene Huskey, David Lane, Thomas Owen, Richard Rose, and Heinrich Vogel. Finally, I also thank Nilay Akcamak for valuable research assistance and for help in preparing the index.

With due credit thus acknowledged, and with the usual proviso about accepting responsibility for all remaining errors and omissions, we may now proceed to the world of financial markets, a world where movements are swift and memories short, and where the mortal sin of greed may, at times of great hubris, even be touted as inherently good.

Introduction

The sudden onset of the global financial crisis triggered a whole series of shock waves that rippled through the global economy, causing major social and political dislocations along the way. As the media began fielding sweeping accusations of inherent corporate greed, as the root of the evil, financial district streets in New York and elsewhere filled with violent protesters demanding retribution. In consequence, corporate jets were grounded and corporate executives could be seen using high-occupancy vehicle (HOV) lanes when traveling to the U.S. Congress with pleas for taxpayer bailouts. At the height of the storm, financial market operators even elected to dress down in public, for fear of personal reprisals.

Driven by justifiable wrath from the side of those who lost not only jobs but in many cases also homes and life savings, politicians responded with shows of great resolve in hunting down the culprits. A prominent but far from isolated example was the Republican senator John McCain, who used a September 2008 presidential campaign rally to vow that if elected he would "put an end to the reckless conduct, corruption, and unbridled greed that have caused a crisis on Wall Street."[1] Sensing how the winds were blowing, others followed suit.

As such, there was nothing really strange in any of this. The collapse of major multinational corporations, some of which had been widely admired for their prowess, was followed by revelations of lavish bonus schemes and of self-serving corporate behavior that seemed to defeat even the wildest of fantasies. Culminating in the scandals surrounding Bernard Madoff, the perpetrator of the most massive Ponzi scheme ever, public anger broadened to include failures of financial oversight, exacerbated by accounts of

---

[1] See further http://www.motherjones.com/mojo/2008/09/mccain-attacks-wall-street-greed-while-83-wall-street-lobbyists-work-his-campaign (accessed on May 12, 2009).

whistleblowers allegedly having been ignored. The general atmosphere of *furore* against financial market sharps brought back literary memories of how Dante once placed those guilty of greed in the fourth circle of Hell.

Beyond the immediate outpouring of anger and emotional calls for retribution, the global financial crisis also resulted in more fundamental discussions about the nature of capitalism and of the modern market economic system. Erupting in the wake of the failure of neo-liberal economic reforms in Russia, it provided new momentum to long-standing criticism of neo-liberal economic policies more generally. Given the combined seriousness of the global recession of 2008–9, and of the preceding hyperdepression that ravaged Russia in the 1990s, it is rather understandable that familiar old debates about the eventual fate of capitalism would re-emerge, with some even expressing glee at its pending demise. We shall have more to say about this later.

Less politicized settings were marked by more balanced reflection on matters such as the increasing attraction of Keynesianism over monetarism. Anticipating the dawn of a new era of greater government intervention in the market, some expressed worries that such intervention would overshoot, resulting in impediments to growth. More broadly, arguments were also made on the superior virtues of, say, German "social market economy" over the alleged greed of Wall Street.

We shall have no ambition here to follow in any of these tracks. Aiming to penetrate beyond such largely political and ideological debates that concern a poorly defined "crisis of capitalism," we shall prefer instead to probe for causes of systemic failure that are inherent, and firmly rooted, in the set of institutional arrangements that constitutes what we know as market economy. The scope of the investigation will in consequence be much broader than simply financial markets.

Speculating on the role of capitalism beyond the subprime mortgage crisis, Amartya Sen notes, "The question that arises most forcefully now concerns the nature of capitalism and whether it needs to be changed." Arguing that the "idea of capitalism did in fact have an important role historically," but that "by now that usefulness may well be fairly exhausted," he points to a need to discuss what "kind of economics … is needed today."[2]

Our approach in this text will depart from the latter part of this statement. More specifically, it will investigate how economics has grappled with the inherent contradiction between self-interested behavior that is value

---

[2]   Sen, Amartya (2009), "Capitalism beyond the Crisis," *New York Review of Books*, vol. 56, no. 5, p. 1 (cited from www.nybooks.com/articles/22490, accessed on May 14, 2009).

adding, and that tallies well with the ideal of Smithian laissez-faire, and the opposite case of behavior that degenerates into pure greed, with broad – and presently all too obvious – repercussions for the stability and functioning of the market economic system.

It will be argued, rather boldly, that the global financial crisis combined with the previous experience of failed systemic transformation in post-Soviet Russia – and indeed with several decades of failed ambitions to promote development in the Third World – to bring home the need for a new departure in social science as a whole. As evidenced by the rather dismal outcomes, the theoretical and practical tools that have been available to deal with problems inherent in these processes have simply not been up to the task. Above all, this has been true with regard to the role of cultural and historical specificity in determining how actors will respond to changes in opportunity sets.

The core of the theoretical challenge that emerges here may be captured in Lionel Robbins's statement that "the pursuit of self-interest, unrestrained by suitable institutions, carries no guarantee of anything but chaos."[3] Culled from his *The Theory of Economic Policy in English Classical Political Economy*, it harbors three broad research questions. The *first* asks why it is that the Smithian call for deregulation, and the associated belief in the workings of the invisible hand, may not always lead to salutary outcomes. The *second* queries how we should understand those "suitable institutions" that may prevent chaos; and the *third* investigates if, having identified what is needed, we also have a theory that may help in devising successful deliberate intervention, aimed at securing a high-performance economy.

Although the book will make frequent reference to the main forces that served to generate what has come to be known as the "Rise of the West," and to questions regarding why this experience has not been easily replicated in the Third World, empirical illustrations will in the main be drawn from Russian tradition. The reasons are simple. While the global financial crisis may offer plentiful input for a discussion on how legitimate self-interest may degenerate into pure greed, with devastating outcomes, it will fall far short of providing the combined insights inherent in Russia's long-term record of market-contrary governance, and in its proudly pronounced ambition, following the collapse of the Soviet Union, to implement radical "systemic change."

[3] Robbins, Lionel (1952), *The Theory of Economic Policy in English Classical Political Economy*, London: Macmillan, p. 56.

Recalling how firmly the latter project was rooted in a belief in the superiority of markets over physical planning and how firmly those advocating reform by way of "shock therapy" were united in calling for sweeping deregulation as a panacea to free up healthy market forces, we are faced with a serious need to explain how the actual outcome could be hyperdepression, hyperinflation, mass pauperization and a serious public health disaster.[4]

Part of the answer will surely rest in the fact that a variety of vested short-term interests were successful in corrupting the reform process and that measures actually implemented in consequence fell far short of visions projected by the reformers. More fundamentally, however, we shall argue that the design of such reform proposals that were associated with the "Washington Consensus," of which we shall have more to say later, reflected fundamental theoretical misperceptions that call for a reassessment of our understanding not only of central economic planning but also of the ideal of functioning market economy.[5]

Our ambition to undertake such reassessment shall proceed within the broad realm of new institutionalism, with particular emphasis on the interaction between formal rules, informal norms, and mechanisms of enforcement that has been suggested by Douglass North.[6] Seeking to explain the root causes of the global financial crisis and of the failure of post-Soviet deregulation to secure the envisioned efficiency gains, we shall navigate between the emphasis of new institutional economics on the role of transaction costs in determining choices between market and hierarchy, as laid out by Oliver Williamson,[7] and the fundamental argument of new

---

[4]	Hedlund, Stefan (1999), *Russia's "Market" Economy: A Bad Case of Predatory Capitalism*, London: UCL Press.

[5]	A somewhat similar argument on theoretical misunderstanding was made by Joseph Stiglitz in the spring of 1999, in the wake of the August 1998 Moscow financial meltdown. His claim, however, referred to a lack of appreciation of developments within modern economics, and a lack of understanding of the special conditions of transition. See Stiglitz, Joseph E. (1999), "Whither Reform? Ten Years of the Transition," available on http://siteresources.worldbank.org/INTABCDEWASHINGTON1999/Resources/stiglitz. pdf (accessed on October 1, 2009).

[6]	North, Douglass C. (1990a), *Institutions, Institutional Change and Economic Performance*, Cambridge: Cambridge University Press. See also North, Douglass C. (1986), "The New Institutional Economics," *Journal of Institutional and Theoretical Economics*, vol. 142, no. 1, North, Douglass C. (1991), "Institutions," *Journal of Economic Perspectives*, vol. 5, no. 1, and North, Douglass C. (1993a), "Institutions and Credible Commitment," *Journal of Institutional and Theoretical Economics*," vol. 149, no. 1.

[7]	Williamson, Oliver E. (1975), *Markets and Hierarchies: Analysis and Antitrust Implications*, New York: Free Press, Williamson, Oliver E. (1985a), *The Economic Institutions of Capitalism*, New York: Free Press, Williamson, Oliver E. (1985b), "Reflections on the New Institutional Economics," *Journal of Institutional and Theoretical Economics*, vol. 141,

economic sociology, originally suggested by Mark Granovetter, that motivation for action is embedded in social structures.[8]

The Russian experience is eminently suited to help in our search for answers to the questions posed here for one major reason: for centuries before the Soviet experiment, Russian tradition was consistently market-contrary, and economic performance in consequence was below par. Given that every instance of relaxing control and repression was followed by reversal of the *status quo ante*, at times after periods of major dislocation and predatory behavior, we may conclude that the "suitable institutions" called for by Lionel Robbins were never successfully put into place. Given, moreover, that repeated attempts to implement change were devised as deliberate top-down interventions, we have substantial empirical illustration of what types of obstacles may arise to impede success in such endeavors.

The more specific ambition of this text to capture the role of culture and history will expand on the author's previous ambition to formulate a theory of Russian path dependence.[9] It will do so by combining theories of historical institutionalism suggested by political scientists[10] with arguments by economists on historical economics and historical specificity.[11] Overall, the search will be implemented against a background of the old American school of institutionalism and of the broader evolution of social science over the past couple of centuries.

Before proceeding to the account proper, we shall expand on what was said in the preface about invisible hands and about Russian experience. On the former count, a review of the global financial crisis will be made and contrasted against earlier discussions on crises of capitalism. On the latter, a

---

no. 1, Williamson, Oliver E. (1996), *The Mechanisms of Governance*, New York: Oxford University Press.

[8] Granovetter, Mark (1985), "Economic Action and Social Structure: The Problem of Embeddedness," *American Journal of Sociology*, vol. 91, no. 3. See also White, Harrison (1981), "Where do Markets Come From?," *American Journal of Sociology*, vol. 87, no. 3.

[9] Hedlund, Stefan (2005), *Russian Path Dependence*, London: Routledge.

[10] Thelen, Kathleen (1999), "Historical Institutionalism in Comparative Politics," *Annual Review of Political Science*, vol. 2, no. 1, Pierson, Paul (2000), "Increasing Returns, Path Dependence, and the Study of Politics," *American Political Science Review*, vol. 94, no. 2.

[11] David, Paul A. (1993), "Historical Economics in the Long Run: Some Implications of Path Dependence," in Graeme D. Snooks (ed.), *Historical Analysis in Economics*, London: Routledge, David, Paul A. (1994), "Why Are Institutions the 'Carriers of History?' Path Dependence and the Evolution of Conventions, Organizations and Institutions," *Structural Change and Economic Dynamics*, vol. 5, no. 2, Hodgson, Geoffrey M. (2001), *How Economics Forgot History: The Problem of Historical Specificity in Social Science*, London and New York: Routledge, Hodgson, Geoffrey M. (2004), *The Evolution of Institutional Economics: Agency, Structure and Darwinism in American Institutionalism*, London and New York: Routledge.

review of Russian experience of post-Soviet reform will be added, focusing on how the freeing up of markets produced not increased value added but instead a hyperdepression and a host of social ills.

All will be done with the intention of setting the stage for approaching in more theoretical terms the fundamental conflict between legitimate self-interest and pure greed that constitutes the mainstay of the account as a whole.

INVISIBLE HANDS

Approaching the sensitive question of greed, we shall have to make a caveat. Although our purpose is not to moralize but to theorize, morality does play an important role in determining individual action. Much emphasis shall in consequence have to be placed on such processes of public norm formation that may inhibit or encourage individual self-interest seeking, beyond what Adam Smith once had in mind. In order to prepare the ground for incorporating such considerations, we shall start our journey in Hollywood.

When Greed Was Good

On December 11, 1987, the motion picture *Wall Street* was released in 730 theaters across the United States. It grossed $4.1 million over the opening weekend, and then went on to make a total of $43.8 million in North America.[12] Directed by Oliver Stone, it featured Michael Douglas as Gordon Gekko, a highly successful but totally unscrupulous corporate raider, and Charlie Sheen as Bud Fox, an ambitious young stockbroker who starts out idolizing Gekko and ends up in the hands of the Securities and Exchange Commission, accused of having leaked insider information.

The picture is relevant for our present purpose simply because it so admirably captures the ethics and morals – or rather lack thereof – among Wall Street movers and shakers in the heady days of the 1980s.[13] In one of its key

---

[12] See http://www.boxofficemojo.com/movies/?id=wallstreet.htm (accessed on November 5, 2008).

[13] With an uncanny sense of timing, in September 2009 Oliver Stone began shooting a sequel, titled *Wall Street 2: Money Never Sleeps*, which, given the events following September 2008, held every promise of attracting an even greater audience (http://www.nytimes.com/2009/09/08/movies/08stone.html, accessed on January 18, 2010). It was somehow symptomatic that while the original had acquired cult status on U.S. financial markets, when Stone wanted access to bank offices and trading rooms as background for shooting the sequel, he would have to turn to the Royal Bank of Canada.

scenes, Gekko addresses the board and shareholders of a fictitious company called Teldar paper:

The point is, ladies and gentlemen, that greed, for lack of a better word, is good. Greed is right. Greed works. Greed clarifies, cuts through and captures the essence of the evolutionary spirit. Greed, in all of its forms, greed for life, for money, for love, knowledge, has marked the upward surge of mankind, and greed, you mark my words, will not only save Teldar paper, but that other malfunctioning corporation called the USA.[14]

An important reason that this statement has been so widely cited is that it evokes a long tradition of condemnation in Western culture, and especially in the Christian faith. Harking back to the biblical saying that "the love of money is a root of all kinds of evil,"[15] greed has been traditionally listed as one of seven deadly sins that may lead to eternal damnation.[16] In his *Summa Theologica*, which summarizes the arguments on most if not all points of Western Christian theology, Thomas Aquinas wrote that greed was "a sin against God, just as all mortal sins, in as much as man condemns things eternal for the sake of temporal things."[17]

What happened among theologians gradually also made inroads into the secular world. Beginning in the early fourteenth century, the time when the *Summa* was written, writers and painters began to develop the theme of the seven deadly sins, as a result of which the latter became ingrained into the broader cultural patterns of what would come to be known as Western civilization.

---

[14] See http://www.youtube.com/watch?v=JaKkuJVy2YA (accessed on November 5, 2008). Stone allegedly had found inspiration for Gekko's speech in a commencement address by U.S. financier Ivan Boesky, held at the UC Berkeley School of Business Administration on May 18, 1986. In his address, Boesky informed hopeful market operators that "Greed is all right; by the way, I think greed is healthy. You can be greedy and still feel good about yourself." Boesky himself would move on to serve two years in prison and pay a $100 million fine for insider trading, in addition to which he was barred for life from working in the financial markets. (See further http://www.answers.com/topic/ivan-boesky, accessed on November 11, 2008.)

[15] 1 Timothy 6:10.

[16] The Catholic Church draws a line between venial sins that are relatively minor and mortal sins that can lead to eternal damnation – unless either absolved through the sacrament of confession or forgiven through perfect contrition on the part of the penitent. The seven deadly sins are pride (*superbia*), greed (*avaritia*), lust (*luxuria*), envy (*invidia*), gluttony (*gula*), wrath (*ira*), and sloth (*acedia*).

[17] The *Summa* was written over the years 1265–1274 and was left unfinished when its author passed away. For a modern edition, see Aquinas, Saint Thomas (1981), *Summa Theologica: Complete English Edition in Five Volumes*, London: Sheed & Ward. The quote may in this edition be found in volume three, p. 1680.

8 *Introduction*

An outstanding example is Dante Alighieri, whose magnum opus, the *Divina Commedia*, earned its author a prominent place in history.[18] The background to the emergence of this work is of particular importance here. At the time of its writing, Florence was badly afflicted by internal strife between families affiliated with the pro-Papal party, known as the Guelphs, and the party that supported the Holy Roman Emperor, the Ghibellines.[19] Having ended up on the wrong side in these conflicts, Dante was exiled and condemned in his absence to be burned should he ever return to Florence. His literary vengeance would secure him a place in the Hall of Fame of Western writers.

Throughout the *Commedia,* Dante consistently castigates greed, together with pride and envy, as the main causes of Florentine ethical and political corruption, and he does so with much gusto. In its first part, the *Inferno*, he is taken by Virgil on a tour of Hell, which is divided into nine concentric circles.[20] As he descends from one circle to the next, he encounters personages who in life had been high and mighty but in death are suffering eternal punishment. It is in the fourth circle that he meets those, including well-known popes and cardinals, who had committed the deadly sin of greed and are now so tortured and transfigured that they are barely recognizable. (Note how Dante, in his vivid and merciless descriptions of their eternal torment, himself may have committed the deadly sin of lust.)

The impact of Dante's portrayal of the deadly sins has been profound. Unsurprisingly, leftist writers have been particularly fond of citing his lustful depiction of the eternal sufferings of bankers in the Inferno. Yet, from a social science perspective, it is imperative not to succumb to the lures of

---

[18] The *Commedia*, which was Dante's own short title, consists of three parts – *Inferno*, *Purgatorio*, and *Paradiso* – that were published separately in, respectively, 1317, 1319, and 1320. It was only in 1472 that the three were published jointly, and only in the mid-sixteenth century that the work appeared as the *Divina Commedia*.

[19] The names are of German origin, having emerged during struggles between the dukes of Bavaria (Welfs) and the Hohenstaufens of Swabia (from Waiblingen). They were introduced into Italian in the twelfth century, during the reign of Frederick Barbarossa. The respective affiliations were partly determined by wealth, with mercantile interests tending to side with the Guelphs, who were in opposition to the Imperial power, but practical considerations also played a part. Cities that were under threat from the Papal States would side with the Ghibellines, and those that felt Imperial pressure would side with the Guelphs. After the final defeat of the Ghibellines, in 1289, the Guelphs broke up into White and Black factions that started fighting each other.

[20] Four of these are devoted to mortal sins; the second to lust, the third to gluttony, the fourth to greed, and the fifth to wrath. At the very bottom of the ninth circle we may find those guilty of the most infamous cases of treachery in history, namely Judas, the betrayer of Christ, and Cassius and Brutus, the betrayers of Julius Caesar.

indiscriminate accusations of greed, understood as an inherent moral quality that dictates economic behavior. We do not, after all, live in an entirely Hobbesian world that is marked by the war of all against all.

This is certainly not to say that greed is good, or that Gordon Gekko was right in claiming that it "captures the essence of the evolutionary spirit." What it does say is that actions that are being construed as driven by greed must be viewed as consequences of systemic defects, of market imperfections that place actors in situations of temptation that – to some, albeit not to all – may prove to be simply irresistible.

The core of the matter concerns the crucial role of self-interest, without which it would make little sense to speak of market economy. As will be shown in subsequent chapters, thinkers from Adam Smith onward have been conscious that some restraints need to be in place here. More recently, Kenneth Arrow has noted that "ethical elements enter in some measure into every contract; without them no market could function."[21] Similarly, James Buchanan wrote that "Life in society, as we know it, would probably be intolerable if formal rules should be required for each and every area where interpersonal conflict might arise."[22] The general need of well-functioning markets for what we shall refer to as a "golden rule" of morality has been well formulated by Jean-Philippe Platteau, who argued that "the pervasive presence of generalized morality in a society can prevent the enforcement costs of the rules of honesty from being excessively high."[23]

With some seeming regularity, financial markets in particular tend to shift into a mode of overdrive where legitimate self-interest that respects the golden rule degenerates into pure greed, with fatal consequences. It is the task of regulators to fine-tune intervention so that such lapses can be precluded – without stifling the pursuit of legitimate self-interest. The reality, however, that was reflected by Oliver Stone in the screen presentation of Wall Street was rife with illustrations of just how difficult that task can be. Once the herd mentality of brokers and corporate executives eager for short-term gain at any risk and cost has taken over, the outcome is bound to be complete abandonment of restraint, and in the end disaster.

As an extreme illustration of what regulators and oversight agencies have been tasked with preventing, we may usefully expand on the case of

---

[21] Arrow, Kenneth J. (1973), *Information and Economic Behavior*, Stockholm: Federation of Swedish Industries, p. 24.

[22] Buchanan, James M. (1975), *The Limits of Liberty – Between Anarchy and Leviathan*, Chicago: Chicago University Press, p. 118.

[23] Platteau, Jean-Philippe (1994), "Behind the Market Stage Where Real Societies Exist – Part II: The Role of Moral Norms," *Journal of Development Studies*, vol. 30, no. 3, p. 756.

Bernard Madoff. He served for many years on the board of NASDAQ and in the process built a solid reputation on Wall Street, but in the end he could not resist temptation. Using his investment firm, Bernard L. Madoff Investment Securities LLC, as a platform, he proceeded to build the most spectacular Ponzi scheme in the history of financial fraud. When he was arrested by the FBI, on December 12, 2008, banner headlines claimed that his investors, including several major European banks, had lost a staggering total of $50 billion.[24] Even more astounding were allegations that over a period of many years, whistleblowers had tried to push the Securities and Exchange Commission into taking action, but to no avail.[25] Madoff had, quite obviously, been above suspicion.

The Madoff case may certainly be dismissed as one of outright criminal fraud, with little relevance to the more routine tasks of financial oversight. There is, however, no shortage of other illustrations that show how difficult those tasks may be. In order to drive home how greed may serve to inflate financial bubbles, which in the end also cause massive losses, it may suffice here to recall toxic cases like those of Enron, WorldCom, and Arthur Andersen.[26]

Enron was a Houston-based energy company created in 1985. When it filed for Chapter 11 bankruptcy protection, on December 2, 2001, it was the seventh largest corporation in the United States, with 21,000 employees in more than forty countries. Most important, right up until the very end it was also the darling of financial market operators who were mesmerized by a stock that traded at fifty-five times earnings.[27] Its bankruptcy broke all previous records in losses, and the revelations that followed, of highly creative accounting practices, caused a huge scandal.

Less than eight months later, on July 22, 2002, another darling of the financial markets, telecom giant WorldCom, with 85,000 employees in

---

[24] For an in-depth account of the story as a whole, which in the end finished at $65 billion and won Madoff a 150-year prison sentence, see http://www.ft.com/indepth/madoff-scandal (accessed on July 15, 2010).

[25] http://money.cnn.com/2009/02/04/news/newsmakers/madoff_whistleblower/index.htm (accessed on October 1, 2009). For an interview with one of those who tried long and hard to expose the scam, see http://www.guardian.co.uk/business/2010/mar/24/bernard-madoff-whistleblower-harry-markopolos (accessed on July 15, 2010).

[26] In a broad and harshly critical background to these events, Paul Krugman asks "how it was possible for a country with so much going for it to go downhill so fast," and argues that it is "a story about leadership – incredibly bad leadership, in the private sector and in the corridors of power" (Krugman, Paul (2003), *The Great Unraveling: Losing Our Way in the New Century*, New York: Norton, p. xvi).

[27] When Enron collapsed, it had just been named "Most Innovative Company in America" for the sixth consecutive year by *Fortune Magazine* and been ranked in the top quartile in the same magazine's list of "100 Best Companies to Work For."

sixty-five countries, presented markets with even greater losses, causing an equal or perhaps even greater outcry.[28] And in the wake of these calamities followed the collapse of the global accounting firm Arthur Andersen, with 100,000 employees worldwide. Having vouched for the quality of Enron and WorldCom accounts, Andersen found its credibility irretrievably compromised.

What is so striking here is that despite huge financial losses and massive public scandals, so little apparently was learned and so much rapidly forgotten. As markets rebounded, and as opportunities for short-term profit again began to proliferate, market dazzle swamped any potentially lingering realization of the need to restrain the scope of actions motivated by pure greed. This time, the highway to hell would be paved with fanciful financial instruments, the nature and effects of which even their originators had trouble grasping in full. Happily humming along to the tunes of "Don't Worry! Be Happy!" both markets and the general public yet again were lulled into believing that greed was good.

When the global financial avalanche was unleashed, in the early fall of 2008, the price to be paid was manifested in collapsing corporations that right up until the very end had enjoyed glory stature and superior credit ratings. Following the stunning and highly controversial bankruptcy of venerable investment firm Lehman Brothers, founded in 1850, the U.S. Congress was reluctantly compelled to provide a massive bailout for insurance giant AIG.[29] Triggered by revelations of bonus schemes that were simply rife with moral hazards, causing an insatiable appetite for unwarranted risk, accusations of greed and a general lack of morality once again became the stuff of banner headlines. And then there was the case of Bernard Madoff.

---

[28] When WorldCom filed for Chapter 11 bankruptcy protection, it had $107 billion in listed assets, making it the largest bankruptcy in United States history. Enron's listed assets had been "merely" $63.4 billion. (See further http://money.cnn.com/2002/07/19/news/worldcom_bankruptcy/, accessed on November 12, 2008.)

[29] On June 2, 2008, Standard & Poor's downgraded Lehman Brothers from A+ to A, and on September 9 it added a negative outlook, to A–. This was still investment grade, that is, well above "junk bonds," albeit with a caveat that "economic situation can affect finance." A mere week later, on September 15, Lehman filed for Chapter 11 bankruptcy protection. With assets of $639 billion, it surged way past the previous WorldCom loss record. In the case of AIG, S&P downgraded it from AA to AA– on May 12, still representing the fourth highest investment grade. On September 16, the day after Lehman filed for Chapter 11 protection, AIG was downgraded to A–. On the following day, the U.S. Congress had to come to the rescue with an $85 billion emergency loan. In contrast to Lehman, AIG was apparently considered too big to be allowed to fail.

Crises of Capitalism

The main question to be asked here concerns what should be made of all of this. Is it, to begin with, the case that capitalism harbors within itself the seeds of its own destruction? Although Karl Marx may have been the first to make this argument, he has certainly not been alone in doing so. Nor is it, as we shall see momentarily, entirely a thing of past debates. Even a cursory glance at how capitalism has been presented and debated over the past century will show that we are faced here with a case of contradictory invisible hands, working simultaneously both to produce wealth and to undermine the grounds for the system as such.

In *The Great Transformation*, published in 1944, Karl Polanyi famously predicted that internal social contradictions would cause the market economy to self-destruct: "Robbed of the protective covering of cultural institutions, human beings would perish from the effects of social exposure; they would die as the victims of acute social dislocation through vice, perversion, crime and starvation."[30] What to some may have been ideologically tinted wishful thinking, to others was a source of great concern. In his classic 1942 book *Capitalism, Socialism, and Democracy*, Joseph Schumpeter posed one of his most quoted questions and answers: "Can capitalism survive? No. I do not think it can."[31]

Where Karl Marx had predicted that capitalism would be destroyed by those it exploited, Schumpeter believed that it would be destroyed by its successes. His reason was that it would lead to the emergence of a class of intellectuals who made their living by attacking the very bourgeois system of private property and freedom that supported their existence. In sharp contrast to Marx, who welcomed the destruction of capitalism, Schumpeter viewed this possibility as a calamity: "If a doctor predicts that his patient will die presently, this does not mean that he desires it. One may hate socialism or at least look upon it with cool criticism, and yet foresee its advent. Many conservatives did and do."[32]

An important driving force in predictions – and worries – of this kind was the experience of nineteenth-century American Robber Barons having run wild, and of the emerging culture among the noveaux riches of flaunting their wealth. The latter, inter alia, inspired the founding father of

---

[30] Polanyi, Karl (1944), *The Great Transformation*, New York: Farrar & Rhinehart, p. 73.
[31] Schumpeter, Joseph A. (1942), *Capitalism, Socialism, and Democracy*, New York and London: Harper & Brothers, p. 61.
[32] Ibid.

American institutionalism, Thorstein Veblen, to pen his most famous work, *The Theory of the Leisure Class*. Appearing in 1899, it introduced the subsequently well-established notion of "conspicuous consumption."[33] Although the Great War intervened to put an effective damper on the capitalist extravaganza, in the subsequent "roaring twenties" bootleggers and capitalists jointly produced the glitter and glamour of the "jazz age" that was so eloquently captured by F. Scott Fitzgerald in his 1925 novel *The Great Gatsby*. Then followed the collapse on Wall Street and the Great Depression.

Given this somber background, it was not surprising that the American school of economic institutionalism, which espoused grave concerns about the social consequences of American capitalism, would gain such a broad following. Given, moreover, the subsequent rise to complete hegemony of the neoclassical economic tradition, it bears noting that in the first decades of the twentieth century it was the institutional school that represented American economic orthodoxy, controlling all the prestige journals and big name schools.[34]

Writing in 1917, Veblen had expressed a great deal of pessimism about the future prospects of capitalism, suggesting that emerging social tensions would produce an "eventual cleavage" between those who own and those who do not. Faced with the rise of socialism, the outcome would have to be either a demise of the market economy or a restoration of ownership rights by force of arms.[35]

In the interwar years, driven by a powerful urge to promote reform, the prominent institutional economist John Commons announced that he wanted to save capitalism by convincing it to "make a profit by doing good."[36] If we consider that his main work on institutional economics was published in 1934, it is perhaps not so strange that he found grounds to worry about economic developments at large.[37] As his colleague Wesley

[33] Veblen, Thorstein (1899), *The Theory of the Leisure Class: An Economic Study in the Evolution of Institutions*, New York: Macmillan, ch. 4 and passim.

[34] Veblen won an appointment at Chicago University in 1892 and while there served as managing editor of the still today highly prestigious *Journal of Political Economy*. The scene would begin to change only in the 1930s, and with the publication, in 1936, of John Maynard Keynes's *General Theory*, it would be completely transformed. As the institutionalists fell silent, debates would rage instead between Keynesians and monetarists, but that, as they say, is a completely different story.

[35] Veblen, Thorstein (1917), *An Inquiry into the Nature of Peace and the Terms of its Perpetuation*, New York: Macmillan, pp. 366–67.

[36] Commons, John R. (1934b), *Myself*, New York: Macmillan, p. 143.

[37] It may also be worth noting that his first major work was devoted to legal regulation. See Commons, John R. (1924), *Legal Foundations of Capitalism*, New York: Macmillan.

Mitchell phrased it, he was far from sure that it would actually be possible to save capitalism by making it good.[38] In his own words, he saw it as "doubtful whether, under modern conditions, a decision can be reached as to which is the better public policy – the Communism of Russia, the Fascism of Italy, or the Banker Capitalism of the United States."[39]

In the post–World War II era, the rise of Keynesianism and the move toward building welfare states, including Lyndon Johnson's "Great Society," caused worries about the fate of capitalism to subside and give way to hopes for convergence between the two systems. The parallel trends of increasing state regulation in the market economies of the West and of increasing reliance on markets in the planned economies of the East were taken by some as evidence that the two systems were about to merge into one.[40] By the end of the 1980s, however, as the Soviet system was breaking down, such hopes in turn gave way to predictions of the end of history and a sense of triumphant capitalism.[41]

With the global financial crisis we had, according to some, come full circle, back to worries about, and perhaps even hopes for, a pending collapse of capitalism. As a prominent illustration, we may listen to a lengthy BBC interview that was aired on October 18, 2008. Here the Marxist historian Eric Hobsbawn, introduced as "one of the towering veterans of the British Left," recognized that he and other representatives of the Left did feel a certain *Schadenfreude* in being vindicated in their views:

> It is certainly the greatest crisis of capitalism since the 1930s.... As Marx and Schumpeter foresaw, globalization, which is implicit in capitalism, not only destroys heritage and tradition, but is incredibly unstable. It operates through a series of crises.... This is the dramatic equivalent of the collapse of the Soviet Union: we now know that an era has ended.[42]

Although declaring that an era has ended may have been something of an overstatement, it did reflect the impact of the crisis on public perceptions

---

[38] Mitchell, Wesley (1935), "Commons on Institutional Economics," *American Economic Review*, vol. 25, no. 4, p. 649.

[39] Commons, John R. (1934a), *Institutional Economics: Its Place in Political Economy*, New York: Macmillan, p. 903.

[40] The most widely cited proponent of this theory was the Dutch economist Jan Tinbergen, who received the Nobel Prize in economics in 1969. See Tinbergen, Jan (1961), "Do Communist and Free Economies Show a Converging Pattern?," *Soviet Studies*, vol. 12, no. 4.

[41] Fukuyama, Francis (1989), "The End of History?," *National Interest*, no. 16, summer, and Fukuyama, Francis (1992), *The End of History and the Last Man*, New York: Free Press.

[42] See http://news.bbc.co.uk/today/hi/today/newsid_7677000/7677683.stm (accessed on November 11, 2008).

of the role of the state. Much as the Great Depression served to trigger both Keynesianism and Roosevelt's New Deal, the subprime mortgage crisis and the ensuing freeze of interbank lending served – at least for a time – to discredit the neo-liberal wave of free marketeering. Having begun with Milton Friedman's monetarism, it prepared the ground for programs of mass privatization and culminated in sweeping deregulation of global financial markets. With the sluice gates having thus been opened wide, and with public norms being increasingly supportive of hedonistic self-enrichment, the stage was set for inherent greed to produce a global financial crisis.

Given the magnitude of losses suffered at this time, both by financial markets and by the real sector, there has been no shortage of blame to go around. The current problematic, however, is considerably more complex than that concerning a pending doom of capitalism. What must be regarded as its true core may be viewed against the background of Sen's question cited earlier regarding what kind of economics is needed today.

Since greed has surely always been present, it cannot be held up as a sole driving force. Simply put, a constant cannot in itself be used to explain variation. Something else must be needed; something that goes beyond a failure to constrain by formal means the scope for self-interested action in conflict with the common good. That something else can only be construed as the presence (or absence) of norms compelling actors to follow the golden rule of not doing to others what you do not want them to do to you.

From Max Weber we have learned that the presence of a "Protestant ethic" will be conducive to superior economic performance. The main thrust of his argument was that a good Calvinist must evolve and embrace a set of norms that are in line with the faith. If this in turn leads to the accumulation of wealth, that is an added bonus, not an objective in itself. The objective must be the way of life.[43] In a less well-known account of "Protestant sects and the spirit of capitalism," based on impressions from travel in America in 1904, he also provided interesting insights into how people tended to establish credentials of trust by introducing themselves as members of a certain faith or a specified church.[44] In the Indian territories

---

[43] Weber, Max (1904/5), "Die protestantische Ethik und der Geist des Kapitalismus," *Archiv für Sozialwissenschaften und Sozialpolitik*, vol. 20, no. 1, and vol. 21, no. 1. For an English version, see Weber, Max (2001), *The Protestant Ethic and the Spirit of Capitalism*, London: Routledge. For a short summary, see Weber, Max (1961), *General Economic History*, New York: Collier Books, ch. 30.

[44] Weber, Max (1946b), "The Protestant Sects and the Spirit of Capitalism," in H. H. Gerth and C. Wright Mills (trans. and eds.), *From Max Weber: Essays in Sociology*, New York: Oxford University Press, p. 303.

that Weber visited, the rule of law was probably weakly developed at best. Transacting within a network based on honesty and loyalty would go a long way toward compensating for this.

More recently, Francis Fukuyama has included in his grand exposition over the role of trust and social virtues a speculation about the effects of long-standing efforts by North American Protestantism to evangelize in traditionally Catholic Latin American countries. Suggesting that this constitutes a "laboratory for measuring the consequences of cultural change," his conclusion is that the mainly Pentecostal conversions have been associated with "significant increases in hygiene, savings, educational achievement, and ultimately per capita income."[45]

For fear of allowing the present argument to turn into a debate about the merits of Weber's highly controversial thesis as such, we shall return to the broader question of the role of norms as restraints.[46] More specifically, we may note Sen's further statement that "Profit-oriented capitalism has always drawn on support from other institutional values."[47] While the power of religious norms in achieving both coordination and cooperation cannot be questioned, what remains to be seriously questioned is the extent to which other types of norms can be deliberately introduced to fill the same function. Our following account will grapple with this challenging issue, contrasting the agency view that is common in economics and in new institutionalism against the structural view that marks sociology and old institutionalism.

Without mentioning, or perhaps even considering, new institutionalism, Sen pinpoints exactly what the approach is all about: "What is also needed is a clearheaded perception of how different institutions actually work, and of how a variety of organizations – from the market to the institutions of the state – can go beyond short-term solutions and contribute to producing a more decent world."[48]

Recalling Robbins's caveat regarding deregulation and chaos, we may ask what it is that determines when actors will choose strategies that aim for value adding contributions toward the common good, resulting in a more

---

[45] Fukuyama, Francis (1995), *Trust: The Social Virtues and the Creation of Prosperity*, New York: Free Press, pp. 44–45. For a fuller account of this argument, see also Martin, David (1990), *Tongues of Fire: The Explosion of Protestantism in Latin America*, Oxford: Blackwell.

[46] For a balanced approach to the discussion of Weber's thesis, see Marshall, Gordon (1982), *In Search of the Spirit of Capitalism: An Essay on Max Weber's Protestant Ethic Thesis*, London: Hutchinson Education.

[47] Sen, "Capitalism beyond the Crisis," p. 3.

[48] Ibid., p. 6.

decent world, and when they will prefer redistributive efforts that include corruption, rent seeking, and state capture, all of which consume real resources, stifle economic performance, and in consequence detract from the common good. In line with what has been said, the question may be phrased as how to combine promotion of the pursuit of legitimate self-interest with maintaining safeguards against excesses driven by pure greed.

The reason this is such a complex issue is because different subdisciplines of the social sciences have such different perceptions of what drives human action. In the liberal economic tradition, forward-oriented pursuit of self-interest is generally viewed as the main driving force. From the side of sociology, however, things look fundamentally different. Jon Elster speaks here of one of "the most persisting cleavages in the social sciences," namely, the "opposition between two lines of thought conveniently associated with Adam Smith and Émile Durkheim, between *homo economicus* and *homo sociologicus*." While the former is supposed to be guided by instrumental rationality, the behavior of the latter is dictated by social norms: "The former is 'pulled' by the prospect of future rewards, whereas the latter is 'pushed' from behind by quasi-inertial forces."[49]

The truly fundamental difference in approach that is reflected here may be led back to a difference between the methodological individualism of economics that views institutions as rules of the game, and the methodological holism of sociology where motivation for human action is held to be embedded in social structures. We shall have ample reason in subsequent chapters to return to these matters. In particular, we shall argue that a closer reading of the works of Adam Smith will reveal a message that is considerably more complex than that of simply liberating markets.

THE RUSSIAN EXPERIENCE

Here we shall proceed to the more specific case of Russia's most recent encounter with capitalism. The true and sordid hallmarks of this process have been greed and callousness taken way beyond the pale, combined with patterns of conspicuous consumption that surpass anything that the Great Gatsby may have ever dreamed of. Given that this brutal outcome stands in such stark contrast to the envisioned emergence of a modern democratic Russia, built on a rules-based liberal market economy, some serious questions must be asked.

---

[49] Elster, Jon (1989a), *The Cement of Society: A Study of Social Order*, Cambridge: Cambridge University Press, p. 97.

Before proceeding, note that we have no intention here of rehashing familiar old debates on shock therapy versus gradualism, or indeed of suggesting what could or should have been done instead. On the contrary, we shall maintain our previous distinction between the imagery of radical and sweeping reform that was projected by the proponents of the Washington Consensus, and such limited reforms that actually were implemented. Viewing the former as a theoretical exercise aimed at achieving a rapid transition from central planning to market economy, we may identify one truly crucial question that should have been asked but was largely ignored.

That question concerns what may be reasonably expected to happen if markets that have long been subjected to stifling control and effective suppression by the state are suddenly and completely deregulated, under conditions where there are substantial state-owned assets available to grab and strip. May actors then be expected to seize the opportunity to form ventures that improve governance and add value, or will they prefer to go on the rampage and loot, ideally in cahoots with representatives of the government? The answer will hinge critically on what we believe about the choice between rule-abiding and rule-avoiding behavior.

In order to appreciate why the question was never formulated as such, and why the seemingly obvious answer was never really taken into account, we must begin by considering the true complexity of devising and implementing what was then presented as "systemic change." The main reason that so many economists in particular failed to appreciate the true dangers that lurked here, of unleashing outright predatory behavior, may be derived from the fact that the project represented something way out of the ordinary of economic analysis.

The standard approach of neoclassical economic theory is to assume marginal change under conditions of ceteris paribus and perfect information. If these assumptions are met, there will be good predictive power. In the Russian case, however, reformers were faced with extra-marginal change occurring simultaneously on multiple margins, in a non-routine situation that was marked by pervasive uncertainty.

The response to the challenges that were implied here may be captured in Napoleon's classic maxim, *On s'engage, et puis on voit.* In good keeping with Russia's tradition of "maximalism," of which more will be said later, Boris Yeltsin's reformers were bent on first destroying as much as possible of the old system.[50] Only then could the ground be prepared for something new to arise. The task of erecting the complex scaffolding of institutions that jointly

---

[50] In the words of one of the leading foreign advisors to the Gaidar government, "it must be remembered that there is an abyss between a command economy and a market economy…

make up functioning market economy was viewed as rather simple. It was to be achieved mainly if not exclusively via deregulation of state controls and sweeping privatization of state property. Although it may come across as an unwarranted slur, one is tempted here to compare this with Lenin's simplistic view on the complexities of administering a command economy, infamously drawing a parallel to the running of a post office.[51]

The hype that surrounded the launch of "shock therapy" was heavily laced with ideological pronouncements on the superiority of market economy and on the perceived need to excel in liberating markets. Russia's "young reform economists" were astute in reading what Western media, markets, donors, and political types in general wanted to hear, and they were richly rewarded for what they delivered. Over the span of a few months, a group of previously unknown young men were catapulted into the role of global superstars of emerging market dazzle. With fame came riches and a rather casual attitude toward problems of moral hazard.[52] *who engaged?*

The main reason the free market rhetoric would be so immensely successful in shaping outside perceptions of Russia's adjustment to a post-Soviet existence was that it was so well attuned to fundamental beliefs within the economics profession. Given everything that was known, or thought to be known, about *transition* the gross inefficiencies of central economic planning, undertaking a transition *costs* to market economy would simply have to produce efficiency gains.[53]

An important driving force in creating the mentality and expectations of what a leading foreign economic advisor to the Russian government referred to as a "Coming Russian Boom"[54] was derived from the belief in a set of "laws of economics" that are somehow assumed to transcend cultural and historical differences between nations. The reason this must be viewed as problematic has been highlighted by Jozef van Brabant, in a major work on the political economy of transition: "Unlike legal principles (with their

first the old system must be destroyed ... then the foundations of the new market economic house must be built on the other side of the abyss." (Cited in Johnson, Juliet Ellen (1994), "The Russian Banking System: Institutional Responses to the Market Transition," *Europe-Asia Studies*, vol. 46, no. 6, p. 973, footnote 11.)

[51] The correct quote is to "organize the *whole* national economy on the lines of a postal service" (Lenin, V. I. (1976), *The State and Revolution*, Peking: Foreign Languages Press, p. 61).

[52] Wedel, Janine R. (1998), *Collision and Collusion: The Strange Case of Western Aid to Eastern Europe 1989–98*, New York: St. Martin's, Wedel, Janine R. (2000), "Tainted Transactions: Harvard, the Chubais Clan and Russia's Ruin," *National Interest*, no. 59, spring.

[53] For a balanced overview of the debate, see Roland, Gérard (2000), *Transition and Economics: Politics, Markets, and Firms*, Cambridge, MA: MIT Press, ch. 15.

[54] Layard, Richard and John Parker (1996), *The Coming Russian Boom: A Guide to New Markets and Politics*, New York: The Free Press.

normative laws) or objective findings (as in physics), an economic law can exist only through human activity."[55]

The bottom line, as sociologists would immediately agree, is that economic decision making can never be viewed as entirely divorced from the social setting. We shall have much more to say about this crucial connection in subsequent chapters. Accepting for the moment that there is considerable disagreement on how the social context shall be defined and on how the causal influence on decision making shall be understood, it will have to remain a fact that when economists proceeded to implement systemic change based on shock therapy, there was little if any consideration of matters relating to the social or indeed the cultural and historical context.

The clarion call for the approach of mainstream economics to the challenge of highly complex institutional transformation was sounded at a World Bank seminar, held in Bangkok in October 1991. At this critical juncture in Russian political transformation, only weeks after the failed August putsch, Lawrence Summers, then chief economist at the World Bank, had the following to say: "Spread the truth – the laws of economics are like the laws of engineering. One set of laws works everywhere."[56]

Unsurprisingly, Russia's young reformers, who were now being appointed government ministers, were quick to jump onto a heavily media-driven bandwagon. In February 1992, for example, the very same view on laws of economics was proclaimed by Pyotr Aven, then Russian minister for foreign economic relations: "There are no special countries from the point of view of economists. If economics is a science, with its own laws – all countries and all economic stabilization plans are the same."[57]

As it began to transpire that things were perhaps not going exactly according to plan, the main reaction was denial and a series of retrenchments. The first line of defense was to claim that numbers showing a drastic decline in GDP were attributable to statistical illusion, derived from discrepancies between Soviet-style and market-based national accounting. Then followed claims that much of what had been produced in the command economy had been of so little value that the lower output of the post-Soviet economy actually represented an improvement, and in the end recourse was made to simple predictions of an imminent boom around the corner.

---

[55] Brabant, Jozef M. van (1998), *The Political Economy of Transition: Coming to Grips with History and Methodology*, London: Routledge, p. 27.

[56] Quoted by Keegan, William (1993), *The Specter of Capitalism: The Future of the World Economy after the Fall of Communism*, London: Vintage, p. 109.

[57] Quoted by Goldman, Marshall (1994), *Lost Opportunity: What Has Made Economic Reform in Russia So Difficult?*, New York: Norton, p. 106.

While all of this was going on, Russia's modern-day Robber Barons were running wild, grabbing and stripping assets and amassing vast private fortunes – all at the expense of the Russian state and of the tens of millions of ordinary Russians who were not invited to the looting party.[58]

The outcome may be viewed as a clear case of out of the ashes and into the fire. Out of a Soviet reality of stagnation and gradual decay, Russia was thrown into a near-decade of chaotic and deeply destructive "wild" capitalism that brought hyperinflation, hyperdepression, financial collapse, mass pauperization, and a demographic meltdown that prompted American demographer Nicholas Eberstadt to speak of Russia as "The Sick Man of Europe." Contending that the country was in "the grip of a steadily tightening mesh of serious demographic problems, for which the term 'crisis' is no overstatement," he found that this "crisis is altering the realm of the possible for the country and its people – continuously, directly and adversely."[59]

The main reason that so many got it all so wrong is deeply revealing of the shortcomings of social science analysis that are at the focus of the present text as a whole. It will be attributed in the following to a combined failure of understanding the true nature of central planning and of appreciating what it is that sets functioning market economy aside from its variously perverted alternative apparitions – ranging from rent-seeking robber capitalism and state capture to outright kleptocracy. On both counts, the argument will focus on the link between rules and motivation.

As Avner Greif puts it, "behavioral prescriptions – rules and contracts – are nothing more than instructions that can be ignored. If prescriptive rules of behavior are to have an impact, individuals must be motivated to follow them." His understanding of "motivation," moreover, goes to the very core of the matters at hand: "By motivation I mean here incentives broadly defined to include expectations, beliefs, and internalized norms."[60]

OUTLINE OF THE STUDY

The questions that are to be addressed in the following chapters of this study will revolve around precisely this problematic, seeking to establish how and when the pursuit of legitimate self-interest will be conducive to the common good, and when it may degenerate into excesses in pure greed.

---

[58] Goldman, Marshall (2003), *The Piratization of Russia: Russian Reform Goes Awry*, London: Routledge.

[59] Eberstadt, Nicholas (2005), "Russia, The Sick Man of Europe," *Public Interest*, winter, p. 1.

[60] Greif, Avner (2006), *Institutions and the Path to the Modern Economy: Lessons from Medieval Trade*, Cambridge: Cambridge University Press, pp. 7–8.

Our use of invisible hands in the plural sense is intended to reflect that we shall need to focus not only on micro-level adjustment by individual actors but also on the role of the state in creating conditions under which good outcomes may result.

It will be necessary but far from sufficient for government agencies to engage in what was described earlier as fine-tuning of regulation, that is, seeking to preclude lapses into short-term greed without stifling such legitimate risk-taking that is necessary for good long-term economic performance. The state will also, and more importantly, have to act as caretaker of such macro-level processes of public norm formation that feed into micro-level internalization of private norms. It is only when there is a smooth link between these two levels that we may expect private norms to emerge that support good economic performance.

Our ambition to capture the influence of culture and history on current decision making will proceed by mapping out how important sets of norms and organizational structures may be reproduced over time, even in cases where such reproduction is clearly inferior on grounds of technical efficiency. As noted earlier, the argument will expand on previous theories of path dependence and of new institutionalism more generally. It will be built in the following eight steps.

Chapter 1 sets the stage, by taking a closer look at the belief in opportunity and self-interest that forms such an integral part of the liberal economic tradition. Chapter 2 adds to the background by looking at how social science has approached over time the core problem of how institutions determine individual action. Chapter 3 introduces the case of central economic planning and argues that in discussions of this "alternative system" too much emphasis was placed on formal rules and restrictions, as opposed to informal norms and collusive influence games. Chapter 4 departs from the fact that command economy was a Russian innovation and argues that many of its formative institutional traits may be reasonably assumed to have emerged out of Russian tradition. Chapter 5 recognizes that markets may be found everywhere and calls for emphasis to be placed not on the presence of markets as such but rather on the quality of supporting institutions. Chapter 6 deals with limits to government intervention, emphasizing the difference between evolutionary institutional change and deliberate institutional choice. Chapter 7 reflects on the role of history in social science analysis, arguing that the increasing focus on formal modeling has resulted in a loss of perspective, where it has been easy to abstract from the crucial interplay between rules and norms. Chapter 8, finally, provides a summary discussion of the argument and Chapter 9 reflects on the implications.

1

Opportunity and Self-Interest

Ever since Adam Smith presented the world with his immortal classic *The Wealth of Nations*, liberal market economy has been based on the centrality of opportunity. If only markets can be sufficiently deregulated, and the state can be kept at bay, good things will follow. Entrepreneurs and consumers will seek out and act on their best available opportunities for profit and utility maximization, competition will make sure that all resources are allocated to their best uses, and welfare will be maximized.

Based on such premises, it is not surprising that over time economics has developed into a science that is fundamentally geared toward an optimistic view of market forces driven by the pursuit of self-interest. This stands in some considerable and interesting contrast to the epithet of a "dismal science" that was once ascribed to political economy by the Victorian writer Thomas Carlyle.[1] The reason then was the dire predictions of pending population checks and food shortages that were issued by Thomas Malthus and David Ricardo.[2] That, however, was soon to change.

---

[1] Carlyle is primarily known for his major work on the French revolution (Carlyle, Thomas (1837), *The French Revolution: A History*, Vols. 1–3, London: Chapman and Hall). He is also commonly alleged to have come up with the notion of the "dismal science" as a comment on Malthus. While it is true that he did use the word "dismal" to portray the prediction of population crises, it should be noted that his attack on political economy as a whole appeared in an 1849 article in *Frazier Magazine*, titled "Occasional Discourse on the Negro Question," where he argued for the reintroduction of slavery as a way of regulating the labor market in the West Indies. His thesis was that the free market forces had caused the former slaves to suffer serious moral and economic consequences. Carlyle's good friend, the liberal economist John Stuart Mill, was opposed forcefully to this suggestion. Four years later, the original magazine publication appeared as a book, with an even less palatable title (Carlyle, Thomas (1853), *Occasional Discourse on the Nigger Question*, London: Bosworth).

[2] While Malthus worried that population growth would outstrip economic growth and thus lead to recurring "checks" on the size of the population, to be known as "Malthusian

Under the combined influence of rapid technological development and the neoclassical revolution in economics, a firm belief began to emerge that economic growth would quite simply take care of itself. The previous "dismal" views that had emphasized natural constraints on the market forces could thus be forgotten, and the role of liberal government could be reduced to keeping out of the way. Given the almost axiomatic assumption that economic men are instrumentally rational, in the sense of being concerned with outcomes and thus forward-looking, mainstream economists have come to expect that features of history and culture really do not, and should not, enter into the calculus.

Is there a problem with this? While many colleagues both in the humanities and in the other social sciences would say yes, most economists would say no, and within their own realm they would be right. The point here is not to take sides in interdisciplinary disputes over pecking orders, and it is not to present a caricature of modern economics. The discipline as such is certainly more analytically profound than a few clips from an undergraduate textbook might lead the casual observer to believe. It is also the case that much valuable work has gone into qualifying the standard assumptions, thus rendering mainstream theory successively more amenable to analyzing the problems of observable reality.[3]

This said, we shall maintain that the strong orientation of modern economics toward instrumentally rational forward-looking behavior does harbor a problem. That problem, however, is not one of economics versus the rest. On the contrary. The fundamental role that is played by the notion of economic man in economic theory will be used here as a sign, or perhaps as a symptom, of a long-standing trend of specialization that has rendered social science at large increasingly insensitive to some of the really great issues that surround us all.

Without going into detail at this point, the latter may be broadly captured in two rather provocative questions. The first asks why it is that poor countries tend to stay poor, and the second if history really matters. Both are highly controversial; the former in the sense that it brings into focus acrimonious debates about venality and deliberate exploitation of the poor

---

checks," Ricardo foresaw that increasing population pressure would lead to successively poorer lands being taken into cultivation, thus raising the cost of living and acting as a brake on economic growth. Both failed to appreciate the dynamic effects of technological change.

[3] See further Eggertsson, Thráinn (1990), *Economic Behavior and Institutions*, Cambridge: Cambridge University Press, and Williamson, Oliver E. (1985a), *The Economic Institutions of Capitalism*, New York: Free Press. ·

by the rich, and the second simply because different scholarly disciplines have such widely different views on the topic. Not the least among the latter concerns how history – and even more so culture – shall be defined. How indeed, and to what purpose?

Before continuing on our journey into the universe of social science, it may be worth noting that the ambition of the present text shall not be to present, or even look for, conclusive answers to any of the questions just posed. Such a venture would represent considerable academic over-stretch. Our more limited ambition shall be to map out fault lines and to see how questions that span disciplines may be formulated, in the hope that further research may add more pieces to the puzzle of how to achieve reintegration.

The aim in the present chapter shall be to set the stage for the following discussion, and we shall do so in three broad steps. The first will provide a background for discussing the emergence and importance of internal lines of division within the social sciences. The second will address the problem of how to account for the growing "development gap" between rich and poor nations, and the third will approach the issue of why it is that only *some* poor countries tend to stay poor.

THEORETICAL FAULT LINES

Beginning with the question of divergence within the social sciences, we may recall Jon Elster's portrayal of a "persisting cleavage" between economics and sociology. The implications are that economists will formulate their models based on the expectation that economic men will always be on the prowl for opportunity, will always be ready to adapt, and will be jointly led by an "invisible hand" to maximize collective welfare. To sociologists, on the other hand, models of human behavior will depart from a view of man as being locked into the past, as a mindless plaything whose actions are insensitive to prospects of opportunities for future gain. To the former, history does not matter. To the latter, history is everything. Can both really be right at the same time?[4]

---

[4] The distinction may be anecdotally reflected in the following quip by economist James Duesenberry: "I used to tell my students that the difference between economics and sociology is very simple. Economics is all about how people make choices. Sociology is all about why they don't have any choices to make" (cited in NBER (1960), *Demographic and Economic Change in Developed Countries: A Conference of the Universities-National Bureau Committee for Economic Research*, Princeton: Princeton University Press, p. 231).

Objections might certainly be raised here, to say that this is an oversimplified way of presenting differences between two distinguished scholarly disciplines. The answer to such objections would be that we are not comparing the disciplines as such, but rather stereotypes of fundamental assumptions about human behavior. As the latter may, however, be safely assumed to have a substantial grip on the minds of practitioners in the respective fields, it seems reasonable to claim that we are indeed faced here with a real problem. To the extent that fundamental assumptions about human behavior do promote the emergence of something akin to a belief system regarding such behavior, the ability to look for causes and effects will be correspondingly biased or circumscribed.

From the economics point of view, we may assume that the bias toward beliefs in opportunity and deregulation has given rise to expectations, tacit or otherwise, that market forces are capable on their own of solving most if not all of the problems that surround us. In the introduction to his provocatively titled work *The Wealth and Poverty of Nations*, David Landes formulates this worldview as follows: "This is the classical economists' view: increase is natural and will occur wherever opportunity and security exist. Remove the obstacles, and growth will take care of itself."[5]

The main reason we have chosen to place such emphasis here on Adam Smith and on the notion of economic man is that modern economics has come to assume such a special role, not only vis-à-vis the humanities, where culture and history figure prominently, but also in relation to the other social sciences, where it is sometimes held that the assumptions and models of economics fail to capture real-world problems.

This should not be taken to imply that all economists are insensitive to matters of culture and history, or that all of "the rest" take a dim view of the formal modeling that is so characteristic of modern economics. The problem that we seek to capture is that while there may be areas of mutual understanding, trends within the various subdisciplines of social science have diverged so far from each other that the foundations on which to build interdisciplinary undertakings have been rendered rather shaky.

To Douglass North, economic historian and winner of the 1993 Nobel Prize in economics, the growing trend of specialization within economics, and the similarly growing trend of divergence within the family of social sciences, gives rise to considerable concern. Since his caution is of great relevance to the argument that is pursued here, it may be worth citing at some length:

---

[5] Landes, David (1999), *The Wealth and Poverty of Nations: Why Some Are so Rich and Some so Poor*, New York: Norton, p. 31.

Economics is a theory of choice – so far so good. But the discipline neglects to explore the context within which choice occurs. We choose among alternatives that are themselves constructions of the human mind. Therefore how the mind works and understands the environment is the foundation of this study. But what is the environment? The human environment is a human construct of rules, norms, conventions, and ways of doing things that define the framework of human interaction. This human environment is divided by social scientists into discrete disciplines – economics, political science, sociology – but the constructions of the human mind that we require to make sense out of the human environment do not coincide with these artificial categories.[6]

The main purpose of North's statement is to enter a powerful plea for the merits of neo-institutional theory, of which North himself is one of the founding fathers. What is of particular importance from our point of view, however, is that the quote also serves to illustrate precisely why the analytical gap between economics and the other social sciences must be taken so seriously.

If we accept that human behavior is indeed conditioned by "rules, norms, conventions, and ways of doing things," which does seem rather plausible, then we have moved some distance away from the neatness of economic man and into what Elster refers to as the "jungle" of social norms.[7] The main implication is that if we observe outcomes that are different from what might have been expected, can we then really be sure that we have the proper tools with which to explain the underlying causes of the deviation?

Let us put it more specifically. If it really were the case that the havoc to be wreaked on the Russian economy by the misguided policy of economic shock therapy *could* have been predicted with tools from within the realm of standard neoclassical economic theory, how could it then be that so many took so long to realize that things were going so seriously awry? If, on the other hand, the latter failure was due to an inability of the theory to capture and deal with the looming hazards, what conclusions should then be drawn?

Given that the social sciences harbor such widely different assumptions on what determines how individuals respond to changes in their environments, it may not only be that we have insufficient tools with which to comprehend human action and interaction. Even worse, if our understanding of pressing problems rests on shaky foundations, then our ability to prescribe

---

[6] North, Douglass C. (2005), *Understanding the Process of Economic Change*, Princeton: Princeton University Press, p. 11.

[7] Elster, Jon (1989a), *The Cement of Society: A Study of Social Order*, Cambridge: Cambridge University Press, p. 100.

remedies for social ills will also have to be called into doubt. Even a quick glance at the social realities that surround us would surely lend strong support to a rather pessimistic view of the role that is played by social science in these regards.

Where an economist, for example, would believe in opportunity and call for deregulation to free up presumably healthy market forces, a sociologist might look for the causes of the problem in past actions and seek to recommend more broad-based social or cultural change. Can we determine who would be right? Or, is it perhaps that some problems are possible to remedy only with tools out of the economics box, and others only with approaches from sociology, or indeed from political science? If so, who is to determine which doctor to call?

We may perhaps even be faced with situations in which we have institutional arrangements, chiefly but not exclusively ones that are lodged in the informal dimension of a country's institutional matrix, which give rise to problems that we do not really know how to approach. This may be understood in two formally separate ways, that on closer reflection really only represent different ways of looking at the same problem.

One is to look for the presence of formal rules that allow destructive behavior – such as rent seeking, corruption, or outright fraud – or for the absence of informal norms that might serve to block such behavior. The other is to identify social improvements that are potentially within reach, and look for the presence of harmful institutions, formal or informal, that hinder such improvement, or for the absence of helpful institutions that might facilitate and support a move in the "good" direction.

We are not suggesting here that we are faced with things that simply *cannot* change, or *be* changed. That would clearly not represent acceptable scholarship. Our analytical thrust will rather be aimed at identifying situations where the root causes of variously defined social ills are poorly understood, and where, as a result, suggested remedies will at best be without effect. At worst, under certain conditions even the most well-intended policy interventions may end up producing unanticipated and seriously negative outcomes.

The case of attempted Russian systemic change provides ample illustration. As social science was confronted with the fallout of the collapse of the Soviet order, there was a general understanding that this represented a gigantic laboratory of sorts. For the first time ever, social scientists would be able to undertake a full-scale experiment, with real people and real societies. It did not quite reach the controlled and replicable environment of the hard sciences, but it did come close, very close. It could even be construed as what Jared Diamond and James A. Robinson have referred to as a "natural experiment of history."[8]

Given the presumed uniqueness of the opportunity, one might perhaps have thought that the tasks at hand should have been approached with open minds and without professional biases and vested interests. The rather deplorable outcome was "transition," a policy that presumes the outcome of an unprecedented experiment in societal transformation to be known in advance.

As mentioned earlier, Chapter 2 shall have much to say about the evolution of the social sciences, from the time of the classical economists and onward. Here we shall return more specifically to the combined belief in opportunity and self-interest and to the implications for undertaking sweeping deregulation. Is it reasonable to assume that one set of policies of liberalization will have the same effect everywhere, irrespective of historical legacy and/or cultural context?

FORGING AHEAD AND FALLING BEHIND

If the world really *had* worked according to the stylized rules of textbook economics, a great many things would have been very different, mainly in the sense that we would then have been right in expecting to see convergence. Even if some countries had gotten off to a bad start, the freeing up of trade should have led to factor price equalization, and the increasing mobility of both labor and capital should have led to improved factor allocation, in both cases with reduced differences in performance, wealth, and welfare as a result. If we look, however, at the way in which the real world has developed, there is precious little evidence that such convergence is taking place.

Looking back at the past couple of centuries, we may find two remarkable patterns that drive home the importance of these points. One is the extraordinary spurt of development that would give rise to accounts such as *The Rise of the West*,[9] *The Rise of the Western World*,[10] *The Unbound*

[8] Diamond, Jared and James A. Robinson (eds.) (2010), *Natural Experiments of History*, Cambridge, MA: Belknap Press of Harvard University Press.
[9] McNeill, William H. (1963), *The Rise of the West: A History of the Human Community*, Chicago, IL: University of Chicago Press.
[10] North, Douglass C. and Robert Paul Thomas (1973), *The Rise of the Western World: A New Economic History*, Cambridge: Cambridge University Press.

Prometheus,[11] *How the West Grew Rich,*[12] and *The Origins of Capitalism and the "Rise of the West."*[13] The other is the failure of the less successful to catch up with, to emulate, or even to imitate the successes of the West, a failure that would give rise to the somewhat derogatory caption of "The West and the Rest."[14]

While the nineteenth century was a time of colonialism and imperialism, factors that would later be held up as alleged causes of underdevelopment of the Third World, it was only in the twentieth century that the gap between rich and poor, or between North and South, really began to open up. According to calculations by Angus Maddison, as late as 1820 the average gross domestic product (GDP) per capita in the then "underdeveloped" world was still about half of that in the developed world. By 1998, however, the "development gap" had widened to no less than seven times. Looking more specifically at the relation between the United States and Africa, the gap had widened to a depressing 20:1, and it was continuing to expand.[15]

How do we account for this? There are two questions, or even challenges, involved here. The first and most basic is to explain why countries have performed so differently over time. In his main work about institutional change, cited in the introduction, North highlights precisely this question: "The central puzzle of human history is to account for the widely divergent paths of historical change."[16]

His own pointed question goes straight to the heart of the economists' beliefs in opportunity and self-interest: "Wouldn't the political entrepreneurs

[11] Landes, David (1969), *The Unbound Prometheus: Technological Change and Industrial Development in Western Europe from 1750 to the Present,* Cambridge: Cambridge University Press.
[12] Rosenberg, Nathan and L. E. Birdzell, Jr. (1986), *How the West Grew Rich: The Economic Transformation of the Industrial World,* New York: Basic Books.
[13] Mielants, Eric H. (2007), *The Origins of Capitalism and the "Rise of the West,"* Philadelphia, PA: Temple University Press.
[14] The notion as such has been around for some time, gaining particular prominence in relation to debates on Samuel Huntington's thesis on the "Clash of Civilizations" (Huntington, Samuel P. (1993), "The Clash of Civilizations," *Foreign Affairs,* vol. 72, no. 3, and Huntington, Samuel P. (1996), *The Clash of Civilizations and the Remaking of World Order,* New York: Simon and Schuster). Most recently, and explicitly, it appears in Scruton, Roger (2002), *The West and the Rest: Globalization and the Terrorist Threat,* Wilmington, DE: ISI Books.
[15] Maddison, Angus (2001), *The World Economy: A Millennial Perspective,* Paris: OECD, p. 17. The category of "developed world" (Group A) includes Western Europe, Western Offshoots (United States, Canada, Australia, and New Zealand), and Japan. The "underdeveloped world" (Group B) comprises the rest.
[16] North, Douglass C. (1990a), *Institutions, Institutional Change and Economic Performance,* Cambridge: Cambridge University Press, p. 6.

in stagnant economies quickly emulate the policies of more successful ones? How can we explain the radically different performance of economies over long periods of time?"[17] The very same question is asked by Avner Greif, in a discussion of the role of cultural beliefs: "Why do societies fail to adopt the institutional structure of more economically successful ones?"[18] Why indeed?

North's answer to questions such as these is provocative, partly because he assigns the blame so squarely to shortcomings in the development of suitable theory: "The disparity in the performance of economies and the persistence of disparate economies through time have not been satisfactorily explained by development economists, despite forty years of immense effort. The simple fact is that the theory employed is not up to the task."[19] While the formulation as such may seem harsh, it does bring out an important problem.

The fundamental reason we are faced here with such controversy goes beyond simple fault finding. The real provocation to mainstream theory is that the failure of poor countries to catch up with the rich goes against the grain of firmly entrenched beliefs in the power of market forces to iron out differences in achievement, simply by rewarding success and by penalizing failure. As North puts it, development over time should be marked by feedback mechanisms whereby "competition would weed out inferior institutions and reward by survival those that better solve human problems."[20] This, moreover, should apply to entrepreneurs in the economic as well as the political spheres. The simple logic is that there should be no room for inferior solutions to endure.

In a somewhat broader perspective, the failure of market forces to produce convergence between countries also goes against the grain of firmly entrenched beliefs in catch-up growth. From Alexander Gerschenkron onward, there has been a strong belief that being late is good, that the latecomer will have the benefit of being able to simply copy the achievements of the rich and to avoid their prior mistakes.[21] If only obstacles can be removed and economic agents can be allowed to freely seek out opportunity, then the development gap in itself should act as a powerful engine of growth. Since

---

[17] Ibid., p. 7.
[18] Greif, Avner (1994a), "Cultural Beliefs and the Organization of Society: A Historical and Theoretical Reflection on Collectivist and Individualist Societies," *Journal of Political Economy*, vol. 102, no. 5, p. 912.
[19] North, *Institutions*, p. 11.
[20] Ibid., p. 7.
[21] Gerschenkron, Alexander (1962), *Economic Backwardness in Historical Perspective*, Cambridge, MA: Harvard University Press.

neither of these beliefs has been possible to square with actual development, there are firm grounds on which to question the general validity of the theory.

Proceeding to the second of our two questions, we are faced with even more of a challenge. Here we must go beyond the failure of the market forces to get the job done on their own, and ask how it can be that the combined outcome of first decolonization, then massive development aid, and then globalization has been such a gross disappointment. With some significant exceptions, it has clearly failed to produce any form of significant impact on the size of the development gap.

Returning to Maddison's calculations, we may find several interesting patterns.[22] The first is that the period 1950–73 comes across as a "golden age of unparalleled prosperity." World GDP rose by nearly 5 percent per year, and world GDP per capita by nearly 3 percent per year. Although some grew more than others, there was increasing prosperity in all regions, and even some convergence (although the latter mainly concerned a narrowing of the gap between the United States and other capitalist nations).

In the subsequent quarter century, things changed dramatically for the worse. The overall growth in world GDP per capita was reduced to less than half, and there was growing divergence in performance between regions.

On the positive side, a small number of countries in Asia (mainly China and India), comprising half the world's population, achieved even faster growth than under the golden age. Based on the performance of this "resurgent Asia" group alone, one might have claimed to have found strong empirical support for the belief in catch-up growth.

On the negative side, however, the same period also saw the emergence of a group of 168 "faltering economies," comprising about one-third of the world's population, that were falling behind rather than catching up. Over the years 1973–98, Africa recorded no advance in per capita income, Eastern Europe and the Former Soviet Union experienced a drop by a quarter, and in Latin America and in many Asian countries, income gains were a mere fraction of the golden age. While the case of the "transition economies" must be viewed as rather special, and although some calculations of the global Gini coefficient across households (a measure of what share of households receives what share of incomes) have shown some decrease in global inequality, the fate of the 168 that are "faltering" does represent a trend that is nothing short of depressing.

[22] Maddison, *The World Economy*, pp. 22–23.

Three important conclusions are to be drawn from these numbers. The *first* notes that those countries that have achieved economic development and a sustained reduction in deprivation are not to be found among the ones that have been the most pampered by foreign aid and assistance. This indicates that under certain conditions market forces will work far better than foreign aid. It is rather striking, for example, that from 1961, when the prosperous British colony Tanganyika gained independence, until 1998, when Tanzania was counted among the world's poorest countries, the country's GDP per capita rose from 418 to 553 constant international dollars. Meanwhile, GDP per capita in South Korea rose more than tenfold, from 1,124 to 12,152 constant international dollars.[23] While Tanzania had pursued self-reliant "African socialism," backed by massive foreign aid, South Korea had opted for a strategy of export-led economic growth.

The *second* conclusion is rather paradoxical, in the sense that those "winners" that have performed in accordance with the belief in opportunity and self-interest have not in the main been taken as proof of the theory. Instead they have been labeled as "miracles" – ranging from the German *Wirtschaftswunder* under Konrad Adenauer, to the strong growth in various Asian "tiger economies." There has been much controversy around how to explain the latter cases, in particular with respect to attempts at finding econometric proof for what growth factors may have been the most important. Perhaps the most sobering contribution, however, has been made by Paul Krugman, suggesting that there has been nothing miraculous at all involved here – only more and harder labor.[24]

The *third*, and perhaps most depressing, conclusion concerns the dismal performance of the "faltering economies." In sharp contrast to the previously widely spread beliefs in convergence and catch-up growth, we are presently faced with a world that is distinctly divided into winners and losers. Landes portrays it as follows, in his own very blunt manner: "This world is divided roughly into three kinds of nations: those that spend lots of money to keep their weight down; those whose people eat to live; and those whose people don't know where their next meal is coming from."[25]

It was in the midst of mounting pessimism about the prospects for promoting development in the Third World that the Second World was suddenly

---

[23] Ibid., pp. 304, 326. The measuring standard is 1990 Geary-Khamis purchasing power converted dollars. On the latter, see further, Maddison, Angus (1995), *Monitoring the World Economy 1820–1992*, Paris: OECD Development Centre, pp. 164–79.

[24] Krugman, Paul (1994), "The Myth of Asia's Miracle," *Foreign Affairs*, vol. 73, no. 6.

[25] Landes, *The Wealth and Poverty of Nations*, p. xix.

and unexpectedly thrown into chaos. As the centrally planned economies of Eastern Europe and the Soviet Union collapsed, and as Communist Party power melted away, a "window of opportunity" was seen to open up for "systemic change" to be undertaken. Again, the general thrust of expectations would be pinned on the forces that rest in opportunity and self-interest, to be freed up by deregulation.

Although it was never formulated as such, it did at times seem as though the "Washington Consensus"[26] on how reform should be pursued rested on a deep belief that democracy, market economy, and the rule of law jointly and simply represent a sort of societal default position – if only all obstacles can be removed, success will be guaranteed. The rhetoric of reform was highly reflective of this attitude, expressing hopes, for example, that the "grabbing hand" of the state should be entered into the "velvet glove" of privatization.[27]

Yet again, however, the outcome would leave quite a lot to be desired. Far from recording rapid economic recovery and catch-up with the West, all of the transition economies were plunged into transformational recession with ensuing social dislocations that in some cases would be serious indeed.[28] In the case of the Russian Federation, it would not be until 2007 that the country's GDP had managed to crawl back up to the level achieved in 1990.[29] Something very clearly had gone wrong, very wrong. The question is what.

Speaking at the Woodrow Wilson Center in Washington, D.C., in June 1997, Federal Reserve Chairman Alan Greenspan offered the following verdict over the beliefs in systemic change and shock therapeutic

---

[26] The notion was originally coined by John Williamson to capture the type of advice that was being offered by the World Bank and the IMF in support of economic reforms in Latin America in the late 1980s (Williamson, John (ed.) (1990), *Latin American Adjustment: How Much Has Happened?* Washington, DC: Institute for International Economics). Subsequently, it would become something of a household expression in discussions of reforms in the Former Soviet Union – used appreciatively at first, and then increasingly as a slur. See also Williamson, John (1993), "Democracy and the 'Washington Consensus,'" *World Development*, vol. 21, no. 8, 1329–1336.

[27] Shleifer, Andrei and Robert Vishny (1998), *The Grabbing Hand: Government Pathologies and Their Cures*, Cambridge, MA: Harvard University Press.

[28] It should be recognized that there was a good deal of variation, with Poland, for example, suffering an output decline lasting a little over two years after which strong growth ensued (Hanson, Philip (2002), "Barriers to Long-Run Growth in Russia," *Economy and Society*, vol. 31, no. 1, p. 64 and *passim*).

[29] Over the years from 1989, which was the last year of growth in the USSR, until 1998, when financial markets collapsed, GDP fell by 43.7 percent. By the end of 2006, it was still 5.5 percent below 1989 (data available on http://www.ebrd.com/country/sector/econo/stats/sei.xls).

deregulation: "Much of what we took for granted in our free market system and assumed to be human nature was not nature at all, but culture."[30] We shall have reason, in subsequent chapters, to return to his understanding of "culture."

Here we may conclude by noting that facts on the ground, in the Third World as well as in the transition economies of the Former Soviet Union, have come to deviate rather strikingly from what the belief in opportunity and self-interest might have led us to predict. Even more so, given the often rather substantial efforts that have been made to promote development and/or transition via advice, aid, and assistance from the outside, results again have fallen far short of what might have been reasonably expected, had the world worked according to the market ideal.

The case of Russia may be viewed as a case in point. Compared to other transition economies, Russia received an inordinate amount of both aid and credits, coupled with political support that entailed turning a blind eye toward a whole range of matters that rightly could and should have been severely criticized.[31] In the latter list it may suffice to include Boris Yeltsin's unconstitutional suppression of the Supreme Soviet, in October 1993; his decision to launch the first war in Chechnya, in December 1994; and the various shenanigans that resulted in his reelection in the summer of 1996.

All of these constitute illustrations of severe moral hazards, that is, of the dangers of counterproductive fallout that are involved in maintaining silence about negative behavior out of unwarranted fear that critique might make things even worse. Was it really wise to maintain silence about Yeltsin's methods in suppressing the country's parliament, in the vain hope that this would restore him to a more democratic path? Or, to take an even more

---

[30] Greenspan, Alan (1997), "Remarks by Chairman Alan Greenspan," available at http://www.federalreserve.gov/boarddocs/speeches/1997/19970610.htm, accessed on January 19, 2010. It may be worth noting here that his speech was presented well over a year before the financial meltdown that struck Moscow in August 1998. If Western fund managers had been ready to listen to Greenspan, whose word normally was not to be questioned, losses of many billions in defaulted Russian securities and credits might perhaps have been avoided. Unfortunately, Greenspan's message on Russia was too far out of sync with the prevailing hype on the market.

[31] What Russia actually did receive was far less than the $30 billion in annual support over the first five years of reform that was deemed necessary by Jeffrey Sachs, one of the leading foreign advisors to the Russian government, in discussions on what came to be known as the "Grand Bargain." Although many of those involved have since argued that assistance of that magnitude would have made a big difference and that the failure of the West to provide it was hence something of a betrayal, it will have to remain an iffy issue. It is surely more likely that additional billions in aid would have simply disappeared – in the same manner as those billions that were provided.

pronounced example, was it really wise to maintain silence about the policy of literally unrestrained lending pursued by the International Monetary Fund (IMF), even though the Kremlin brazenly broke all agreements and deliberately redirected credits to purposes such as the war in Chechnya and the campaign to reelect Yeltsin?[32]

A particular form of collateral damage from this policy of silence was that the Kremlin's spin doctors would have an easy time indeed projecting an image of success that had very little to do with facts on the ground. It may suffice to recall the events of August 1998, when the Russian ruble was devalued and when the country's financial markets collapsed. The massive losses that were sustained by Western investors must be at least partly understood as a consequence of faulty analysis in the times leading up to this crash.[33]

The commercial and political backlash that ensued was surely to some extent motivated by how blatantly the Russian government and Central Bank favored its own insiders, at the expense of foreign investors. It is, however, hard to leave out completely that the anger may also have been at least partly conditioned by feelings that one really should have known better, that too many pundits had been too self-serving and too eager for short-term profit to face up to the dangers of total meltdown that were involved in Russia's financial market mismanagement. The name of the game yet again was greed, and the outcome was predictable.

WHY *SOME* POOR PEOPLE STAY POOR

Given that so much has been at stake, ranging from the plight of poor people, to aid that has been misspent, and organizational and political prestige that has been wagered and lost, it is not surprising that there have been some rather heated exchanges of opinion regarding what has gone wrong, and who might be rightly to blame.[34] We shall steer well clear of such debates

---

[32] Hedlund, Stefan (2001), "Russia and the IMF: A Sordid Tale of Moral Hazard," *Demokratizatsiya*, vol. 9, no. 1, pp. 104–36.

[33] The immediate effect was that the Russian government defaulted on $40 billion in treasury bills, known as GKOs, to which may be added credits to Russian banks that also went into default, and other sundry items, few of which would be repaid at face value. The exact share lost by foreign creditors in this meltdown is hard to figure out, for the very simple reason that many deals had been done via creative channels, but it most certainly was quite substantial.

[34] In the specific case of Russian transition, the blame game even penetrated into the realm of high politics. In the campaign for the 2000 presidential election, where Al Gore was running against George Bush, an all-Republican committee in the U.S. Congress, chaired

and seek instead to probe the more fundamental question of why it is that only *some* countries that have been poor have succeeded in breaking out and in generating substantial growth, while others have remained in abject poverty.[35]

The main problem that must be approached here is that addressing the question of why a country got off to a bad start is very far from the same as explaining why it has since failed to break out of its predicament. To drive this point home, a little digression may be helpful. Many different cases might be usefully advanced to illustrate, but given our focus on Russia, we shall remain within the Russian tradition.

An added reason for this choice may be that Russia is so often depicted as essentially different from the rest of Europe – indeed in some accounts even as sui generis, not to be compared with any other case.[36] We shall postpone commenting on such views, which will figure prominently in Chapter 4, and rest content with noting that the main reasons advanced to explain Russian difference relate to climate and religion. In superficial terms, these are commonly accepted.

It is a fact that Kievan Rus, which preceded Muscovy and subsequent Russia, adopted Orthodox Christianity toward the end of the tenth century. It is a fact that large parts of what would become Russia are marked by a seriously inhospitable climate, and it is a fact that Muscovy got off to a bad start. Against this background, it is not surprising that any standard text on

by Representative Christopher Cox, put together a massive report, titled "Russia's Road to Corruption," that purported to detail "How the Clinton Administration Exported Government Instead of Free Enterprise and Failed the Russian People" (text available on http://www.globalsecurity.org/wmd/library/news/russia/2000/russia/index.html). Given the involvement of Vice President Gore in the highly controversial Gore-Chernomyrdin Commission, the obvious intention was to damage his foreign policy credentials and thus also his electoral prospects. To what extent the "Cox Report" may actually have influenced the outcome of the election is clearly impossible to tell, but it surely cannot have done much to help Gore.

[35] Needless to say, the issue of persistent Third World poverty is one that has attracted a huge literature. Absent any ambition to provide even a brief overview, two works may be usefully mentioned. One is Paul Collier's award-winning *The Bottom Billion: Why the Poorest Countries Are Failing and What Can Be Done About It* (Oxford University Press), which castigates at length rich governments and donor agencies, claiming they have simply elected to forget about those countries – with a combined population of about one billion people – that are at the very bottom. The other is Gregory Clark's book, *A Farewell to Alms: A Brief Economic History of the World* (Princeton University Press, 2007), which suggests that culture – rather than exploitation, geography, or resources – explains the wealth and poverty of nations. Both, implicitly and explicitly, challenge the prevailing notion that poor countries can be developed by outside intervention.

[36] For example, Pipes, Richard (1974), *Russia under the Old Regime*, New York: Charles Scribner's Sons, p. 23.

Russian history will devote a section to the harshness of nature and to the adoption of Orthodox Christianity.[37]

Some may certainly object to such accounts by arguing that other countries, such as Greece, have adopted Orthodox Christianity without being locked into the special path that was to be Russia's, and that some countries, such as Canada, are located in equally inhospitable climates, again without going down the Russian path.

Objections of this kind may be partly deflected by arguing that Orthodoxy and the harshness of nature were necessary but not also sufficient conditions for Russian specificity to arise. To complete the explanation, we might add a third factor, also an undisputable fact, namely, that of serious security problems.

To the Russian historian Vasily Kluchevsky, it was a question of keeping the nomadic tribes along the eastern frontier at bay: "Every year during the sixteenth century thousands of the frontier population laid down their lives for their country, while tens of thousands of Moscow's best warriors were dispatched southwards to guard the inhabitants of the more central provinces from pillage and enslavement."[38] To the less impassioned Canadian historian William McNeill, it was a question of standing up to Western powers that wielded far superior military technology.[39]

In both cases, we may recall the emphasis that was placed by Landes on the combination of opportunity *and* security. In neither case, however, have we succeeded in explaining why Russia would also *remain* "backward," long after the time when the Empire had achieved both strength and security, and when the call for lifelong service by the nobility had been abolished.

The message that is conveyed by this Russian example may be broken down into two central questions. First, if it is the case that we perceive striking institutional continuity over time, do we then have the theoretical tools with which to explain how and why institutions are being reproduced? Attempts to answer this question have given rise to theorizing around multiple and inferior equilibria, institutional lock-in effects, and possible path dependencies. We shall have much more to say about this in Chapter 6, which will argue that history matters.

The second of our two questions is even more challenging. To the extent that perceived institutional continuity is viewed as a problem, which is

[37] For example, Billington, James H. (1970), *The Icon and the Axe: An Interpretive History of Russian Culture*, New York: Vintage, and Pipes, Richard (1974), *Russia under the Old Regime*.
[38] Kluchevsky, V. O. (1912), *A History of Russia*, Vol. 2, London: J. M. Dent & Sons, p. 118.
[39] McNeill, *The Rise of the West*, pp. 604–11.

clearly not the case in the success story of the "Rise of the West," do we then have the appropriate tools that may help devise a way of breaking out of the bad equilibrium? Attempts to theorize around this question will not only have to focus on endogenous rather than exogenous factors. It will also be necessary to deal with the informal rather than the formal dimensions of a country's institutional matrix, thus again bringing into play the whole complex of why and how history matters.

The core of the argument maintains that several decades of ambitions by the rich industrialized countries to promote development in the Third World, and more lately to achieve "transition" in the Former Soviet Union, have rested, quite explicitly, on no more than a partial understanding of the tasks at hand. This in turn has led to a narrow focus on getting the formal institutions right – ranging from beliefs in the sufficiency of deregulation to promote catch-up growth, to active promotion of IMF-sponsored structural adjustment programs, and the transfer of billions in aid and soft credits. As we may recall from Maddison's numbers cited earlier, the outcome has not been a great success.

What is really at stake here, from an economics point of view, is the extent to which countries may succeed in realizing their full potentials. The technical dimension of this question may be captured in the notion of a production possibility frontier, the point of which is that countries may restructure the composition of their output by simply reallocating resources between different uses. Based on technologically defined production functions, the production possibility frontier will show how much of one good will have to be given up to produce an extra unit of another good. In a general equilibrium framework, countries may choose freely at which point on this frontier they desire to be, and – most important – they will always be at some point on this frontier.

Needless to say, this understanding does not tally with observable reality. For a somewhat provocative approach to explaining why, we may turn to a classic article by Mancur Olson, titled "Big Bills Left on the Sidewalk: Why Some Nations Are Rich and Others Poor."[40]

His point of departure is a familiar anecdote about a professor and a graduate student walking down the street. When the latter bends down to pick up a $100 bill, he is held back with the caution that if the note had been real it would have been already picked up by someone else. The anecdote is funny, at least to economists, in the sense that it captures the belief

---

[40] Olson, Mancur (1996), "Big Bills Left on the Sidewalk: Why Some Nations Are Rich and Others Poor," *Journal of Economic Perspectives*, vol. 10, no. 2, pp. 3–24.

in opportunity, and in maximization on all margins, assuming that recontracting will continue until all deals have been made and there are no more $100 bills left to be picked up.

Olson's pointed question concerns why so many of the nations in this world have allowed their sidewalks to remain littered with $100 bills, that is, why they have failed to even approach their production possibility frontiers. He also provides a staggering estimate of output thus forgone: "The sums lost because the poor countries obtain only a fraction of – and because the richest countries do not reach – their economic potentials are measured in the trillions of dollars."[41]

Let us add to this deadweight loss that really high rates of growth will never be recorded in the already rich nations but only in a select group of poor nations. The real challenge then becomes to determine what it is that decides *which* of the poor nations shall be successful in escaping poverty, and which of the transition economies will be successful in reaching their predetermined destination of liberal market economy. If the answer is seen to rest in building good institutions and in conducting good policies, as Olson maintains, then it may be tempting to agree that "the best thing a society can do to increase its prosperity is to wise up."[42] The question that remains to be answered is what this should be taken to mean, more specifically.

For a somewhat different approach to the same problem, we may turn to Joel Mokyr's work on the role of technological creativity in economic progress. While to Olson the problem was to explain why countries fail to achieve their full production possibilities, Mokyr instead chooses to ask under what conditions technological change may increase a country's productive potential, understood by economists as an outward shift in the production possibility frontier.

In his book, he sets out by noting how unfairly the odds of success are distributed across the world: "There is very little in common between the quality of life that can be expected by an average person born in, say, rural Cameroon or urban Java, and one born in Greenwich, Connecticut or Oslo, Norway."[43]

While this may seem trivial at first sight, there is implied in his argument a dimension that is very far from trivial. Insisting that technological change

[41] Ibid., p. 22.
[42] Ibid., p. 21.
[43] Mokyr, Joel (1990), *The Lever of Riches: Technological Creativity and Economic Progress*, New York: Oxford University Press, p. 3.

is tantamount to a free lunch, in the sense that it represents "an increase in output that is not commensurate with the increase in effort and cost necessary to bring it about," he deliberately challenges economic orthodoxy, and he proceeds to make it worse: "The question I am interested in here is not why some individuals are more creative than others, but why were and are there societies that have more creative individuals in them than others."[44]

By thus framing the endlessly discussed problem of how to explain technological change as a *social* phenomenon, embedded in what we may refer to as the cultural dimension of a society's institutional matrix, he moves the challenge of explanation firmly into the institutional field. He also offers a suggestion, lifted from economic historian Ross Thompson, that "technical change is like God. It is much discussed, worshipped by some, rejected by others, but little understood."[45]

If we accept that explanation must aim for endogenous rather than exogenous factors, we shall have come part of the way, but we will still not be out of the woods. As Landes points out, there are two very different ways of looking at the problem of underdevelopment. His argument recalls what was said earlier about something akin to a belief system within economics, and it implies that endogenous explanations may be sought in two rather different ways:

One says that we are so rich and they so poor because we are so good and they so bad; that is, we are hardworking, knowledgeable, educated, well-governed, efficacious, and productive, and they are the reverse. The other says that we are so rich and they so poor because we are so bad and they so good; we are greedy, ruthless, exploitative, aggressive, while they are weak, innocent, virtuous, abused and vulnerable.[46]

The main difference between these two diametrically opposed approaches to the very same problem concerns not only the controversial role of venality but even more so the role of belief systems that cause policy makers to look in specific directions. This operates on two levels, one concerning what party may be assumed to be at fault, and the other in what part of the institutional matrix causes of problems must be sought. Let us begin with the former.

If we assume, for example, that the root causes of unequal development are to be found in Brussels, then we do have a fair idea of what it would take

[44] Ibid., p. 8.
[45] Ibid., p. 6.
[46] Landes, David S. (1990), "Why Are We So Rich and They So Poor?," *American Economic Review*, vol. 80, no. 2, p. 1.

to find a cure. Accepting that the Third World would benefit more from scrapping the protectionist European common agricultural policy than from being the recipient of compensatory foreign aid, we may conclude that the cure rests in breaking up vested interests and in getting ready to deal with irate French farmers. While this may indeed present an insurmountable political obstacle, making it preferable to dish out further billions of taxpayer euros in compensatory foreign aid, there are no serious theoretical problems involved.

If, on the other hand, we assume that the problem is lodged in, say, the political culture of Dar es Salaam, then we do have a major theoretical problem. If it is the case, as Lawrence Harrison suggests, that obstacles to achieving a sustained reduction in deprivation reside in the part of the institutional matrix that we may refer to as "culture," then we are faced with a major complexity: "If some cultural values *are* fundamental obstacles to progress – if they help explain the intractability of the problems of poverty and injustice in a good part of the Third World – then there is no alternative to the promotion of cultural change."[47]

While this statement clearly takes us to the second of our two levels, asking in what dimension of the institutional matrix we must look for solutions to the problems that we face, the remaining question is where this all leaves us. Shifting attention from the formal to the informal dimension may seem intuitively appealing, but it also opens a Pandora's box of both theoretical and methodological complications.

If we leave aside for the moment all potential objections holding that we have no moral right to argue for cultural change, it will remain a troublesome fact that the policy implications are very far from clear. Harrison not only recognizes that "culture *is* difficult to deal with both politically and emotionally." He also notes that it is "difficult to deal with intellectually because there are problems of definition and measurement and because cause-and-effect relationships between culture and other variables like policies, institutions, and economic development run in both directions."[48]

Returning to the case of Russia, we may recall Greenspan's insistence that the cause of the failure of Russian transition was that the culture and infrastructure of the market were missing, and listen to the continuation of his statement: "There is a vast amount of capitalist culture and

[47] Harrison, Lawrence E. (2000b), "Why Culture Matters," in Lawrence E. Harrison and Samuel P. Huntington (eds.), *Culture Matters: How Values Shape Human Progress*, New York: Basic Books, p. xxxi.

[48] Ibid., p. xxxii. See also Harrison, Lawrence E. (2000a), *Underdevelopment Is a State of Mind: The Latin American Case*, Lanham: Madison Books.

infrastructure underpinning market economies that has evolved over generations: laws, conventions, behaviors, and a wide variety of business professions and practices that have no important functions in a centrally planned economy."[49]

While it is easy enough to sympathize with his point of view, it does raise the same problem that we encounter when political scientists argue that countries with high trust, or with high social capital perform better than those less well endowed.[50] The observations may be correct, but the causality is unclear and the policy implications remain shrouded in mystery. We shall have ample reason in subsequent chapters to return to these matters.

Turning now to wrap up the first part of our argument on opportunity and self-interest, we may recall the time when the Soviet order collapsed and emphasize the role of social science in conceptualizing the tasks that lay ahead. Noting that strategies of at times predatory short-term self-interest seeking would come to deviate so substantially from what many observers had expected, we must concluded that we are faced here with substantial analytical shortcomings.

In subsequent chapters we shall seek to show that mainstream theorizing had failed to grasp what the reality of command economy was all about, that it had literally refused to consider the weight of Russia's historical legacy, and that it had nurtured an overly idealized vision of what liberated markets would be able to achieve. The rude awakening that was to follow has been captured as follows by Greenspan, who better than most may be viewed as the true incarnation of free market economy:

Until the wall fell and the need to develop market economies out of the rubble of Eastern Europe's central-planning regimes became apparent, few economists had been thinking about the institutional foundations that free markets need. Now, unintentionally, the Soviets were performing an experiment for us. And some of the lessons were startling. The collapse of central planning did not automatically establish capitalism, contrary to the rosy predictions of many conservative-leaning politicians.[51]

---

[49] Greenspan, "Remarks by Chairman Alan Greenspan."

[50] Both of these notions have attracted substantial scholarship across the social sciences. On the former, see in particular Fukuyama, Francis (1995), *Trust: The Social Virtues and the Creation of Prosperity*, New York: Free Press. The notion of "social capital" is normally ascribed to sociologist James Coleman (see esp. Coleman, James S. (1990), *Foundations of Social Theory*, Cambridge, MA: Harvard University Press, ch. 12). The first to introduce it, however, was Glenn C. Loury (1977), "A Dynamic Theory of Racial Income Differences," in Phyllis A. Wallace and Annette M. La Mond (eds.), *Women, Minorities and Employment Discrimination*, Lexington, MA: Lexington Books, p. 176.

[51] Greenspan, Alan (2008), *The Age of Turbulence: Adventures in a New World*, New York: Penguin, p. 139.

If we add that the rude awakening would afflict not only "conservative-leaning politicians" but also numerous mainstream theorists who were involved in formulating policy for the transition, the bottom line will have to be that we need to reconsider our understanding of the driving factors of self-interest seeking – ranging from beliefs and expectations to deeply embedded social norms.

Let us now look at the reasons that social science at large, and economics in particular, came so ill prepared to deal with the tasks that emerged when the doors to the great "reform laboratory" were opened.

2

Scope and Tradition of Social Science

Since time immemorial, discovery and exploration have formed integral parts of human existence. On a mundane level, humans have strived tirelessly to improve their lot by coming up with better practices and by searching for better places to make their living. The outcome has been a steady process of low-tech innovation and of a gradual colonization of new lands. On a more spectacular level, such endeavors have been associated with great names, with individual explorers and inventors whose contributions live on in the history books.

The history of science and exploration most certainly is a fascinating one. At the superficial level it is quite simply a good story. It is hard indeed not to be captured by the adventures of the great explorers, who set out to discover India and China, who delved deep into the heart of Africa, and who raced to be the first to reach the North and the South Poles. Similarly, it is hard not to be captured by the lives and works of the great scientists, who gave us breakthrough knowledge in fields like mathematics, astronomy, physics, and medicine, to mention but a few. Along both of these tracks it is quite clear that humans have been possessed, across cultures, by a drive to discover and to improve.

At a more fundamental level, however, it will immediately be evident that the good story is rife with complications and with important questions that are still looking for answers. Why, for example, has technological progress has been so uneven across cultures? Why did the Chinese and the Arabs, once so far ahead of the Europeans, so "suddenly" drop out of the race? Are there features that make some cultures more hospitable to science and discovery than others? Is Joel Mokyr correct in asking "what kind of social environment makes individuals innovative, what kind of

45

stimuli, incentives, and institutions create an economy that encourages technological creativity?"[1]

Are we, on the other hand, sure that we have told the full story of how an immense spurt of technological creativity suddenly catapulted a few European nations onto the growth trajectory that would become known as "The Rise of the West?"[2] Have Douglass North and Robert Thomas got it right when they link this process narrowly to markets and property rights?[3] Can we really explain why the steam engine would have to wait for James Watt, although the underlying technology had been known already in ancient Egypt?[4] And are we really in agreement that 1750 is a correct timing for the takeoff that created "the West"?[5]

This chapter does not seek to answer any of these questions. Our ambition is more narrowly focused on the emergence and evolution of organized scholarship and on the eventual rise of what would come to be known, in the early nineteenth century, as "social science."[6] As we proceed along this track, however, it will be useful to consider the questions just asked.

Throughout most of history there has been a clear link between science and discovery, on the one hand, and the betterment of the condition of human existence, on the other. Although we must recognize that the story also has a dark side, in the striking human capacity for devising new and

---

[1] Mokyr, Joel (1990), *The Lever of Riches: Technological Creativity and Economic Progress*, New York: Oxford University Press, p. 8.

[2] Landes, David (1969), *The Unbound Prometheus: Technological Change and Industrial Development in Western Europe from 1750 to the Present*, Cambridge: Cambridge University Press; Rosenberg, Nathan and L. E. Birdzell, Jr. (1986), *How the West Grew Rich: The Economic Transformation of the Industrial World*, New York: Basic Books.

[3] North, Douglass C. and Robert Paul Thomas (1973), *The Rise of the Western World: A New Economic History*, Cambridge: Cambridge University Press.

[4] The first inventor was the Greek physicist Hero of Alexandria, who is believed to have lived in the first century BC. Although based on the same principle as the steam engine, his invention of a steam ball that could be made to rotate never found much practical use.

[5] Based on his previously cited calculations of world GDP for the past millennium, Angus Maddison challenges conventional wisdom and suggests that the real transition to high growth did not take place until 1820 (Maddison, Angus (2001), *The World Economy: A Millennial Perspective*, Paris: OECD, p. 45). A further support is that none of the classical economists, who were active in the second half of the eighteenth century, mentioned anything about a pending acceleration in growth.

[6] The term as such first appeared in an 1824 book by William Thompson, titled *An Inquiry into the Principles of the Distribution of Wealth, Most Conducive to Human Happiness; Applied to the Newly Proposed System of Voluntary Equality of Wealth*. The book is available in reprint as Thompson, William (1963), *An Inquiry into the Principles of the Distribution of Wealth, Most Conducive to Human Happiness*, New York: Augustus M. Kelley. This term appears in the chapter on "Preliminary observations."

better ways of inflicting harm on others, it is impossible not to be amazed at all the ways in which human inventiveness has served over time to improve the quality of life of successive generations of humans. At the very least, this applies to the hard sciences.

Once we shift the focus of our attention to matters that are of more immediate relevance to the present text, matters that concern improvements of the social order, the story will come across as considerably different. Here, as Albert Hirschman underlines, potential ambitions to strive for betterment are of more recent origin: "Once upon a time, not all that long ago, the social, political and economic order under which men and women were living was taken for granted."[7] The causes of misery and injustice were long viewed as unchangeable, such as human nature or the will of God. Only in the eighteenth century did thinkers begin to suggest that human happiness could be *engineered* by changing the social order, a task that was captured in Saint-Just's famous phrase: "The idea of happiness is new in Europe."[8] This was the time of "Enlightenment" and of the first steps toward social science.

The main question that will be asked in the following is to what extent *modern* social science really lives up to the ideal of striving for the betterment of human existence. Is it perhaps the case that the broader trends in the social sciences over the past few decades have been pointed in the wrong direction, toward *ars gratia artis*, rather than toward socially useful contributions to knowledge and understanding? The question is deliberately provocative, and answers may possibly not live up to the challenge. It does, however, serve to focus our attention.

In the following we begin by taking a brief look at the European Enlightenment. Arguably the most profound of all the various mental transformations that have combined to shape Western civilization, it will provide a suitable context for our discussion of systemic differences. The main reason it still remains a source of great controversy is that the idea of a "perfectible social order" arose at about the same time people began to realize the unintended effects of human actions and decisions. While the former was a product of the French Enlightenment, the latter was a principal contribution of the Scottish moralists.[9] Friction between these two approaches would have a major impact on how subsequent thinkers

[7] Hirschman, Albert O. (1982), "Rival Interpretations of Market Society: Civilizing, Destructive, or Feeble?," *Journal of Economic Literature*, vol. 20, no. 4, p. 1463.
[8] Ibid.
[9] Ibid., pp. 1463–64.

perceived capitalism and the market economy – as something that promoted or eroded good manners and morals.

It is within this context that we shall outline how the once unified human and social dimensions of scientific discovery were transformed into multiple and increasingly specialized subdisciplines, which over time have moved further and further apart. In conclusion, we shall also review briefly how an increasing ambition by the social sciences at large to imitate the "hard" sciences has become path dependent and may prove difficult indeed to reverse.

EUROPEAN ENLIGHTENMENT

What has come to be known as the Enlightenment was the outcome of efforts by a rather small group of men in a rather short span of time. Most of the outstanding works that are normally associated with this important phase in European cultural history were published within a few years, from 1748 until 1751.[10] Before we look in more detail at these contributions, note that European Enlightenment emerged out of times that were troubled indeed.

The preceding phase of Reformation and Counterreformation had resulted not only in turbulent relations between church and state, with many of the worldly powers vacillating in their allegiances, but also the Thirty Years' War, which utterly devastated large parts of what is now eastern Germany. Even after that war had been concluded with the formative peace of Westphalia in 1648, relations between monarchs and their subjects remained conflict-ridden. In England, it culminated in the Glorious Revolution of 1688–89. In France, the outcome was a consolidation of absolutist monarchy. For an emerging class of "enlightened" European intellectuals, there was plenty to think about.

The core of the Enlightenment movement was made up of a group of French, English, and Scottish thinkers, who came to be known in the French case as the *philosophes*. Their clearly stated ambition was to work for the betterment of the human condition, and their thinking suggested various ways in which this could be achieved. Although some were prone to look

---

[10] It began with the publication of Montesquieu's *De l'esprit des lois* in 1748, continued with Rousseau's *Discours sur les sciences et les arts* in 1750, and culminated in the appearance of first edition of Denis Diderot's monumental *Encyclopédie* in 1751. (In total, the latter work would comprise thirty-five volumes, with 71,818 articles and 3,129 illustrations. The first twenty-eight volumes, edited by Diderot, were published between 1751 and 1766. The final installment, a two-volume index, appeared in 1780.)

back to a nobler past – notably Rousseau but also Adam Ferguson – most were united in a firm belief in progress and in the need to show tolerance of people with different faiths.[11] One might say that this was a time when science became truly "social," in the sense of being clearly focused on matters of practical importance for human existence.

While it is true that the star performers among the *philosophes* were French – men like Voltaire, Rousseau, Montesquieu, and Diderot – a deeper understanding of the phenomenon requires that we also take into account several streams of important prior influence from England and Scotland. We may trace four such streams, three of which would have a profound impact also south of the Channel.

The first derived from the "scientific revolution"[12] and may be associated here with Isaac Newton. In his masterpiece, *Philosophiæ Naturalis Principia Mathematica*, often known only as the *Principia*, which was published in 1687, he introduced the theory of universal gravitation and the laws of motion that laid the foundations for classical mechanics. A frequently used metaphor that is associated with Newton depicts the universe as a great clock, where all movement is understandable by reason and thus predictable. This should not be construed as atheism. Newton was a religious man, and he actually warned against understanding his view of the universe as a mere machine, as if akin to a great clock: "Gravity explains the motions of the planets, but it cannot explain who set the planets in motion. God governs all things and knows all that is or can be done."[13] While he would thus maintain that it was God who had created the clock and set it in motion, the important message remained: the world could be understood with reason alone, without recourse to religion or mysticism.

The impact on Enlightenment thinking would be profound. In more general terms a belief emerged holding that Newton's use of natural philosophy to create order in the universe could be replicated within political

---

[11] Voltaire forms something of a case in point here. His *Traité sur la tolerance*, published in 1763, was written to exonerate a Protestant man by the name of Jean Calas, who had been falsely accused of having murdered his son before the son could convert to Catholicism. The case caused a public uproar, but despite being savagely tortured, and eventually strangled to death, the accused never admitted his guilt. Largely thanks to Voltaire, he would be posthumously rehabilitated. (See Voltaire (2000), *Treatise on Tolerance*, New York: Cambridge University Press.)

[12] Among historians of science, the very notion as such is controversial. It is used here merely to suggest the important influence that ran from a series of discoveries in the natural sciences to the emerging belief that the human sciences could be approached in a similarly ordered and orderly way.

[13] Tiner, John H. (1975), *Isaac Newton: The True Story of His Life as Inventor, Scientist and Teacher*, Milford, MI: Mott Media, p. 107.

philosophy, that is, that rational thinking could create order also in matters regarding politics and the economy. On a more practical level, this belief would be formulated in one of the most important principles of the Enlightenment, namely, that of "deism," which issued a firm challenge to the church by putting reason firmly before religion.[14]

The second stream of influence was that of English empiricism,[15] of which Newton himself was a prime example. Rooted in Aristotelian philosophy, it was reintroduced into European culture by John Locke. In *An Essay Concerning Human Understanding*, published in 1690, he suggested that the human mind was a clean slate. In his own words, it was "white paper" upon which a person's experiences are inscribed as life progresses.[16] The philosophical implication is that there can be no pure reason and that knowledge may be derived only by *induction* based on experience.

While Locke won a broad and lasting following in his own country, including luminaries like George Berkeley in the seventeenth century, David Hume in the eighteenth, and John Stuart Mill in the nineteenth, the Continental intellectual tradition would remain dominated by rationalism, holding that knowledge can be derived only by way of *deduction* from known truths. Taking its cue from Plato, this tradition was associated with big names like Descartes, Leibnitz, and Spinoza. Among the French *philosophes* it was only Voltaire who sought to champion the cause of empiricism, and for him it was an uphill battle. Subsequent French empirical science owes a large debt to the lonely struggles of this man.

The third of our four English influences concerns the nature of relations between the state and its subjects and may be led back to Thomas Hobbes. His point of departure was that in the absence of a society humans would

[14] It should be noted here that like Newton, the *philosophes* were not atheists. They remained convinced of the role of God as Creator and actually suggested introducing a Cult of the Supreme Being that would be freed of the mystical and supernatural aspects of religion. After all, if God had created a rational universe then he too must be rational, and that precluded any recourse to mysticism. It has been suggested that their deism may have been merely a pose, designed to escape prosecution for atheism, which was a crime at the time. In such a case, Voltaire's passionate pleading for tolerance would come across as partly, or even wholly, self-serving. This shall have to remain speculation.

[15] For some of the more influential texts, see *The Empiricists*, Garden City, NY: Anchor Books, 1974.

[16] Locke's own formulation reads as follows: "Let us then suppose the Mind to be, as we say, white Paper, void of all Characters, without any *Ideas*; How comes it to be furnished? Whence comes it by that vast store, which the busy and boundless Fancy of Man has painted on it, with an almost endless variety? Whence has it all the materials of Reason and Knowledge? To this I answer, in one word, from *Experience*: In that, all our Knowledge is founded; and from that it ultimately derives itself" (Locke, John (1975), *An Essay concerning Human Understanding*, Oxford: Clarendon Press, p. 104). Emphasis in the original.

live in an imaginary "state of nature" where all have the same natural rights, including that of causing harm to others for personal gain. Under such conditions, the inevitable outcome would be a "war of all against all," a *bellum omnium contra omnes*, where life becomes "solitary, poor, nasty, brutish, and short."[17] It was to prevent this dreadful outcome that humans had formulated, sometime in distant history, a "social contract" whereby the subjects chose to surrender their rights and freedoms to an absolute power, the *Leviathan*, who was able to maintain order.

While the "social contract" that was suggested by Hobbes was carved in stone and could not be subject to revision, Locke chose to develop a more genuinely contractual view. The main difference between the two lies in the view of the "state of nature," which is central to all theories of social contracts. To Hobbes, this was an absolutely dreadful state, and any form of absolute rule, no matter how despotic, would be preferable. Locke, in contrast, viewed the state of nature as one of peace and harmony. Since it could be threatened by the outbreak of war, which might become long-lasting, there were grounds on which to establish a sovereign ruler.[18] Crucially, this ruler would retain his legitimacy only for as long as he protected and upheld the rights of his subjects. If these rights were violated, the contract would be voided and the subjects would have a right to rebel.[19] In sharp contrast to Hobbes, Locke thus recognized that some forms of tyranny might be worse than the state of nature.

In France, Jean-Jacques Rousseau more than anyone else would come to be associated with the social contract. For him, the state of nature was an original state of blissful existence that had been gradually corrupted by modernization; although he never used the term himself, he is often

---

[17] Given the importance of this truncated half-line citation, it may be worth repeating here in full: "In such condition there is no place for industry, because the fruit thereof is uncertain: and consequently no culture of the earth; no navigation, nor use of the commodities that may be imported by sea; no commodious building; no instruments of moving and removing such things as require much force; no knowledge of the face of the earth; no account of time; no arts; no letters; no society; and which is worst of all, continual fear, and danger of violent death; and the life of man, solitary, poor, nasty, brutish, and short" (Hobbes, Thomas (1968), *Leviathan*, Harmondsworth: Pelican, p. 186).

[18] Locke sees here "one great reason of men's putting themselves into society, and quitting the state of nature: for where there is an authority, a power on earth, from which relief can be had by appeal, there the continuance of the state of war is excluded, and the controversy is decided by that power" (Locke, John (1821), *Two Treatises on Government*, London: R. Butler, p. 204).

[19] Locke states that whenever the end for which power was given "is manifestly neglected, or opposed, the *trust* must necessarily be *forfeited*, and the power devolve into the hands of those that gave it, who may place it anew where they shall think best for their safety and security" (ibid., p. 317). (Emphasis in the original.)

credited with having invented the notion of the "noble savage." His views on the corruptive influence of civilization were presented in two installments. In *Discours sur les sciences et les arts*, published in 1750, he argued that the arts and sciences had been driven by pride and vanity, and that the growth in knowledge had paved the way for government that crushed individual freedom and creativity. In *Discours sur l'origine et les fondements de l'inégalité parmi les hommes*, which appeared in 1754, he presented a more detailed account of how the introduction of private property and the division of labor, so fundamental to the thinking of Adam Smith, had led to the emergence of an essentially warped social contract that favored the rich and the powerful.[20]

It was in response to this arrangement that Rousseau published his most celebrated work. In *Du contrat social, ou Principes du droit politique*, he argued that the social contract must be reformulated. He not only maintained, as did Locke, that there must be genuine reciprocity. Any government that failed to live up to its obligations to protect and uphold the rights and freedoms of its subjects must be considered in breach of the contract that forms the basis of its political authority. He also emphasized that the contract must be based on the rights and freedoms of all, not just of the rich and the powerful.[21]

The fourth and final strain of influence from England was the Glorious Revolution itself.[22] The outcome of the conflict that led to the removal of King James II, and the accession of William of Orange to the throne, was

[20] Both these works were submitted to essay contests that were sponsored by the Academy of Dijon. The first, translated into English as *A Discourse on the Moral Effects of the Arts and Sciences*, actually won Rousseau a prize. The second, *Discourse on the Origin and Foundations of Inequality among Men*, was far too long and too controversial to even be seriously considered. (For translations, see Rousseau, Jean-Jacques (1993), *The Social Contract and the Discourses*, New York: Alfred A. Knopf.) Perhaps the most striking feature of these discourses is the negative attitude that they display to knowledge, progress, and private property. Together with his complicated personality, this made Rousseau something of an outsider among the *philosophes*.

[21] This surely is not the place to outline the full complexity and provocative nature of the *Contrat social*. It may, however, be useful to note that its publication was closely followed by the appearance of another of Rousseau's major works, *Émile, ou de l'éducation*. In the latter, he suggested a radical system of education that would enable his uncorrupted "natural man" to live within a corrupt society. The book was immediately ordered to be burned, both in Paris and in the Republic of Geneva where Rousseau was a citizen. The combined effect of these two controversial books, appearing within months of each other, was to turn Rousseau into a refugee from the law.

[22] On the series of events that surrounded this watershed in English – and European – historical development, see Vallance, Edward (2006), *The Glorious Revolution, 1688: Britain's Fight for Liberty*, London: Little, Brown.

that Parliament succeeded in having the incoming monarch accept a set of rules that transformed England into a constitutional monarchy, subsequently to become a parliamentary democracy. The document that laid out these rules was the "Bill of Rights," arguably the most important document in English political history since the Magna Carta.[23] The bill contained provisions for a number of positive rights for citizens as well as a list of constraints on the exercise of power by the monarch. It may also be seen as the first – implicit – arrangement for a tripartite division of power into executive, legislative, and judicial functions or branches.

To the French Baron de La Brède et de Montesquieu, who by chance was born in 1689, the example of this "revolution" in state-building provided great inspiration. In his famous work *De l'ésprit des lois*, published in 1748, he laid the foundations for all subsequent theorizing around the separation of powers in government. As the cornerstone in his thinking was that of political liberty, he was much concerned with introducing what would subsequently come to be known as "checks and balances." Inspired by Locke's reasoning in the second of the two treatises on government, Montesquieu argued that the executive, legislative, and judicial functions of government must be assigned to different bodies, so that attempts by one branch of government to infringe on political liberty might be restrained by the other branches.[24]

These efforts by the *philosophes* would directly influence two great experiments in state-building that followed within the span of a mere three decades after the publication of their great *oeuvres*. This was most clearly the case with the French Revolution in 1789; despite all its spectacular atrocities, it must also be remembered for introducing the catalogue of rights that were listed in the *Déclaration des droits de l'homme et du citoyen*. This stood in stark contrast to the way in which the *philosophes* had

---

[23] The full title of this important document, which was enacted by Parliament in 1689, was *An Act Declaring the Rights and Liberties of the Subject and Settling the Succession of the Crown*. It was preceded by a set of twenty-three *Heads of Grievances*, reformulated as a *Declaration of Rights*, that were presented to William before he accepted the throne. At the time of coronation, he was compelled to swear an oath to uphold the laws that were made by Parliament. See further Schwoerer, Lois G. (1981), *The Declaration of Rights, 1689*, Baltimore: Johns Hopkins University Press, which also contains the full texts of the documents concerned.

[24] Montesquieu, Charles de Secondat, Baron de (2002), *The Spirit of Laws*, Amherst, NY: Prometheus Books. See, in particular, Book XI: "Of the Laws Which Establish Political Liberty, with Regard to the Constitution," which highlights "the tranquility of mind arising from the opinion that each person has of his safety," and establishes that "there is no liberty, if the judiciary power be not separate from the legislative and executive" (ibid., pp. 151–52).

been treated under the monarchy. Their critique of the church and their staunch defense of civil liberties resulted in severely strained relations with the royal authorities. Montesquieu was forced to publish his *De l'esprit des lois* anonymously. Voltaire spent much of his life in exile, and following the publication of the *Contrat social*, Rousseau was forced to flee in order to escape arrest.[25]

This said, it is indisputable that by far the most important illustration of how Enlightenment thinking could be transformed into political action was played out not in France but in America, in the shape of the American Revolution. In drawing up the Declaration of Independence in 1776, Thomas Jefferson was clearly inspired by Rousseau (viz. the latter's opening statement in the *Contrat social*: "Man is born free; and everywhere he is in chains").[26] The American Constitution that was adopted in 1787 drew heavily on Montesquieu's notions of a division of powers and of checks and balances, and in formulating the Bill of Rights in 1789, James Madison was inspired by Voltaire. It would be no exaggeration to say that the "Founding Fathers" of the American republic built in practice what the *philosophes* had merely envisioned in writing. It is also intriguing to note that another Frenchman, Alexis de Tocqueville, would pen one of the most important works on what the Americans had achieved.

We may round off this account with a striking parallel between Tocqueville and another famous French traveler, the Marquis de Custine. Having read Tocqueville's famous prophecy, in *Democracy in America*, that the future belonged to America and Russia,[27] Custine decided to become what some have referred to as "the Tocqueville of Russia." The outcomes of the efforts of these two men could not have been more different, however. Tocqueville had journeyed to America to study democracy, and returned inspired by

---

[25] Given the tremendous impact that Rousseau would have on subsequent generations of thinkers and state builders, it may be worth noting that his position among his fellow *philosophes* was estranged. During the last fifteen years of his life, he was clinically ill, developing a paranoia that caused him repeatedly to bite the hands that were trying to feed him. His own experience is summarized in three autobiographical works, where he attempts to justify his life and his work (*Les confessions, Dialogues de Rousseau: juge de Jean-Jacques,* and *Les Rêveries du promeneur solitaire,* the latter of which was unfinished).

[26] Rousseau, *The Social Contract,* p. 181. The French original reads as follows: "L'homme est né libre, et partout il est dans les fers."

[27] Appearing at the very end of volume 1, the passage reads as follows: "There are at the present time two great nations in the world, which started from different points, but seem to tend towards the same end. I allude to the Russians and the Americans. Both of them have grown up unnoticed; and while the attention of mankind was directed elsewhere, they have suddenly placed themselves in the front rank among the nations, and the world learned their existence and their greatness at almost the same time" (Tocqueville, Alexis de (1945), *Democracy in America,* New York: Alfred A. Knopf, vol.1, p. 434).

what he had seen. When Custine set out to study Russia, in 1839, he hoped to find a better alternative to the French regime but returned a deeply disillusioned man. His work, *Empire of the Czar: A Journey through Eternal Russia*, still retains its stature as a classic on Russian nineteenth-century autocracy.[28]

The contrast between the works of Tocqueville and Custine is important for our subsequent discussion mainly as it captures the crucial importance for building liberal democracies and rules-based market economies of matters that are encapsulated in the social contract. In so doing, it also points at a fundamental reason that Russian development would follow such a profoundly different trajectory. We shall have much more to say about these matters in later chapters. Let us turn now to the more narrowly economic track that would produce modern-day economic thinking and theorizing.

THE NEOCLASSICAL REVOLUTION

While the contributions of the French *philosophes* were mainly concerned with state-building and with securing civil rights and liberties, by far the most important contribution of the English and Scottish side was that of economic liberalism. As we have noted previously, the main received message of Adam Smith was that of laissez-faire, of allowing markets to develop with as little interference by the state as possible. To this we may add the impact of Newtonian mechanics, which, as we have also noted, convinced many Enlightenment thinkers that political and economic systems could be understood in much the same way as gravity and the laws of motion, that is, as human versions of the planetary system, or of the Newtonian "great clock."

This was a potent brew, the consequences of which would be far-reaching indeed. Before we outline how the heritage from Smith would be transformed into a narrowly specialized discipline of "economics," it may be helpful to know the general context in which Smith and the other classical economists worked.

While Smith is normally held up as the founder of the school of classical economics,[29] the label in use from the seventeenth century onward was

---

[28] Custine, Astolphe, Marquis de (1989), *Empire of the Czar: A Journey through Eternal Russia*, New York: Doubleday. The original was published in 1843, as *Lettres de Russie*. Banned in Russia, it would go through six editions in France and be translated into English. See also Kennan, George F. (1971), *The Marquis de Custine and His Russia in 1839*, Princeton: Princeton University Press.

[29] The first group of scholars to call themselves "economists" was actually the French physiocrats, whose chief ambition was to argue against mercantilism. Their call on government

"political economy,"[30] indicating that the object of study was not markets in isolation but rather the more encompassing economy of states, of the *polities*. Other well-known members of this tradition were David Ricardo,[31] whose interest in economy was awakened by Smith's *Wealth of Nations*, and Thomas Malthus, who in 1805 was appointed to England's first chair in political economy.[32] In 1821, James Mill, the father of John Stuart Mill, even founded a Political Economy Club, which served as a meeting place for reading papers and exchanging thoughts.

The strong emphasis that was placed by this school on the role of the state, and thus of politics, in the creation of common rules of the game implied that no firm line of division could be drawn between what we now know, respectively, as economics and as political science. The neoclassical revolution would entail a complete break with this tradition. Under the impression of Smithian laissez-faire, implying that the state should not intervene in markets, a parallel train of thought emerged holding that the separation of politics from the economy should be reflected also in the scholarly world, such that economists could devote more specialized attention to the workings of markets.

In the following we shall see how the tradition of classical and political economy was transformed into neoclassical economics that would be increasingly based on mathematical modeling, and how this change in course gave rise to opposition from very different quarters. In the conclusion of the chapter, we shall also have a few words to say about the state of tribal warfare that would ensue between representatives of the various emerging subdisciplines of social science.

to further industry and commerce was expressed in the classic phrase *laissez faire et laissez passer*. They also maintained that the wealth of nations was derived from agriculture, and that cities were essentially parasitic. Only agricultural labor could produce value. The main contribution of this school was François Quesnay's *Tableau Économique*, published in 1758 (Quesnay, Francois (1980), *Tableau Économique*, Tokyo: Bibliothèque de la Facultè des sciences èconomiques, Universitè Nihon. See also Kuczynski, Marguerite and Ronald L. Meek (eds.) (1972), *Quesnay's Tableau économique*, London: Macmillan).

[30] The term was introduced in 1615, in a work by the French poet-economist Antoine de Montchrestien, titled "Traicté de l'œconomie politique: dedié en 1615 au roy et à la reyne mere du roy." (See Montchrestien, Antoine de (1999), *Traicté de l'oeconomie politique*, Genève: Droz.)

[31] Ricardo's main work, *On the Principles of Political Economy and Taxation*, was published in 1817. It is here that he lays out his previously mentioned theory on the link between population pressure and ground rents, and also the fundamental principle of comparative advantage that explains why all nations can profit from free trade.

[32] The appointment was made at the East India Company College, which was closed in 1858. Malthus's most important work was *An Essay on the Principle of Population*, first published in 1798, in which he made his previously cited "dismal" prediction that population growth would outpace food supply.

From Smith to Marshall

There are good reasons indeed why Smith remains to this day something of an icon in the economics tradition. His strong conviction of the benefits to be derived from specialization and the division of labor still constitutes the core not only of economic theory as such but also of the more policy-oriented case for free trade. His famous account of the pin factory, which makes up much of the first chapter in *The Wealth of Nations*, also retains its powerful appeal. With ten specialized workmen producing 48,000 pins per day, the output per person came to 4,800 pins per day. If each worker had undertaken the whole process of production, he might not have produced twenty, perhaps not even a single pin in a day.[33]

It is easy to understand why Smith would be so fascinated by this example and why it still remains a standard quote in undergraduate economics texts. The theoretical case as such is both strong and uncontroversial. The point where problems begin to emerge concerns not the potential gains that are involved in specialization and division of labor, but rather the associated belief in the mystical powers of the equally famous "invisible hand." To what extent can we assume that economic actors will be instrumentally rational, in the sense of exploiting all available opportunities for future gain, and that they will pursue short-term profit and utility maximization under the assumptions of what we have referred to as the "golden rule" – that is, not strive for personal gain at the expense of others?

While most modern economists would agree that the answer to these questions can be at best conditionally positive, they will also maintain that it does not really matter much. It is sufficient that most actors behave as prescribed at most times. The problems that may arise will be mere deviations from the norm, and they can still be handled within the standard paradigm. Modeling cannot be and certainly cannot usefully be a complete picture of everything. We shall have more to say about this in Chapter 7.

From the point of view of sociologists, however, modern as well as classical, it is precisely this type of question that – allegedly – illustrates why modern economics has rendered itself largely irrelevant. Economic actors cannot be viewed, or modeled, in isolation from others. The choices that are made by *homo sociologicus* will not be derived from a clinically pure calculus of relative costs and benefits. They will rather emerge out of a dense and noisy environment of social relations that are marked by norms, traditions,

[33] Smith, Adam (2000), *The Wealth of Nations*, New York: The Modern Library, pp. 4–5.

habits, resentments, obligations, and plain irrational behavior. As we shall see in the following, economists would take little notice of such objections.

The point of departure for the "marginal revolution" was the assumption that all economic actors maximize on all margins. More specifically, this implies that consumers will extend consumption until the (decreasing) utility derived from, say, the last cup of coffee is precisely equal to the price paid, and that producers will extend production until the (increasing) cost of the last unit produced is precisely covered by the price received. In consequence, the central notions of this new theory would be those of *marginal utility* and of *marginal cost*. More generally, this revolution in economic thinking may also be viewed as a first step toward the system of general equilibrium that long constituted the core of modern economics.[34]

One of the most prominent of the "founding fathers" of this new departure was the French economist Léon Walras. He is remembered most of all for the notion of *tâtonnement*, of an imaginary auctioneer who keeps calling out changing prices until markets everywhere have adjusted to positions where supply equals demand.[35] He was, however, not the only father of the "marginal revolution." Quite independently of each other, Stanley Jevons in England and Carl Menger in Austria had been pursuing the very same lines of thought.[36]

Important as these earlier contributors were, it would be up to the English economist Alfred Marshall to enter his name into the annals of the history of economic thought as the man who transformed political economy into economics. His *Principles of Economics* not only introduced the very notion of "economics." It may also be viewed as the true starting point for

---

[34] The classic formulation of the general equilibrium model is due to Nobel Prize laureates Kenneth Arrow and Gérard Debreu (Arrow, Kenneth and Gérard Debreu (1954), "The Existence of an Equilibrium for a Competitive Economy," *Econometrica*, vol. 22, no. 3, pp. 265–90). See also Debreu, Gérard (1956), *Theory of Value*, New York: Wiley.

[35] Walras, Léon (1874), *Éléments d'économie politique pure ou Théorie de la richesse sociale*, Lausanne: Imprimerie L. Corbaz. It bears noting that the subsequent introduction and proliferation of game theory caused a substantial drop of interest in general equilibrium.

[36] Their respective main works are Jevons, W. Stanley (1871), *Theory of Political Economy*, London: Macmillan; and Menger, Carl (1871), *Grundsätze der Volkswirtschaftslehre*, Wien: W. Braumüller. The contours of the central theory on marginal utility could be discerned already in an earlier work by Jevons, titled *General Mathematical Theory of Political Economy*, which appeared in 1862. (Originally presented as a short and largely unknown lecture, four years later it would appear in Jevons, W. Stanley (1866), "Brief Account of a General Mathematical Theory of Political Economy," *Journal of the Royal Statistical Society*, vol. 29, June, pp. 282–87.) Menger differed from the others not only in the sense of having founded his own "school," the subsequently famous Austrian School. He was also much less prone to presenting his ideas in mathematical formulae. Some have taken this as grounds for placing him in a category of his own.

the neoclassical tradition that in recent decades has been totally dominant in the field.[37]

This was the time when economic theoreticians began laying the foundations for modern economics, with its strong emphasis on general theory and on formalized mathematical modeling. While most if not all modern economists would maintain that this has been a healthy and useful process, it also signaled the onset of an ever more complicated relation between economics and the more prestigious "hard" sciences, mainly, physics and mathematics.

This development must be viewed against the previously mentioned background of the scientific revolution. In the ancient world, no distinction was made between hard sciences such as mathematics and the study of politics and economy, or even poetry. Aristotle could approach them all with the same philosophical methodology. Even in the time of Thomas Hobbes, there was a belief in the unity of science as descriptive, allowing him to argue that Leviathan represented a scientific description of a political commonwealth.[38]

The impact of Newtonian mechanics was to change all this. With the growing conviction that the laws of motion could adequately explain the universe, there followed, as we have noted, a growing conviction that the same must hold also for the economic and political spheres. And since the natural sphere could be explained with laws expressed in mathematical terms, there was growing pressure also for the human sciences to develop laws of their own. This was the starting point for the subsequently long and thus far inconclusive struggle of the social sciences to mutate from "soft" to "hard" sciences.

As an illustration of the problems that are involved here, we may note that the approach of many economists to the task of undertaking "systemic change" in the Former Soviet Union would be heavily predicated on the existence of a well-defined set of "laws of economics" that have general applicability. The outcome, as we may also recall, was not a great success. In the often acrimonious debates that ensued, some elected to explain the failure

---

[37] Marshall, Alfred (1890), *Principles of Economics*, London: Macmillan. It may be added here, for the sake of completeness, that with the passage of time a consensus would emerge that the one who first formulated the theory of marginal analysis, and who should thus be rightly recognized as its founder, was the German economist Herman Heinrich Gossen (Gossen, H. H. (1854), *Entwicklung der Gesetze des menschlichen Verkehrs und der daraus fließenden Regeln für menschliches Handeln*, Braunschweig: Vieweg).

[38] Hobbes's alleged attitude is quoted here from an article on "Social sciences," published in the *Wikipedia* (http://en.wikipedia.org/wiki/Social_sciences).

by referring to the warped belief in economics as a "hard" science, which can be viewed and applied in isolation from social and cultural realities.

Rather than revisit these debates, we shall prefer here to contrast the belief in laws of economics that was so firmly entrenched in the early postcommunist 1990s against the atmosphere of doubt and disillusionment that was spreading at the beginning of the twentieth century. The latter is captured as follows by a contemporary observer, the economist Henry Moore:

> In the closing quarter of the last century great hopes were entertained by economists with regard to the capacity of economics to be made an "exact science." According to the view of the foremost theorists, the development of the doctrines of utility and value had laid the foundation of scientific economics in exact concepts, and it would soon be possible to erect upon the new foundation a firm structure of interrelated parts which, in definiteness and cogency, would be suggestive of the severe beauty of the mathematico-physical sciences. *But this expectation has not been realized.*[39]

Arguing that "there must have been something fundamentally wrong," Moore suggests that the "explanation is found in the prejudiced point of view from which economists regarded the possibilities of the science and in the radically wrong method which they pursued." That prejudice and faulty method rested in assuming "gratuitously" that economics could be modeled on the mathematical sciences: "Economics was to be a 'calculus of pleasure and pain,' a 'mechanics of utility,' a 'social mechanics,' a '*physique sociale*.'"[40] For neoclassical economics, and economists, these were not good times.

The Opposition

Opposition to the neoclassical revolution emerged from several quarters, by far the most venomous of which was the nascent American institutional school. The outright hostility that was shown by Thorstein Veblen toward neoclassical economics may be reflected in his sweeping condemnation of the notion of economic man, penned in 1898: "The hedonistic conception of man is that of a lightning calculator of pleasures and pains, who oscillates like a homogenous globule of desire of happiness under the impulse of stimuli that shift him about the area, but leave him intact."[41]

[39] Moore, Henry L. (1914), *Economic Cycles: Their Law and Cause*, New York: Macmillan, pp. 84–85. (Emphasis added.)

[40] Ibid., p. 85.

[41] Veblen, Thorstein (1898), "Why Is Economics Not an Evolutionary Science?," *Quarterly Journal of Economics*, vol. 12, no. 4, p. 389.

While the approach of Veblen was to simply dismiss, without much discussion, others chose to take a more serious approach. A methodologically important challenge against the marginal revolution was issued by German economists in the "historical school." Under the formative influence of Wilhelm Roscher, they developed an approach that rejected the formulation of general theoretical systems.[42] Arguing that economic "laws" could not be viewed out of context, they called instead for detailed empirical studies, the purpose of which would be to find laws of historical development.[43] Only based on such knowledge would it be possible to formulate more narrowly "economic" theories.

The implications of this *inductive* approach were not limited to rejecting the narrow specialization of economics and to calling instead for an essentially interdisciplinary effort that would have to include both history and sociology. More fundamentally, the "historicists" also rejected the methodological individualism that was at the heart of the marginal revolution, arguing instead for methodological holism or collectivism. At the core of this argument lies questioning the nature of knowledge that we have touched on earlier.

In an assessment of the scope and method of political economy, published in 1890, John Neville Keynes (father of the more famous John Maynard Keynes) contrasts "two broadly distinguished schools, one of which describes political economy as positive, abstract, and *deductive*, while the other describes it as ethical, realistic, and *inductive*."[44] He also notes that while both of these schools had invoked the authority of Adam Smith to support their respective cases, a correct reading would show that Smith was careful to pursue both deductive and inductive reasoning, that is, constructing a theory and proceeding to verify as far as possible whether it could hold water. The more specialized deductive method in political economy would be developed by Ricardo and, in particular, by John Stuart Mill.[45]

By insisting on an inductive approach, the historicists broke with the English tradition and set out to chart a course all their own. The problems

---

[42] The central methodological work of this school is Roscher, Wilhelm G. F. (1843), *Grundriss zu Vorlesungen über die Staatswirtschaft nach geschichtlicher Methode*, Göttingen: Dieterich.

[43] Reflecting his emphasis on the need to undertake serious mining of historical detail, Roscher made a distinction between "craftsmen" (*Handwerker*) and "masters" (*Künstler*) of history, where the former would do the collecting and the latter the analysis.

[44] Keynes, John Neville (1917), *The Scope and Method of Political Economy*, 4th ed., London: Macmillan, pp. 9–10. (Emphasis added.)

[45] Mill, John Stuart (1844), *Essays on Some Unsettled Questions of Political Economy*, London: J. W. Parker.

they would encounter were formidable. Since repeated observation is not really possible in social science, Roscher suggested a holistic approach that would generate knowledge by mapping and comparing the economic development of all nations. This is not the place to go into the more philosophical issues of knowledge and method that this approach raised.[46] We may, however, note the scope of the task they placed before themselves:

> Since nations have their own customs, habits and traditions, which create their unique history and determine the presently existing social structures, Roscher held that the task of economics is not to explain regularities which somehow emerge from the rational behavior of individuals. Its primary task is instead to analyze the historical development of such "wholes" as nations, economic systems and classes, and to detect their historical laws of development: the social sciences are the theory of history.[47]

The main implication of the latter statement was to draw a firm line in the academic sand: "It is the major claim of the historical school that the social sciences are historical sciences and quite different from the natural sciences."[48] Even more provocatively, the historicists maintained that "social sciences are not sciences *sui generis* but the theory of history, and thus belong to history. Among the positive sciences one may distinguish between science and history only."[49] Given this orientation, it is not surprising that the influence of the German historical school on the subsequent development of economic theory would be negligible, nor that their efforts would evoke a great deal of attention both in history and in the other social sciences. At home, however, they exerted tremendous influence over more than one generation of German economists.[50]

In the 1880s, the historicists had such an overpowering grip over German academic life that any form of influence from either classical or neoclassical economic theory could be excluded. Beginning in 1883, however, they got involved in a vicious battle over methodology, the famed *Methodenstreit*,

---

[46] See further Milford, Karl (1995), "Roscher's Epistemological and Methodological Position: Its Importance for the *Methodenstreit*," *Journal of Economic Studies*, vol. 22, nos. 3/4/5.

[47] Ibid., p. 39.

[48] Ibid., p. 38.

[49] Ibid., p. 31.

[50] Wilhelm Roscher is normally considered part of the "old" historical school, which also included Bruno Hildebrand and Karl Knies. The leading figure in the "younger" historical school was Gustav von Schmoller, who around 1900 was arguably one of the most distinguished European economists. Today he has been largely forgotten. Among other prominent scholars who considered themselves to be affiliated with the German school we may find Max Weber. Some would also hold that the works of Joseph Schumpeter constitute a continuation of the efforts of this school.

which would be decisively won by Carl Menger and the Austrian school.[51] Despite having lost this debate, the historicists not only succeeded in maintaining their positions in Germany but they also managed to extend their influence into the American academic world. When the American economist Richard T. Ely, who was educated in Heidelberg, joined with John R. Commons and Wesley C. Mitchell in founding the American institutional school, their inspiration was drawn heavily from the German historical school, and for a couple of decades at the outset of the twentieth century they were highly successful.[52]

Returning again to the end of the nineteenth century, while Austrian and German economists were slugging it out over methodology, yet another line of critique against the neoclassical revolution emerged, one, moreover, that still retains its power to cause important divisions within the social sciences. Developed independently in Germany and France, by Max Weber and Émile Durkheim, "economic sociology" entered the stage.[53]

Like Ely, Weber was educated at Heidelberg, where, needless to say, he was introduced to the teachings of the German historical school. When he was appointed to a chair in political economy at Freiburg, in 1895, he would refer to himself as one of the younger members of this school, and in the following year he would return to Heidelberg where he received a

---

[51] The first round in this battle was fired with the publication, in 1871, of Menger's previously mentioned *Grundsätze der Volkswirthschaftslehre* (Wien: W. Braumüller). As part of the "marginal revolution," it introduced a subjective theory of value that completely contradicted the classical theory of value. The real eruption arrived in 1883, when Menger approached more broadly the issue of methodology in the social sciences, aiming quite clearly to put historicism in its place (Menger, Carl (1883), *Untersuchungen über die Methode der Socialwissenschaften und der politischen Ökonomie insbesondere*, Leipzig: Duncker & Humblot). From the German side, Gustav von Schmoller wrote a demolition review of Menger's work, suggesting that it was simply irrelevant (Schmoller, Gustav von (1883) "Zur Methodologie der Staats- und Sozial-Wissenschaften," *Schmoller's Jahrbuch*, vol. 7, no. 3, pp. 975–94). Menger responded in 1884, with the publication of *Die Irrthümer des Historismus in der deutschen Nationalökonomie* (Wien: A. Hölder). The ensuing fight would rage for a couple of decades. Menger's devastating critique of the "historical method" and his defense of economic theory are still regarded as the winning argument in the debate. See also Haller, Markus (2004), "Mixing Economics and Ethics: Carl Menger vs Gustav von Schmoller," *Social Science Information*, vol. 43, no. 5, and Schumpeter, Joseph A. (1954), *History of Economic Analysis*, London: Allen & Unwin, pp. 800–19.

[52] For a detailed account, see Hodgson, Geoffrey M. (2004), *The Evolution of Institutional Economics: Agency, Structure and Darwinism in American Institutionalism*, London and New York: Routledge.

[53] For a concise overview, see Smelser, Neil J. and Richard Swedberg (1994), "The Sociological Perspective on the Economy," in Smelser and Swedberg (eds.), *The Handbook of Economic Sociology*, Princeton, NJ: Princeton University Press.

similar appointment as full professor of political economy.[54] Weber's most celebrated, and criticized, work was his previously cited *Die protestantische Ethik und der Geist des Kapitalismus*, which appeared in 1904–5 and certainly reflected his own upbringing by an orthodox Calvinist mother.[55]

Of greater importance for the case at hand, however, was his appointment, in 1908, as editor of a monumental handbook in economics, the *Grundriss der Sozialökonomik*, which would appear in twelve volumes. Weber's ambition was decidedly interdisciplinary, including contributions from the fields of economic theory, economic history, and economic sociology, and – most significantly – both sides in the still raging *Methodenstreit* were invited to participate. The editor's own contribution to this series, *Wirtschaft und Gesellschaft*, contains what Neil Smelser and Richard Swedberg refer to as "a kind of founding document in economic sociology."[56] In it he places heavy emphasis on the role of social relations in determining interaction in the marketplace. The title – "Economy and Society" – also indicated that the neoclassical revolution had not yet succeeded in completing the separation of the market from its social context.

Émile Durkheim comes across as a stark contrast to Weber, perhaps mainly so because he never studied or taught political economy, or indeed economics. What he did know he had absorbed on his own, and it is doubtful whether he knew much about the ongoing marginal revolution. Perhaps this conditioned, or was conditioned by, his rather negative general attitude toward economics: "Durkheim disliked much of what he read in economics – no doubt because of his antipathy toward utilitarianism, individualism, and speculative thought."[57]

In his famous lecture on "sociology and the social sciences," published in 1909,[58] Durkheim leads off by paying homage to Auguste Comte, who is generally held to have introduced sociology as a science of society. There were good reasons for Durkheim to be fascinated by this positivist thinker. Anticipating the program of formalization that would be pursued by the neoclassical economists, Comte's vision was that sociology would become

[54] Weber's brief tenure of the Freiburg chair is remembered most of all for his "Freiburg address," which established his liberal credentials.

[55] For a translation, see Weber, Max (2001), *The Protestant Ethic and the Spirit of* Capitalism, London: Routledge.

[56] Smelser and Swedberg, "The Sociological Perspective," p. 10. Weber, Max (1922), *Wirtschaft und Gesellschaft*, Tübingen: J. C. B. Mohr (P. Siebeck).

[57] Smelser and Swedberg, "The Sociological Perspective," p. 11.

[58] Durkheim, Émile (1909), "Sociologie et sciences sociales," in H. Bouasse et al., (eds.), *De la méthode dans les sciences*, Paris: F. Alcan.

a "social physics," a *physique social*. Echoing Comte's belief that sociology would eventually come to occupy the very pinnacle of a hierarchy of sciences, Durkheim had only scorn for the role and position of economics: "By becoming a branch of sociology, economic science will naturally be wrenched from its isolation at the same time that it will become more deeply impregnated with the idea of scientific determinism."[59]

Perhaps the most crucial point of difference between Durkheim and the neoclassical economists rested in his refusal to accept the latter's strong emphasis on the role of the individual, as embodied in the notion of *homo economicus*. To him, this was tantamount to creating a world that does not exist, with serious consequences for the discipline of political economy:

It remained an abstract and deductive science, concerned not with the observation of reality, but with the construction of a more or less desirable ideal. For this abstract man, this systematic egoist whom it describes, is solely a creature of reason. Real man – the man whom we all know and whom we all are – is complex in a different way: he is of a time, of a country; he has family, a city, a fatherland, a religious and political faith; and all these factors and many others merge and combine in a thousand ways.[60]

Of all the different forms of opposition to the neoclassical revolution in economics that emerged in the last decades of the nineteenth century, the challenge that was issued by Comte and Durkheim must be placed in a class of its own. Transcending mere disagreements on points of methodology, it was aimed squarely at confrontation, at deciding once and for all which of the two disciplines would be considered superior to the other. The outcome may be viewed as a state of tribal warfare that would mark social science for decades to come, and has still to be resolved.

TRIBAL WARFARE

Before we proceed to look in more detail at the nature and consequences of this unfortunate conflict, it may be useful to recapitulate very briefly the general background, from the classical economists onward. Although Adam Smith is rightly known as the father of the discipline of economics, his repertoire, as we have noted above, was much broader than looking

---

[59] Translation cited from Durkheim, Émile (1978), *On Institutional Analysis*, Chicago: University of Chicago Press, pp. 81–82.

[60] The statement originally appeared in an opening lecture, "Cours de science sociale: Leçon d'ouverture," that was published in 1888, in *Revue internationale d'enseignement*. Translation cited here from Durkheim, *On Institutional Analysis*, pp. 49–50.

simply at markets. Smith rather stands out for his ability to combine economic theory with insights into social relations and institutions.[61] Writing at a time when the world had not yet been introduced to a division between economics and sociology, it did seem natural to take such a broad view. According to John Stuart Mill, no thoughtful person would deny that "a person is not likely to be a good economist who is nothing else. Social phenomena acting and reacting on one and another, they cannot rightly be understood apart."[62]

Economy *and* Society?

This ambition of combining an interest in the economy with an awareness of its social and historical context was to be maintained in German scholarship, well past the time when the neoclassical revolution had caused economics to be narrowly focused on markets, and on economic men. Although Karl Marx developed his very own notion of economics, he had no problem combining it with sociology. Weber, as we have also noted, stressed both economy and society, and he made a point of turning the *Grundriss der Sozialökonomik* into an interdisciplinary undertaking. Even more important, perhaps, Joseph Schumpeter, who is known primarily as a prominent Austrian economist, was no stranger to giving lectures on sociology.[63] In his posthumously published work *History of Economic Analysis*, he chose

---

[61] It is symptomatic that despite their animosity toward political economy, many of the early sociologists would show great admiration for Smith. Some even would claim him to have been a sociologist rather than an economist. As an illustration, the prominent Chicago sociologist Albion Small opens his book about Smith with the following statement: "If one were to come upon *The Wealth of Nations* for the first time, with a knowledge of the general sociological way of looking at society, but with no knowledge of economic literature, there would be not the slightest difficulty nor hesitation about classifying the book as an inquiry in a special field of sociology." And he goes on to claim that "sociologists have kept alive the vital spark of Smith's moral philosophy." (Small, Albion W. (1907), *Adam Smith and Modern Sociology: A Study in the Methodology of the Social Sciences*, Chicago: University of Chicago Press, pp. 1, 4.)

[62] Cited by Marshall, *Principles of Economics*, p. 73.

[63] While Schumpeter was a fine economic theorist, who identified with the Austrian neoclassical school of economics, he also cooperated with Weber and was a member of the German Sociological Association. In an article on Pareto, who also straddled the divide between the two disciplines, he noted that "there is nothing surprising in the habit of economists to invade the sociological field. A large part of their work – particularly the whole of what they have to say on institutions and on the forces that shape economic behavior – inevitably overlaps the sociologist's preserves" (Schumpeter, Joseph A. (1951), "Vilfredo Pareto, 1848–1923," in Schumpeter, *Ten Great Economists: From Marx to Keynes*, New York: Oxford University Press, p. 134).

to present economics as being composed of four fields, namely, economic history, statistics, theory, and economic sociology.[64]

The real challenge to this tradition was fielded by Auguste Comte, decades before Alfred Marshall introduced "economics." Comte's main ambition was to promote the philosophy of positivism, an endeavor that resulted in his encyclopedic undertaking *Cours de philosophie positive*, published over the years 1830–42.[65] It was in volume four of this work, published in 1839, that he introduced the notion of "sociology," to replace his previous "social physics,"[66] and it was here that he laid out his infamous onslaught against the "alleged science" of political economy. What he referred to as "our economists" were (erroneously) said to have emerged from the ranks of lawyers and writers. They were strangers to the very idea of scientific observation, and their vain and childish contestations were nothing but sterile forms of metaphysics that lacked any scientific value.[67]

For all of its factual and analytical shortcomings, there was a distinct logic to Comte's attack. The main thrust of the philosophy that was laid out in his *Cours de philosophie positive* was that the accumulation of knowledge is an evolutionary process that proceeds in three stages; beginning in a theological stage, it proceeds to a metaphysical one and reaches completion in a scientific, or positive, stage that is marked by complete understanding. This holds for all the different branches of science. According to Comte's "encyclopedic law," science evolves in a fashion in which each successive step builds on the previous. The ordering begins with mathematics, is followed by astronomy, physics, chemistry, and biology, and culminates in social science. As it would serve to integrate the findings of all previous science, the *physique social* that Comte renamed *sociologie* would represent the culmination of all knowledge. It would be the "queen of all sciences." Political economy could simply be discarded.

---

[64] Schumpeter, *History of Economic Analysis*, pp. 12–24. The role of economic sociology in relation to the other fields was defined as being based on a division of labor, where "economic analysis deals with the questions how people behave at any time and what the economic effects are they produce by so behaving; economic sociology deals with the question how they came to behave as they do" (ibid., p. 21).

[65] Comte, Auguste (1830–42), *Cours de philosophie positive*, vols. 1–6, Paris: Bachelier.

[66] Comte, Auguste (1869), *Cours de philosophie positive*, 3d ed., vol. 4, Paris: Ballière, p. 185. The notion is introduced in a footnote, where he claims that this is "exactement équivalent à mon expression, déjà introduite, de physique sociale." The latter notion, in turn, had been introduced in a little-known article from 1822, titled "Plan des travaux scientifiques nécessaires pour réorganizer la societé" (Reprinted in Comte, Auguste (1883), *Opuscules de Philosophie Sociale, 1819–1828*, Paris: E. Leroux).

[67] Comte, *Cours de philosophie positive*, pp. 193–204.

Needless to say, those who were at the receiving end of this scalding criticism did not take it lightly. Prominent economists like John Stuart Mill, John Cairnes, and Alfred Marshall all reacted strongly, condemning Comte for his superficial and ill-founded criticisms.[68] In his previously cited book on the scope and method of political economy, John Neville Keynes summed up the sentiments regarding sociology that prevailed among leading British economists around the turn of the century: "Comte charged political economy with being radically sterile as regards results. But what results has sociology, conceived as a master science, dealing with man's social life as a whole, yet to show?"[69] The general conclusion, provoked by Comte's attack, was that sociology in a scholarly sense was useless, having nothing to offer economics.

Reactions on the American side of the Atlantic were similarly marked by animosity over perceived turf infringement. Much as Durkheim was struggling hard to establish sociology in France,[70] the early American sociologists were encountering great difficulties persuading universities to introduce sociology as a field of study. Their situation was not improved by the difficulty in reaching an agreement on what sociology really was. At a meeting of the American Economic Association, held in New York in 1894, it even came to an open confrontation, where the sociologists present were informed that they had "no right to stake off for themselves a portion of social science without the consent of the economists."[71]

---

[68] Mill, John Stuart (1865), *Auguste Comte and Positivism*, London: Trübner, pp. 80–83; Cairnes, John (1873), "M. Comte and Political Economy," in Cairnes, *Essays in Political Economy: Theoretical and Applied*, London: Macmillan, esp. pp. 283–84, Marshall, Alfred (1885), *The Present Condition of Economics*, London: Macmillan, pp. 34–38; Marshall, 1890, *Principles of Economics*, pp. 72–74.

[69] Keynes, *The Scope and Method of Political Economy*, p. 139.

[70] Durkheim received an appointment at the University of Bordeaux in 1887, where he joined the department of philosophy. Making education his field of specialization, he strove to win acceptance for sociology as a field of its own. After nine years at Bordeaux, he was promoted to a full professorship in "Social Science," the first such position in France. In 1898, he founded a journal, *L'Année Sociologique*, that became a platform for his ambition. In 1902, he was called to the Sorbonne. At first this was a demotion, from professor to a mere *chargé du cours de Science et de l'Éducation*, but in 1906 he was again made professor, this time in "Science of Education." In 1913, the name of Durkheim's chair was changed by a special ministerial decree to "Science of Education and Sociology." He died four years later, in 1917.

[71] Swedberg, Richard (1990), *Economics and Sociology: Redefining Their Boundaries: Conversations with Economists and Sociologists*, Princeton, NJ: Princeton University Press, p. 10. On the broader background of the standoff between economists and sociologists at this time, see also Swedberg, Richard (1987), "Economic Sociology: Past and Present," *Current Sociology*, vol. 35, no. 1, pp. 17–20.

Realizing that their only chance of getting sociology accepted as a discipline in its own right would have to proceed via support from the economists, the sociologists decided to back off the economic and political spheres. This was a decision that essentially meant accepting being relegated to "such unclaimed subjects as the family, deviance, crime, and urban pathology."[72] In later correspondence, the Chicago sociologist Albion Small would refer to sociology as a "convenient label for left-overs within the range of human knowledge that cannot be classified under any other head."[73]

Eventually, the sociologists would get their own university departments, and in 1905 they also succeeded in establishing the American Sociological Society. The effective retreat by sociology from the field of economic study would, however, have two unfortunate consequences. It not only set the stage for an enduring animosity that would seriously constrain all further ambitions to undertake interdisciplinary ventures. By ceding to the economists a de facto monopoly on study of the marketplace, it also put an end to the Weberian tradition of studying economy *and* society.[74]

By the late 1940s, it would have come to the point that, as Swedberg puts it, "economists and sociologists knew little about each other's works and were often hostile to each other."[75] In his previously cited history of economic analysis, Schumpeter frames it even more pointedly, arguing that

ever since the eighteenth century both groups have grown steadily apart until by now the modal economist and the modal sociologist know little and care less about what the other does, each preferring to use, respectively, a primitive sociology and a primitive economics of his own to accepting one another's professional results – a state of things that was and is not improved by mutual vituperation.[76]

It was, however, not exclusively a matter of turf battles. At the bottom of the conflict that set economics and sociology onto different trajectories were serious differences of opinion on matters of methodology. As the experience of the *Methodenstreit* had clearly shown, these are issues that may

---

[72] Granovetter, Mark (1990), "The Old and the New Economic Sociology: A History and an Agenda," in: Roger Friedland and A. F. Robertson (eds.), *Beyond the Market Place: Rethinking Economy and Society*, New York: Aldine de Gruyter, p. 89.

[73] Swedberg, "Economic Sociology," p. 20.

[74] As Roger Friedland and A. F. Robertson note, it was not only sociology that was pushed out of the marketplace. The emerging discipline of anthropology became preoccupied with nonmarket relations, and political science fixed on the institutions and dilemmas of popular participation in the nation-state (Friedland, Roger and A. F. Robertson (1990), "Beyond the Market Place," in Friedland and Robertson (eds.), *Beyond the Market Place: Rethinking Economy and Society*, New York: Aldine de Gruyter, p. 5).

[75] Swedberg, *Economics and Sociology*, p. 13.

[76] Schumpeter, *History of Economic Analysis*, pp. 26–27.

touch the very raison d'être of a discipline. Returning to Schumpeter, we are cautioned never to forget that genuine schools are sociological realities, akin to living beings:

They have their structures – relations between leaders and followers – their flags, their battle cries, their moods, their all-too human interests. Their antagonisms come within the general sociology of group antagonisms and of party warfare. Victory and conquest, defeat and loss of ground, are in themselves values for such schools and part of their very existence.[77]

While the attitude that emerged among economists would view sociology as a pseudoscience, sociologists would fret about "economic imperialism." One way of approaching the root cause of the methodological differences that produced such feelings was suggested early on by the Italian economist Vilfredo Pareto, in his *Trattato di Sociologia Generale*.[78] According to Swedberg, "His basic premise was that economics studies rational action, and sociology studies non-rational action – or, in Pareto's terminology, 'logical' action and 'nonlogical' action."[79] Interestingly, this view would also find its way into Paul Samuelson's classic *Foundations of Economic Analysis*, where it is noted that "many economists, well within the academic fold, would separate economics from sociology upon the basis of rational or irrational behavior, where these terms are defined in the penumbra of utility theory."[80]

There were those who, like Schumpeter, sought to maintain open lines of communication, but theirs was a losing struggle. An excellent example is Talcott Parsons. Trained as an economist, he crossed the line to become one of the foremost American sociologists. Setting himself the task of continuing Weber's thinking on economy and society,[81] he proceeded to devote much of his work to elaborating on the relation between the two disciplines. The central theme in his *The Structure of Social Action*, published in 1937, was that of a division of labor. While economics should focus on the means-ends chain that involves rational adaptation of scarce means to alternative ends, the role of sociology would be to study that part of the chain which involves ultimate values.[82]

---

[77] Ibid., p. 815.

[78] Pareto, Vilfredo (1916), *Trattato di sociologia generale*, Firenze: G. Barbèra.

[79] Swedberg, *Economics and Sociology*, p. 11.

[80] Samuelson, Paul (1947), *Foundations of Economic Analysis*, Cambridge: Harvard University Press, p. 90.

[81] In 1956 he co-authored a book with precisely that title (Parsons, Talcott and Neil J. Smelser (1956), *Economy and Society: A Study in the Integration of Economic and Social Theory*, Glencoe, IL: Free Press).

[82] Parsons, Talcott (1937), *The Structure of Social Action: A Study in Social Theory with Special Reference to a Group of Recent European Writers*, New York: McGraw Hill, p. 771.

As Mark Granovetter notes, Parson's approach was counterproductive in two ways. By launching an attack on the institutional economists, he helped burn potential bridges, and by suggesting a formal division of labor between economics and sociology, he helped solidify their separation: "If economics was fully adequate within its own domain, one separate from that of sociology which was to treat value systems and the institutional preconditions of economic action, there was little motive for economists to pay attention to sociology unless they were concerned with such matters, as few were in this period."[83]

As a prominent reflection of the growing animosity that came to mark relations between economics and sociology,[84] we may briefly invoke the example of Karl Polanyi, who is most well known for having pioneered the notion of "embeddedness."[85] In good tradition from Durkheim, his writings were permeated by a clearly expressed antipathy toward economics. He was convinced that the spread of what he referred to as a "market mentality" would lead to a demolition of society: "For Polanyi, the very idea of a totally unregulated labor market was repulsive, and he considered the market ideology of the British economists as a kind of evil utopia."[86]

Once we proceed beyond what Schumpeter referred to as "mutual vituperation," it will become quite clear that the ambition of creating economic sociology as a joint venture of sorts between economics and sociology was

---

[83] Granovetter, "The Old and the New Economic Sociology," p. 91.

[84] For fear of leaving an impression of a one-sided animosity that only has sociologists exhibiting ill feelings about economics, we may note a few prominent voices in the other direction, gleaned from interviews conducted by Richard Swedberg. Commenting on the work of Talcott Parsons, by far the leading U.S. sociologist in the 1950s and early 1960s, Gary Becker notes that "reading Parsons soured me on sociology"; Kenneth Arrow uses such words as "empty and grandiose," "preposterous," "void of all empirical content," "tautological" and "just awful"; and Robert Solow speaks of "bad metaphors" that left him "really quite unhappy" (Swedberg, *Economics and Sociology*, pp. 29, 135, 271).

[85] The introduction of this term is normally associated with his previously cited *The Great Transformation*. Given the subsequent importance to sociological analysis of "embeddedness," it bears noting that in Polanyi's main work, which runs over 300 pages, it appears only twice, namely on pp. 57 and 61 (Barber, Bernard (1995), "All Economies Are 'Embedded': The Career of a Concept, and Beyond," *Social Research*, vol. 62, no. 2, p. 401). A striking parallel may be drawn here to Adam Smith, whose "invisible hand" appeared only once in *The Wealth of Nations*. In both cases, what would become household expressions in their respective disciplines were used by their originators as shorthand for ways of thinking. In Polanyi's case, the underlying method may be most clearly seen in Polanyi, Karl (1957), "The Economy as an Instituted Process," in Karl Polanyi, Conrad M. Arensberg, and Harry W. Pearson (eds.), *Trade and Markets in Early Empires: Economies in History and Theory*, Glencoe, IL: Free Press. We shall return to these matters at greater length in Chapter 6.

[86] Smelser and Swedberg, "The Sociological Perspective on the Economy," p. 14.

a tall order indeed. Recall what Jon Elster referred to as a "persisting cleavage" in the social sciences. At the bottom of the long-standing contradiction between *homo economicus* and *homo sociologicus* lurk diametrically opposed views on a whole range of issues where that of methodological individualism must occupy center stage. (This also was a pivotal issue in the *Methodenstreit*, separating inductive from deductive approaches to the acquisition of knowledge.)

While the approach as such was originally formulated by Carl Menger, as part of his attack on the German historical school, it was Schumpeter who introduced the label and made clear what it meant. In his 1908 work *Das Wesen und der Hauptinhalt der theoretischen Nationalökonomie*, he devoted a whole chapter to drawing a line between political and methodological individualism, stating that the latter only meant that "when describing certain economic processes we must depart from the actions of individuals."[87] This stands in stark contrast to the sociological perspective, where individuals cannot be separated from their social context, however that may be described.

Over time, as the neoclassical tradition gained an ever stronger grip over the economics profession, methodological individualism would achieve an almost axiomatic status. Writing in 1994, Kenneth Arrow noted "It is a touchstone of accepted economics that all explanations must run in terms of the actions and reactions of individuals."[88] In his concise and perceptive handbook, *Nuts and Bolts for the Social Sciences*, Elster simply notes that the view of individual human action as "the elementary unit of social life" – that is, methodological individualism – is "trivially true."[89]

From the other side of the fence, however, the view has been very different. In his monumental *Foundations of Social Theory*, published in 1990, James Coleman takes issue with what he refers to as a "fiction" in economics, offering the following summary verdict over economic man as a focus of analysis:

This fiction is that society consists of a set of independent individuals, each of whom acts to achieve goals that are independently arrived at, and that the functioning of the social system consists of the combination of these independent individuals. This

[87] Schumpeter, Joseph A. (1908), *Das Wesen und der Hauptinhalt der theoretischen Nationalökonomie*, Leipzig, Duncker & Humblot, pp. 90–91.

[88] Arrow, Kenneth J. (1994), "Methodological Individualism and Social Knowledge," *American Economic Review*, vol. 84, no. 2, p. 1.

[89] Elster, Jon (1989b), *Nuts and Bolts for the Social Sciences*, Cambridge: Cambridge University Press, p. 13.

fiction is expressed in the economic theory of perfect competition in a market, most graphically in Adam Smith's imagery of an "invisible hand."[90]

A Pecking Order

Perhaps the most distinctive, and regrettable, feature in the fragmentation of social science that began toward the end of the nineteenth century has been the emergence of a strictly enforced pecking order. Superficially, it may be viewed as an outgrowth of the claims by Comte that sociology represented a master science. On closer inspection, however, we will find that the root cause goes back to Newtonian mechanics and the associated belief that social science could and should be pursued with the same rigor as the natural sciences.

It is deeply symptomatic that the distinction between "hard" and "soft" sciences has also been viewed as a distinction between "real" science and the rest, and that those who have been relegated to the latter category have strived hard to qualify for an upgrade. The outcome has been an implicit pecking order, where status has been increasingly linked to theoretical and methodological refinement. In practice, this has produced a belief that "real" science must be shrouded in complex mathematics – the harder it is to penetrate the formulae, the higher the degree of theoretical sophistication. (The fact that professional mathematicians remain unimpressed by the ambitions of social scientists to copy their trade is a fact that is rarely commented upon.)

Since economics has been the most amenable to this type of formalization, it is not surprising that colleagues in other fields have delighted in faulting economists for their allegedly unrealistic assumptions, on which the success of their models hinges critically. More telling, however, is that some of the elders within the economics profession have also found reason to speak up against the trend toward increasingly formalistic specialization.

Writing about the troubled relation between economics and economic history, Nobel Prize laureate Robert Solow, one of the fathers of economic growth theory, utters a stern admonition – "I suspect that the attempt to construct economics as an axiomatically based hard science is doomed to fail" – and proceeds to echo Comte's belief in a *physique social*, albeit with a sarcastic twist: "My impression is that the best and the brightest in the

---

[90]   Coleman, James S. (1990), *Foundations of Social Theory*, Cambridge, MA: Belknap Press of Harvard University Press, p. 300.

profession proceed as if economics is the physics of society. There is a single universally valid model of the world. It only needs to be applied."[91]

Nobel Laureate Ronald Coase is just as harsh, when he speaks of the increasingly narrow focus on the technical dimension of how prices are determined, and the associated neglect of all other aspects of the economic system: "Sometimes, indeed, it seems as though economists conceive of their subject as being concerned only with the pricing system and anything outside this is considered as no part of their business."[92]

In more general terms, Elster simply notes that "the social sciences are light years away from the stage at which it will be possible to formulate general law-like regularities about human behavior." His suggestion is that instead of developing elaborate grand theory, social scientists should focus on "specifying small and medium sized mechanisms for human action and interaction – plausible, frequently observed ways in which things happen."[93] Uttered by one of the leading figures in the development of rational choice theory, this admonition should not be taken lightly.[94]

The main reason we have chosen here to speak of "tribal warfare" is that the pecking order has evolved not only between economics and the other social sciences, but even more so within economics itself. Reserving for themselves the place of a master science that Comte once tried to claim for sociology, economists have imposed on their own community a peculiar culture of internecine rivalry where mathematical sophistication is the measure of status and prestige. There can be no better illustration of this self-imagery than the classic anthropological essay about "Life among the Econ" that was once penned by Axel Leijonhufvud.[95]

The humor of the piece lies in depicting a small but hardy tribe – the "Econ" – whose members are divided into castes known as "fields," each of which makes its own distinctive totems that are known as "modls." Living in villages known as "depts," the Econ are ruled by elders who allow the young to pass into adulthood only after having produced a modl of

[91] Solow, Robert (1985), "Economic History and Economics," *American Economic Review*, vol. 75, no. 2, pp. 328, 330.

[92] Coase, Ronald H. (1992), "The Institutional Structure of Production," *American Economic Review*, vol. 82, no. 4, p. 714.

[93] Elster, Jon (1989a), *The Cement of Society: A Study of Social Order*, Cambridge: Cambridge University Press, p. viii.

[94] See further Elster, Jon (ed.) (1986), *Rational Choice*, New York: New York University Press.

[95] Leijonhufvud, Axel (1973), "Life among the Econ," *Western Economic Journal*, vol. 11, no. 3. (Reprinted in Joshua S. Gans (ed.) (2000), *Publishing Economics*, Cheltenham: Edward Elgar.)

acceptable quality. Joint control over the tribe as a whole is exercised at traditional tribal midwinter councils.[96] Rivalry within the tribe is marked by a strong rank-ordering. While the relative status of the Micro and the Macro is undecided, all bow to the priestly caste of the Math-Econ, who make the most elaborate modls, and all look down on the lowly caste of the Develops, who are castigated for associating with alien tribes, such as the Polscis and the Sociogs, and for endangering the moral fiber of the tribe by placing insufficient emphasis on modl-making.

For as long as practitioners within the various subdivisions of social science remain focused on narrowly defined problems that are amenable to analysis with the tools of their respective trades, it may be argued that all is well. It is when we are confronted with persistent inability to break out of poverty traps, or with great experiments in social engineering, such as that of attempted systemic change in the Former Soviet Union, that we must consider the implications of having moved ever further away from the inquisitiveness of Smith and the classical economists, not to mention the *philosophes* more generally.

While the process of increasing specialization and methodological refinement has served to provide the social sciences with an increasing aura of catching up with the hard sciences, it also has led to the emergence of what may be referred to as a huge hole in the middle. Closer consideration shows that answers to many of the great questions we are faced with today must be sought in the voids that have opened up between, say, economics, sociology, and political science. The prospects for this hole to be filled by serious interdisciplinary scholarship seem regrettably slim.

As described by Leijonhufvud with respect to economics, each of the social sciences has developed its own internal pecking order where careers are made – and broken. The ambition to imitate the hard sciences, often known as "physics envy," has resulted in an emphasis on formalization and on mathematical refinement that has become clearly path dependent and will likely prove to be difficult to reverse, even if such an ambition should emerge, of which there is presently no indication. These remarks, moreover, still have not even begun to question the wisdom of leaving history and culture out of the analysis, a topic to which we shall return in Chapter 7.

We began the present chapter with fascination over the human drive to explore and discover, to constantly look for ways of bettering the condition of human existence. We have also seen how much intellectual development

---

[96] For the benefit of the non-economist, these councils are the annual meetings of the American Economic Association, traditionally held at the beginning of January.

has been geared into supporting precisely this cause, in the "hard" as well as in the "soft" sciences. We are forced to end on a somewhat different note, to ask again if social science is becoming increasingly focused on *ars gratia artis*, on developing models and approaches that may never please anyone outside of a small circle of like-minded friends and colleagues.

Writing as early as in 1973, when mathematical sophistication had only begun to make its inroads into the social sciences, Leijonhufvud found reason to end his humorous piece on the Econ on a rather somber note: "It is true that virtually all Econographers agree that the present modl-making has reached aesthetic heights not heretofore attained. But it is doubtful that this gives cause for much optimism."[97]

Let us proceed now to look at the role of markets under a regime of central economic planning, a topic that will be of great relevance to our subsequent discussions of attempted systemic change and of the fundamental need to make a distinction between (exogenous) institutional choice and (endogenous) institutional change.

---

[97] Ibid., p. 337.

3

Markets under Central Planning

During the Cold War, the study of economic systems was heavily marked by the bifurcation of Europe and of the global security architecture more generally, into two mutually hostile "blocks" or spheres of interest. While the "free world" was associated with liberal market economy, the communist counterpart was seen to practice central economic planning. The Third World, in consequence, was divided into countries that had been dragooned into the Soviet-type system and those that were viewed simply as underdeveloped versions of the West.

Although sporadic attempts were made to introduce nuance – for example, by presenting Japan as a distinct "model" of its own – economic thinking remained dominated by the perception of plan and market as the respective hallmarks of two mutually exclusive economic systems.[1] The tradition of comparative economics that emerged with discussions of market socialism in the 1930s was in consequence devoted to comparison of the respective mechanisms of resource allocation that were associated with socialism (central planning) and capitalism (the market). The main ambition was to investigate the circumstances under which either of the two could be held to produce greater efficiency.[2]

The sudden collapse of Soviet economic planning put an abrupt end to such discussions. The impact on the academic world was profound and unavoidably marked by the general sense of elation, celebrating the victory

---

[1] For an exception to the rule within the literature on comparative economic systems, which explicitly recognized the role of values and contrasted the Soviet economy against those of America, Japan, and China, see Haitani, Kanji (1986), *Comparative Economic Systems: Organizational and Managerial Perspectives*, Englewood Cliffs, NJ: Prentice-Hall.

[2] Djankov, Simeon, Edward Glaeser, Rafael La Porta, Florencio Lopez-de-Silanes, and Andrei Shleifer (2003), "The New Comparative Economics," *Journal of Comparative Economics*, vol. 31, no. 4, pp. 595–96.

of democracy and liberal market economy, in some cases even hypothe-
sizing the end of history. The following verdict is symptomatic: "Socialism
produced misery and inefficiency, not to mention mass murder by several
communist dictators who practiced it. Capitalism, in contrast typically produced growth and wealth."[3] The "new comparative economics" in consequence would be focused on "varieties of capitalism," of which more will be
said in subsequent chapters.

Here we shall remain with the nature of the legacy of central planning
that would come to play such a vital role in the postcommunist ambition
to undertake a transition to a market economy. In a world where market
economy assumed the role of single surviving economic system, it was easy
enough to make two unwarranted assumptions, namely (a) that all those
who had practiced central planning would now be keen on undertaking
a full transition to market economy, and (b) that this transition could be
achieved in the main by simply removing the regulatory parts of the old
system.

The main purpose of this chapter will be to challenge such assumptions.
By investigating the role of such market activities that did and do take place
even under the most rigid forms of central economic planning, we will pave
the way for a discussion of the type of forward-looking instrumental rationality that is normally associated with a well-functioning market economy
and the role of such embedded norms and beliefs that must underpin systems of formal rules and that have proven to be less amenable to change.

Before we proceed to these tasks, we shall have to make a brief digression, aiming at capturing the terminological disarray that has come to mark
both political and academic exchange in the post-Soviet world and that
has clouded insights into what really matters for successful institutional
change.

TERMINOLOGICAL DISARRAY

First, note that the triumph of market economy remains incomplete. Five
remaining communist states have persisted in adhering to versions of the
Soviet-type system. In addition to the prominent case of China, we have
those of Vietnam, Laos, Cuba, and North Korea. The intriguing question
that emerges here is to what extent these holdouts may be reasonably viewed
as representative of an economic system that remains fundamentally different from market economy.

[3] Ibid., p. 596.

Ever since Deng Xiaoping's introduction of cautious reforms in 1978, the Chinese case has been marked by a steadily increasing reliance on elements of market economy. Inspired by the economic rewards, Vietnam and Laos have been moving in that same direction. In stark contrast, Cuba and – more extremely so – North Korea feature regimes that have balked at paying the political price for reaping the potential economic rewards. To further complicate the picture, we also have born-again totalitarian Venezuela that is moving away from rather than toward market economy.

The novelty of the situation as a whole may be reflected in the emergence of an at times amusing labeling game, where pundits as well as governments have excelled in coming up with fanciful sets of qualifiers for both democracy and market economy. The list is long and familiar and needs no reproduction here. What is important, however, is that inventiveness has been driven by two very different types of motivation, reflecting our distinction between institutional choice and institutional change.

One marks governments in present and formerly communist nations that seek to rationalize the retention of state controls by referring to their own systems in terms such as "sovereign democracy," "authoritarian market economy," and indeed "market economy with Chinese characters." The other may be found with pundits introducing labels of their own, aiming to describe observed idiosyncrasies in political as well as economic systems that are somehow viewed as being in transition toward democracy and market economy. The former reflects an ambition to prevent a complete transition, the latter a failure to achieve the same.

The main problem with this labeling game is that it adds to rather than dispels confusion. Reflected in the rapid growth of qualifying labels is the presence of fundamental conceptual disarray, derived from a lack of consensus concerning what we are or should be focusing on. To some considerable degree, this may be led back to the previous association of economic systems with ideology and superpower rivalry. This association was unfortunate in the sense that discussion of planned versus market economies tended to spill over into at times acrimonious debates on the respective merits and demerits of socialism versus capitalism.[4]

---

[4] . It bears noting that an important distinction could be made between the respective notions of socialism and communism. While both may be found represented as ideologies and as political movements in countries across the globe, once we approach the political system that was built in the Soviet Union it would make sense to follow Archie Brown's suggestion to speak not of socialism but of Communism with a capital "C" (Brown, Archie (2009), *The Rise and Fall of Communism*, London: Vintage Books, p. 11). Given, however, that the Soviets referred to their own system as "socialist" and that Western debates on capitalism

Among the first victims of such exchanges was the fact that core systemic features such as free markets and rights to property appeared as ideological litmus tests of what side you were on. To the extent that professing allegiance took precedence over seeking understanding, the stage was set for trouble. The cost, for example, of allowing private property to become an overriding objective in itself would be manifested in neglect of how and whether privatization can be implemented without causing substantial collateral damage. Needless to say, all of this clouded the prospects for a dispassionate analysis that would reveal what, more fundamentally, *did* make the two systems different.

Even more unfortunate was the corollary effect of the self-proclaimed ideological triumph of the West. The catchy slogans of speedy liberalization and privatization that surrounded the introduction of Russian "shock therapy" were deeply revealing of a general reluctance to appreciate the true extent of the challenges that lay ahead. Mesmerized by the prospects of huge investment and business opportunities, pundits and serious observers alike evolved powerful beliefs that the collapse of communism would somehow automatically produce a successful transition from planned to market economy. The consequences for the formulation of marketizing reform would be profoundly negative.

The main problem with this approach was that it neglected the crucial dimension of such pervasive albeit corrupted markets that *did* exist under central planning, and in the absence of which the system surely would not have been able to "muddle through" for as long as it did. When the Soviet Union finally and suddenly did collapse, and Russia joined its many newborn neighbors in professing an ambition to undertake a swift transition to liberal market economy, economics in particular came ill-prepared to the table.

Returning to the labeling game, it is of essence to draw a line between normative ambitions that focus on pleading a case for more or less government intervention in the market, and positive ambitions that seek to highlight how real world markets *do* rather than *should* function. On the former count, we have a long prior tradition of debate on the nature of capitalism.

Beginning with notions of "state capitalism" that were in use among both German and Russian socialists before the Russian revolution in 1917,[5]

---

have tended to invoke socialism rather than communism, we shall stick here with the established contrast between capitalism and socialism.

[5] The notion as such has been traced back to the Russian anarchist Mikhail Bakunin and would subsequently be used both by the German socialist Wilhelm Liebknecht and by the Russian Bolshevik Nikolai Bukharin. With the passage of time, it would become a

in the 1930s members of the American institutional school added that of "banker capitalism,"[6] and subsequent Western radical intellectuals would favor attacking "monopoly capitalism."[7] While all of these were predicated on a conflict between capitalism and socialism, following the collapse of central planning scholars also began exploring "varieties of capitalism" *within* the world of non-socialist market economies. Contrasting "liberal" against "coordinated" economies, the main focus in this latter literature has been on developed market economies with different types of institutional composition.[8]

While many interesting things have been said along these various lines, they all have as common point of departure the presence of a basically market-oriented economic system. The use of qualifying labels has served to focus attention not on the fundamentals of the market as such, but rather on normative discussions concerning government intervention.

It is not our purpose here to grapple with the normative aspects of how to deal politically with free markets, or indeed with mainly political questions concerning what economies may be rightly classified as market economies for world trade purposes. The point, rather, is to approach the basic understanding of what constitutes market economy and to investigate what must be in place for good economic performance to result.

As will be argued at greater length in Chapter 5, markets may be found everywhere, even under the most rigid forms of central planning. Even in Albania under Enver Hoxha, arguably the most repressive of all European communist states, and in North Korea under Kim Jong Il, it would surely be possible to find some elements of voluntary horizontal exchange. The argument on a distinct difference between systems must in consequence depart not from a formal dichotomy between plan and market, but rather from the

frequently used epithet in critique of economic systems across the board. Significantly, when the Russian economist Andrei Illarionov resigned from his post as advisor to President Vladimir Putin, in December 2005, he did so in protest against Russia's "embracement of state capitalism" (*International Herald Tribune*, January 25, 2006). For ample further reference, see http://en.wikipedia.org/wiki/State_capitalism, accessed on January 18, 2010.

6 John Commons viewed the development of capitalism as a process in three stages, from merchant capitalism and employer capitalism to banker capitalism (Commons, John R. (1934a), *Institutional Economics: Its Place in Political Economy*, New York: Macmillan, p. 763).

7 Baran, Paul A. and Paul M. Sweezy (1966), *Monopoly Capital: An Essay on the American Economic and Social Order*, New York: Monthly Review Press.

8 Hall, Peter A. and David Soskice (2001), "An Introduction to Varieties of Capitalism," in Hall and Soskice (eds.), *Varieties of Capitalism: The Institutional Foundations of Comparative Advantage*, Oxford: Oxford University Press.

specific set of state interventions that caused markets in what came to be known as "command economy" to be infused with a set of highly distinctive norms.[9]

To appreciate the importance of such norm formation, we may recall Alec Nove's words about "feasible socialism," namely, that "if it is assumed that all will identify with the clearly visible general good, then the conflict between general and partial interest, and the complex issues of centralization/decentralization, can be assumed out of existence."[10] In short, if the Communist Party really had been successful in creating a breed of "Soviet Men," then command economy might perhaps have been workable after all.

As it turned out, however, Soviet citizens remained overwhelmingly faithful not to the socialist utopia but rather to Adam Smith's famed "propensity to truck, barter and exchange one thing for another."[11] The problem they encountered was that the state found such ambitions to be disagreeable, and their reaction was to evolve a set of norms to support and rationalize actions taken against the state interest. It is the latter that will be viewed here not only as the main cause of Russia's troubled encounter with capitalism but also as an important call for lessons to be learned concerning embeddedness versus forward-looking instrumental rationality.

What makes the Russian case so analytically important is that mandatory economic planning was a Russian innovation. The first Five Year Plan ever to be introduced was launched in the USSR in October 1928, to be concluded ahead of time at the end of 1932. Subsequently, this model would be copied in a large number of other countries, near and afar, but it was in Soviet Russia that it all began. The literature, scholarly and otherwise, that would emerge on its various aspects is nothing short of massive. Needless to say, we shall have no desire here to undertake any form of in-depth revisitation of its technical aspects.[12]

Our ambition in the following shall be different, namely, to explore how the Russian experience of command economy may help in understanding what generates functioning market economy and good economic performance. We shall focus on the presence of pervasive albeit corrupted markets

---

[9] The notion of a "command economy" was first introduced in Grossman, Gregory (1963), "Notes for a Theory of the Command Economy," *Soviet Studies*, vol. 15, no. 2, pp. 101–23.

[10] Nove, Alec (1983), *The Economics of Feasible Socialism*, London: George Allen & Unwin, p. 10.

[11] Smith, Adam (2000), *The Wealth of Nations*, New York: Modern Library, p. 14.

[12] For broad overviews, see Gregory, Paul R. and Robert C. Stuart (1974), *Soviet Economic Structure and Performance*, New York: Harper & Row, and Nove, Alec (1977), *The Soviet Economic System*, Boston: Allen & Unwin.

and look for historical roots of the associated collectivism, and we shall do so in three steps.

The first will be devoted to an exploration of the Bolshevik program of building socialism, where a contrast must be made between the ideological context of the project as a whole, which attracted so much attention, and the more narrow scholarly dimensions of intellectual origins of "collectivist economy" and of central planning perceived as a set of technical problems.

Having established this general framework, we shall proceed to the question of how command economy *did* work, behind its variously decorated façade. Here we shall argue that state interdiction of voluntary horizontal exchange caused the emergence of a set of "irrepressive" markets that provide fertile ground indeed for investigating the emergence of highly distinctive norms, beliefs, and expectations.

In conclusion, we shall outline the role of such perceptions and priorities that may be assumed to have been prevalent among the system managers. This is of great importance not only in highlighting how the USSR differed from the West but also, and more important, in bringing home the awareness that our understanding of "systemic failure" needs to be qualified in several respects.

To begin with, clearly the very notion of "failure" as such harbors an important normative component. From an *economics* point of view it may seem clear-cut. If a system does not live up to the criteria of efficiency that are associated with maximizing behavior, then we are faced with failure, be it of the market or of government. From a *moral* point of view it is more complex. Here one might set as an objective that a system should achieve a sustained reduction of deprivation, which would condemn many cases as distinct failures, but the objective also might be a certain type of social order – say, socialism or capitalism, or indeed fundamentalist Islam – in which case the question of success versus failure becomes muddled. A third possibility is that of *elite preferences*, which is clearly relevant to the USSR. If rulers are willing to accept reduced economic efficiency as a price to be paid for achieving other objectives, then the question of failure to ensure a reduction in deprivation will have to be assessed against popular perceptions of the system as such. As Archie Brown notes, "failure has to be *perceived* as failure, and any such perception is culturally conditioned, as is attribution of the causes of what is identified as failure."[13] We shall have ample reason in the following chapters to return to these distinctions.

---

[13] Brown, Archie (2006), "Cultural Change and Continuity in the Transition from Communism," in Lawrence E. Harrison and Peter L. Berger (eds.), *Developing Cultures: Case Studies*, New York: Routledge, p. 388.

Let us now look at the challenges that were involved in introducing the Soviet order, to be understood here as the first of two Russian twentieth-century ambitions to undertake radical systemic change.

BUILDING SOCIALISM

The Bolshevik attempt at post-imperial state-building was exceptional in many ways, not the least of which concerned the associated degree of violence. The story of these sordid events has been told many times elsewhere and needs no repetition here.[14] What is important, however, is that the project of "building socialism" emerged out of a state of true chaos where improvisation and crisis management was the order of the day.

When Lenin and his cohorts assumed power, not only had they had no blueprint to guide them; Karl Marx, as we all know, had precious little to say about what would come after the final collapse of capitalism. More pressing was that a terrible civil war made it imperative to secure not only power but also sufficient food supplies for the Red Army and for the cities under its control. While the former entailed deliberate Red Terror, the latter was associated with a system of forced requisitioning (*prodrazverstka*) that resulted in pitched battles with armed peasants. Overall, the period came to be known as War Communism.[15]

It was only as the situation stabilized and as power was consolidated that two patterns of great importance for the future could be discerned. One was that the project of state-building came to be associated with the projection of utopia. As this fed into ongoing debates on capitalism versus socialism, it attracted a great deal of enthusiasm from socialists near and afar. The other was that the foundations of a new type of economic system began to emerge. Rooted in Lenin's fascination with the German state-controlled war economy, it proceeded via experimentation with a limited scope for market forces and culminated in the introduction of mandatory economic planning. The latter would remain the hallmark of the Soviet system up until its final demise.

Proceeding now to look at both of these in turn, we shall keep in mind our reservations about normative discussions on capitalism versus socialism, that is, that such exchanges have tended to cloud our understanding of how markets, understood in the sense of voluntary horizontal exchange,

---

[14] See Rosefielde, Steven (2009), *Red Holocaust*, London: Routledge.

[15] See further Nove, Alec (1969), *An Economic History of the U.S.S.R.*, Harmondsworth: Pelican, ch. 3.

really do work, under conditions that range from mandatory central economic planning to a liberal free market environment.

Projecting Utopia

From a systems-oriented perspective, it is important to note that the Soviet Union the Bolsheviks set out to construct was conceived not as a state in any traditional sense of the word but rather as a political and ideological project designed to build socialism. Despite all the vehement rhetoric that had been aimed by Lenin at the Russian Empire as a "prison of nations," and despite all the calls that had been made for national self-determination, once they had secured power for themselves the rulers of the new Soviet state would pay no more than lip service to such matters.

It is true that the Soviet Union was constitutionally construed as a union of ethnically defined Soviet republics and of ethnically defined autonomous units within those republics. In fact, however, there was no ethnically *Russian* Soviet republic, which underscored that from a Russian point of view it was all thought of as being Russian anyway.[16]

Our understanding of the Soviet state as an ideological project rather than a more traditional state may be reflected in the first paragraph of the 1977 "Brezhnev" constitution, which stated: "The USSR builds socialism" (*SSSR stroit sotsializm*). Several important points may be derived from this understanding, which was accepted practice long before it became constitutional law. As there was no question of a state built on either nation or territory, ethnicity was rendered peripheral, as were borders. Center stage instead was occupied by the Communist Party, which had placed itself in charge of the building. The infamous sixth paragraph of the same constitution granted the party a "leading role," the more precise meaning of which was never made clear.[17] In line with the same logic, the state security service, known at the time of the collapse of the USSR as the KGB, was viewed as the sword and shield of the party, charged not with protecting state or territory but rather with safeguarding the ongoing project.

The main thrust of these observations is that this was not a case of state-building at all but rather of an ambition to create a new world order, one

---

[16] For clarity's sake, it should be noted that the Russian Socialist Federative Soviet Republic, the RSFSR, in itself was a peculiar federation of ethnically defined autonomous republics and territorially defined regions, the point being that no single part of this federation was ethnically defined as "Russian."

[17] The somewhat hazy principle that was established for party-state relations was that the party was charged with "leading" but not with "governing" (*rukovodit no ne upravlyayet*).

moreover that would be carried forward on a huge wave of enthusiasm, internal as well as external. The formation of norms, beliefs, and expectations in consequence would play a crucial role. While Soviet workers took pride in being part of building the future, being dispatched to showcase building projects such as the giant Magnitogorsk steelworks and the series of hydroelectric power stations that were erected along the Volga river, Western radical intellectuals rejoiced over what they viewed as an emerging new civilization, freed of the injustices and oppression of the capitalist order.

A typical example of the latter was the American radical journalist Lincoln Steffens, who visited Soviet Russia in 1919. Dazzled by what he had been shown by his friendly guides, upon his return to America in 1921 he famously stated that "I have been over into the future, and it works."[18] Like so many others, he would soon become disillusioned and retreat to being a mere reformer. Another illustration of the same was the American (Lithuanian-born) anarchist Emma Goldman, who was repeatedly arrested, eventually jailed, and then deported from America to Russia. At first enthusiastic over what the Bolsheviks were doing, she also became disillusioned, left Russia, and proceeded to lead a wandering life that would include participating in the Spanish civil war.[19]

As the early contours of the economic system of the USSR began to emerge, the circle of admirers no longer was limited to radicals and revolutionaries. On the contrary, there were numerous intellectuals on the European and North American Left who greeted the new system with enthusiasm, viewing it as a superior alternative to the instability and gross social injustices of the market economy. Some, like Maurice Dobb, argued that the benefits of introducing a socialist system were so large that considerations of detail in its feasibility would have to be secondary.[20] Others, like the Fabian socialists Sidney and Beatrice Webb, even viewed it as a "New Civilization."[21]

Needless to say, the 1929 collapse on Wall Street and the onset of the Great Depression not only contributed greatly to the general spread of such

---

[18] A more frequently quoted version of the same appears on the title page of a book published by his wife in 1933: "I have seen the future and it works" (Winter, Ella (1933), *Red Virtue: Human Relationships in the New Russia*, New York: Harcourt, Brace). See also Steffens, Lincoln (1931), *The Autobiography of Lincoln Steffens*, New York: Literary Guild.

[19] Her impressions were laid out in Goldman, Emma (1923), *My Disillusionment in Russia*, Garden City, NY: Doubleday, Page.

[20] Dobb, Maurice (1933), "Economic Theory and the Problem of a Socialist Economy," *Economic Journal*, vol. 43, no. 172, pp. 588–98.

[21] Webb, Sidney and Beatrice (1935), *Soviet Communism: A New Civilisation?*, London: Longmans, Green. In a subsequent edition, published in 1937, the authors would drop the question mark in the title.

sentiments and expectations but also provoked scholars as diverse as Karl Polanyi and Joseph Schumpeter into making predictions, based on hopes as well as on fears, of a pending demise for capitalism. And we may recall the Schadenfreude that was exhibited by Eric Hobsbawm in response to the global financial crisis that erupted in September 2008.

Returning to the 1930s, we may note how the early sense of enthusiasm came up against a reality where utopia was being transformed into dystopia.[22] The decade opened with the horrors of mass collectivization, which resulted in the death of millions. Then followed the "Great Terror," which killed additional millions, and the infamous Moscow show trials during which the last remnants of opposition to Stalin were eradicated.[23] Needless to say, to the extent that the truth about these events became known, it served to put a damper on the enthusiasm of all but the most ardent believers. Then, however, followed the wartime alliance against Nazi Germany, when "Uncle Joe" was suddenly taken to heart and Soviet power was viewed as a lesser threat.

During the ensuing Cold War, when relations between Moscow and the West again were tense, a second wave of enthusiasm was to follow, driven by what Paul Hollander has castigated as "political pilgrims."[24] Much as the members of the first wave had been captivated by hopes for a new world order, those of the second were motivated more by critique of the capitalist order than by a true ambition to understand what the Soviet system was really about. As captured in the subtitle of the second edition of Hollander's study, it was a case of "Western Intellectuals in Search of the Good Society."[25]

The main problem with much if not most of this admiration was that it focused so narrowly on projections rather than on realities. The building of Soviet socialism appeared to be of interest not for its own sake but merely

---

[22] The term "utopian" was originally introduced by John Stuart Mill, in a speech before the House of Commons castigating the government's Irish land policy. Given the horrors that would mark the Soviet 1930s, one might perhaps even be justified in using Mill's alternative of "cacotopian."

[23] Conquest, Robert (1986), *The Harvest of Sorrow: Soviet Collectivization and the Terror-famine*, New York: Oxford University Press, and Conquest, Robert (1968), *The Great Terror: Stalin's Purge of the Thirties*, London: Macmillan. A revised version of the latter book, called *The Great Terror: A Reassessment*, was issued by Oxford University Press in 1990, when Conquest had been able to amend the text, having consulted recently opened Soviet archives.

[24] Hollander, Paul (1981), *Political Pilgrims: Travels of Western Intellectuals to the Soviet Union, China, and Cuba, 1928–1978*, New York: Oxford University Press.

[25] Hollander, Paul (1998), *Political Pilgrims: Western Intellectuals in Search of the Good Society*, New Brunswick, NJ: Transaction.

as a source of arguments against the capitalist system. This being the case, it was logical that little interest would be devoted to how economic actors actually adjusted to the experiment in replacing free markets with mandatory planning. Maintaining that this flaw would be of great consequence for our understanding of plan versus market, we shall proceed now to take a brief look at how the Bolsheviks actually approached the problem of managing their socialist economy.

Managing the Economy

At the time of the Russian revolution, economists had already been toying for some time with the notion of a "collectivist" economy. One of the first to do so was the Italian economist Vilfredo Pareto, who together with his French colleague Léon Walras made up the Lausanne school in economics. Importantly, Pareto underscored that a collectivist economy would have to rely on the very same economic categories as a market economy, namely, prices, wages, interest rates, and so on. They would be differently named and differently determined, but without them a hypothetical "Ministry of Production" would be groping in the dark, not knowing how to organize production.[26]

In 1908, Pareto's idea was picked up by the Italian economist Enrico Barone, who presented an elegant mathematical formulation of a system of equations that could be solved to arrive at an optimal set of prices and quantities. While private ownership would be suppressed, the information function of the price system could be maintained via a system of "equivalents" that were to be determined by the ministry with the help of the equations. Barone's main recognition, however, was that the rationing function of flexible market-determined prices could not be filled by solving technically determined equation systems. To minimize costs and maximize welfare, large-scale experiments would be needed.[27] The crucially important question of how such experiments were to be organized in practice was, however, left unanswered.

When the Bolsheviks began their rule, they had little time to consider the niceties of such theorizing. It was imperative to secure immediate food

[26] Pareto, Vilfredo (1896), *Cours d'économie politique professé à l'Université de Lausanne*, Lausanne: F. Rouge.

[27] Barone, Enrico (1908), "Il ministerio della produzione nello stato collettivista," *Giornale degli Economisti*, September/October, 2, translated and reprinted in Hayek, Friedrich A. von (1935), *Collectivist Economic Planning: Critical Studies on the Possibilities of Socialism*, London: G. Routledge.

supply, and the means chosen was to use force. This departure is important as it casts doubt on what may have been the original intentions in systems-building. While subsequent Soviet propaganda would project an image of "scientific socialism" that rested on central economic planning, there was nothing preordained about this outcome.[28] Given that reality at the outset was marked by a chaotic search for practical solutions, different interpretations are possible.

Some have argued that the initial use of force was conditioned by necessity, that subsequent liberalization reflected an ambition to allow a mixed form of economy, and that the forceful introduction of mandatory planning was Stalin's work. Others have argued, more credibly, that the initial use of force demonstrated to the Bolshevik leadership how the party could extend control over the economy, that liberalization was in effect a retreat, and that the introduction of planning was a return to the original principles of War Communism.[29] Although the issue as such will surely never be fully resolved, it is important in the sense that it highlights the conflict between political control and economic efficiency that would come to stand as something of a hallmark of command economy.

What we do know is that as the early phase of War Communism gave way to Lenin's New Economic Policy, it seemed for a while as though state control would coexist with at least some leeway for market relations.[30] It was symptomatic of this development that the initial tasks assigned to the Gosplan, the subsequently notorious State Planning Commission that was founded in 1921, had little indeed to do with planning in its subsequent sense. In its first years, Gosplan was tasked merely with providing sets of annual "control figures," representing projections of anticipated developments that served as input into the policy process. The decisive step toward central economic planning as we now know it was taken in 1927, when the control figures were transformed into mandatory commands. From 1928 onward, this mode of operation would constitute the capstone of the Soviet order.

Given what has been said earlier about intellectual support and enthusiasm for the Soviet experiment, it should be noted that the ambition to

---

[28] It may be noted that the notion of "scientific socialism" has been is use among socialists since its introduction by the French anarchist Pierre-Joseph Proudhon (Brown, *The Rise and Fall of Communism*, p. 16).

[29] The latter is laid out with great clarity in Szamuely, László (1974), *First Models of the Socialist Economic Systems: Principles and Theories*, Budapest: Akademiai Kiadó.

[30] The change in course took place under the gallows. As peasants responded to forced requisitioning by reducing sowings, famine ensued and in February 1921 Lenin made an about-face, abolishing many of the extractive measures.

promote socialism and socialist economy did not proceed without opposition. One of its earliest critics was the eminent Austrian economist Ludwig von Mises, who had argued already in 1920 that the suppression of market-determined prices would render impossible any form of rational "economic calculation." Efficiency in consumption would still be possible; the beer drinker and the teetotaler would, for example, still have incentives to undertake mutually beneficial exchange. But the crucial relation between producers would be marked by an absence of valuation that precluded any form of efficiency. He also pointed at the problem of managerial incentives, in a situation where the link between effort and reward was severed, and at the problem of banking in the absence of money markets, both of which would come to loom large in actual Soviet life.[31]

A scholarly counterargument was provided in the 1930s, when the Polish Marxist economist Oskar Lange contributed an outline of how the information problem could be solved. The trick was to allow an imaginary auctioneer in the Ministry of Production to mimic Walrasian *tâtonnement*. Given a set of decision rules, consumers and managers would react to prices announced by the auctioneer in much the same fashion as they do in a market environment. Since, moreover, the Ministry of Production would be able to place joint before private interests, the socialist economy would be both more efficient (avoiding monopolies and negative external effects) and more equitable than the market economy.[32]

The main problem with Lange's widely acclaimed argument was that it merely demonstrated the theoretical *possibility* of a socialist economic system that suspended private property rights. What it left out was the crucial dimension of how it might also be implemented. Points similar to those raised by von Mises would be subsequently raised by Friedrich von Hayek, who argued strongly that for reasons relating mainly to problems of information, central planning would always remain inferior to market economy,[33] and by Abram Bergson, whose main critique was that enterprise managers would not be sufficiently motivated to play by the rules of the bureaucracy that was to take the place of the market.[34]

---

[31] Mises, Ludwig von (1920), "Die Wirtschaftsrechnung im sozialistischen Gemeinwesen," *Archiv für Sozialwissenschaften*, vol. 47.

[32] Lange, Oskar (1936, 1937), "On the Economic Theory of Socialism," *Review of Economic Studies*, vol. 4, nos. 1–2. See also Lippincott, Benjamin (ed.) (1938), *On the Economic Theory of Socialism*, Minneapolis: University of Minnesota Press.

[33] Hayek, Friedrich A. von (1944), *The Road to Serfdom*, Chicago: University of Chicago Press.

[34] Bergson, Abram (1967), "Market Socialism Revisited," *Journal of Political Economy*, vol. 75, no. 5, pp. 655–73.

The decades that followed the introduction of mandatory planning would be marked by an ongoing effort to work out optimal planning techniques, including the development of input-output tables, linear programming, and mathematical optimization theory. Underlying this work was the insight of Pareto, Barone, and Lange that a collectivist economy would need to imitate its market counterpart. In 1975, Leonid Kontorovich and Tjalling Koopmans were awarded the Nobel Prize in economics for their formulation of the "duality theorem," which provided formal proof of the *equivalence* of perfect planning and perfect markets.[35]

By then, expectations were also being formed that the development of powerful computers would help alleviate the information-processing problem and thus make optimal planning practically feasible. Economists affiliated with Moscow's elite Central Economic Mathematical Institute began elaborating a "System for an Optimally Functioning Economy," or simply SOFE, which for a few years served to breathe new life and optimism into the profession.[36]

Soon enough, however, it became apparent that no matter how large the computers, the practical planning problem would remain insurmountable, and optimism began to give way to disillusionment. It was becoming painfully obvious that there was a world of difference between perfect planning and what was being practiced in real Soviet life.

The widening gulf between perfect and actual planning was clearly indicative of the practical irrelevance of the scholarly search for a system of optimal planning. While it is true that some countries still practice forms of central economic planning, the track record is not inspiring and the system as such no longer represents a perceived alternative to market economy, capable of generating a scholarly literature on "alternative systems."[37]

This makes it highly unlikely that anything resembling the formal structures of the Soviet Model of planning will ever be reintroduced in Russia; more important, given the difficulties that Russia has experienced in

---

[35] Kantorovich, Leonid (1968), *The Best Use of Resources*, New York: MacMillan, Koopmans, Tjalling and Michael Montias (1971), "On the Description and Comparison of Economic Systems," in A. Eckstein (ed.), *Comparison of Economic Systems*, Berkeley: University of California Press. See also Weitzman, Martin (1974), "Prices versus Quantities," *Review of Economic Studies*, vol. 41, no. 4, pp. 477–91.

[36] Sutela, Pekka (1984), *Socialism, Planning and Optimality: A Study in Soviet Economic Thought*, Helsinki: Finnish Society of Sciences and Letters.

[37] An exception to this rule, which incorporates culture as an important determinant of systemic difference, is Rosefielde, Steven R. (2002), *Comparative Economic Systems: Culture, Wealth, and Power in the 21st Century*, Malden, MA: Blackwell.

seeking to abandon this system, we are again prompted to make a distinction between the formal system of planning that was embodied in bureaucracies and planning documents and the informal dimension of individuals evolving strategies to cope with the daily routine of deeply dysfunctional mandatory planning.[38]

More precisely, we must ask how much of central planning as it *did* unfold was derived from intellectual efforts to conceive an optimally functioning system of collectivist economy, and how much was due to traditional Russian patterns of organizing economic exchange. In the following, we will argue that once we look behind the modern façade of sophisticated planning techniques, we will find a reality that was marked by striking continuity with age-old institutional patterns.

Making this argument will be of crucial importance to our subsequent discussion on the role of culture and history in shaping current decision making. It will call not only for a digression into Russia's troubled historical legacy, which will be the topic of the following chapter, but also for a discussion of what we understand by the benchmark of markets and market economy, which in turn will be outlined in Chapter 5.

With the benefit of hindsight, we may conclude that while Oskar Lange may have won the theoretical argument on the feasibility of socialist economy, and while the duality theorem may have proven the equivalence of perfect markets and perfect planning, those who argued that in actual practice planning would remain inferior to liberal market economy have been proven largely right, at the very least on efficiency grounds. It would take some time, however, before the latter insight became standard knowledge.

Well beyond the point where the USSR was being variously derided as a "banana republic without bananas" or as an "Upper Volta with nuclear weapons," outside observers remained impressed by the inherent mobilization potential of the Soviet economy. It was after all a fact that Soviet industrialization had made it possible to halt and defeat the Nazi German war machine. There was no denying that the Soviets took the first strides in

---

[38] Soviet propaganda would often refer to the victory in World War II as vindication of the system of economic planning that was built under Joseph Stalin. Seeking to demolish this argument, Holland Hunter and Janusz Szyrmer have undertaken a computer-assisted analysis of the first five-year plans, concluding that the system of planning was so irrational that a non-centralized system would have generated far higher levels of output than what actually occurred (Hunter, Holland and Janusz M. Szyrmer (1992), *Faulty Foundations: Soviet Economic Policies, 1928–1940*, Princeton, NJ: Princeton University Press). I am indebted to Tom Owen for drawing my attention to this work.

the space race, and it was generally recognized that the USSR kept abreast with the United States in the Cold War arms race. To the average Soviet citizen, moreover, daily life in the 1970s was clearly very different from daily life in the 1920s.

A striking manifestation of such beliefs in the Soviet Model may be found in the fact that as late as in 1989, both official Soviet and CIA statistics showed Russia catching up with American living standards. Both suggested that Russian per capita GDP (valued in dollars) was 68 percent of the U.S. level. Yet, a mere two years later the figure, computed at the market rate of exchange, had dropped to 14.7 percent.[39] By suggesting that seven decades of catching up had thus been erased, more or less over night, this also illustrated that there is something fundamentally problematic with the numbers game.

Given the latter background, it was perhaps not so surprising that many would remain convinced, up until the very end, that the Soviet system would indeed be able to "muddle through" for quite some time yet to come. Had it not been for the reforms of Mikhail Gorbachev and the subsequent vendetta between him and Boris Yeltsin, it is not inconceivable that the system might have done precisely that for at least another decade or so. The main question is where this all leaves us.

Are we really justified in describing the Soviet experiment with central economic planning as a case of systemic failure? As noted earlier, our understanding of "failure" needs to be qualified. If measured according to Western yardsticks, the answer would seem to be a given affirmative, but are we really correct in applying Western criteria? Was it perhaps that the two sides were simply keeping score in different games? Entailed here we may find not only the provocative question of presumed universal superiority of liberal market economy. Of even greater importance is the implied role of political priorities that may impact negatively on economic efficiency.[40] Before we grapple with these core issues, we need to take a closer look at what command economy was really about.

---

[39] Rosefielde, Steven (1998), *Efficiency and Russia's Economic Recovery Potential to the Year 2000 and Beyond*, Aldershot: Ashgate, Table S1, p. xxii.

[40] The simple fact that the economic system of the USSR was designed to promote resource mobilization over and above efficiency in resource utilization adds further complexity. To what extent overall output suffered will have to be judged against the level of repression that was needed to maintain a high rate of extraction, making the system seem more efficient under Stalin than under Brezhnev. For a balanced account of the system's postwar performance, see Hanson, Philip (2003), *The Rise and Fall of the Soviet Economy: An Economic History of the USSR from 1945*, London: Longman.

COMMAND ECONOMY

There can, to begin with, be little doubt that the introduction of central economic planning was one of the truly formative events of the twentieth century. It made a big impression on the superpower confrontation, and it had a major impact on the search for alternatives to the prevailing system of market-based capitalism. As we proceed now to outline how the system really did work, we shall leave those dimensions behind. Accepting that the actual pursuit of command economy was widely different from the ideal world of central economic planning, we shall ignore technocratic visions about finding optimal solutions to planning problems. Recalling, moreover, what has been said earlier about the normative aspects of capitalism versus socialism, we also shall disregard ideological projections regarding the superiority of the socialist economy.

The following discussion shall retain in focus our overriding ambition to contrast beliefs in the salutary effects of invisible hands against repeated and varied observations of systemic failure. We shall in consequence approach from a perspective of individual adjustment to government interdiction of economic opportunity, and we shall seek to establish that, as is the case in a market economy, individual action in the command economy remained clearly motivated by self-interest.

At a casual glance there can be no denying that central economic planning did represent a very special case, distinctively different from market economy. Importantly, however, the presence of such difference was limited to those formal rules that were introduced to suppress freely negotiated horizontal exchange, and to such public agencies that were built to formulate and enforce the commands. While the functioning of this formal apparatus did attract a great deal of scholarly interest, and quite rightly so, from an institutional perspective it represented no more than the rules of the game and its enforcement characteristics.

The crucial third dimension that would make or break the system as such was very different. In brief it may be defined as the presence of motivation for economic actors to abide by or to evade or even avoid the rules. It is when we look at such informal determinants of actual economic behavior that we shall find opportunity and self-interest to be no less important, albeit differently manifested, under central economic planning than under the ideal of market economy.

The main point of the following argument in consequence is that we must focus not on the formal rules and enforcement agencies that were so characteristic of this system, but rather on the informal context of those pervasive albeit corrupted markets that could be found beneath the surface. In so doing, we shall make good use of Douglass North's previously cited institutional triad consisting of formal rules, informal norms, and enforcement mechanisms.

Rules of the Game

The core feature of the command economy, which also provided the rationale for the label as such, was the criminalization of such voluntary horizontal exchange that constitutes the essence of market economy. Although ambitions at first were to extend this legal suppression to all forms of horizontal exchange, practical considerations caused the scope to be limited to exchange between producers. Soviet reality in consequence came to be marked by full command economy for inter-enterprise relations, and by quasi-markets for labor and consumer goods. While the latter would have an important impact on how actors adjusted, for the moment we shall focus on the former.

The decision to suppress market coordination between producers had a whole series of consequences that jointly would make up a distinctly new set of rules of the game. Seeking to understand how Soviet enterprise managers adjusted was, however, greatly complicated by the fact that Soviet economic language was permeated by a number of false cognates. In books and articles about the Soviet economy, frequent reference was made to most of those institutional features that make up the fundamental building blocks in a market economy, ranging from money and prices to banks and capital, and indeed enterprises.

Given that the functions that were associated with these labels in the command economy were very different from those of their market counterparts, the stage was set for confusion. Was it, to be specific, in any sense reasonable to speak about a Soviet "enterprise," or should a different terminology have been used? Let us begin by looking at the questions of price formation, which constitutes the core of the market mechanism, and of money, without which it makes no sense to talk of economy in the first place.

In a market economy, freely determined prices provide actors with information concerning changing opportunities, and budget constraints linked to the threat of bankruptcy add incentives to act on this information. If, for example, demand for a certain good or service should go up, a rise in the price will communicate to producers that output should be increased and to consumers that consumption should be decreased. For as long as prices are indeed allowed to move freely, this "market mechanism" will ensure that all markets are in continual movement toward equilibrium, and that in consequence thereof all resources are always used efficiently.

In the vision of Langean optimal socialist economy that was outlined earlier, prices were no longer to be determined via horizontal market exchange, which presupposes private ownership, but rather by a fictitious auctioneer. The main point, however, is that prices were still assumed to fill the very same function as providers of information. As previously argued by Pareto, with reference to the hypothetical "collectivist economy," optimal socialism in this sense was assumed to function in the very same way as market economy.

In Soviet reality, where producers were legally prohibited from engaging in horizontal market exchange, information was provided in the form of commands formulated in physical terms. Given, however, that it was considered unfeasible to evaluate performance based on physical indicators alone – that is, comparing apples and pears – "prices" were assigned based on which values could be computed and compared. As these values were to be used as a measuring rod, it followed in turn that the prices they were based on would have to remain constant over long periods of time.

Even if such prices might at the outset have had some small relation to real-life conditions, over time they would be rendered less and less relevant as providers of such information. The main consequence was that producers would have to operate in an environment of seriously distorted information, where evaluation of performance would rest on nonmarket considerations the nature of which will be outlined in greater detail later in the chapter.

Proceeding to the question of the Soviet currency, note that the role of money in a market economy is normally divided into three, namely, to serve as a measure of value, as a means of exchange, and as store of value. The role of money in the Soviet economy was nowhere close to any of these.

First, given that prices were fixed arbitrarily, it made little sense to talk of measuring "value"; indeed, when the Soviet economy collapsed, a fair share of total industrial production was actually value subtracting, known in Soviet parlance as "cannibalistic production," or *samoedskaya produktsiya*.[41] *Second*, since voluntary horizontal exchange between producers was

---

[41] In a study made at the time of the Soviet breakup, 7.7 percent of Russian industrial production was found to be value subtracting in the short run. If longer term considerations were to be made, say, of depreciation of the capital stock, the figure would be a stunning 35.8 percent (Senik-Leygonie, Claudia and Gordon Hughes (1992), "Industrial Profitability and Trade among the Former Soviet Republics," *Economic Policy*, vol. 7, no. 2, pp. 360, 364).

illegal, only two situations remained where money could serve as a means of exchange, namely, in disbursing wages and in spending household income. As neither of these had any impact on producer decision making, they must be referred to at best as quasi-markets. *Third*, although ruble deposits could be made to accounts in the state savings bank, the Sberbank, there were no other ways in which money could serve as a store of value.

The latter observation forms part of a broader realization that the Soviet banking system could in no reasonable way be compared to its market-based cognate. Given that producers could not turn to banks for credit, and indeed were not allowed to use the official currency as legal tender in support of transactions, it followed that banks could not appear in their fundamental role as intermediary between savers and investors. From this in turn followed that money in circulation represented a closed system, with zero (legal) impact on the real side of the economy.

In accordance with instructions in the plan, the state bank would allocate to producers a certain volume of cash rubles that management was charged with disbursing as wages. Employees would then have a choice between spending and saving. In the former case, "money" would be exchanged for goods in state retail stores, from which it was then returned to the state bank. In the latter, "money" would be deposited in accounts with the state savings bank, from which it again was returned to the same pool.

Much ink has been spilled seeking to establish a link between this peculiar form of money supply and Soviet inflation. Given that prices were inflexible, there could be no question of open price inflation. Instead, experts toyed with the notion of "hidden" inflation, which captured various roundabout ways of redefining quality specifications so as to get a higher price for essentially the same good, and with a "ruble overhang," defined as involuntary saving of rubles that could find no goods or services to purchase.

We shall refrain here from commenting on these ambitions, over and above stating that money printing by Moscow in the final Soviet year of 1991 assumed such proportions that it actually exceeded the total accumulated volume of rubles printed over the preceding three decades.[42] In consequence, price liberalization in January 1992 was simply bound to unleash a spiral of inflation that rapidly turned into hyperinflation, wiping out savings and offering well-placed insiders vast opportunities for short-term speculation.

---

[42] Total money printing in 1991 amounted to 137.3 billion rubles, as compared to an accumulated total of 133.8 billion for the period 1961–90 (*Ekonomika i zhizn*, no. 10, 1992, p. 9).

Thus accepting that the Soviet command economy was based on neither prices nor money, we may proceed to the core question posed earlier, namely, how one should understand the presence of what was known as a Soviet "enterprise," a *predpriyatie*. Two dimensions are of great importance here.

One follows from the suppression of voluntary horizontal exchange. Since producers would not be involved in either sales or purchasing, but merely in receipts and deliveries of goods according to plan, no needs would arise for marketing, cost accounting, or other components of modern business administration.[43] As what remained was a production facility with a personnel department, the main tasks of management would have little indeed to do with "economy." The overriding managerial priority was to bargain with those who could issue certificates for allocation of much needed inputs. The task, in short, was to bribe suppliers, not customers.

The other dimension concerns the absence of property rights and is more fundamental. Given that enterprises did not appear as legal subjects, it was not only the case that all possibility of motivating managers and workers with increases in share values was forfeit; of even greater importance was the implication for legal regulation. The absence of a threat of bankruptcy and the inability to take on debt in proportion to risk were of fundamental importance for the legal system as such. This brings us over to the question of enforcement.

Enforcement Mechanisms

The visions of a collectivist economy that have been outlined above were similar to general equilibrium theory in the sense that no formal enforcement was needed. Under the assumptions that all actors are identical, that all share the same preferences, and that all abide by given rules, optimality will be ensured. The main problem with such assumptions was that they assumed out of existence the very core of the problem, namely, that actors will respond to interdiction of economic choice by resorting to evasion and avoidance.

Proceeding now to outline the problem of enforcement under the rules of command economy we shall take as a point of departure the presence of serious internal inconsistencies in the planning process, due mainly to systemic distortion and concealment of information. Given that formal

---

[43] For the sake of accuracy, if nothing else, it should be noted that the Soviet economy did have special trading organizations that depended on supplying consumers with goods that at times were simply impossible to sell at any price. For such organizations, marketing efforts were important. The main point, however, is that (legal) relations between producers were fully regulated by commands, rather than by consumer influence.

commands issued to producers would in many cases present them with obstacles that bordered on insurmountability, managerial self-interest would simply have to dictate obfuscation and rule evasion.

The multitude of enforcement agencies that were introduced to counter such responses would be plagued by the absence of accepted yardsticks. Since prices did not and could not reflect economic reality, measuring enterprise performance in value terms was rife with problems. As penalties and rewards in consequence would have to be linked to physical output indicators, the field was opened up for all kinds of manipulation. Relations between principals and their agents would in consequence be based on complex bargaining, where distortion and withholding of information constituted vital strategic assets.

The bottom line of the argument as a whole is that enforcement of the rules of the command economy foundered because the criteria for evaluation were so fuzzy. In lieu of classic legal principles of transparency, consistency, predictability, proportionality, and equality, the command economy in consequence would be marked by opacity, inconsistency, unpredictability, and willfulness, all of which could only serve to undermine the prospects for successful formal rule enforcement.

The prominence of rule evasion and avoidance was both triggered and reinforced by the traditional weakness of the Russian legal system, which had always been perceived by the subjects as a set of tools in the hands of those in power. The absence of a truly independent judiciary, and the refusal of the rulers to accept accountability, had produced a legal culture in which morality was consistently placed before the law and where those in power reserved for themselves the right to interpret what at any given moment might be consistent with morality. The tremendous staying power of such norms, beliefs, and expectations that emerged within government enforcement agencies may be reflected in President Dmitry Medvedev's frequent reference to traditional Russian "legal nihilism."

In short, we may conclude that the agencies and institutions that were built to enforce the rules of the command economy were bound to place economic actors in very special situations of choice, widely different from the assumptions of autonomy and of trust in the impartiality of impersonal government agencies that underpin the market economy.

Endogenous Adaptation

From these observations follow what must be viewed as the true core of the command economy, namely, distinctive patterns of endogenous adaptation to pervasive willfulness. Accepting that the Soviet state failed in its proclaimed ambition to create Soviet Men, and that Soviet citizens remained bent on exploiting opportunity and self-interest, it follows that our main focus must be aimed at *how* they set about organizing their ambitions to truck and barter. The solution, as suggested earlier, rested in rule evasion.

Being ever fearful of unexpected events that could jeopardize plan fulfillment, or for various other reasons that could lead to harsh sanctions being imposed, enterprise managers were forced into building buffers of protection. While these could and did include wasteful hoarding of inputs, it was mainly focused on building dense personal networks based on bribery, favors, and obligations, known in Russian as *blat*, that could help reduce risks.[44] As such collusive networks would include managers as well as bureaucrats, operating in cahoots to devise clandestine ways of circumventing the formal commands issued by the planning bureaucracy, they would work to counter the interest of the state in resource mobilization. Enforcement agencies in consequence would have to develop ever more intrusive means of surveillance, and the system as a whole would be rife with corruption.[45]

The practical outcome was a dual system of operations, where all were obliged to play according to the formal rules, but where all were at the same time also placed in a situation where the practice of rule evasion and rule avoidance was simply necessary for survival. While a certain volume of the official production of goods and services would thus be transacted according to plan directives, that is, produced and delivered in exchange for plan fulfillment credits, a parallel volume of – often higher quality – output would be transacted on the side, *na levo*, as part of an unofficial economy that was technically illegal but also crucial to the functioning of its official counterpart.

From the shop floor all the way up to the Kremlin, actors would be involved in playing these dual games. Higher quality sausage that was sold on the side in state stores would fetch a higher price, thus generating a surplus that went into a common pool of cash to be used for unofficial side payments. Bureaucrats could use their powers of license and exemption to extract such side payments, and managers who were regularly allocated faulty deliveries of inputs would employ special facilitators, known as *tolkachi*, who could trade on the side with other producers.

[44] Ledeneva, Alena V. (1998), *Russia's Economy of Favors: Blat, Networking and Informal Exchange*, Cambridge: Cambridge University Press.
[45] See further Olson, Mancur (2000), *Power and Prosperity: Outgrowing Communist and Capitalist Dictatorships*, New York: Basic Books, ch. 8.

The reality that is depicted here was one of a bewildering set of warped markets that were characterized by varying degrees of illegality. The first to portray this reality was the Soviet economist Aron Katsenelinboigen, in a 1977 article titled "Colored Markets in the Soviet Union."[46]

Turning now to capture the impact of these various types of warped market activity on vital processes of network building and of norm formation, we shall introduce the notion of an "irrepressive market." In a general sense, this refers to cases of voluntary horizontal exchange that are interdicted by the government on moral grounds. Classic examples refer to sex, drugs, and gambling. By introducing laws that prohibit specific practices in relation to these types of activities, the government causes a new type of market to emerge, one that is marked by lingering desires by segments of the population to engage in the now illicit practices.

The persistence of such demand will have two types of consequences. One derives from the fact that the increasing risk associated with the prohibition will cause the price of the good or service to rise, as a result of which income and wealth will be shifted from consumers to providers. The rise of organized crime syndicates may be viewed as the epitome of this transformation and as an important part of the cost to society of undertaking such interventions.

The other concerns the process of law enforcement and captures the fact that while enforcement in "normal" cases will exist to protect one party against potential predations by others, in the case at hand both parties will desire the state to stay out. The upshot is that since neither side will have any interest in reporting transgressions of the law to the relevant authorities, enforcement will have to depend on roundabout means such as purchased information, provocations to commit crimes, and outright denunciations, all of which will impact negatively on the quality of the rule of law. Given these clearly troublesome side effects, and given the fact that the state will incur substantial costs from the prosecution and incarceration of offenders, it is not surprising that voices have been raised pleading for legalization.[47]

---

[46] Katsenelinboigen, Aron (1977), "Colored Markets in the Soviet Union," *Soviet Studies*, vol. 29, no. 1, pp. 62–85.

[47] This has been especially true in the United States, where at the outset of 2009 a staggering 7.3 million Americans, representing one in every thirty-one adults, were inside the nation's prison system. The number includes those in jails and prisons, on parole, on probation, or under other forms of correctional supervision. In fiscal year 2008, U.S. states were estimated to have spent more than $52 billion to incarcerate and monitor the prison population, representing a more than 300 percent increase over 1988 spending (http://www.wsws.org/articles/2009/mar2009/pris-m04.shtml, accessed on October 13, 2009).

In a democratic setting, the obvious rationale for introducing bans on the kinds of activities referred to here is that the state reserves for itself both a right and an obligation to protect its citizens from the consequences of immorality.[48] While libertarian thinkers will argue that the state does not have any right to interfere in this way, this is clearly not the place to engage in philosophical speculation over the role of the state vis-à-vis its subjects. Let us proceed instead by recognizing that while the irrepressive markets just mentioned represent a mere island in a sea of legitimate economic exchange, central economic planning took this type of repression to its extreme.

By de facto criminalizing all voluntary horizontal exchange between producers, the system managers caused the entire economic playing field to be fundamentally reconfigured. This had far-reaching implications not only for the management of production. The associated shortages that were so typical of the command economy would have equally profound consequences for the daily life of consumers. As citizens in general were constantly forced to engage in a variety of illegal transactions, simply to make it through the day, the system was rife with irrepressive markets with varying degrees of illegality and socially disruptive consequences.

The consequences of thus pushing actors into a context where all were forced to undertake criminal actions may be viewed as a generalization of the effects of the irrepressive market that were outlined above, that is, roundabout means of enforcement that rest on intrusive surveillance and denunciations that seriously undermine both the legitimacy of the state and the potential for interpersonal trust to emerge and to promote a build-up of productive social capital.

The bottom line is that while the official side of the system was "clean" and easily amenable to technical analysis in mathematical form, the command economy also had an unofficial side that was distinctly "messy." Marked by dense personal networks, embedded in complex social structures, this dimension was considerably more difficult to model and thus also to understand. Perhaps, as suggested by Richard Rose and Ian McAllister in an article about post-Soviet household survival strategies, we are faced here with idiosyncratic characteristics best identified by anthropological studies.[49]

---

[48] It might of course also be argued that the costs to society from allowing an unbridled legal trade in sex, drugs, and gambling would actually exceed the costs of enforcing a ban, but that is beside the point here.

[49] Rose, Richard and Ian McAllister (1996), "Is Money the Measure of Welfare in Russia?," *Review of Income and Wealth*, vol. 42, no. 1, p. 88.

Given that systemic performance will in the end be determined by how individual actors adjust to changing rules of the game, it is in precisely this dimension of adjustment that we must be looking for causes and explanations of systemic failure. As this in turn brings into focus the role of the state as the originator and caretaker of how changes in the rules are devised and implemented, we shall conclude our discussion on markets under central planning with a look into questions of perception, priorities, and systemic reformability.

PERCEPTIONS, PRIORITIES, AND REFORMABILITY

Let us begin by recalling what was said earlier about a need to qualify our understanding of the core notion of "systemic failure." The very fact that in the end the Soviet system did collapse, and that during its final decades it clearly underperformed its market rival in the provision of welfare, will clearly have to be contrasted against what priorities the system managers may have had.

For the moment, we can disregard whether and to what extent the Soviet leaders actually believed that central economic planning was superior to the market economy in efficiency terms, or if they really did nurture any hopes that enhanced computing capacity would eventually overcome the information problem. What it all boils down to may be reflected in the following statement by Alexander Yanov, culled from a book about his experiences of attempted Soviet agricultural reform in the 1960s: "Inevitably the answer to the question 'Does the system work?' depends on what one means by 'work.' If it refers to political control, then the kolkhoz system works very well; if it refers to food production, then the system does not work, for it was not designed to."[50]

The relevance of Yanov's point must be viewed against the background of a contrast between the unquestionable ability of the command economy to achieve macro-level forced mobilization of resources and the equally unquestionable price that had to be paid in terms of micro-level loss of economic efficiency and global competitiveness. Adding the associated support provided by this system for political agendas of securing military power and providing privilege for the elite, it may be suggested that micro-level inefficiency was a price willingly paid. This will be explored further in the account of Russia's historical legacy that follows in Chapter 4.

[50] Yanov, Alexander (1984), *The Drama of the Soviet 1960s: A Lost Reform*, Berkeley: CA: Institute of International Studies, p. 22.

Remaining with our argument that Russian elites may have been keeping score in a game of their own, we shall suggest here that an agenda of military power and elite privilege has effectively trumped any considerations of economic efficiency in either static or dynamic terms. This view is supported by the fact that command economy offered three substantial political advantages, relating to mobilization, extraction, and privilege, all of which must be weighed against any potential realization of economic inefficiency.

In the *first* of these, by suppressing consumer sovereignty and by making producers exclusively dependent on physical allocation of inputs, the share of consumption in GDP could be firmly controlled. Whether consumers were happy with what they got was a political problem that had no bearing on the actual management of production. If it was decided to make machines that made machines that made machines, as one of the metaphors of the time would have it, then that was something the consumers would simply have to accept. The true hallmark of this system was producer rather than consumer sovereignty.

The *second* and clearly related political advantage of command economy was that within the share of GDP that was set aside for capital accumulation, the choice of priority investment projects could also be politically determined. If, for example, the system managers decided that the USSR must keep up with the United States in the arms race, and perhaps even take the lead in the space race, then they could simply allocate the necessary funds. If this resulted in military expenditure that was multiples of the U.S. level, measured as share of GDP, or if it resulted in a crowding out of productive investment in civilian projects that could have made Soviet non-military goods competitive on world markets, then so be it.

The *third* and to the elites perhaps most important advantage of command economy was that the effective suppression of money exchange resulted in a serious loss of transparency with regard to the distribution of welfare. As noted, the USSR did have an official currency and workers received wages in this currency, but that constituted no more than a small part of the picture. Given that the vast bulk of household consumption was simply allocated, via various administrative systems of preference and rationing, the Soviet ruble was de facto limited to function as an expanded form of food stamps. It offered consumer choice only for certain non-allocated goods and it was not legally convertible into market-based currencies.

The lack of transparency was important not only in providing the privileged members of the once famed Soviet *nomenklatura* with vast opportunities for a clandestine lining of their own pockets.[51] Even more important, it provided the foundations for such relations of dependence and loyalty, resting on the provision of selective favors and rewards, that constituted the core of the governance model. The price to be paid was measured in a loss of accountability and in the emergence of such forms of corruption and influence games that were to become the true hallmarks of the system.

All of these may be viewed as generic consequences of the main principles of command economy, consequences that were clearly observable in all Soviet-type economies. The situation may have been worse in some places than in others, with pragmatic Hungary being jocularly referred to as the "happiest barracks in the camp," but these were differences of degree rather than of principle. From a purely formal perspective, the system was solid. Even in the best performers, the track record of attempted partial reforms was not a happy one.

The real test of just how deeply the formal rules of the command economy were rooted in the informal dimension of each individual country's institutional matrix would follow once the grip from Moscow had been relaxed, and the Soviet system as such had finally collapsed. Recalling that central planning was a Russian invention, we may proceed here to add that the various informal dimensions of norms, beliefs, and expectations that would provide the formal model with a content of motivation for human action must in consequence have been at least partly rooted in Russian tradition.

While the cause of building socialism did attract a broad following that was the same across nations and cultures, we shall maintain that some of its fundamental principles were of a more distinctly Russian origin. It will be the task of the following chapter to take a closer look at this historical legacy, to identify its main patterns of institutional reproduction, and to establish the essential continuity that was carried over into the formation of the Soviet system.

From a general perspective of reformability, the Soviet system could be viewed as a set of formal rules and enforcement mechanisms that was fairly homogenous across all Soviet-type economies. Although the Bolshevik revolution was not unique in the sense of emerging from within and from below – as opposed to communist rule being imposed from without and from above – the case of Russia is arguably distinctive in the sense that the formal rules and enforcement mechanisms that would come to be known as

[51] Voslensky, Michael (1984), *Nomenklatura: The Soviet Ruling Class*, Garden City, NY: Doubleday.

the "Soviet Model" emerged within a Russian context. Although there were some small variations, communist followers would largely and faithfully copy this model. The importance of this observation rests in the associated fact that those informal norms that underpin and determine the performance of the formal system, that is, cultural and historical legacies, were substantially different between countries.

A tentative combined conclusion will be that while in Russia rules and norms evolved endogenously, in a process of mutual reinforcement, in other cases rules were imposed from above, on a set of norms that were bound to resist that imposition. The fact that post-Soviet adjustment would exhibit a pattern of major divergence in development paths between countries provides strong evidence of the role of culture and history in determining such paths.

It was highly symptomatic that while pretty much all new governments that were established to undertake post-Soviet reforms would adhere publicly to the same formal goals of building democracy and rules-based market economies, elites within different countries would have very different perceptions and priorities regarding what actually could and should be done. In some cases, there was a community of interest that was helpful in implementing painful but necessary reforms. In others, good intentions on the part of some reformers were simply hijacked by more powerful predatory elites, and in the most unfortunate cases one may reasonably suspect that westernizing reform was never really in the cards at all.

What could be observed in the years that followed the Soviet collapse was the emergence not of a common transition to liberal market economy but rather of striking diversity. Out of a world of superficially homogeneous command economies, all of which had been patterned on the Russian/ Soviet Model, there emerged an array of divergent development paths. In line with what was just said, some would extricate themselves with but a reasonable amount of trouble and be rewarded with membership in the European Union. Others would get stuck in limbo, where it remains unclear if institutional change in some form is still ongoing, and yet others would collapse into or near to failed states.

The fact that the Russian Federation would be found in the middle category of states locked into institutional limbo is striking not only due to the inordinate share of attention, advice, and assistance that was mentioned above, and that might perhaps have been expected to smooth the way toward successful westernizing reform. Even more striking was the enthusiasm with which Russia's reformers embraced the perceived need for a radical break with the past that was implied by the policy of shock therapy.

While the latter did serve to cement expectations among outside observers that Russia really was on track toward a successful integration into the West, we shall argue that the drastic switch was in itself a sign of how Russia remained in the grip of her own past. The powerful embrace of marketizing rhetoric may be viewed here as a manifestation of what Yurii Lotman and Boris Uspenskii have referred to as an age-old Russian cultural pattern of *maximalism*, of an inability to find a neutral middle ground between extremes.[52]

Looking back at Russian tradition, we may find as one of its main distinctive traits that the pendulum always tends to swing to its extremes, before it reverts. So it was when Lenin set out to eradicate tsarism, and so it would be when Yeltsin set out to eradicate communism. Given this track record, it does come across as rather important to consider whether Russian elites at the time of the Soviet breakup really did perceive a need to reform.

The key question must concern whether the downside of the old system, which may have seemed so obvious to outside observers, was sufficient also for insiders to warrant its replacement by something new. There can be little doubt that ambitions among the country's westernizing intelligentsia were serious enough, but then again that had been the case since the days of Alexander Herzen, and it had always been a fringe phenomenon. Perhaps we would be better advised to take seriously then President Putin's infamous remark in a speech to the Russian Federal Assembly in April 2005, that "the collapse of the Soviet Union was a major geopolitical disaster of the century."[53]

Realizing that a serious program of westernizing reform, including core features such as accountability in government and impartial law enforcement in the business world, would have constituted a serious threat to the rent-seeking ambitions of the country's elites, we shall suggest here a rather different interpretation of the pursuit of opportunity and self-interest.

While it is true that the collapse of the Soviet order represented massive opportunity for change, it is not as clear that there really was a communality of both insight and ambition regarding how to deal with such opportunity. A more likely interpretation is that outside the ranks of the westernizing intelligentsia, elites perceived an unprecedented opportunity

---

[52] Lotman, Yurii M. and Boris A. Uspenskii (1984), "The Role of Dual Models in the Dynamics of Russian Culture (Up to the End of the Eighteenth Century)," in A. Shukman (ed.), *The Semiotics of Russian Culture*, Ann Arbor: University of Michigan.

[53] http://archive.kremlin.ru/eng/speeches/2005/04/25/2031_type70029type82912_87086. shtml, accessed on October 12, 2010.

to loot, to make hay while the sun was still shining. Beyond such ambitions, it is debatable to what extent they really were desirous of serious change.

The ease with which President Putin would succeed in suppressing – de facto if not de jure – pretty much all of the work that was begun already under Mikhail Gorbachev to promote democratic institution-building does illustrate that the cause of westernizing reform may not have had much of a following after all.[54] This is supported by opinion surveys from the time that showed broad popular support for most if not all of the main principles of his authoritarian restoration. In a survey of polls undertaken in the first term of Putin's rule, Richard Pipes found that Russians overwhelmingly felt that democracy was a fraud, that private property was a façade for corruption, and that outsiders were not to be trusted. They felt comfortable with a one-party state, placed order before freedom, and had little problem with censorship of the media. Above all, they wanted Russia to be a great power again, and they saw more government involvement in the country's economic life as a way to reach that goal.[55]

Turning now to take a brief look at Russia's historical legacy, we may recall what has been said about the ideological clash between capitalism and socialism. Embedded in this clash we may find a fundamental opposition between individualism and collectivism, an opposition that goes to the very heart of the contrast between central economic planning and liberal market economy. The main question that emerges here concerns the line of causality between planning and collectivism. Was it, simply put, that the strongly collective nature of the command economy was produced by the newly introduced ideology of socialism, or was it perhaps rooted in prior long-term Russian history?

The latter view is well formulated in Kanji Haitani's insistence that "the Soviet government's indoctrination efforts have not *created* the collectivist

---

[54] Although Boris Yeltsin has been widely associated with sweeping Russian reform, aiming to introduce democracy and market economy, a balanced account will have to recognize that it was Mikhail Gorbachev who took the first vital steps toward dismantling the Soviet system. Without his personal ideals and commitment, and the leadership he provided in the early years of perestroika, the world might never even have come to know Yeltsin, whose personal commitment to the ideal of democracy and a rules-based economy would be found seriously wanting. Gorbachev's tragedy was that dismantling the Soviet system also led to a collapse of the Soviet state. Whether this could have been avoided shall never be known. For a powerful argument in support of Gorbachev as the true reformer, see Brown, Archie (2007), *Seven Years that Changed the World: Perestroika in Perspective*, Oxford: Oxford University Press.

[55] For a summary of the results of several polling organizations, see Pipes, Richard (2004), "Flight from Freedom: What Russians Think and Want," *Foreign Affairs*, vol. 83, no. 3, pp. 9–15.

orientation of the Russian people; rather, they have merely preserved, nurtured, and expanded the traditional collectivism that has been developed by centuries of living under autocratic rules."[56]

The distinction is far from trivial. If a country has a long-term cultural heritage of norms that promote collectivism and acceptance of autocratic government, may we then still retain a belief that simple deregulation will automatically result in liberal market economy? Bearing this rather brutally formulated question in mind, let us proceed now to see what insights a perusal of the Russian experience may contribute.

[56] Haitani, *Comparative Economic Systems*, p. 40.

4

Russia's Historical Legacy

In the account thus far we have placed much emphasis on the combined role of opportunity and self-interest, as determinants of economic development, and we have recognized a need to go beyond the assumptions of hedonism and rationality that underpin the neoclassical economic tradition. In line with our ambition to capture the broader institutional context of transactions, we have also suggested that a distinction will have to be made between forward-looking instrumental rationality and such informal types of motivation that are somehow embedded in social structures.

It is when we investigate how the latter may influence the way in which choices are made that it becomes necessary to incorporate the role of factors we may refer to as "cultural." As this in turn entails considering the long run and possible path dependence, the essentially ahistoric focus of transaction cost analysis must be completed with insights into the driving forces of historical progression. For such insights to be of real value, it is, moreover, essential that they be distinctly different from the common Western tradition that has produced what we presently know as democracy and rules-based market economy.

As we have repeatedly argued, the case of Russia is admirably suited to fit this ticket. It offers poignant illustrations of critical junctures, of pressures for reform that lead to actions followed by reversal, of causes that drive institutional reproduction over time, and of governance that is distinctly market-contrary. In short, it serves to provide a provocative context where opportunity and self-interest produce outcomes that are widely different from those normally associated with invisible hands and good economic performance. Designed to provide important background for discussion in subsequent chapters, the following account will be presented in four chronological steps.

The *first* will detail the emergence, in the fourteenth and fifteenth centuries, of an institutional matrix that was very different from developments in the rest of Europe.[1] The reasons were linked to a set of special circumstances, and for all its inherent "difference" the arrangement was rationally suited to the needs of the time.

The *second* step will outline how a transformation over time of the unfavorable initial conditions would cause mounting pressures for the matrix to be adjusted, and how such pressures would fail to produce sustainable results. This is a story that is rife with controversy, relating mainly to institutional continuity and to subjective understandings of the causes of reversal.

The *third* step will argue that the creation by the Bolsheviks of the Soviet order may be interpreted not as the introduction of a utopian new order but rather as a reconstitution of deeply rooted Muscovite institutional patterns, which had been dislocated during the period of what came to be known as the "Great Reforms."

The *fourth* and final step will look at post-Soviet developments, arguing that the dismal consequences of sweeping liberalization under Boris Yeltsin illustrate why opportunity and self-interest may not always be sufficient for good economic performance, and that the ensuing authoritarian restoration under Vladimir Putin constituted yet another reversion to age-old institutional patterns.

Before proceeding to these main undertakings, we shall, however, provide a brief account of ways in which Russia has been viewed as somehow inherently different from the rest of Europe. Recalling what has been said about systemic failure, emphasis will be placed here on such undeniable achievements that have fed into Russian self-imagery and that may perhaps be viewed still as important factors conditioning further developments.

RUSSIA IS DIFFERENT

One of the most striking features of Russian history is that there was so little in the cards to suggest that a small settlement at a bend in the Moscow River would emerge, eventually, as the capital city of a superpower with global reach. The odds against such an outcome were formidable, including

---

[1] Geoffrey Hosking opens his account of "Russia and the Russians" by stating, "The north Eurasian plain is not only Russia's geographical setting, but also her fate" (Hosking, Geoffrey (2001), *Russia and the Russians: A History from Rus to the Russian Federation*, Harmondsworth: Penguin Press, p. 1). For a more neutral account of Russia's emergence at the eastern steppe frontier, see, for example, McNeill, William H. (1963), *The Rise of the West: A History of the Human Community*, Chicago, IL: University of Chicago Press.

a harsh climate, poor resource endowments, and great distance from both markets and trade routes, not to mention living in a tough neighborhood. Logically, the outcome should have been something very different. As Richard Pipes puts it, "On the face of it, nature intended Russia to be a decentralized country formed of a multitude of self-contained and self-governing communities."[2] The simple fact that Muscovy did not merely survive but even proceeded to transform itself into an empire, must hence be viewed as a remarkable achievement.

The main reason it is essential to bear this achievement in mind is that a cursory glance at Russian history will not generate much optimism about the country's future. In a book with the telling title *The Agony of the Russian Idea*, Tim McDaniel sums up what amounts to a track record of persistent systemic failure: "Reform in Russia: over the centuries it has always failed, sometimes to be replaced by a reactionary regime (Alexander III's reversal of Alexander II's 'great reforms' of the 1860s and 1870s), and sometimes culminating in the collapse of the system (1917 and 1991)."[3]

The contrast between these two approaches, between achievement and persistent failure, lies at the very core of the frequently advanced understanding of Russia as being somehow inherently "different." Analytically, the story of achievement is the most readily accessible. Departing from a set of inauspicious initial conditions, it details how very specific measures were taken to overcome serious obstacles. The point where controversy will arise is defined not by what in some sense may be viewed as objective facts relating to measures taken, but rather by subjective perceptions of those measures and of their outcomes.

An important trend in forming outside perceptions was set already by the first Western travelers to visit Muscovy, men like Giles Fletcher and the Baron Sigismund von Herberstein. Experiencing a sixteenth century that was heavily marked by Ivan the Terrible, they returned with stunning accounts of a "rude and barbarous kingdom" marked by tyranny and despotism.[4] Much the same would be reflected in the previously cited nineteenth-century account by the Marquis de Custine, whose book *Empire of the Czar*

---

[2]   Pipes, Richard (1974), *Russia under the Old Regime*, New York: Charles Scribner's Sons, p. 19.

[3]   McDaniel, Tim (1996), *The Agony of the Russian Idea*, Princeton, NJ: Princeton University Press, p. 174. I have been taken to task on this point by Archie Brown, underscoring that what collapsed in 1991 was the Soviet *state*, not the Soviet *system*. The Communist system, with a capital "C," was dismantled under Mikhail Gorbachev, arguably during the course of 1989. For a detailed presentation of this argument, see Brown, Archie (2007), *Seven Years that Changed the World: Perestroika in Perspective*, Oxford: Oxford University Press, ch. 7.

[4]   This immortal phrase was originally formulated by Richard Chancellor, whose Muscovy Company did brisk trade with Ivan the Terrible. See further Berry, Lloyd E. and Robert

was banned in Russia; and in his classic "long telegram" from 1946, which introduced the Cold War policy of containment, George Kennan argued that Soviet behavior was conditioned by traditional Russian paranoia.[5]

The list of negative imagery could be made much longer, and it could be made to include such considerably more optimistic interpretations that have been advanced by many radical Western intellectuals.[6] Recalling, however, what was said earlier about perceptions and priorities, a deeper understanding of how Russia's historic legacy may influence current developments can be attained only by considering how generations of not outsiders but of Russians themselves have perceived their own very specific problems and solutions.

If what outsiders have viewed as systemic failure has been viewed by many Russians as great achievements, then we have a major source of misunderstanding. Given our emphasis on the interplay between formal rules and informal norms, it is of critical importance that the account of measures taken and outcomes recorded be made to incorporate, as far as possible, a dimension of such internal perceptions that will impact on the formation of norms.

Before we proceed to these tasks, let us say just a few added words about the understanding of achievement. In subsequent chapters we shall have much to say about developments in the remainder of Europe, developments that Russia would not form part of or even succeed in emulating. Viewed from a perspective of norms and perceptions, it is imperative that the account of what was missed can be accompanied by an account of what the Russians did instead. Only thus may we approach the crucial issue of interpretation, and of how collective memories of the past may continue to exert influence over actions in the present.

In his classic account of "Muscovite political folkways," Edward Keenan warns his readers against being taken in by what he refers to as the "deprivation hypothesis," that is, all those developments in Western Europe that Russia opted to stay out of. His argument is quite to the point: "The

---

O. Crummey (eds.) (1968), *Rude and Barbarous Kingdom: Russia in the Accounts of Sixteenth-Century English Voyagers*, Madison: University of Wisconsin Press, and Poe, Marshall T. (2000), *"A People Born to Slavery." Russia in Early Modern European Ethnography, 1476–1748*, Ithaca, NY: Cornell University Press.

[5] Kennan's subsequently famous telegram was at first published anonymously, under the pseudonym "X" (Kennan, George F. ["X"] (1947), "The Sources of Soviet Conduct," *Foreign Affairs*, vol. 25, no. 4, pp. 566–82).

[6] For a more detailed account, and discussion, of what Russia is and is not, see also Poe, Marshall (2003), *The Russian Moment in World History*, Princeton, NJ: Princeton University Press, ch. 1.

deprivation hypothesis has little explanatory power with regard to the political culture that did arise in Muscovy, nor does it address the question of why that culture was – despite features that Westerners might consider unattractive or 'deficient' – so effective and, apparently, so admirably suited to Muscovy's needs."[7]

Keenan's main point is that the survival and even vigor and demographic vitality of the Slavs could be assured by "a remarkably congruent and tenacious set of practices and attitudes." He concludes that "the creation of a distinctive and strikingly effective political culture in the hostile and threatening environment that was the womb of Russia's political culture was that nation's most extraordinary achievement."[8] While the Russians may have failed to imitate the West, it is in consequence not entirely clear on what grounds their own solution may be rightly viewed as inferior.

A similar approach to highlighting the achievements of the Muscovites, in a "singularly inopportune environment," is suggested by Marshall Poe. Noting that the grand princes, supported by a tiny boyar elite, were faced from the very beginning with "the unenviable task of knitting together an expansive, poor, sparsely populated region of far northeastern Europe and mobilizing it for constant defense against a host of aggressive neighbors," he underlines that "not only did the Russians survive, they prospered, creating in the span of a bit over a century an empire that stretched from Archangelsk to Kiev and from Smolensk to Kamchatka."[9]

Even more important, he also follows Keenan in emphasizing the tenacity over time of those institutional solutions that were once generated to deal with the highly specific problems of the time: "By almost any standard, Muscovite political culture proved to be quite durable, lasting in its pristine form for almost two centuries and, according to the opinions of some continuity theorists, well into modern times under one guise or another."[10]

Rounding off the argument, there can be little disagreement about the rational foundations of what Poe calls the "logical adaptive strategy that permitted the Muscovite elite to build an empire under the most trying of conditions."[11] What does remain to be addressed is a very different question, one that may also be taken to represent the main analytical challenge of the continuity approach as a whole.

[7] Keenan, Edward (1986), "Muscovite Political Folkways," *Russian Review*, vol. 45, no. 2, p. 119.
[8] Ibid., p. 122.
[9] Poe, *"A People Born to Slavery,"* p. 220.
[10] Ibid., p. 219.
[11] Ibid., p. 226.

How could a set of highly specific institutional arrangements that emerged under a set of equally specific circumstances show such durability over time? To put it more specifically, how was it possible for the core features of what we may refer to as the institutional matrix of Muscovy to remain largely intact for so long, long after the time when those arrangements may have been instrumentally rational – and to the great detriment of future generations?

These are core questions that will be dealt with here in a preliminary fashion only, leaving for Chapter 7 to undertake a more general in-depth consideration of the role of history and of possible path dependence. Let us turn now to the historical account proper, and begin with the emergence of a coherent institutional matrix.[12]

THE MUSCOVITE MATRIX

The first organized state to emerge on the territory of the Eastern Slavs, known as Kievan Rus, or *Kievskaya Rus,* was centered on Kiev, the present capital of Ukraine. Long before Moscow began its rise to power, Kiev had already risen to become one of the largest cities in Europe, deriving much gain from lucrative trade with Byzantium. According to some, its rapidly growing wealth and splendor placed it on equal footing even with Constantinople.[13]

An important problem with Kievan historiography is that the sources are so poor. With some insignificant exceptions, historians really only have one available source, namely, the *Primary Chronicle,* or the *Povest vremennykh let,* which is believed to have been compiled at the beginning of the twelfth century.[14] It is, in consequence, difficult to say anything of greater substance about how Kievan society and economy were organized.

---

[12] The long story is told in Hedlund, Stefan (2005), *Russian Path Dependence,* London: Routledge. For a more succinct presentation, see also Hedlund, Stefan (2006), "Vladimir the Great, Grand Prince of Muscovy: Resurrecting the Russian Service State," *Europe-Asia Studies,* vol. 58, no. 5, pp. 781–85.

[13] Blum, Jerome (1964), *Lord and Peasant in Russia: From the Ninth to the Nineteenth Century,* New York: Atheneum, p. 15, quotes several contemporary sources to this effect, notably Adam of Bremen (d. 1076) who wrote that Kiev rivaled Constantinople.

[14] Cross, Samuel H. (ed. and transl.) (1953), *The Russian Primary Chronicle,* Cambridge, MA. Even the authorship of this document has been hotly debated. At first it was ascribed to a monk by the name of Nestor, but in later scholarship it has been presented as a compilation of several documents. The presumed compiler was a certain Silvester, Abbot of the Viebuditsky Monastery in Kiev. See further, for example, Kluchevsky, V. O. (1911), *A History of Russia,* vol. 1, London: J. M. Dent, ch. 1.

What we do know is that beginning in the twelfth century, a steadily worsening security situation caused an increasing migration toward the north, to the forested and largely unpopulated Volga-Oka basin. Then, following the plunder of Constantinople by the Venetians during the Fourth Crusade, in 1203–4, Kiev was effectively shut out from the Mediterranean trade, and in 1240 the Mongols put a conclusive end to Kievan Rus, by simply razing the city to the ground. It would take a century or more for it again to resemble a city. Our story shall thus have to begin not with Kiev but with Moscow.

Introducing Autocracy

The notion of "Muscovy" is normally used with reference to the regional great power that emerged, during the fourteenth and fifteenth centuries, to succeed Kievan Rus in the north. Given that these were times when the land of Rus, the *russkaya zemlya*, as a whole was dominated by the Mongols, and when numerous tiny principalities were constantly feuding with each other, creating unity was a tall order indeed. The first obstacle to be overcome, in dealing with the common enemy, thus had to be that of creating unity in command.

The problem here was rooted in the heritage from Kievan times, when all members of the one princely family, claiming descent from the legendary Viking chieftain Rurik, who may or may not have been a historic person, were jointly in control of the lands. Under the highly complex "rota system," princes would be promoted between cities, up a ladder of increasing importance where the post of Grand Prince of Kiev represented the very top.

As the center of gravity shifted toward the north, and as the power of Kiev waned, the bonds of the old hierarchy were eroded. As a result, relations between princes and their cities became increasingly complicated. Given the importance of death and inheritance in determining the distribution of both power and property, this era would come to be known as *appanage* Russia. Upon the death of a prince, his possessions would be shared among his sons, thus perpetuating fragmentation and weakness.

The main challenge to this system was issued by the Moscow house of princes, and it was successful for two sets of reasons. One was pure fluke, in the sense that the Moscow princes were long-lived and had few surviving sons. The other was pure skill, mainly in lobbying the Mongol overlords. Moscow's real rise to power began under Prince Ivan I, also known as Kalita or "moneybags," who succeeded in winning from the Mongols a right to act as tax collector for all of Rus. According to the Russian historian Vasily Kluchevsky, no prince "more often went to pay his respects to the Mongol potentate than did Ivan Kalita, nor was he ever aught but a welcome guest, seeing that he took care never to come empty-handed."[15]

The crowning achievement was reached in 1328, when the Metropolitan of the Orthodox Church decided to move his see from the older and more prestigious principality of Vladimir to Moscow, which in consequence assumed the combined role of secular and spiritual leader of Rus. Still being nominally Grand Prince of Vladimir, Ivan marked the occasion by expanding his title to "Grand Prince of Moscow and all Rus." Over the coming century, his successors would absorb by peaceful means all the other northern principalities but one. The exception was that of Novgorod, which would be subjected to a drawn-out military conquest. Beginning with a limited campaign under Ivan the Great in 1471, it ended in total destruction at the hands of Ivan the Terrible in 1570.

The essence of the rise to prominence of the Moscow house of princes may be captured in the transformation of an order where the grand prince had been a *primus inter pares*, a first among equals within the princely family, into one of genuine autocracy, where there were no formalized means by which the ruler could be held to account.[16] This stands in sharp contrast to the strongly contractual and rights-based system of contemporary west European feudalism, and may serve as the true hallmark of the Muscovite model.

Conditional Property Rights

As the principle of autocracy was being firmly established, the logical next step was to transform the system of traditional hereditary property, known from Kievan times as *votchina*, into a system of lands offered in return for service, to be known as *pomestie*. Although it is something of a misnomer, in the sense that it assumes a two-way bargain, we shall refer to the latter as one of conditional property rights.

The origin of the *pomestie* system was linked to military needs. As Muscovy expanded toward the east, it absorbed vast stretches of territory

---

[15] Ibid., p. 286.
[16] Given what has been said about false cognates, it may be worth noting that the original Greek notion of rule by an autocrat (*autokrator*), which would be translated into the Russian *samoderzhave*, denoted a form of self-rule in which the Byzantine emperor recognized no external – that is, foreign – constraints on his power. In Muscovy, the understanding would be that the grand prince recognized no limitations whatsoever, external or internal.

that were only partly settled and cultivated. This caused an entirely new concept to take shape. By settling these areas with military servitors, these men "would become converted into a landowning class, and so act as a living rampart against raids from the steppes."[17]

At the outset, there was nothing at all remarkable about this. Given that there were many different princes to serve and that boyars retained other holdings in the form of hereditary *votchina* lands, the ability of the grand prince to impose compulsory service was effectively constrained.

The real transformation would occur in two overlapping steps, both of which were related to the gathering of the lands. The first was linked to the shrinking number of princes to serve, a development that eroded the effective freedom of the boyars, and the second to the increasing availability of vacant lands, which followed from expropriations and allowed the victorious Moscow princes ever greater latitude in awarding service lands.

Slow at first, the process gained true momentum after Moscow's victory against Novgorod. As the vanquished population of this geographically expansive principality was being either killed or deported en masse, plenty of vacant land was made available for the grand prince of Muscovy to hand out to his servitors. Surviving Muscovite boyars would find that they now had only one master to serve, and no remaining lands that they could call truly their own. This was the origin of what Richard Hellie has referred to as a Russian "service state," of which we shall have more to say in a moment.[18] Over the coming century, the formal distinction between *votchina* and *pomestie* was eroded, and in 1731 it was abolished altogether.

The consequences of thus combining unaccountable power with the introduction of conditional property rights would be far-reaching indeed. When he needed resources to go to war, the Muscovite ruler would not have to engage in bargaining with landed nobles. He could simply command and commandeer. The reason we have said that "conditional" is a misnomer is that it presumes a right for nobles to refuse service, at the cost of forfeiting their *pomestie*. No such right existed. The very essence of the new system was that of transforming service into a universal obligation.

It is here that we may find the true key to the rise of Muscovy, and it is here that we may also find reasons to presume that despite inferior economic efficiency, both Muscovite and subsequent Russian rulers, arguably

---

[17] Kluchevsky, V. O. (1912), *A History of Russia*, Vol. 2, London: J. M. Dent, p. 119.
[18] Hellie, Richard (1977), "The Structure of Modern Russian History: Toward a Dynamic Model," *Russian History*, vol. 4, no. 1, pp. 1–7.

including Vladimir Putin, may have come to view this arrangement as a sine qua non for survival.

Legal Regulation

In the early days of appanage Russia, there was a legally recognized right for boyars to choose whom to serve and to move between princes at will. In surviving princely treaties of the time we find a standard phrase being employed, saying that "the boyars and servitors who dwell among us shall be at liberty to come and go."[19] As such rights were being increasingly circumscribed, and eventually fully suppressed, the boyars were not alone in finding their conditions of life transformed. For the princes, and eventually the single remaining grand prince, two types of consequences resulted.

The first was related to the mounting danger of defection and betrayal that followed from increasing compulsion. Seeking to make sure that servitors would indeed show up for battle when called upon to do so, the Moscow princes began to interfere with the right of departure. Both boyars and lesser princes in their service were forced to take oaths never to leave service and to offer bondsmen to vouch for their loyalty.[20] Over time, such demands would increase substantially, with regard both to the number of bondsmen required and to the fines that would have to be paid in case of defection. Under Ivan the Terrible there would be cases of suspected boyars having to put up literally hundreds of surety bonds, being liable for fines of up to 25,000 rubles.[21]

The main effect was to introduce among the leading strata of the boyar class a system of overlapping collective responsibilities, whereby individual defection would lead to collective punishment. There was some historical precedence for this, in the form of *krugovaya poruka*, a system that had originally denoted networks of mutual assistance and of joint responsibility. Under the Muscovite princes, *poruka* acquired a political dimension of dependence and subordination that would become deeply ingrained and long-lived.

To this system of internalized mutual control was added an ever expanding obligation to report and denounce. Originally an essential part of all

---

[19] Kluchevsky, *A History of Russia*, vol. 1, p. 263.
[20] On the early roots of this system, see Dewey, Horace W. and Ann M. Kleimola (1984), "Russian Collective Consciousness: The Kievan Roots," *Slavonic and East European Review*, vol. 62, no. 2, pp. 180–91.
[21] Dewey, Horace W. (1987), "Political Poruka in Muscovite Rus," *Russian Review*, vol. 46, no. 2, p. 128.

inter-princely treaties, with princes agreeing to inform each other of all possible threats and disloyalties, the centralization of power to the grand prince implied an important change. The obligation would now be for all subjects to "inform against anyone who spoke to them in any way detrimental to the interests of the grand prince, his wife, his children or their lands."[22]

As with so many other important transformations of Muscovy, the formal dimension would be slow in coming. According to the infamous law on "word and deed" (*slovo i delo*), which was formally introduced in the Ulozhenie law code of 1649, all subjects were required under penalty of death to report immediately any form of criticism against the tsar.[23]

The second consequence of locking the boyars into service was related to the fact that with increasing control from above they were successively deprived of ways of securing their own livelihood. For the grand prince, who was faced with a general absence of both trade and resource wealth, this implied a serious challenge. Having little or no money to hand out as wages, he would have to find alternative ways of remunerating his servitors.

The solution was found in the practice of *kormlenie*, of allowing officials to "feed" off the lands they were tasked with administering. The main impact of this system, which alleviated the resource constraint, was that it also replaced a contractual relation of being paid fixed wages with a system of dependence on being allocated lucrative postings where the "feeding" would be good.

A system of legal regulation that had included rights to hereditary property and to free departure was thus transformed into an unregulated obligation to serve, with contractual rights to wages for work replaced by handouts awarded on the basis of the goodwill of the ruler. It is hard to imagine a system that is more stifling of private entrepreneurship and of innovation from below.

Forced Mobilization

Throughout the Muscovite era, the true driving force behind the process of institution-building was linked to considerations of security. At the outset,

---

22 Kleimola, Ann M. (1972), "The Duty to Denounce in Muscovite Russia," *Slavic Review*, vol. 31, no. 4, p. 765.

23 James Billington maintains that this "probably represents an extension to the public at large of the rigid obligations to report fully any wavering of loyalties inside Josephite monasteries" (Billington, James H. (1970), *The Icon and the Axe: An Interpretive History of Russian Culture*, New York: Vintage, p. 64).

there were valid grounds for such considerations. In Kievan times, the Rus had been constantly harassed by peoples of the steppe, who at times penetrated even into the city itself. With the subsequent "Mongol Storm," they were given added reason to fear both material destruction and risks of being carried off as slaves.

Writing about the consequences of having to put up a defense against threats that lasted even after the Mongols had been defeated, Kluchevsky comes close to sentimentalizing: "Every year during the sixteenth century thousands of the frontier population laid down their lives for their country, while tens of thousands of Moscow's best warriors were dispatched southwards to guard the inhabitants of the more central provinces from pillage and enslavement."[24]

As Muscovy gained strength, one might have thought that a sense of added security should have led to a change in direction, allowing greater freedom for the serving nobility. The opposite would prove to be true. Following his first defeat of Novgorod, Ivan the Great presided over the emergence of a political culture that was imbued with a powerful sense of true xenophobia. Borders were sealed, and those foreigners who were admitted would be kept under constant guard, making sure that there could be no contact with the local population.

Being convinced that they were surrounded by enemies and that survival was indeed constantly at stake, the Muscovites built a model that was eminently suited to promoting forced mobilization of resources for defense. In so doing, they not only built a system in which the state would function as the sole engine of growth. They also made the presence of an enemy a prerequisite for maintaining the practice of constant mobilization of resources. Both represent patterns that would remain all too familiar down to and throughout the Soviet era.

To capture the essence of this process, we may return to Hellie's previously mentioned notion of a Russian "service state." Assuming that the main driving force rests in perceived security threats, the logic shows how strong rulers trigger programs of mass mobilization in support of defense that entail strict hierarchical bonds of allegiance and obedience. Long-term Russian history has been marked by three cases of such "service class revolutions," occurring under Ivan the Terrible, Peter the Great, and Joseph Stalin.[25]

The historical dynamics of this model predict that periods of authoritarian economic growth and force projection, which follow upon the respective

---

[24] Kluchevsky, *A History of Russia*, Vol. 2, p. 118.
[25] Hellie, "The Structure of Modern Russian History."

"revolutions," will be concluded by "times of trouble" that in turn lead up to an authoritarian restoration of the old order.[26] The core implication is that Russian historical development exhibits a fundamental institutional continuity that prevails even in the face of drastic upheavals.

REFORM AND REVERSAL

Looking now at the tenacity over time of the institutional arrangements that emerged in Muscovy, we must begin by recognizing that the measures taken constituted rational responses to pressing needs of the time. The story of achievement that is detailed by Keenan, Poe, and others would scarcely have been possible under a different sort of arrangement. The real puzzle lies in explaining how a subsequent transformation of initially inauspicious conditions could fail to result in a re-ordering of the core dimensions of the institutional matrix. Proceeding to grapple with this issue, we shall find that Russian historiography may be divided into two opposing schools.

The most clearly pronounced, and consistent, of the two is based on the "continuity theory" that is normally associated with previously mentioned scholars like Richard Hellie, Edward Keenan, Richard Pipes, and Marshall Poe. Borrowing from Max Weber the notion of a patrimonial state, where the line between power and property is erased, Pipes even argues that Russia evolved into a sui generis state that is not to be compared to any other country or system: "The patrimonial regime ... is a regime in its own right, not a corruption of something else."[27]

The opposite school is associated with Martin Malia, who claims that from the time of Peter the Great until the October revolution in 1917, Russia was on the same track as the rest of Europe, only with a fifty-year lag.[28] From his perspective, the imposition of Bolshevik rule was a watershed event that served to derail Russia from her path toward Europe: "Soviet Russia ...

---

[26] This understanding of repeated "times of trouble" as interludes, or as punctuations, between cycles of repression and liberalization, is central also to Alexander Yanov's theory on the origin and evolution of Russian autocracy (Yanov, Alexander (1981), *The Origins of Autocracy: Ivan the Terrible in Russian History*, Berkeley and Los Angeles: University of California Press). See especially his presentation of the "Political Spiral" (on pp. 59–65).

[27] Pipes, Richard (1974), *Russia under the Old Regime*, New York: Charles Scribner's Sons, p. 23. Writing in 1996, he said: "The sense of isolation and uniqueness bequeathed by Orthodox Christianity unfortunately survives. Present-day Russians feel themselves to be outsiders, a nation *sui generis*, belonging neither to Europe nor Asia" (Pipes, Richard (1996), "Russia's Past, Russia's Future," *Commentary*, June, p. 35).

[28] Malia, Martin (1999), *Russia under Western Eyes: From the Bronze Horseman to the Lenin Mausoleum*, Cambridge, MA: Harvard University Press, pp. 418–19.

represents both maximal divergence from European norms and the great aberration in Russia's own development."[29]

The problem in assessing which of these views may offer the better interpretation of essentially the same set of events is that while the former is mainly concerned with measures taken to surmount obstacles, the latter focuses on perceptions, mainly by outsiders, of those same measures. Given our focus on economic performance, it is of some importance to note Malia's attitude: "In fact, the economic dimension of the process is the one least relevant to deciding modern Russia's fate: ideology has been much more crucial."[30]

The following account will expand on this opposition, seeking to capture how a trend of ambitions to introduce liberalizing rules would come into repeated conflict with a parallel trend of tenacity in fundamental norms, illustrating our previous argument that opportunity and self-interest may not always be sufficient for good economic performance to result.

Peter the Great

The person of Peter the Great incarnates the very essence of the contradiction between the two approaches. To some, he stands as a great liberal reformer, as the man who was famously seen by Pushkin to open a window on Europe, and who set Russia irreversibly on a path toward the West. To others, he was the Antichrist, the founder of the Russian police state and the originator of command economy. All of this is wrapped into one man.

To appreciate the reasons behind such widely different interpretations, it must be understood that the latter part of the seventeenth century was a time of great turmoil in Russia. The country was heavily marked by fallout from the "great schism," the religious confrontation that resulted from the Church Synod in 1666. Bent on introducing reform that would return the church to the true roots of Orthodoxy, Patriarch Nikon provoked opposition from within that well-nigh tore the church apart. James Billington justifiably characterizes this as a *coup d'église*, comparable in importance to the Bolshevik *coup d'état* that was to follow 250 years later.[31]

The reason the schism would have such profound effects is rooted in developments in the former part of the century, when effective co-rule between

---

[29] Ibid., p. 12.
[30] Ibid., pp. 13–14.
[31] Billington, *The Icon and the Axe*, p. 121.

Tsar Mikhail and his father, Patriarch Filaret, led to the emergence of a system of theocratic power over the state. Reflecting the legitimating role of norms, when the clerics proceeded to destroy that construct from within, they logically also succeeded in shaking the very foundations of the state.

When Peter embarked on his program of modernization, the church was an easy victim. By calling for the introduction of modern European fashion in dress and for beards to be shaved off, he made a symbolic attack on the iconographic tradition of the church. To this were added more tangible measures, such as holding drunken parties – known as the "Most Drunken Synod" – at which the clergy were derided and humiliated, and by deciding not to appoint a new patriarch when the incumbent Patriarch Adrian died in 1700.

By this time, the church was so weakened by internal strife that it was no longer able to resist: "The *coup de grace* was dealt a victim so drained of all vitality that it hardly twitched; there were no protests, only silent submission. No Church in Christendom allowed itself to be secularized as graciously as the Russian."[32]

While the attack on the church did constitute an important part of Peter's program, its more fundamental dimension related to modernization of the state. Driven by his urge to break with the country's byzantine past, in 1697–98 Peter undertook a long tour of study abroad, to be known as the Grand Embassy. Traveling incognito, under the name of Peter Mikhailov, the tsar and his entourage visited a number of European countries, most important Holland and England, where they studied shipbuilding and modern administration.

Called home by urgent dispatches of rebellion by old believer circles within the army, Peter had to begin by putting the house in order. A big and powerful man, said to be capable of decapitation by a single blow with the axe, he took a personal part in the repression. According to the Marquis de Custine, "He has been seen in a single evening to strike off twenty heads with his own hand, and has been heard to boast of his address."[33]

Exiting the torture chamber, the tsar proceeded to work on his reputation as a great westernizer, by streamlining the bureaucracy and by toying with the separation of the crown from the state. Introducing notions such as "the common good" and "the benefit of the whole nation," Peter actively sought to promote a sense of connection between private and public good.

[32] Pipes, *Russia under the Old Regime*, p. 240.
[33] Custine, Astolphe, Marquis de (1989), *Empire of the Czar: A Journey through Eternal Russia*, New York: Doubleday, p. 440.

The most concrete manifestation of the ambition for modernity and rationality was a new and more professional bureaucracy that was copied from the Swedish college system. With the "general regulation," the *generalnyi reglament*, of 1720, the multitudes of old Muscovite *prikazy* were replaced by – initially – nine administrative colleges that were organized on functional rather than geographic or simply historical lines.

The true essence of modernization rested in increased efficiency of command and control rather than in allowing more initiative from below. Thus, while Peter did introduce the first program of secular education ever in Russia, seeking to teach young nobles mathematics and other useful sciences, this was done with the aim of improving their qualifications in military matters like navigation and gunnery.

The absence of any ambition to allow true entrepreneurship from below was reflected in the "Table of Ranks," the *Tabel o rangakh*, that was introduced in 1722. Replacing old internal systems of rank and promotion that had been upheld by the nobles themselves, the new system introduced a mandatory lifelong service obligation that was based on merit rather than on blood.

Continuing the Muscovite tradition of controlling the population at large, Peter also proceeded to complement the previous legislation on "word and deed" by introducing a separate political police. As phrased by Marc Raeff, the *Preobrazhenskii prikaz* was set up to "ferret out, prosecute, and punish all those suspected of political subversion."[34] To Pipes, the "scope of its operations and its complete administrative independence mark it as the prototype of a basic organ of all modern police states."[35]

By the end of the Petrine era, the Russian state had been essentially secularized and modernized. The grip of the clergy had been broken. The bureaucracy had been streamlined, industries were being built, and a blue water navy was being constructed. In short, Peter had succeeded in harnessing all his subjects behind a modernizing project of empire-building. He had done so, however, with essentially Muscovite means, achieving what Pipes refers to as "the apogee of tsarist patrimonialism."[36]

The core of Hellie's previously cited understanding of the time of Peter the Great as a second "service class revolution" lies in the link between security concerns and the imposition of command and control, with the aim of

---

[34] Raeff, Marc (1976), "Imperial Russia: Peter I to Nicholas I," in Robert Auty and Dimitri Obolensky (eds.), *An Introduction to Russian History*, Cambridge: Cambridge University Press, p. 142.

[35] Pipes, *Russia under the Old Regime*, p. 130.

[36] Pipes, Richard (1999), *Property and Freedom*, New York: Alfred A. Knopf, p. 187.

facilitating mass mobilization of all resources for defense. Peter succeeded in defeating both Sweden and Turkey and in proclaiming himself Emperor, a clear sign of achievement of the Muscovite model.

This achievement, however, was not without cost. Raeff attributes Peter's economic policies to the then prevailing principles of mercantilism: "Not only did the government provide most of the purchasing power and investment capital, but it also set rigid standards of production, dictated methods of manufacturing, and made available a good part the labor force by attaching serfs to mines and factories."[37] An even better understanding would be to view it as the first case in history of the introduction of command economy.

The Post-Petrine Era

The first real test of whether Russia was on the same track as Europe, as argued by Malia, would arrive in the post-Petrine era. With the conclusion of the Great Northern War, in 1721, Peter had secured what was now an empire and thus also removed the previous constant fears of survival. In consequence thereof, it was logical for the nobility to question the need for lifelong service. From the side of the autocracy, moreover, there was little reason to resist. Aiming to build a modern bureaucracy of professional civil servants, it could do without often incompetent nobles. In 1730, Empress Anna reduced the service obligation to twenty-five years, and in 1762 Peter III removed it altogether.

Under the subsequent rule of Catherine the Great, the position of the nobility was further advanced. With her Charter of the Nobility, issued in 1785, nobles were granted rights to property and due process, not to mention an end to corporal punishment. In further reflection of the German-born empress's personal convictions, she also toyed with the idea of ending serfdom, which she found to be reprehensible. Events, however, would overtake her ambitions and cause retrenchment rather than reform.

First and foremost was the bloody Pugachev rebellion, in 1773–75. The horror that Catherine experienced at these events was further enhanced by the French revolution, which led to the murder, in 1793, of her friend Marie Antoinette, and by the assassination of her first cousin, Swedish King Gustavus III, in 1792. Having begun as a valiant reformer, who not only befriended and corresponded with the French *philosophes* but also allowed their works to be both read and translated, Catherine ended her rule in a repressive mode.

---

[37] Raeff, "Imperial Russia," p. 126.

The nineteenth century was to be marked by further swings of the pendulum between reform and repression. Following the murder of Catherine's son, the strongly repressive Emperor Paul, his son Alexander I in turn began as a liberal tsar. Restarting the process of reform, he proceeded to defeat Napoleon and to participate at the Congress of Vienna, where Russia emerged as the "gendarme of Europe."

The Napoleonic wars, however, left a heavy impression on the tsar. Becoming ever more convinced of the need to maintain the status quo, Alexander gradually abandoned his resolve to support reform. In consequence, many of those who had pinned great hopes on liberalizing reform were disappointed. By 1825, a group of frustrated guards officers, who had been to Europe and had experienced both constitutional and other developments there, were plotting to kill the tsar. As Alexander happened to die a natural death only months before they could strike, their "Decembrist" uprising instead was aimed at his younger brother and successor, Tsar Nikolai I.

Coming to power in the midst of a revolt, Nikolai would assume the role as Russia's last truly powerful autocratic tsar. His regime would evolve a strange bunker mentality, to be described as "the discipline of the camp – it is a state of siege become the normal state of society."[38] The center of power was a personal chancellery, the most notorious part of which was its Third Section. Headed by General Benckendorff, it was a well-organized political police, set up with a broad mandate: "Foreigners, dissenters, criminals, sectarians, writers – any exponent of ideas would come under its supervision."[39] Like the *Preobrazhenskii prikaz* of Peter the Great, it was exempt from supervision by other government agencies, reporting directly to the tsar himself.

The essence of Nikolai's rule was captured in the trinity of "autocracy, orthodoxy, nationality" that was formulated by his minister of education, Count Uvarov. The proclaimed ambition was for the regime "to serve as an ideological dam that would hold back all critics of the existing order." Uvarov made no pretense about his own limited ambitions: "If I can succeed in delaying for fifty years the kind of future that theories are brewing for Russia, I shall have performed my duty and shall die in peace."[40]

The statement reflects rather clearly the ambivalent nature of the time. Well hidden behind its repressive façade, the autocracy maintained an

[38] Kochan, Lionel and Richard Abraham (1990), *The Making of Modern Russia*, Harmondsworth: Penguin, p. 160.
[39] Ibid., p. 161.
[40] Ibid.

ongoing process of reflection over the need to reform. Benckendorff himself referred to serfdom as a "powder magazine under the state,"[41] and there were other sections of the chancellery that kept alive the process of thinking about matters such as legal reform. Even so, by the time of Nikolai's death, no concrete measures had been taken to promote any form of change in a liberal direction.

The seeds that had germinated below the surface of Nikolai's repressive rule would be brought to full bloom under his successor, Alexander II, arguably the most able and best prepared ruler ever to ascend the throne of Russia. Together with that of Peter the Great, his era constitutes the most important illustration in support of the argument that Russia has been on the same track as Europe.

His Great Reforms included the abolition of serfdom in 1861, the introduction of legal reform in 1864, and the introduction of limited local government (the *zemstvo* movement), also in 1864.[42] While all of these did represent fundamentally important changes in the formal rules of the game, the outcomes would be short-lived and/or represent too little too late. The abolition of serfdom in particular would turn out to have been ill-conceived. This time round, increasing disappointment and frustration spilled over into a wave of terror that culminated in 1881, when the tsar was killed in a terrorist bombing.

Under strong influence of Konstantin Pobedonostsev, the reactionary lay head of the Orthodox Church, Alexander III embarked on a program of authoritarian restoration that was aimed at correcting what Pobedonostsev referred to as the "criminal error" of his father. The gains of the *zemstvo* movement were rolled back, the judicial reform was diluted by the introduction of emergency powers and military tribunals, and talk of easing the mounting debt burden of the peasants was derided as a way of weakening their moral fiber. Most odious of all, the new regime allowed a wave of open anti-Semitism. According to Pobedonostsev, one-third of the Jews must die, one-third emigrate, and one-third assimilate.[43]

The ideology of Alexander's rule represented a continuation of the reactionary trinity of "autocracy, orthodoxy, nationality." The main difference was that Russia had undergone profound change, making it ever more difficult to keep the lid firmly in place. Opposition to the autocracy had been

---

[41]   Ibid, p. 162.
[42]   For example, Eklof, Ben, John Bushnell, and Larissa Zakharova (eds.) (1994), *Russia's Great Reforms, 1855–1881*, Bloomington: Indiana University Press.
[43]   Kochan and Abraham, *The Making of Modern Russia*, p. 225.

reinforced by the reforms under Alexander II, and support for the terrorists had spread into the ranks of both bureaucracy and nobility.

Although realization of the need to reform had been mounting steadily, the very thought of introducing any form of constitutional constraints on the exercise of power remained anathema. Confronted with demands for a national legislative assembly, viewed by the liberals as a "crowning of the edifice," even Alexander II would constantly repeat, in the midst of all his great reforms, a flat refusal: "*surtout, pas d'Assemblé de notables!*"[44]

It was somehow symptomatic that the powerful and strong-willed Alexander III would be followed by a weak but obstinate son. When Nikolai II ascended to power, in 1894, he was perhaps the most reluctant tsar ever to do so. Being convinced that maintaining the autocracy was his personal duty to God, Nikolai would remain insistent that constitutional reform was simply out of the question. On one occasion, when approached on the matter, he would simply denounce such thoughts as "senseless dreams."[45]

What might have been a truly important break with the past was begun in earnest in the last decade of the nineteenth century. Under firm and highly competent leadership by minister of finance Sergei Witte, the Russian economy entered a phase of rapid growth. Spreading across several sectors, it resulted in more than a doubling of industrial production as a whole. By the turn of the century, Russia was the world's leading producer of oil, the ruble was convertible, and foreign investment was gushing in. The building of the Trans-Siberian Railway was of particular importance, in the sense of spreading market relations and of thus increasing the monetization of the Russian economy.

Importantly, however, it all represented a case of industrialization that went against the logic of the market. The main challenge to Witte rested in the absence of domestic capital, which created a need for foreign investment. The solution was found in imposing heavy taxation on the peasantry. By forcing them to produce a surplus that could be exported, much-needed capital goods could be imported. The cynical underlying logic of this policy was reflected in a classic statement made already by Witte's predecessor as minister of finance, I. A. Vyshnegradskii: "We will be underfed, but we will export" (*Ne doedim, no vyvezem*).[46]

---

[44] Malia, *Russia under Western Eyes*, p. 168.

[45] Kochan and Abraham, *The Making of Modern Russia*, p. 232.

[46] Volin, Lazar (1970), *A Century of Russian Agriculture: From Alexander II to Khrushchev*, Cambridge, MA: Harvard University Press, p. 63.

What made this case so special was that it represented a stark deviation from the "normal" pattern of industrialization, in which increasing productivity in the primary sector allows for a transfer of resources into the secondary manufacturing sector. In the Russian case, agricultural productivity had failed to reach the level where such transfer of resources could be initiated without damage to the primary sector. Ignoring this fact, Witte introduced a policy of forced extraction, which generated substantial short-term results at equally substantial long-term cost. Already heavily burdened by mounting arrears in paying redemption fees for land they had acquired with emancipation, peasants would now also have to shoulder the added burden of heavy taxes.

Toward Revolution

The twentieth century opened with famine and disorder, culminating in the revolution of 1905, an event that forced Nikolai II into accepting substantial concessions. His rightly famous "October Manifesto" provided for elections to Russia's first State Duma and for the introduction of a Basic Law that secured a full catalogue of rights and freedoms. In the following year, Prime Minister Pyotr Stolypin launched an ambitious program to promote private farming.

The question is whether this package of reforms may be rightly viewed as a final breakthrough for Russia in establishing a rules-based market economy. Many have argued that endogenous reasons would have caused it to run out of steam even if Russia had been spared the internal turbulence that resulted from the outbreak of the Great War. Others have balked at the implied counterfactual speculation and suggested that "the question of whether Russia would have become a modern industrial state but for the war and the revolution is in essence a meaningless one."[47]

While the point on the futility of counterfactual speculation is valid, it is a fact that we are faced here with a major attempt at transforming Russia in a westernizing direction, one, moreover, that on formal grounds looked most promising. Exactly why it failed is a question that hinges on what we believe about the prospects for a corresponding transformation of informal norms, which will have to remain speculative. What we do know is that the Great War paved the way for the Bolsheviks, and that their introduction of the Soviet order put a definitive end to all hopes, this time round, for continued Russian movement toward Europe.

---

[47] Nove, Alec (1982), *An Economic History of the USSR*, Harmondsworth: Pelican, pp. 43–44.

The main question that does arise here concerns the impact of the program that the Bolsheviks proceeded to implement, once they had secured power. The standard view is that of radical systemic change, in the direction of building a new utopian world order. What we suggest is that it really was a case of moving backward into the future. Setting out to suppress all of those trends toward democratic institution-building and a rules-based market economy that had been unfolding over the past half century, beginning with the Great Reforms of Alexander II, Lenin and his cohorts actually succeeded in reviving a historical legacy marked by long-term Muscovite path dependence.

In the following we shall frame the introduction of the Soviet order as a contrast between modernizing and westernizing. While it is undoubtedly true that the Soviet era was a time when Russia did undergo broad processes of modernization, and that the heavily industrialized Soviet Union did represent a stark contrast to the predominantly rural imperial Russia, it is also true that there was a great deal of institutional continuity. We must thus be wary of taking modernization as conclusive evidence that the core dimensions of the country's deeply rooted institutional matrix were also undergoing fundamental change.

THE SOVIET ORDER

Seeking to capture the essence of the Bolshevik program, we shall make use of a model developed by János Kornai to explain the emergence of the socialist economic system. His logic, very briefly summarized, is presented in biological terms, where taking one step leads to another, then a third, and so on. More specifically, the introduction of a monopoly on power leads to the suppression of private property, which in turn eliminates market exchange, which produces a distinct quantity drive, and so on.[48]

Kornai's main argument is focused on the parallel introduction of a powerful ideology of totalitarianism, which in a sense provided the system with a purpose and a will of its own. Without this system of powerful public norms, the formal introduction of new rules regarding power and property relations would not have resulted in the very special case that was the socialist economic system. In line with the biological analogy, he views the combination of rules and norms as "the body and soul" of the system.[49]

---

[48] Kornai, János (1992), *The Socialist System: The Political Economy of Communism*, Oxford: Clarendon Press, esp. ch. 15.
[49] Ibid., p. 361.

Quite in line with the logic suggested by Kornai, the first step in the Bolshevik program was to suppress the movement toward political liberalization and to re-introduce a system of autocracy. From a practical perspective, it entailed starting with a ban on all non-socialist parties, proceeding to a showdown with the socialist rivals, and finally centralizing all power within the sole surviving party, soon to become known as the Communist Party of the Soviet Union, the CPSU.

Although it would be cloaked in terms of collective leadership and of a nominal co-habitation between party and state, the true essence of one-party rule could be captured in two fundamental principles. The first was that all power effectively rested with the party leadership, and the second was that this power was wielded according to no formal rules and with no formal mechanisms of impartial outside enforcement. For all its outer differences in décor, the Soviet political system would thus retain the same core of unaccountability that had emerged in old Muscovy, and it would do so up until the very end.

Having established their monopoly on power, the Bolsheviks proceeded to suppress such limited private property relations as had been introduced during the decades of reform. Nominally, this was carried out in the guise of sweeping nationalization, with the aim of introducing "people's property." That, however, was a notion without real meaning. What is owned by everyone is de facto owned by no one. The real implication was to suppress the legal and economic institution of property as such.

The vital importance of making this seemingly technical distinction would be made clear when the time came, following the Soviet collapse, to privatize nominally state-owned enterprises. If those enterprises had remained legal entities, with ownership vested in the hands of the state, privatization would have been reducible to a technical exercise, reminiscent of the broad privatization programs that had raged in many European countries in the 1980s. As it turned out, however, the first step toward Russian privatization would have to be reintroducing the very understanding of "property" in productive assets and of proceeding to generate respect for the legal rights of others to such property. As is well known, that would prove to be a tall order indeed.

Turning now to the third step in Kornai's chain, his focus was aimed at how the suppression of both money and property created a need to come up with some visible "mechanism of coordination" that might replace the invisible hand of Adam Smith. The formal solution was found in the introduction of the colossal bureaucracy of central planning, the intricacies and idiosyncrasies of which were discussed in the previous chapter.

Placing this story into historical context, we may see quite clearly that once the Bolsheviks had suppressed monetary exchange, they would revert to old Muscovite modes of remunerating their servants by offering both *kormlenie* and *pomestie*. Local party bosses would be allowed to line their pockets in much the same way as the *kormlenshchiki* of old, and senior servitors within the new service state would be transformed into modern *pomeshchiki*, being offered conditional use of state properties of various kinds, in ways that recalled the landed estates of boyars and indeed of monasteries in Muscovy. The way in which military commanders would be allowed to use recruits as free labor, at times even to be hired out on the side to enterprises in need of labor, also recalled the old system of "allocated," or *pripisnye*, serfs.

Given the fundamental role that is played in a rules-based market economy by legal regulation and by contractual relations, it is of quite some importance to note how drastically the Bolsheviks distanced themselves from the process of increasing legality that had marked the final decades of the Russian Empire. As one of its very first acts of legislation, the Bolshevik government issued its "Decree No. 1," which said that old laws would be observed "only insofar as they had not been repealed by the Revolution and did not contradict revolutionary conscience and the revolutionary concept of justice."[50] By thus placing morality before the law, and by reserving for themselves the right to determine the understanding of morality, the new regime began its rule by making mockery of the most basic principles of the rule of law.

The fourth and final step on the path toward erecting a Soviet order also is that which best reflects Hellie's presentation of the Stalin era as a third service class revolution. Faced with a perceived need for military modernization, derived from a sense of being surrounded by enemies, Stalin launched a massive campaign for industrialization that yet again rested on tried and tested methods. Like Witte, but in vastly more brutal ways, he imposed heavy tribute on the agricultural sector, which suffered incalculably, and like so many of his predecessors he chose to legitimate his policy of forced extraction by reinstating official xenophobia, to the point even of resurrecting the old myth about Moscow as a Third Rome.[51]

---

[50] Yakovlev, Alexander M. (1995), "The Rule-of-Law Ideal and Russian Reality," in Stanislaw Frankowski and Paul B. Stephan III (eds.), *Legal Reform in Post-Communist Europe: The View from Within*, Dordrecht: Martinus Nijhoff, p. 10.

[51] The latter was so successful that as late as 1984 German Chancellor Helmuth Kohl would explain that the Russian "drive for expansion and … belief that Mother Russia will bring salvation to

Harking back to the policies of Ivan the Great following the defeat of Novgorod, he closed borders to the outside world again and severely circumscribed contacts with foreigners. The familiar old practice of political *krugovaya poruka* was reasserted, in the form of collective responsibilities and the holding of friends and family members as hostages, and the Communist Party slid easily into the equally self-appointed role of fifteenth-century monasteries as producers of ideology, notably xenophobia and support for the autocracy.

The true core of this process as a whole rested in a deliberate use of images of the enemy to legitimate forced mobilization of resources for the military-industrial complex. The outcome was a formidable increase in military power. Quite in line with Hellie's portrayal of both Muscovite and Imperial Russia as a "garrison state," it used to be said that the USSR did not *have* a military-industrial complex, but that it *was* a military-industrial complex. As outlined by Kornai, the combination of repressive formal rules and a totalitarian ideology had provided the system with a clearly defined purpose.

Recalling from the account in Chapter 3 that all the fundamental aspects of the model that was created by Stalin would survive until the time the construct as a whole finally collapsed, what we have here is a powerful illustration of systemic resistance over centuries to westernizing reform, entailing transfer or imitation of the institutions of a rules-based market economy.

Retaining our fundamental assumption that Soviet citizens were just as keen as any others to truck and barter and exchange one thing for another, the question to which we shall now turn concerns what would happen when they were suddenly allowed to do so freely and openly. Would deregulation and privatization of the command economy bring about functioning market economy and good economic performance?

OUT OF THE ASHES

The true test of just how deeply rooted the practice of command economy was in national norms, beliefs, and expectations would arrive once the formal system had collapsed, which happened literally overnight. The outcome was great divergence, suggesting that some countries found it easier than others to simply shrug off the legacy of communism and of central economic planning.

the world" could be traced to the idea of "Moscow as the Third Rome, after Byzantium" (cited by Poe, Marshall T. (2001), "Moscow the Third Rome: The Origins and Transformation of a 'Pivotal Moment,'" *Jahrbücher für Geschichte Osteuropas*, vol. 49, no. 3, p. 428).

Here we shall conclude by taking a brief look at the process of Russian adjustment to visions of a post-Soviet world of democracy, market economy, and the rule of law. Focusing on the interplay between formal rules and informal norms, we shall argue that sweeping liberalization under Boris Yeltsin resulted in a huge disconnect between a set of radically different rules and surviving sets of norms, beliefs, and expectations, and that authoritarian restoration under Vladimir Putin brought about a new synthesis.

Whether the Russian government under Yegor Gaidar really could have pursued a different economic policy is beside the point here. What matters is that deregulation and privatization opened up a vast field of opportunity, where self-interested actors faced a stark choice. Would a rational course of action be to place trust in the emerging institutions of the new market economy, and in consequence to opt for value-adding activities? Or would it be more rational to anticipate the dominant strategy to be that of predation, and in consequence to opt for rent seeking and other essentially redistributive forms of activity?

The answer, as we all know, would be overwhelmingly in the latter category, and the consequences would be hugely negative. The story is well known, has been touched upon earlier, and needs no repetition here. What is mainly important, aside from the mass looting of state assets, is that despite the formal introduction of market economy, household coping strategies would remain mired in the old practice of reliance on networks and other forms of nonmarket activity. The tenacity of such practices has been amply documented by Alena Ledeneva.[52] Using survey data from the "New Russia Barometer," Richard Rose even found reason to characterize Russia well into the postcommunist era as an "anti-modern society."[53]

While experience from the Yeltsin era may thus be taken as confirmation of our argument that opportunity and self-interest may be necessary but not also sufficient for good economic performance to result, assessing what would come to pass under Vladimir Putin is slightly more complex. The main and obvious reason is that a spike in oil prices caused such a massive inflow of petrodollar wealth that all other economic factors were reduced to insignificance.[54]

---

[52] Ledeneva, Alena V. (2006), *How Russia Really Works: The Informal Practices that Shaped Post-Soviet Politics and Business*, Ithaca: Cornell University Press.

[53] Rose, Richard (1999), "Living in an Anti-Modern Society," *East European Constitutional Review*, vol. 8, nos. 1–2, pp. 68–75.

[54] Over the decade from 1999 to 2008, Russia registered an accumulated total surplus on the current account of $587.4 billion (http://www.cbr.ru/eng/statistics/credit_statistics/).

In the dazzling days of the Putin presidency, a casual visitor to Moscow would have found it hard indeed *not* to agree that Russia had finally succeeded in achieving its long-awaited transformation into a modern market economy. To the image of striking urban renewal, including shopping malls, luxury hotels, and flashy casinos, one could have added things like stylish dress, frequent foreign travel, and an equally striking modern jargon, in politics as well as in the media and in advertising.

While there could be no denying that in all of these respects Russia had indeed come to resemble a modern urban Western society, this also is where one must be wary of confusing the superficial with the more fundamental. Caution must go beyond recognizing that showcase Moscow is worlds away from provincial Russia, which remains mired in a pre-modern past. The pivotal question concerns whether Russia's booming capitalist economy, with seemingly unlimited potential for foreign investment and growth in stock market valuations, could also be reasonably construed as a successful market economy.

To Vladimir Putin personally, the timing of his two terms as president could not have been more opportune. He moved into the Kremlin when the Russian economy was just about to stage a spectacular rebound, and he moved out just before the global financial crisis caused that rebound to hit the proverbial brick wall. The eight intervening years of petrowealth and of high economic growth provide us with a challenge in assessing whether it really was a case of genuine systemic transformation being concluded.

What it essentially boils down to is whether modernization, which was unquestionable, could also be construed as westernization. If the latter is understood as the successful introduction of the full set of institutions normally associated with a high-performance market economy, the proposition not only remains questionable from a theoretical perspective. It also agrees poorly with observable facts on the ground.

To see that the image of economic achievement under Putin was mainly façade, note the following three items. *First,* and according to official statistics, only in 2007 did the Russian economy finally succeed in crawling back up to the level attained in 1990, implying that average annual economic growth over the years 1990–2007 had been just about zero.[55] Compare this to around 10 percent average annual growth in China since 1978.

International reserves held by the Central Bank would in consequence peak at $596.6 billion in August 2008 (http://www.cbr.ru/eng/hd_base/mrrf/?C_mes=01&C_year=2008&To_mes=04&To_year=2010&x=32&y=6&mode). Only China and Japan had more.

[55] By the end of 1998 GDP had fallen by 43.7 percent, and by the end of 2006 it was still 5.5 percent below 1989 (http://www.ebrd.com/country/sector/econo/stats/sei.xls).

Second, according to numbers presented by the Organization for Economic Cooperation and Development (OECD) in 2006, the share of fixed capital investment in Russian GDP over the good years 2000–2005 came to no more than 18 percent, as opposed to 40 percent in China, indicating that investment was way too low to make up for the gross neglect during the Yeltsin years.[56] *Third,* given the tremendous brain power that was once housed in the Soviet military-industrial complex, it is symptomatic of the failure of transition that most of this capital would be simply squandered. According to multiple accounts, by the time Dmitry Medvedev moved into the Kremlin the prospects for Russian industry to achieve the type of innovation and technological change that would be needed to ensure global competitiveness had been reduced to a very low order of probability.[57]

While all of this may serve to deflate the positive spin that surrounded the Putin years, our focus must be aimed not at the ideological and business-driven dimension of creating a Russian market economy but rather at the micro level of motivation to engage in value-adding entrepreneurship. The core challenge here is to explain why the replacement of dysfunctional command economy with technically superior market economy did not result in superior performance. More specifically, we shall look for the underlying reasons that combined to prevent a successful transition to a high-performance rules-based market economy.

If we take into account the massive inflow of petrodollar wealth, it is especially significant that so little was achieved, or even attempted, in terms of upgrading technology and infrastructure. Even within the energy complex, where serious funds *were* available for exploration and technological advance, there was a clear pattern of opting for short-term gains, that is, picking the proverbial low-hanging fruit rather than investing in operations with long-term yields. Most if not all of this may be explained with reference to those deeply rooted features in the institutional matrix that were outlined in the previous chapter.

Much as the old USSR could be shown to exhibit basic institutional continuity from the days of Muscovy, it may be argued here that the Russian Federation of the early twenty-first century exhibits a number of striking resemblances with the very same. Such resemblances range from an autocratic mode of government and fuzzy property rights, to the emergence of a modernized form of service nobility that is dependent on the good will

---

[56] OECD (2006), *Economic Survey of the Russian Federation 2006*, Paris: OECD, pp. 26–27.
[57] For example, Cooper, Julian M. (2006), "Can Russia Compete in the Global Economy?," *Eurasian Geography and Economics*, vol. 47, no 4, pp. 407–25; Desai, Raj M. and Itzhak Goldberg (eds.) (2008), *Can Russia Compete?,* Washington, DC: Brookings Institution.

of the ruler, and a growing sense of xenophobia that feeds an increasing emphasis on security and patriotism.

The implied argument on long-term path dependence will be left for discussion in Chapter 7. Here we shall conclude by noting that while Russia has been officially recognized as a market economy, both by the EU and by the United States, that recognition has been withheld from China. In contrast, China is a member of the World Trade Organization, and Russia is not. As China's track record is one of close to 10 percent annual economic growth over three decades, while Russia has a record of zero annual growth over 1990–2007, it calls into doubt what purpose is served by the labeling game.

Does it really add to our understanding of fundamental economic processes to learn that following seven decades of command economy Russia has now become a market economy? The following chapters will penetrate behind the labels and seek to capture what institutional features may secure or indeed hinder good economic performance.

5

Markets Everywhere

Thus far we have argued that markets may be found everywhere, even under the most repressive forms of command economy. We have suggested that the implied dichotomy between plan and market, which made up the core of theories on alternative economic systems, was partly misleading, and we have indicated a need to provide nuance by focusing more closely on the *informal* institutional context of transactions. The subsequent two chapters will be devoted to a combined investigation first of how informal norms may impede ambitions to promote a high-performance economy, and then of how such norms may be reproduced over centuries, even when the effects are seriously detrimental to economic efficiency.

In this chapter we shall set the stage for that investigation, by taking a closer look at the second part of the juxtaposition of plan versus market. To the previous argument on misunderstandings of what central economic planning was really about we shall add a number of qualifications regarding the textbook ideal of an instrumentally rational forward-looking market economy that is free of historical and cultural context.

Ever since the days of Adam Smith, the liberal economic tradition has rested on his portrayal of a natural "propensity to truck, barter and exchange one thing for another."[1] The presence of a strong urge to trade with others has been taken as evidence that individuals are always on the prowl for ways to improve their situation, and proponents of free trade have remained convinced that the associated expansion of markets will secure efficiency and economies of scale, thus making everybody better off. Does this not apply in equal measure to all countries and cultures? To answer this crucial question, we shall take a closer look at the institutional environment that surrounds the situation of exchange.

[1] Smith, Adam (2000), *The Wealth of Nations*, New York: Modern Library, p. 14.

First we shall present evidence that Adam Smith had a far more sophisticated view of the world than would appear from the liberal economic tradition associated with his name. This will illustrate the main tenets and limitations of the liberal economic tradition and show that over time economics has increasingly lost touch with its Smithian roots.

Then we shall introduce a distinction between simple markets and a more encompassing market economy, which hinges on the crucial role of the state in providing good governance. This will identify the preconditions that must be in place for simple market exchange to result in a high-performance economy, stressing that the standard view of what constitutes a "market" is in serious need of qualification.

The third step will place the discussion as a whole into a framework of markets versus hierarchies, highlighting the role of nonmarket decision making, in general terms as well as in the context of the command economy, and in conclusion we shall outline trends in the larger pattern of evolution of economic thinking, from Isaac Newton to Oliver Williamson.

THE LEGACY OF ADAM SMITH

Beginning with the legacy of Adam Smith, it may be useful to note that in his times there were good reasons indeed to argue the case for opportunity and self-interest, or for deregulation and free trade. Being the son of a customs official and having had experience of his own in that same line of work, Smith not only had theoretical skills but also practical firsthand experience upon which to formulate his attacks on the prevailing system of mercantilism.

While the victory of market liberalism did bring tremendous benefits, in the form of free trade and limited government, it also would have a darker side. As noted in our previous discussion about greed, the ideological dimension of laissez-faire has at times had a less healthy impact on the formation of norms in general, and of business ethics in particular. The purpose of this section is to show that there are excellent grounds for taking a dim view of how Smith has been dragooned into serving as a hostage of sorts for pleading the case for unregulated self-interest.

Despite all his subsequent fame as an economist, Smith after all held a chair in moral philosophy. As such, he was likely quite capable of differentiating between self-interest that is conditioned by suitable norms, and self-interest that degenerates into pure greed, representing a mortal sin. In his preface to the edition of *The Wealth of Nations* that we are citing here, Robert Reich displays an understandable sense of indignation: "One of the

ironies in the history of ideas is that *The Wealth of Nations* – a book ded-
icated to improving the welfare of the common man rather than just the
merchants or nobility – should have been used by a rising class of industri-
alists as theoretical justification for *not* seeking to remedy these and related
social ills."[2]

In a somewhat similar vein, Amartya Sen argues that the global financial crisis that erupted in September 2008 was at least partly generated by
a "huge overestimation of the wisdom of market processes." He suggests
that Smith would have seen clearly the dangers of the associated collapse of
trust in financial markets and in businesses in general: "As it happens, these
problems were already identified in the eighteenth century by Smith, even
though they have been neglected by those who have been in authority in
recent years, especially in the United States, and who have been busy citing
Adam Smith in support of the unfettered market."[3]

To be sure, Smith was very clear in stating that it is up to every man to
care for himself. In his first major work, *The Theory of Moral Sentiment*,
this is presented as follows: "Every man is, no doubt, by nature, first and
principally recommended to his own care; and as he is fitter to take care
of himself, than of any other person, it is fit and right that it should be
so."[4] He was also convinced that human beings, in contrast to animals,
are possessed by an inner drive to better their condition by trading with
other humans. This belief was captured in his formulation of a propensity
to truck and barter.

Known to all, cited by many, and read by few, *The Wealth of Nations* still
stands as something of a hallmark of the liberal economic tradition, and
of the case for free trade. It is here that we may find, in the introductory
account of the pin factory, the first presentation of the benefits that can be
derived from the exploitation of comparative advantage.

It was Smith who established what would come to be one of the central
tenets of liberal market economy, namely, the positive role of self-interest
as a driving force in human actions. His own formulation was poignant and
has become something of a must to cite in economics texts: "It is not from
the benevolence of the butcher, the brewer, or the baker, that we expect our
dinner, but from their regard to their own self-interest."[5]

---

[2] Ibid., p. xix.
[3] Sen, Amartya (2009), "Capitalism beyond the Crisis," *New York Review of Books*, vol. 56,
no. 5, p. 4 (cited from www.nybooks.com/articles/22490, accessed on May 14, 2009).
[4] Smith, Adam (1976), *The Theory of Moral Sentiments*, Indianapolis: Liberty Classics,
p. 161.
[5] Smith, *The Wealth of Nations*, p. 15.

The underlying and somewhat paradoxical logic explains how the pursuit of self-interest will be led, as if by an "invisible hand," to promote what is best for all concerned. Smith's own formulation expresses distinct surprise that the outcome of actions by greedy merchants and landowners really can be to the benefit of all: "he intends only his own gain, and he is in this, as in many other cases, led by an invisible hand to promote an end which was no part of his intention."[6]

The relevance of these observations to our concern with matters such as Wall Street greed and Russia's brutal encounter with capitalism proceeds via the derived belief in economics that markets are capable of resolving most if not all problems on their own, and that the state should thus be kept at bay. The real world, as we have suggested in Chapter 1, does not work quite like that. The reasons, moreover, have long been well known.

In sharp contrast to the happy message that has been associated with liberal policies of laissez-faire, we may advance another side of Smith, one that is clearly aware also of the dark side of motivation for self-interested action. In his works, especially *The Theory of Moral Sentiment*, he went to considerable length to warn about the dangers to "the immense fabric of human society" that lurk in allowing a free play for market forces driven by self-interest: "Society may subsist, though not in the most comfortable state, without beneficence; but the prevalence of injustice must utterly destroy it."[7]

His own sense for fair play, so typical of later generations of Scots and Englishmen, was also clearly expressed: "In the race for wealth, and honors, and preferments, he may run as hard as he can, and strain every nerve and every muscle, in order to outstrip all his competitors. But if he should justle, or throw down any of them, the indulgence of the spectators is entirely at an end. It is a violation of fair play, which they cannot admit of."[8]

Even in *The Wealth of Nations*, which is the most frequently quoted in support of Smithian laissez-faire, he cautions against the "mean rapacity, the monopolizing spirit of merchants and manufacturers, who neither are, nor ought to be, the rulers of mankind,"[9] and he warns of the potential

[6]   Ibid., p. 485.
[7]   Smith, *The Theory of Moral Sentiments*, p. 167.
[8]   Ibid., p. 162. The fact that philosophers, much more than economists, have been rediscovering Adam Smith, with particular attention paid to his key concept of an "impartial spectator," provides further illustration of the importance in his work of moral philosophy as opposed to the narrow focus on liberating markets that has captivated generations of economists. I am indebted to Archie Brown for enlightening me on this count. See also Raphael, D. D. (1975), "The Impartial Spectator," in Andrew S. Skinner and Thomas Wilson (eds.), *Essays on Adam Smith*, Oxford: Clarendon Press.
[9]   Smith, *The Wealth of Nations*, p. 527.

consequences of allowing a free rein for self-interest seeking: "People of the same trade rarely meet together, even for merriment and diversion, but the conversation ends in a conspiracy against the public, or in some contrivance to raise prices."[10]

It is somehow symptomatic that in the works cited here, which jointly total around 1,700 pages, the metaphor of the invisible hand appears only *three times* in all, and then merely in passing. There are good reasons indeed to agree with Emma Rothschild's contention, that Smith may have used it merely as an "ironic but useful joke."[11]

Given how deeply entrenched the invisible hand, and the associated belief in opportunity and self-interest, have become in liberal market economy, it may be worth noting that to those who study the works of Adam Smith, his true intentions in producing this metaphor have remained enigmatic. Much thought has gone into brooding over whether Smith had a change of heart, from his focus on norms and morality in *The Theory of Moral Sentiment*, to his apparent embrace of self-interest in *The Wealth of Nations*. In the literature, this is sometimes known as the "Adam Smith problem."[12]

Although the positive message that is contained in *The Wealth of Nations* has greatly overshadowed Smith's previous warnings, in *The Theory of Moral Sentiment*, it remains a fact that the implications for economic policy of allowing unbridled self-interest seeking have long been known and commented upon.

Recalling what has been said earlier concerning Joseph Schumpeter's worries about the demise of capitalism, due to its inherent tensions, we may add the following from his 1949 presidential address to the American Economic Association: "No social system can work which is based exclusively upon a network of free contracts between (legally) equal contracting parties and in which everyone is supposed to be guided by nothing except his own (short-run) utilitarian ends."[13]

As noted *en passant* in our introductory chapter, writing in 1952 Lionel Robbins expanded on the same theme, arguing that "the pursuit of self-interest, unrestrained by suitable institutions, carries no guarantee of

---

[10] Ibid., p. 148.

[11] Rothschild, Emma (1994), "Adam Smith and the Invisible Hand," *American Economic Review*, vol. 84, no. 2, p. 319. See also Rothschild, Emma (2001), *Economic Sentiments: Adam Smith, Condorcet, and the Enlightenment*, Cambridge, MA: Harvard University Press.

[12] See further Macfie, A. L. (1967), *The Individual in Society: Papers on Adam Smith*, London: Allen & Unwin.

[13] Schumpeter, Joseph A. (1950), "The March into Socialism," *American Economic Review*, vol. 40, no. 2, p. 448.

anything but chaos."[14] While the latter insight does emphasize that deregulation will not be sufficient to ensure good economic performance, a
fact that also was pointed out by Douglass North in his 1993 Nobel Prize
lecture,[15] it remains unclear exactly what should be understood by "suitable
institutions."

The very same holds for the continuation of Alan Greenspan's previously
cited statement on nature and culture. While his understanding of a "capitalist infrastructure" may be accepted as fairly straightforward, that does
not hold for "capitalist culture" and for the associated conventions, behaviors and practices. The latter, on the contrary, touch on the very core of what
institutional theory is all about, namely, the interplay between formal rules
and informal norms.

Let us proceed now to look at the emergence of market economy from
the latter perspective, that is, to see how simple exchange was transformed
into what Mancur Olson has referred to as "socially contrived markets."[16]

SOCIALLY CONTRIVED MARKETS

In his previously cited book about markets and hierarchies, Oliver
Williamson sets out building his case by suggesting that "in the beginning
there were markets."[17] In pointed opposition, Geoffrey Hodgson argues that
"the market itself is an institution [that] involves social norms and customs,
instituted exchange relations, and information networks that themselves
will have to be explained."[18] Wedged between these two statements we may
find the whole reason for our following discussion of what it is that may
secure or impede good economic performance.

Stating that markets have always existed is, to begin with, in a sense a tru-
ism. If by a "market" we understand a voluntary transaction between two
individuals seeking to enhance their welfare by trading, then this is surely

---

[14] Robbins, Lionel (1952), *The Theory of Economic Policy in English Classical Political Economy*, London: Macmillan, p. 56.

[15] His exact formulation was that "transferring the formal political and economic rules of successful Western market economies to third world and Eastern European economies is not a sufficient condition for good economic performance" (North, Douglass C. (1994), "Economic Performance through Time," *American Economic Review*, vol. 84, no. 3, p. 366).

[16] Olson, Mancur (2000), *Power and Prosperity: Outgrowing Communist and Capitalist Dictatorships*, New York: Basic Books, p. 183.

[17] Williamson, Oliver E. (1975), *Markets and Hierarchies: Analysis and Antitrust Implications*, New York: Free Press, p. 20.

[18] Hodgson, Geoffrey M. (2004), *The Evolution of Institutional Economics: Agency, Structure and Darwinism in American Institutionalism*, London: Routledge, p. 20.

something that has been going on since the dawn of Mankind. If, on the other hand, we were to understand by a "market" a physical space that has been set aside for such transactions, then we are also looking at a very long history, albeit perhaps not as long as that of simple exchange.

What Hodgson refers to is not the basic process of transacting as such, which constitutes the core of a market economy, but rather the fact that over time the institutional context of transacting has grown increasingly sophisticated.[19] As a result, the transaction has become increasingly entrenched, or embedded, in a dense maze of both formal and informal institutions.

Maintaining in focus the Smithian assumption that all actors are driven by self-interest, the analytical challenge to the social sciences at large lies in decoding precisely what it is in this maze that may secure good performance and what it is that may drive action in the opposite direction. Let us begin by looking at the simplest form of exchange and map out the conditions under which it may be transformed into modern economy, defined here as a case where originally spontaneous markets have evolved into being "socially contrived."

Growth of the Market

Seeking to illustrate the generic foundations of the market economy, authors of undergraduate economics textbooks have often tended to favor the story of how the meeting between Robinson Crusoe and Friday served to replace autarky with mutually beneficial trade. As with Smith's pin factory, the point is to show how division of labor leads to specialization and to increased efficiency, derived from comparative advantage. The underlying logic is well in tune with the success story of how the Western world emerged that was referred to in Chapter 1, and that will be elaborated in Chapter 6.

There is, however, an early stage in economic development, which we may refer to as a bazaar economy, that is different from this positive story.[20] It is important in the sense of capturing a case where actors do engage in

---

[19] According to calculations by Douglass North and John Wallis, the share of the transactions sector (defined as activities that support economic exchange), in U.S. GDP increased from less than a quarter in 1870, to more than 45 percent in 1970, and by extrapolation to more than half in 2000. (See Wallis, John J. and Douglass C. North (1986), "Measuring the Transaction Sector in the American Economy," in Stanley Engerman and Robert E. Gallman (eds.), *Long-Term Factors in American Growth*, Chicago, IL: University of Chicago Press, and North, Douglass C. (2005), *Understanding the Process of Economic Change*, Princeton: Princeton University Press, pp. 91–93.)

[20] See further McMillan, John (2002), *Reinventing the Bazaar: A Natural History of Markets*, New York: Norton.

voluntary horizontal transactions but fail to secure the benefits that are entailed in the dynamics of the positive story. As we shall see in a moment, it also constitutes reality in much of the institutionally poorly developed parts of the Third World. Despite decades of efforts to achieve development by means of outside aid, this type of institutional setting remains stubbornly resistant to change.

What we are talking of here may be characterized as self-enforcing spot-markets. As both parties have full control over the transaction, and as they are likely not looking at a repeated relationship, the need for information about the other side is minute, as is the need for outside assistance in contract enforcement. The illustration is striking in the sense that it again is so in tune with the free market ideal, at least superficially so. Here we may find no states, no controlling bureaucracies, and indeed no corporate boardrooms where greed may pervert decision making. It is a world of free entrepreneurs, striking freely negotiated deals with anonymous counterparts.

The obvious downside is that markets of this kind have very low value added and thus cannot serve as the basis for a modern economy, or indeed a modern society. As an extreme illustration, we may envision the entire population of a country being arranged in one long line, where one disposable razor is being sold down the line, from individual to individual. When the razor reaches the end of the line, we may have clocked a large number of transactions, and thus also large contributions to GDP, but we will still be talking about one single shave.

To capture what happens when low value-added spot-markets develop into more sophisticated markets, featuring increasing division of labor that secures high value added and incentives for technological change, we may distinguish between transformation costs and transaction costs. As the market expands, and as the size of production grows, economies of scale will result in falling costs of *transformation*. On a parallel track, however, the increasing degree of sophistication will also lead to an increase in the costs of *transacting*. As increasing the size of the market will thus be accompanied by costs that are falling on one account and rising on another, the outcome is indeterminate. Given the crucial importance of these observations, we may usefully elaborate.

While the story of specialization and comparative advantage captures how expanding markets *may* generate growth, there are no guarantees that this is what is going to happen. As we have noted repeatedly, the belief in opportunity and self-interest that is so prominent among economists agrees poorly with observations of countries that are trapped in poverty, or with the many shortcomings, and indeed systemic failures, in implementing transition from planned to market economies.

The reasons this is so – that is, why we are faced with repeated cases of systemic failure – cannot be understood without reference to the problems of rising transaction costs. In the real world, there will be untold numbers of deals that cannot be made, untold transactions that would have been mutually beneficial but will not be undertaken, all for the very simple reason that the costs of transacting the deals in question are larger than the potential benefits. This essentially is the story that is told in Olson's previously cited account of "Big Bills Left on the Sidewalk," and it has given rise to much valuable research within the realm of "new institutional economics."[21]

The bottom line is that markets in isolation will be hard put to come up with solutions that may reduce transaction costs and in so doing help smooth the way for further expansion. The very simple reason is that the solutions in question will often have the characteristics of collective goods, that is, of goods – and services – that once provided will be free for all to use. Since the returns to investment in providing such goods will be shared by all, it is difficult to find a way of sharing out the costs. The most common solution is for the state to step in.[22]

Illustrations range from the very trivial, such as providing standardized weights and measures, to the highly complex task of putting into place all the laws and enforcement agencies that jointly constitute the rule of law. The previously cited accounts of the "Rise of the West" rest heavily on charting the interplay between free markets and states appearing as providers of much needed collective goods.[23] As in the case of the role of the invisible

---

[21] For an early comprehensive contribution, see Eggertsson, Thráinn (1990), *Economic Behavior and Institutions*, Cambridge: Cambridge University Press. For later broad overviews, see also Furubotn, Eirik G. and Rudolf Richter (eds.) (1991), *The New Institutional Economics: A Collection of Articles from the Journal of Institutional and Theoretical Economics*, College Station: Texas A & M University Press; Furubotn, Eirik G. and Rudolf Richter (1998), *Institutions & Economic Theory: The Contribution of the New Institutional Economics*, Ann Arbor: University of Michigan Press; Ménard, Claude (ed.) (2000), *Institutions, Contracts and Organizations: Perspectives from New Institutional Economics*, Cheltenham: Edward Elgar; and Ménard, Claude and Mary M. Shirley (eds.) (2005), *Handbook of New Institutional Economics*, Dordrecht: Springer.

[22] As an exception to the rule, we may note Nobel Laureate Elinor Ostrom's long-standing work on governing the commons, which documents cases where common property is surprisingly well managed (Ostrom, Elinor (1990), *Governing the Commons: The Evolution of Institutions for Collective Action*, Cambridge: Cambridge University Press). Her Nobel Lecture is available on http://nobelprize.org/nobel_prizes/economics/laureates/2009/ostrom-lecture.html.

[23] For example, North, Douglass C. and Robert Paul Thomas (1973), *The Rise of the Western World: A New Economic History*, Cambridge: Cambridge University Press, ch. 1.

hand in guiding opportunity and self-interest, there are serious problems of conceptual disconnect here, between what the theory would predict and what we may observe on the ground.

Introducing the notion of a second invisible hand, phrased as an "invisible hand on the left," Olson portrays the state as being driven by encompassing self-interest to provide collective goods that improve market performance – for the very simple reason that this will also enhance the tax base.[24] As in the case of the butcher, the brewer, and the baker, we may thus do without benevolence and place our reliance on state self-interest.

The tentative conclusion to be drawn from the combined invisible hands of Smith and Olson comes across as highly encouraging. Without recourse to any form of altruism, markets and states in joint efforts will make sure that individual action is always consistent with the collective good. Yet what we observe on the ground is that only *some* countries succeed in moving along this path toward prosperity. We shall have more to say about this in a moment. First, however, we shall provide further illustrations, in the form of how long-distance trade was opened up in the Mediterranean.

Mediterranean Illustrations

The triggering factor was the crusades and the associated decline of Muslim and Byzantine naval power in the eastern Mediterranean, toward the end of the twelfth century. As the power of the Byzantine Empire was beginning to wane, and as its grip over trade in the eastern part of the Mediterranean was slipping, vast opportunities for gain were opened up for traders from the western part.[25] The challenge that emerged here was to handle the risks and uncertainties that are associated with long-distance trade, ranging from dangers at sea, emanating from the elements as well as from pirates, to the problems of information and enforcement that arise in trade with unknown parties, in distant and unknown cultures.

Two main groups responded to this challenge, and did so in very different fashions. One was composed of Jewish traders, originally from Baghdad, who had migrated to the Maghreb, an otherwise Muslim Arab

---

[24] Olson, *Power and Prosperity*, p. 13.

[25] What had originally destroyed the "ancient unity of the Mediterranean" was not so much the "Arab assault" as the subsequent Byzantine domination. The gradual weakening of the Byzantines thus was an important factor in allowing the western powers, notably the Venetians, to return to the eastern Mediterranean. (See further Lewis, Archibald R. (1951), *Naval Power and Trade in the Mediterranean, A.D. 500–1100*, Princeton, NJ: Princeton University Press, p. 97 and *passim*.)

community in what is presently Morocco, Algeria, and Tunisia.[26] The other was the subsequently famous city-states of northern Italy, most notably Venice and Genoa.[27] As outlined by Avner Greif, the respective solutions of these two groups could not have been more different. While the Maghrebi chose to rely on relatives and close associates, who were susceptible to informal social sanctions, the Genoese and the Venetians opted for institution-building that rested on the state's assuming responsibility for contracts and property rights. As Greif puts it, they "ceased to use the ancient custom of entering contracts by a handshake and developed an extensive legal system for registration and enforcement of contracts."[28]

For three reasons this example is important to our present account. One is that it illustrates so clearly the crucial role of the state as a third party enforcer. While the Maghrebi would vanish from history, the outcome in the Italian north would be a long period of economic growth and accumulation of wealth. Closer inspection of the latter case may also reveal how the respective princes went about solving the crucial commitment problem, that is, how they succeeded in convincing potential traders that it was rational for them to place trust in the government's willingness, and indeed ability, to live up to its part of the bargain. Our previous account of the traditional absence in Russia of accountability in government serves to further underline the importance of these observations.

The second reason the Mediterranean example is so important lies in the link to what has been said earlier about collectivism versus individualism, that is, in contrasting a collectivist solution resting on informal sanctions against an individualist one that relies on trust in anonymous government agencies. Though unwilling to draw any firm conclusions, Greif indicates that their respective degrees of success may have been determined by the collectivist focus on norms versus the individualist focus on rules. He also finds it "intriguing" that while the Maghrebi solution resembles that of many present-day developing nations, that of Genoa forms a model for the

---

[26] For a more detailed study of the Maghrebi, see Greif, Avner (1993), "Contract Enforceability and Economic Institutions in Early Trade: The Maghrebi Traders' Coalition," *American Economic Review*, vol. 83, no. 3, pp. 525–48.

[27] For a more detailed discussion of the case of Genoa, see also Greif, Avner (1994b), "On the Political Foundations of the Late Medieval Commercial Revolution: Genoa during the Twelfth and Thirteenth Centuries," *Journal of Economic History*, vol. 54, no. 4, pp. 271–87.

[28] Greif, Avner (1994a), "Cultural Beliefs and the Organization of Society: A Historical and Theoretical Reflection on Collectivist and Individualist Societies," *Journal of Political Economy*, vol. 102, no. 5, p. 937.

developed West.[29] Our previous account of a long Russian tradition of collectivist solutions, including the *krugovaya poruka of* collective obligations, again serves to further underline the argument.

By far the most important point in the illustration as a whole is that it brings out a need to focus on the *causes* of protracted divergence. It is striking that while the regions in the Italian north are among the most prosperous in the European Union, those in the south, the *Mezzogiorno*, are among the poorest. The reasons this is so have been subjected to detailed study in Robert Putnam's widely cited book, *Making Democracy Work*, which established a fundamental line of division between the "criminal capitalism" of the south and the "social market economy" of the north.[30]

In the former case, transactions take place in an environment of low trust and low social capital that is reminiscent of Edward Banfield's classic account of "amoral familism."[31] Social relations are highly personalized, and conflict resolution will be undertaken by trusted individuals, or by crime lords. The main implications are that the scope of the market will be seriously constrained and the time horizon for productive investment will be short.

The social market economy, in sharp contrast, is marked by an institutional environment that promotes high trust and high social capital. When actors are willing to place their trust in anonymous government agencies, they will also be prepared to trade with anonymous counterparts; consequently, the scope of the market will expand and economic performance will improve.

Perhaps the most striking feature of Putnam's presentation is that the line of division between north and south in Italy exhibits a path dependence that stretches back to the twelfth century. Despite massive outlays from the *Cassa per il Mezzogiorno*, the modern-day government in Rome has not succeeded in closing the development gap, and resentment in the north has produced political movements for secession, such as the Lega Nord. Knowing what is broken is obviously far from knowing how to fix it.

Maintaining that the case of Palermo may house important clues to understanding that of Moscow,[32] we shall now take a closer look at the role

---

[29] Ibid., p. 943.

[30] Putnam, Robert (1993), *Making Democracy Work: Civic Traditions in Modern Italy*, Princeton, NJ: Princeton University Press. See also Leonardi, Robert (1995), "Regional Development in Italy: Social Capital and the Mezzogiorno," *Oxford Review of Economic Policy*, vol. 2, no. 2.

[31] Banfield, Edward (1958), *The Moral Basis of a Backward Society*, Glencoe, IL: Free Press.

[32] Hedlund, Stefan and Niclas Sundström (1996), "Does Palermo Represent the Future for Moscow?," *Journal of Public Policy*, vol. 16, no. 2, pp. 113–55.

of the state. Recalling from our account in the previous chapter that the absence of a clear line of division between power and property has been one of the true hallmarks of the Russian tradition, we shall retain our focus on the role of the state as an impartial third party enforcer, charged with upholding the sanctity of contracts and of rights to private property.

The Role of Good Government

From an economics perspective, there are two basically different ways of looking at the state. One is to view it as a neutral part of the institutional matrix, as a nesting of contracts or as an impartial agency that is charged with maximizing joint welfare. Along this line of thought, the state will simply dissolve into the market, much as a lump of sugar dissolves into a cup of coffee. It will be there, and it will serve a purpose, but it will not be visible and it will not be an actor in itself.

The opposite approach is to recognize that the state may indeed be an actor in itself, with an agenda that may not be in full agreement with the preferences of its subjects. Extreme versions can be found in models of kleptocracy and predatory states. Short of such extremes, which tend to be self-destructive, we may advance a host of more technical reasons for why the state must be recognized as an actor in and of its own.

We may have situations when a desire to maximize tax receipts causes discrimination between constituencies, simply because some groups will be easier to tax than others. We may have cases when certain groups are afforded preferential treatment because they may appear as supportive or as potential threats, and we may encounter states where the ruler feels so insecure that otherwise rational optimization of taxation over time will be blocked.

All of these, however, represent cases where the state operates within a market context. Given our overriding ambition of addressing what Sen refers to as "the huge limitations of relying entirely on the market economy and the profit motive,"[33] by far the most important role that is being played by our Russian illustrations rests in the tradition of Russian governance having such a long track record of being persistently and genuinely market-contrary.

While the case of central planning was admittedly extreme, in imposing an all-encompassing hierarchy with no option for exit, both the imperial era and the post-Soviet one reflect the presence of governance that

---

[33] Sen, "Capitalism beyond the Crisis," p. 2.

has prompted actors to engage in playing influence games rather than to opt for self-interest seeking according to the Smithian vision of the invisible hand.

Returning to our core question of how spontaneous markets may evolve into socially contrived markets, as reflected in the social market economy of the Italian north, we shall focus more specifically on the role of the state in upholding an impartial judiciary. To link this argument back to transactions, we may borrow here from Williamson's discussion of governance and the distribution of transactions.

Suggesting a three-part division into spot-market trading, long-term contracting, and hierarchy, he argues that neither spot-markets nor hierarchical transactions will need much support from the judiciary: "Disappointed spot-market traders can easily limit their exposure and can seek relief by terminating and turning to other traders. And internal organization is its own court of ultimate appeal. By contrast, transactions in the middle range can be difficult to stabilize."[34]

Williamson's main point is that a failure to organize the judiciary in "an informed and uncorrupted manner" will lead transactions in the middle range to gravitate toward one or the other of the polar extremes:

The upshot is that the quality of a judiciary can be inferred indirectly: a high-performance economy (expressed in governance terms) will support more transactions in the middle range than will an economy with a problematic judiciary. Put differently, in a low performance economy the distribution of transactions will be more bimodal – with more spot-market and hierarchical transactions and fewer middle-range transactions.[35]

Borrowing further from Olson, we may characterize Williamson's middle-range segment as production that is "property-rights intensive." The point here is that "the familiar expression capital intensive obscures the crucial role of enforceable rights."[36] Returning again to our Russian illustrations, we may recall that fuzzy or absent rights to property, resulting from unaccountability in government, have been presented above as the true key to understanding Russian specificity.

The grounds on which this argument has been made may in turn be derived from the persistent absence in Russian tradition of an independent

[34] Williamson, Oliver E. (1995), "The Institutions and Governance of Economic Development," *Proceedings of the World Bank Annual Conference on Development Economics 1994*, Washington, DC: World Bank, p. 181.

[35] Ibid., pp. 181–82.

[36] Olson, *Power and Prosperity*, p. 186.

judiciary. When the rule of men trumps the rule of law, the outcome will have to be generalized rule aversion, prompting actors to opt for personalized influence games that violate the fundamental principle of autonomy in the market.

The implications from a dynamic perspective are fairly substantial. If we accept that a poorly functioning judiciary will cause increasing gravitation toward the extremes of the bimodal distribution of transactions, this will also lead to reduced pressure for such reforms that may support "property-rights intensive" production, which in turn will negatively impact the demand for sophisticated human capital investment. As a result, the economy risks being trapped in a low-performance equilibrium with a poorly functioning judiciary. The latter would seem to be precisely what has happened not only in Russia but also in the Italian *Mezzogiorno*.

The Informal Sector

To elaborate further on the role of the state in relation to the market, we may return here to our previous focus on traditional self-enforcing markets and add a modern version. Known as the "informal sector," it represents a phenomenon that has long been widely known from the Third World and is increasingly so also from the world of postcommunist states. Let us begin with the former.

As a casual visitor to any of the ubiquitous megacities of the Third World will immediately recognize, this is an environment that is simply teeming with activity and entrepreneurship. Still, the value added resulting from such activities remains negligible. The reasons constitute the main focus of attention in Hernando de Soto's treatment of *The Mystery of Capital*, which argues that the main cause of underdevelopment rests in the absence of clearly enforceable rights to property. Based on empirical research, de Soto and his colleagues conclude that the total value of real estate held but not legally owned by the poor of the Third World and former communist nations, referred to as "urban and rural dead capital," is at least $9.3 trillion.[37]

Recalling what was said in Chapter 3 about irrepressive markets, we may note that while both are examples of markets that are self-enforcing, there is a also a fundamental way in which the informal sector is different, one, moreover, that is directly related to the role of the state. Where the former

[37] Soto, Hernando de (2000), *The Mystery of Capital: Why Capitalism Triumphs in the West and Fails Everywhere Else*, New York: Basic Books, p. 35.

arises due to government interdiction, the latter is the consequence of a failure by the state to extend supporting institutions. The following is de Soto's colorful portrayal:

> When you step out the door of the Nile Hilton, what you are leaving behind is not the high-technology world of fax machines and ice makers, television and antibiotics. The people of Cairo have access to all those things. What you are really leaving behind is the world of legally enforceable transactions on property rights.[38]

These illustrations are relevant to the present account mainly in the sense of further emphasizing that deregulation and reliance on free markets will be far from sufficient to secure good economic performance. Russia's attempted transition from planned to market economy provides sordid evidence of a combined need to consider motivation both for individual actors to choose between rule-abiding and rule-evasive strategies, and for the state to assume responsibility for promoting the former over the latter.

It is highly significant that the effective outcome of Russian marketizing reform would be to transform a set of irrepressive markets within a single hierarchy of command into a set of predatory rival hierarchies surrounded by a vast informal sector. In a slight paraphrase of Schumpeter, the effects may be viewed as destructive creation.

While entrepreneurs in the extraction-oriented hierarchies succeeded in capturing the state and stripping it of its assets, entrepreneurs in the informal sector were largely abandoned by the state, being forced to deal on their own with criminal protection rackets and state officials demanding side payments.

Perhaps most important, the absence of secure rights to private property precluded the emergence of financial markets in any sense but short-term speculation. The upshot was that entrepreneurs in the informal sector, who could have created the foundations of a vibrant small business sector, were in practice excluded from credit. In consequence, they were also effectively precluded from growing their businesses. Given, moreover, that retained earnings would serve as the main source of investment, predatory elites were placed in a clear position of advantage over small entrepreneurs.

Looking in greater detail at this outcome, we note that the twin policies of liberalization of markets and privatization of state property that were so ideologically prominent at the outset of the reform process would in the end fall far short of securing good economic performance. The heavy emphasis that was placed by the Russian reformers on "getting the property

---

[38] Ibid., p. 16.

rights right" constitutes a case in point, prompting the following comment by Williamson: "But the deeper problem is that getting the property rights right is too narrow a conception of what institutional economics is all about. The more general need is to get the institutions right, of which property is only one part."[39]

So, when talking about markets and about market economy, we must be explicit in how these concepts are defined and understood. While markets in the trivial sense of actors exchanging nuts for berries at the edge of the forest have always existed, once we start looking for the preconditions that secure good performance, in the form of "socially contrived markets," matters at once get considerably more complex.

Let us maintain our assumption that economic performance will to a large extent be determined by how the state approaches its responsibility to act as a third party enforcer of contracts and as a guarantor of the sanctity of rights to property. There is good reason to place particular emphasis on the latter. As Olson underscores, property cannot be disassociated from government: "Though individuals may have possessions without government, the way a dog possesses a bone, there is no private property without government. Property is a socially protected claim on an asset – a bundle of rights enforceable in courts backed by the coercive power of government."[40]

This, however, still leaves open the question of *how* rights to property are rendered more or less secure. As Greif puts it, "Understanding how property is secured requires knowing why those who are physically able to abuse rights refrain from doing so."[41] The latter pertains not only to individual actors but even more to the state itself. One of the most classic problems in relations between state and market is that a state that is powerful enough to protect private property rights will also be powerful enough to violate those rights.

To summarize the importance of these points, we may usefully introduce Olson's notion of a "market-augmenting government," defined as a government that is strong enough to violate property rights but at the same time sufficiently constrained so as not to do so of its own volition. His conclusion is that "prosperous economies need market-augmenting government."[42] While the success story of the rise of the West that has been outlined earlier

---

[39] Williamson, "The Institutions and Governance," p. 173.

[40] Olson, Mancur (1995), "Why the Transition from Communism Is so Difficult," *Eastern Economic Journal*, vol. 21, no. 4, p. 458.

[41] Greif, Avner (2006), *Institutions and the Path to the Modern Economy: Lessons from Medieval Trade*, Cambridge: Cambridge University Press, p. 7.

[42] Olson, *Power and Prosperity*, p. x.

can be easily made to fit into this picture, the Russian case illustrates the implications of economic development that has no clear line of division between power and property, or between state and market. Let us now place these insights into the context of nonmarket decision making.

MARKETS AND HIERARCHIES

In the "natural" order of things that is superficially derived from *The Wealth of Nations*, economic actors are all assumed to be the same – fully informed, instrumentally rational, and forward looking. Markets are price makers and individuals are price takers. Decisions to maximize utility proceed via quantity adjustment only. In this world of market clearing perfect competition, which ensures steady movement toward a unique global optimum, there is no room for firms, organizations, and states. Still, in real life the latter types of hierarchy that displace the market are both important and omnipresent.

Herbert Simon suggests an image of aliens from Mars looking at Earth through a telescope that reveals social structures. Assuming that firms show up as solid green areas, and market transactions as red lines, the economy as a whole will appear like a spider's web of green areas intersected by red lines. Rather than present this as a "network of red lines connecting green spots," the Martian would prefer "large green areas interconnected by red lines." If he were told that the green areas were called organizations and the red lines market transactions, he'd wonder why the structure as a whole was referred to as a "market economy."[43]

The obvious answer to this seeming paradox is that it is the market that provides the overall rules of the game. Even if the bulk of all transactions in a modern economy will take place within hierarchical organizations, such as households, firms, and governments, that are placed outside the market, they will nevertheless take place within the *context* of markets. As a case in point, we may use the Israeli Kibbutz.[44] Although its internal social organization is collective to the point of being devoid of any market relations such as prices, wages, or indeed pensions, it remains dependent for its success on the surrounding market economy.[45]

---

[43] Simon, Herbert (1991), "Organizations and Markets," *Journal of Economic Perspectives*, vol. 5, p. 27.

[44] Barkai, Haim (1977), *Growth Patterns of the Kibbutz Economy*, Amsterdam: North-Holland.

[45] As a further illustration, we may recall an old Soviet joke saying that the global triumph of the Soviet order would have to stop at the borders of the last capitalist state, for the simple reason that it would be needed in order to determine prices.

The reason we offer these illustrations is that the Soviet case represented the extreme opposite, namely, an all-encompassing hierarchy that suppressed *all* (legal) voluntary horizontal exchange. The implications, as we shall see in a moment, were far-reaching indeed, corrupting rather than resting on the institutions that combine to make up what we understand as functioning market economy. There are important lessons to be drawn here concerning the role of informal norms in supporting or impeding economic progress. Let us begin, however, with the general case.

Vertical Integration

The first to approach the issue of vertical integration from an economics point of view was Ronald Coase, whose celebrated 1937 article titled "The Nature of the Firm" explained why internalization of decisions within a hierarchy may at times serve to economize on transaction costs.[46] In the tradition of "new institutional economics" that we have alluded to, the inspiration from Coase to think about the costs of transacting has loomed large,[47] so large that there is a tendency to forget how important the role of transactions was already to the early American institutional school in economics.[48]

In the theory of institutions that was presented by John Commons in 1934, the transaction was placed squarely at the center of analysis.[49] Although his definition was more encompassing than has been the case in subsequent transaction cost analysis, he was quite clear about why its

[46] Coase, Ronald H. (1937), "The Nature of the Firm," *Economica*, vol. 4, no. 16, pp. 386–405.
[47] The collective debt that is owed to Coase on this account has been generally recognized by all leading representatives of this new field of research, for example, Matthews, R. C. O. (1986), "The Economics of Institutions and the Sources of Growth," *Economic Journal*, vol. 96, no. 384, pp. 903–18; North, Douglass C. (1986), "The New Institutional Economics," *Journal of Institutional and Theoretical Economics*, vol. 142, no. 1, pp. 230–37; and Williamson, Oliver E. (1985b), "Reflections on the New Institutional Economics," *Journal of Institutional and Theoretical Economics*, vol. 141, no. 1, pp. 187–95. See also Hutchison, Terence W. (1984), "Institutionalist Economics Old and New," *Journal of Institutional and Theoretical Economics*, vol. 140, no. 1, pp. 20–29.
[48] When reference is made by new to old institutionalists, it is generally in very condescending terms, arguing that the latter's scorn of theory and analysis caused their whole effort to be largely wasted. James Buchanan sums up this attitude as follows: "Their methodological *naïveté* caused them to think that observation and description somehow automatically give rise to predictive theories, to hypotheses, when, in fact, we now know that almost the reverse holds" (Buchanan, James M. (1979), "An Economist's Approach to 'Scientific Politics,'" in Buchanan (ed.), *What Should Economists Do?* Indianapolis, IN: Liberty Press, p. 147).
[49] Commons, John R. (1934a), *Institutional Economics: Its Place in Political Economy*, New York: Macmillan.

focus was so important: "It is this shift from commodities and individuals to transactions and the working rules of collective action that marks the transition from the classical and hedonic schools to the institutional schools of economic thinking."[50]

Like Hobbes and Locke, Commons viewed the introduction of property rights to scarce resources as a potential source of social conflict, and like Smith he emphasized the dangers that rest in allowing a free rein for self-interested behavior. In contrast to Smith, however, he could not see an invisible hand that would put everything right. As we have noted above, he worried about the fate of capitalism and focused his interest on how explicit rules and sanctions might be introduced to protect individuals from the negative consequences of self-interested behavior by others.[51]

What Commons did not discuss was the degree to which deliberate policy intervention could actually *succeed* in achieving stated ambitions. This not only highlights the fundamental issue of what degree of choice policy makers may have in introducing or amending institutions that are believed to fill certain given functions. It also brings us back to the associated core question of what motivation actors will have to opt for strategies that are based on rule obedience as opposed to rule evasion, with substantial implications for economic performance. We shall elaborate on both of these issues in the following chapter.

In Williamson's previously mentioned account of markets and hierarchies, where he does acknowledge a debt to Commons, emphasis is placed on how transactions are being continually shifted between market and hierarchy, with an intention of minimizing transaction costs. A key component is the notion of "comparative institutional choice," which is introduced to show that organizational adjustment to changing circumstances in the market is indeed an ongoing process driven by self-interest.[52]

The main point is that to understand the factors influencing how the choice between market and hierarchy is made – that is, why firms may at times elect to bypass the market and resort instead to hierarchical modes of organization – it is necessary to focus on a combination of both human and environmental factors.

With respect to the human factors, we may begin by recognizing that individuals make decisions under conditions Herbert Simon has referred to

[50] Commons, John R. (1931), "Institutional Economics," *American Economic Review*, vol. 21, no. 4, p. 652.
[51] Commons, John R. (1924), *Legal Foundations of Capitalism*, New York: Macmillan.
[52] Williamson, *Markets and Hierarchies*, pp. 8–10.

as "bounded rationality."[53] Implied here is that the ability to solve complex problems will be constrained both by neurophysiological limits, restricting the human capacity to process information, and by language limits that complicate communication. To this we may add opportunistic behavior. What Williamson refers to as "self-interest seeking with guile" represents strategic manipulation of information and misrepresentation of intentions, phrased in his own distinctive terms as "selective or distorted information disclosure, or self-disbelieved promises regarding future conduct."[54]

It is, however, not sufficient to consider bounded rationality in isolation. It is only when we add a complex environment that limitations on individual data processing capacity will appear as a constraint. Similarly, it is not sufficient to consider opportunistic behavior as such. With large numbers of actors, opportunistic behavior will not be sustainable. Only in small numbers will opportunism pose a distinct risk.

The main benefits that Williamson associates with vertical integration may be grouped under three headings. *First,* the introduction of hierarchy will ease the constraints associated with bounded rationality. Within a hierarchy, decisions can be made sequentially, based on limited information, and adaptation may take place as the future is permitted to unfold. *Second,* internal organization will attenuate the problems of opportunistic behavior, both by reducing the potential gains and by affording enhanced modes of social and other control. *Third,* the creation of hierarchies will also be associated with softer features, such as the emergence of efficient codes of communication and of convergent expectations, all of which combine to create a special "atmosphere." Corporate culture would fall under this heading.

While all of this may help explain why hierarchies sometimes displace market mediation, we must remain cognizant that functioning market economies are marked by continued competition between the two, indicating that changing circumstances – that is, transaction costs – will determine the choice. The main consequence of introducing command economy was that it effectively suppressed this choice. As this would have far-reaching consequences both for governance and for other institutions that surround transactions, we shall take a closer look at the associated formation of informal norms.

Inside the Hierarchy of Command

We have presented unaccountable government as the core feature of the Muscovite institutional matrix and as the trigger that established its

---

[53] Simon, Herbert (1957), *Models of Man,* New York: Wiley, p. 198.
[54] Williamson, *Markets and Hierarchies,* p. 26.

remaining components, most notably, the suppression of private property. We have also argued that although rulers might have realized that this mode of government impacts negatively on economic efficiency, the associated potential for control and for resource mobilization has greatly outweighed any such considerations. Let us view the persistent refusal by Russian political elites to accept any form of accountability as the true defining feature of the Russian economic model, and proceed to see where that leads us.

Quote 2 success!

Retaining Smith's conviction of the "propensity to truck and barter" and the associated role of self-interest seeking, the main consequence of introducing command economy had to be that of a proliferation of irrepressive markets. Given the risk of detection that is involved in such activities, actors were forced to develop skills in building trust within clandestine networks. As a result, transactions became heavily "embedded" in social structures, and the role of the state as such was reduced to an exogenous source of trouble. Given, moreover, that both collusion and corruption reduce economic efficiency, the state was forced to set aside resources for supervision and to undertake intrusive activities that further undermine its own legitimacy.

In response to being forced into playing redistributive influence games, actors evolved the types of expectations, beliefs, and internalized norms that have been presented as determinants of the choice between rule evasion and rule obedience. At this point we are no longer talking of deliberate institutional choice, in the sense of institutions as rules of the game that is derived from the agency view. On the contrary, we are faced with informal adaptation to the removal of sets of opportunity for legal private entrepreneurship. We shall map out three types of consequences, all of which will be contrasted against the benefits that Williamson associated with vertical integration.

First, with respect to easing the constraint of bounded rationality we may note that the suppression of voluntary horizontal exchange resulted in a loss of such information that is provided to market actors via the price mechanism. This had two serious implications. It not only served to render impossible any form of "rational calculation," as Ludwig von Mises put it. As noted by Abram Bergson and others, it also made it difficult to control managers whose activities could no longer be monitored via budget performance or share price movements. In consequence of the latter, much ink has been spilled seeking to define what objective functions were maximized by Soviet enterprise managers.

The upshot from the present perspective is that while vertical integration of the central planning kind was certainly not designed to economize on transaction costs, it did produce similar consequences with respect to nonmarket decision making. Being forced to operate in an environment of scattered and seriously distorted information, managers responded by resorting to sequential decision making, addressing problems as they emerged, with little or no ambition to look beyond the most immediate. The added fact that willful governance could at any time lead to unexpected changes in penalties and rewards made it even more important to engage in nonmarket forms of influence seeking that could provide insurance against risk. The outcome was to increase transaction costs and to reduce the scope for rational resource allocation.

Second, with regard to the effect of vertical integration in attenuating the problems of opportunistic behavior, in the case of central planning vertical integration was clearly not conducive to reducing the incentive to engage in self-interest seeking with guile. It is true that there is formal similarity. Command economy will remove such opportunities for gain that may be derived from opportunistic behavior in the open market, and it will add authority for the principal to intervene. The absence of a surrounding market, however, ensures that the impact will be very different. When actors are locked into a hierarchy where there is no legal exit and where abilities to influence their own situation are severely circumscribed, there will be every incentive in the world to engage in what Williamson refers to as "strategic manipulation of information and misrepresentation of intentions." Illicit substitution and outright theft must also be included here.

As both planners and managers are forced to engage in the same games of deceit and manipulation, the consequences will be endemic. As the principal will factor in opportunistic behavior by its agents, the agents will find that revealing intentions and capabilities leads to immediate penalties as plan targets are adjusted upward. The resulting costs will again be measured in terms of deteriorating efficiency in resource allocation. The incentive to hoard inputs for safety will cause static efficiency to drop, and the absence of a premium for risk-taking will negatively impact dynamic efficiency.

The *third* and from an informal perspective most important consequence of blocking the scope for voluntary horizontal exchange relates to the "atmosphere" that will emerge within the hierarchy. In Williamson's case of vertical integration, actors were seen to evolve codes of communication and to be marked by a convergence of expectations, all of which supports improved decision making. In the case at hand, there will be similar effects but again no longer to the benefit of the system. Agents who are forced to engage in criminal activities will evolve clandestine codes of communication that enhance their abilities to collude against the principal, and they will be marked by a convergence of negative expectations regarding state intervention in particular. Perhaps the most important feature of this atmosphere, which places a premium on "beating the system," or cheating the state, concerns the proliferation of negative attitudes to entrepreneurship.

In a modern market economy, the small business sector assumes a dual role as mother of invention and as main source of growth. Given, moreover, that small business transactions depend on institutions that support credible enforcement and long-term contracting, it is logical that high-performance economies will be associated with a rapid expansion of the transactions sector.

In the Russian case, small has never been beautiful. Russian tradition also has been marked by the continued absence of a state that is able and willing to assume the role as an impartial third party enforcer. Given the discretionary powers to control and to extort bribes that have consequently devolved to members of the bureaucracy, it is only logical that strongly negative attitudes have emerged toward entrepreneurship and toward such income differentiation that results from private initiative.

From a long-term perspective, we may identify two distinctive Russian characteristics that agree rather poorly with the ambitions of building a rules-based market economy. First, Russian merchants have always been plying their trades in close proximity to predatory government agents. Present-day hoopla surrounding Kremlin-sponsored campaigns against corruption in this sense merely reflects that we are dealing here with a long-term endemic disease. When imperial era merchants were liberated from being de facto serfs, they remained in the claws of sundry bureaucrats. Once the Bolsheviks took over and mercantile activity was formally criminalized, such vulnerability was enhanced, and in the post-Soviet era merchants have labored under the dual burden of corrupt bureaucrats and criminal protection rackets. At no point along the road has there been any reason to expect or to predict the emergence of feelings of trust in anonymous government agencies, as guarantors of contracts and of property rights.

The second, derivative, characteristic concerns the zero sum nature of Russian economic exchange. The dishonesty of imperial Russian merchants was legendary, and there were good reasons for this. Under willful government that preys on whatever activity seems to generate a profit, actors will not stand to gain from transparency and honesty.[55] Although there will

---

[55] Richard Pipes maintains, "In practice, any product which entered into commerce became the subject of a state monopoly," and goes on to note, "It is difficult to conceive of a practice more fatal to the entrepreneurial spirit" (Pipes, Richard (1974), *Russia under the Old Regime*, New York: Charles Scribner's Sons, p. 195).

be powerful incentives to collude against the government, a practice that does require an element of interpersonal trust, there will be no incentive to abstain from cheating partners to a transaction, if the possibility arises. The classic Russian expression *kto kogo*, or "who beats whom," which is so often applied to political games, is equally applicable to business transactions.

Again recalling Williamson's emphasis on factors that generate a special "atmosphere," it may be useful also to cite his argument that transactions cannot be viewed as neutral in and of their own: "Recognition that alternative modes of economic organization give rise to differing exchange relations, and that these relations themselves are valued, requires that organizational effectiveness be viewed more broadly than the usual efficiency calculus would dictate."[56]

What is so vital to recognize at this point is that the whole notion of "entrepreneurship" rests not only on the technical dimensions of secure rights to property and of faith in long-term contracting. Far more important is the associated feeling of being in charge of the whole chain of events – from idea to effort to reward. When this works according to the ideals that have been derived from Smithian laissez-faire, it is logical to assume that entrepreneurship will be imbued with a sense of self-realization that adds important drive to the efforts of the entrepreneur. If, however, surrounding society is marked by social norms that castigate entrepreneurship as "speculation," and that resent incomes and wealth that are derived from such activities, it must be equally clear that the "entrepreneur" will develop rather different attitudes.[57]

These latter consequences must be viewed as particular complications in any attempt at major societal transformation or reconstruction because here we are no longer faced with expectations, which may be altered following a stream of consistent experience that supports new rules. Nor are we talking of beliefs, where the path of change may also be mapped out. Once we enter the realm of internalized norms relating to what is viewed as right and proper, we shall also have to address problems that relate to the category of social norms, an area that Elster simply refers to as a "jungle."[58] We shall have reason to return to these complications in the following chapter. Here we shall briefly summarize and conclude our argument.

---

[56] Williamson, *Markets and Hierarchies*, pp. 38–39.
[57] For an expanded argument on the social and cultural context of entrepreneurship, see Greenfield, Sidney M., Arnold Strickton, and Robert T. Aubey (eds.) (1979), *Entrepreneurs in Cultural Context*, Albuquerque: University of New Mexico Press.
[58] Elster, Jon (1989a), *The Cement of Society: A Study of Social Order*, Cambridge: Cambridge University Press, p. 100.

FROM NEWTON TO WILLIAMSON

In our previous account of social science, we took as our point of departure Isaac Newton's mechanics and the impact that his metaphor of the universe as a "great clock" would have on the "soft" sciences. We have seen how over time social scientists have strived ever harder to frame their own theories in model frameworks that move ever closer to those of the "hard" sciences. In the past three decades in particular, mathematical sophistication has arisen as the true test of quality of scholarly endeavor.

As different branches of social science are differently amenable to such theoretical formalization, the dual processes of increasing distance between disciplines and of enforcing internal pecking orders within disciplines have become ever more pronounced. Talk about interdisciplinary endeavors may at time be used for decorative purposes, but hard realities tell us that rational consideration of prospects for *intra*disciplinary careers ensures that disciplinary boundaries remain firmly drawn.

The main implication that this development has for our present purpose concerns the previously mentioned "cleavage" between economics and sociology. Leaving this crucial problem for a more extensive treatment in the following chapter, here we shall round off with a few additional remarks on how modern economics has increasingly lost sight of what the liberal economic tradition was originally about.

In his highly influential work *The Economic Institutions of Capitalism*, Williamson sets the stage for presenting his own approach to new institutional economics by characterizing how economics developed in the three decades from 1940 until 1970: "The allocation of economic activity as between firms and markets was taken as a datum; firms were characterized as production functions; markets served as signaling devices; contracting was accomplished through an auctioneer; and disputes were disregarded because of the presumed efficacy of court adjudication."[59]

Citing numerous sources that began, in the 1970s, to question the wisdom of the neoclassical approach, he nevertheless finds that introduction of the transactions cost approach, which forms an essential part of the new institutional economics, was sorely needed. With specific reference to Coase's statement that "modern institutional economics is economics as it ought to be,"[60] he laments that neoclassical economics maintains a maximizing

---

[59] Williamson, Oliver E. (1985a), *The Economic Institutions of Capitalism*, New York: Free Press, p. 7.

[60] Coase, Ronald H. (1984), "The New Institutional Economics," *Journal of Theoretical and Institutional Economics*, vol. 140, no. 1, p. 231.

orientation. If all relevant costs had been recognized, that would have been unobjectionable, but the maximizing tradition does not encourage such recognition: "Instead, the role of institutions is suppressed in favor of the view that firms are production functions, consumers are utility functions, the allocation of activity between alternative modes of organization is taken as given, and optimizing is ubiquitous."[61]

With this type of baggage, it was perhaps understandable that economics came so ill prepared to the task of dealing with the wreckage left by the collapsed project of central economic planning. The basic premise of the envisioned transition was that both command economy and its market counterpart were amenable to analysis along the lines of Newton's "great clock," that is, that the game was all about formal rules and enforcement agencies. By professing that for the purpose of economic policy all countries are essentially the same, the Russian reformers refused to even consider the third leg of North's institutional triad: the informal norms that provide legitimacy for the formal rules.

To what extent a more comprehensive analytical approach might have served to prevent the ensuing hyperdepression and the associated host of assorted ills is beside the point here. The point, rather, is to emphasize the crucial role that was played by such beliefs, expectations, and internalized norms that were carried over from the Soviet era, and to some extent even from the deeper recesses of Russian history. The question of whether a different outcome might have been possible hinges critically on what we believe about the scope for deliberate intervention in the area of informal norms, what Williamson refers to as "atmosphere."

A deeper understanding of what Coase views as "economics as it ought to be" must proceed beyond the mechanics of the "great clock" and focus more specifically on the interplay between public and private norm formation. It is in the latter realm that we may find a good deal of the explanation for systemic failures such as the havoc that was caused by Russian shock therapy in the 1990s and the financial meltdown that was to follow on Wall Street a decade later, not to mention the long-standing failure to achieve Third World development.

When Williamson published his work on the economic institutions of capitalism, public debates on economic policy were marked by a rising tide of neo-liberal deregulation, privatization, and minimal government. This was a time when both private and public culture became infused with beliefs that greed is good and that self-enrichment is virtue. With the

---

[61] Williamson, *The Economic Institutions*, p. 45

ensuing collapse of communism and the associated myth of the end of history, such beliefs were further entrenched, and in consequence they helped prod further deregulation and a further lowering of public defenses against predatory financial activities.

As noted in our introductory chapter, at the turn of the millennium these beliefs were so deeply entrenched that the scandals surrounding Enron, WorldCom, and Arthur Andersen caused no more than a minor tremble. It was deeply symptomatic that whistleblowers seeking to draw attention to the brewing Madoff Ponzi scheme were simply ignored. The global financial crisis that began with the collapse of Lehman Brothers was different, at least initially so.

Perhaps it was symptomatic of the growing concerns about the wisdom of the approach of modern economics that the Nobel Prize in economics for the crisis year 2009 was awarded to Oliver Williamson and Elinor Ostrom, both of whom have won their spurs for thinking outside the box. Whether this in turn will have any implications for the further development of the discipline remains to be seen. Let us proceed now to look at the core question of deliberate institutional choice, as opposed to endogenous institutional change.

6

Institutional Choice

In his main presentation of institutional theory, Douglass North writes, "Institutions are the rules of the game in a society or, more formally, are the humanly devised constraints that shape human interaction."[1] There is obvious truth in this. Since time immemorial, humans have strived to regulate their relations to other humans by making rules. Beginning as unwritten codes, conventions, and norms, handed down by tradition, over time this rule making has become increasingly formalized and increasingly complex.

In a modern society, making and enforcing rules and regulations generates substantial employment, often at high incomes, in multiple professions across both the private and the public sectors. This said, one should not be lured into taking the continued reliance of many traditional societies on unwritten rules as a sign of lacking sophistication. As many anthropological studies have shown, the systems of informal norms that mark what is sometimes known as "primitive societies" can be highly sophisticated.[2]

As we have argued, however, from a narrow perspective of economic efficiency there is clear empirical evidence that systems of formal rules, backed by credible and impartial third party enforcement, generate better economic performance than informal systems backed by social censure and sanctions. The contrast between north and south in Italy brings this point home, as does the broader contrast between Russia and the West. The question that must now be approached concerns *why* countries with poorly functioning judiciaries, which persist in generating large informal

---

[1] North, Douglass C. (1990a), *Institutions, Institutional Change and Economic Performance*, Cambridge: Cambridge University Press, p. 3.
[2] For example, Colson, Elizabeth (1974), *Tradition and Contract: The Problem of Order*, Chicago: Adeline.

sectors with low value added, have such long track records of failing to emulate the positive experience of those countries that have been more successful.

We have touched on this crucial question repeatedly in previous chapters, citing questions both by North and by others to the effect that while necessary, opportunity and self-interest have clearly not been sufficient for poor countries to rise out of poverty, or for centrally planned economies to undertake a successful transition to rules-based market economy. Here we may add a similarly crucial question, posed by David Landes in a discussion of why poor people stay poor:

Certainly the incentive is there: the gap between what is and what can be is enormous. And the opportunity. Once (here fill in the appropriate condition) the burden of colonialism is lifted, the government sets growth as the objective, the plans are drawn up, and the requisite resources are mobilized, growth and development should follow as the night the day. Only it has not.[3]

This insight not only goes against the grain of long-standing beliefs in the benefits of being late and of having an easy opportunity to catch up. Even more so, it goes against the grain of beliefs in the salutary effects of markets and competition, in politics as well as in the economy. As North puts it, development over time should be marked by feedback mechanisms whereby "competition would weed out inferior institutions and reward by survival those that better solve human problems."[4]

Turning now to look for possible answers to these questions, we may begin by asking how the notion of "humanly devised" should be understood. Is the institutional matrix of a given society the result of a deliberate introduction of specific sets of rules, designed to achieve clearly pronounced objectives, or is it the outcome of a process of evolution, perhaps even one whereby institutions get established or re-established as by-products of other action?

The implications are substantial. In the final analysis, as Avner Greif points out, it boils down to what we believe "about the degree of choice individuals within a society possess in selecting their institutions."[5] From the side of economics, the answer is straightforward. Assuming that actors are price takers who respond only by making quantity adjustments, that is,

---

[3] Landes, David S. (1990), "Why Are We So Rich and They So Poor?," *American Economic Review*, vol. 80, no. 2, p. 6.

[4] North, *Institutions, Institutional Change*, p. 7.

[5] Greif, Avner (2006), *Institutions and the Path to the Modern Economy: Lessons from Medieval Trade*, Cambridge: Cambridge University Press, p. 12.

by playing according to the rules, institutions are viewed as the rules of the game. Rule making in consequence is viewed as an instrumentally rational process of responding to perceived problems by introducing rules designed to fill specific functions.

Against this "agency" or functionalist view, which is common not only in economics but also in new institutionalism more broadly, we may contrast the approach of sociology, and of old institutionalism, which views the driving forces of human action as being embedded in social structures. According to the latter "structural" or cultural view, institutions are viewed as phenomena that "transcend individual actors and are immutable cultural features of societies that determine behavior."[6]

What we have here is simply another way of formulating what Jon Elster was referring to as a "persisting cleavage" in the social sciences. It is serious not only in the sense that it has precluded much potentially useful interdisciplinary work. It is even more so in the presently critical sense that we do not really have any form of broad scholarly agreement, either on what motivates human action or on how important rules of the game are made and enforced. The remainder of this chapter will be devoted to an investigation into what implications this may have. While our main emphasis shall be on the general case, Russia's troubled encounters with capitalism will again be used as important background illustration.

Let us begin by considering what lessons may be drawn from the main driving forces in the success story of the "Rise of the West" that we have referred to repeatedly in previous chapters, albeit merely in passing.

THE SUCCESS STORY

Given the tremendous impact it would have on the rest of the world, it is not surprising that the emergence of what we may refer to here as Western civilization, or as the Western Model, has provoked a good deal of both writing and discussion. It is after all true that the spectacular economic and technological advances that took off in Europe in the eighteenth century would produce both imperialism and colonialism, not to mention two devastating world wars. Feelings of guilt and shame have in consequence played an important role in conditioning massive efforts of atonement. To date, this has mainly taken the form of putting up substantial amounts of cash, in a thus far largely unsuccessful effort to bridge the gap between the rich and the poor.

---

[6] Ibid., pp. 12–13.

Although the latter are issues that we shall want to stay well clear of here, they do present an important background. This is so not only with respect to the emergence of massive aid bureaucracies. It is even more so concerning the associated and equally unsuccessful attempts by the social sciences to produce useful theoretical models in support of efforts to achieve development. Noting that we still lack a clear understanding of the preconditions for successful institutional transfer, for legal transplants, or for institutional imitation more generally, we shall now look in broad terms at what the less fortunate nations of the world have been called upon to emulate.

It will after all not be sufficient to call on them to simply copy the way the West works. One is easily reminded here of what Robert Lucas once wrote about imitation in the case of the Asian "miracle" economies: "But simply advising a society to 'follow the Korean model' is a little like advising an aspiring basketball player to 'follow the Michael Jordan model.'"[7] If it were that easy, Jordan would be no star; indeed there would be no stars anywhere below the heavens.

Agency versus Evolution

The success story is striking most of all in the sense that it really does not have a beginning. As Marshall Poe puts it, "Historians have worked for decades trying to determine when and how the Europeans set out on the road to modern existence. No compelling answer has been forthcoming because the European road has no salient, recognizable beginning."[8] There is no real agreement on whether the point of takeoff should be dated to 1750 or to 1820, and there has been much debate over what really caused industrialization.[9] It has all been a case of evolution, where numerous tributaries have added to the main flow.

---

[7]   Lucas, Robert E. (1993), "Making a Miracle," *Econometrica*, vol. 61, no. 2, p. 252.
[8]   Poe, Marshall T. (2003), *The Russian Moment in World History*, Princeton, NJ: Princeton University Press, p. 60.
[9]   Absent any form of ambition to venture into the debate as such, we may note that the understanding of institutional change in England in the seventeenth century as the basis of and indeed the explanation for the subsequent industrial revolution has been somewhat controversial. Mancur Olson, for one, is quite specific in stating that the case of British development after 1688–89 is "relatively clear-cut," and that "as almost everyone knows, the consolidation of individual and more or less democratic rights provided during the Glorious Revolution was followed by the Industrial Revolution" (Olson, Mancur (1997), "The New Institutional Economics: The Collective Choice Approach to Economic Development," in Christopher Clague (ed.), *Growth and Governance in Less-Developed and Post-Socialist Countries*, Baltimore: Johns Hopkins University Press, p. 52). For an alternative view of the roots and explanations of Western success, see Clark,

This stands in sharp and analytically important contrast to the Russian experience, where institutional change, or reform, is consistently initiated from above. Beginning with the defeat of Peter the Great at Narva in 1700, a battle that triggered the Great Northern War, there has been a clear pattern of reform as reaction to threats from outside.[10] Major defeats in war, such as those at Narva, in the Crimean War, or in the Russo-Japanese war, have triggered changes aiming to close the gap with the "developed" countries in Europe. At each time, associated with great tsars and/or prominent ministers, the autocracy responded to emergency by seeking to implement top-down reforms based on imported models.

Although technical modernization did sometimes result, as argued in Chapter 4, the threshold to westernization was never crossed, and sustainability never achieved. As an outstanding example we may advance the legislative commission that was summoned by Catherine the Great in 1767. From an intellectual point of view, it did represent an important step. In line with the general spirit of Catherine's at least initially enlightened regime, its members were allowed to read important works such as Beccaria's *Crimes and Punishments* and Montesquieu's *The Spirit of Laws*.[11] While this did promote the emergence of a corps of professional jurists that would maintain the process of thinking about legal reform, over the coming century their work would have no practical outcome. Catherine's commission simply vanished.

Reflected here is what Poe refers to as social engineering *ab novo*. European monarchs bent on change would always have at their disposal

Gregory (2007), *A Farewell to Alms: A Brief Economic History of the* World, Princeton, NJ: Princeton University Press, which maintains that the political and economic institutions normally associated with industrialization had a long prior history, causing over time deep cultural changes that caused people to adopt economic habits such as hard work, rationality, and education. For an interpretation from the radical left, see also Frank, A. G. (1998), *ReOrient: Global Economy in the Asian Age*, Berkeley: University of California Press, ch. 6.

[10] It may be argued that the very same pattern could also be found in earlier Muscovy, for example, when Ivan the Terrible faced Sweden in the Livonian war, with seriously negative consequences. This, however, will not be pursued further here.

[11] Beccaria, Cesare, Marchese di (2006), *An Essay on Crimes and Punishments*, Clark, NJ: Lawbook Exchange; Montesquieu, Charles de Secondat, Baron de (2002), *The Spirit of Laws*, Amherst, NY: Prometheus Books. It may be of some interest to note here that influence on Catherine's reforms flowed not only from the French *philosophes* but also from the Scottish enlightenment. The "Instruction" she issued to the legislative commission drew in part on a proposal written by a certain Semyon Desnitskiy, who had studied under Adam Smith in Glasgow. (See Brown, A. H. [Archie] (1975), "Adam Smith's First Russian Followers," in Andrew S. Skinner and Thomas Wilson (eds.), *Essays on Adam Smith*, Oxford: Clarendon Press, p. 263.)

important modernizing resources, in the form of intermediary bodies such as organized estates, incorporated towns, clerical organizations, guilds, and local parliaments. While these would often act as drags on the executive power, they could at times also be harnessed for important tasks at hand. In Russia, that was never the case. While the autocracy had enviable unity of command, which allowed targeted mobilization, it could never rely on change being driven by social forces from below. At times when change was desired, the necessary resources would have to be put in place from above by deliberate design.[12]

The overall pattern of economic development that resulted from this model would come to assume what Alexander Gerschenkron referred to, in his classic *Economic Backwardness in Historical Perspective*, as a "peculiarly jerky character." Driven by military needs, episodes of state-led mobilization of resources would lead to repeated spurts of rapid economic development, to be followed by repeated crises: "Precisely because of the magnitude of the governmental exactions, a period of rapid development was very likely to give way to prolonged stagnation, because the great effort had been pushed beyond the limits of physical endurance of the population and long periods of economic stagnation were the inevitable consequences."[13]

The main implication of these contrasts is that while Russian tradition has been marked by numerous illustrations of at times most serious interventions from above, interventions that have been quite in line with the agency approach, the response from below has been contrary to the associated belief in instrumental rationality. Rather than adapt to and abide by new sets of rules, actors have persistently preferred to either avoid or to bend them. The outcome, as described in previous chapters, has been irrepressive markets, endemic corruption, and a clear preference for highly personalized influence games.

To gain a better understanding of why these structural patterns have proven so resilient over time, and why market forces have failed to favor solutions that would have yielded economically more efficient outcomes, we shall return to the success story that the Russians have sought so hard over the centuries to copy, for the simple reason that they so repeatedly have found their own model to be inferior in generating military strength. The following will suggest four major milestones.

[12] Poe, *The Russian Moment*, p. 60.
[13] Gerschenkron, Alexander (1962), *Economic Backwardness in Historical Perspective*, Cambridge, MA: Harvard University Press, p. 17.

Milestones of the West

The *first* and most obvious is that of Roman law, which not only introduced the still-practiced legal definitions of private property, namely, the right of use (*usus*), the right to proceeds (*usufruct*), and the right of disposal (*abusus*). In addition, and more fundamentally important, the ancient Romans also drew a firm line of division between the power of the state (*imperium* or *potestas*) and the right of citizens to property (*dominium* or *proprietas*). Thus, for example, Cicero would argue "that government could not interfere with private property because it had been created in order to protect it," and the philosopher Seneca would hold that "to kings appertains the power over all, but property belongs to individuals."[14]

Although the process of "Renaissance," or more properly *Rinascimento*, that began in Tuscany in the fourteenth century has been mainly associated with the fine arts, it also brought back into focus vital components of the classical heritage, such as that of Roman law. The fundamental and lasting importance of this rediscovery is that the old Roman rights to property would be specifically included in the *Déclaration des droits de l'homme et de citoyen* of the French revolution, as well as in the subsequent Napoleonic Code of 1804. In the latter document, as Richard Pipes emphasizes, French law removed all feudal limitations on ownership and returned almost verbatim to the Roman definitions: "Property is the right to enjoy and dispose of objects in the most absolute manner, provided that one does not make use of it in a manner prohibited by laws or regulations. No one can be forced to give up his property unless it is for the public good and by means of a fair and previous indemnity."[15]

The crucial role that has been played by Roman law in the Western tradition may be usefully contrasted here against the absence in Russian tradition of a clear line of division between power and property. It is a fact that Russia was not touched, in any meaningful way, by the Renaissance. Its legal tradition has shown no trace of serious influence by Roman law, and up to the present there has been nothing even resembling the line once drawn by Cicero and Seneca between the power of the state and the property of individuals. Absent a sphere of private property, it makes little sense to talk of a distinction between state and society. Indeed, the very essence of Pipes's previously cited portrayal of Russia as a "patrimonial state" is that the two are blended together.

[14] Pipes, Richard (1999), *Property and Freedom*, New York: Alfred A. Knopf, pp. 12–13, 28.
[15] Ibid., pp. 43–44.

Proceeding to the *second* of our four milestones, we may recall what was said about the opening up of long-distance trade in the Mediterranean. To begin with, there is general agreement that "Western wealth began with the growth of European trade and commerce which started in the twelfth century in Italy."[16] The very same may also be reflected in the mirror of language. It is striking how much of the terminology that is still used in talking of economic matters is derived from the Italian language: *summa, saldo, conto, budgetto, firma, credit* – and indeed *banca rotta*.

The role that was played by Venice and Genoa in this process may be described as one of responding to prospects for gain by building a distinctly novel political system. Quite in line with our emphasis on evolution, Greif concludes that "the history of the Italian city-states of the late medieval period is that of endogenous emergence of political systems explicitly aimed at advancement of the economic interests of those who established them."[17]

While the purely technical solutions – the Dogeship in Venice and the Podestà in Genoa – were somewhat different, they were similar in the sense of achieving a credible commitment by the state to the core task of protecting the sanctity of contracts and of private property.

From the Italian north, this new mode of commercial operations was carried by traders up the Rhône valley, via the Champagne fairs to the Low Countries and to the United Kingdom, where in 1776 it was up to Adam Smith to pen the story of what had happened. It again was a process based on evolution, on a series of endogenous institutional responses that aimed to reduce transaction costs and thus to expand the scope of the market.

The Russian parallel is composed of both contrast and similarity. Although the latter is linked mainly to counterfactual historiography, to what could have been rather than what was, it does constitute a useful backdrop for gaining a better understanding of the contrast.

What was known in Russian medieval times as Lord Great Novgorod (*Gospodin Velikii Novgorod*) presents a striking exception to the subsequent rise to power of Muscovy. Situated at the northern end of the trading route that was opened by the Vikings to reach Constantinople, the merchants of Novgorod were faced with challenges similar to those of their contemporaries in Venice and Genoa. Responding in much the same fashion, they

[16] Rosenberg, Nathan and L. E. Birdzell, Jr. (1986), *How the West Grew Rich: The Economic Transformation of the Industrial World*, New York: Basic Books, p. 35.

[17] Greif, Avner (1995), "Political Organizations, Social Structure, and Institutional Success: Reflections from Genoa and Venice during the Commercial Revolution," *Journal of Institutional and Theoretical Economics*, vol. 151, no. 4, p. 734.

proceeded to build democratic institutions that rested on firm legal regulation. According to Pipes, Novgorod "granted its citizens rights which
equaled and in some respects even surpassed those enjoyed by contemporary Western Europeans."[18] Perhaps most intriguingly, they unknowingly
mimicked the Genoan solution of contracting an outside prince to uphold
the law.[19]

Emerging to become a vital part, albeit not a full member, of the Hanseatic
Trading League, the city and its merchants began to accumulate serious
wealth, the evidence of which may still be traced in splendid archaeological
findings. Extending the parallel previously drawn to Venice and Genoa, the
fourteenth and fifteenth centuries were times when Novgorod, in the words
of Henrik Birnbaum, would constitute the "scene of a pulsating urban life,
complex sociopolitical activities and tensions, and a booming, productive
economy. It was the hub of a far-flung, largely international trade and the
center of a flourishing, many-faceted culture."[20]

In the end, however, Novgorod was destroyed by Moscow. The Hansa
trading yard was shut, the German merchants expelled, and their wares
confiscated.[21] The extended struggle between these two cities, or principalities, may also be viewed as a showdown between two systems. While
Novgorod was a classic example of a trading state, evolving institutions
to support its commercial ambitions, Moscow was the archetypal warrior
state, always ready to sacrifice economic gain to secure political control.
And it was Moscow that emerged victorious.

The importance of the contrast that is entailed here, not only between
Moscow and Novgorod but even more so between Russia and the West,
may be viewed against the background of evidence produced by J. Bradford
De Long and Andrei Shleifer on European city growth before the industrial
revolution. Based on regression analysis of the links between urban growth

---

[18] Pipes, *Property and Freedom*, p. 160.
[19] Beginning in the early fourteenth century, Novgorod was transformed from a principality
into a republic, ruled by a mayor (*posadnik*) and a popular assembly (*veche*). An outside
prince was employed on a contractual basis to serve as commander in chief and as an
anchor in the judicial process. Severe constraints were laid down that included prohibition for the prince to reside inside the city, to own land, or to be involved in commerce.
All of this is highly reminiscent of the earlier Genoan model of employing an outsider,
the Podestà, who would be paid after the termination of his contract and would hence be
above involvement in oligarchic struggles for power and fortune.
[20] Birnbaum, Henrik (1996), *Novgorod in Focus: Selected Essays by Henrik Birnbaum*,
Columbus, OH: Slavica, p. 73.
[21] For a broad account of the rise and decline of the Hansa, see Nash, E. Gee (1929), *The
Hansa: Its History and Romance*, New York: Dodd, Mead.

and types of ruler in Western Europe during the period from 1050 until 1800, they conclude that "strong princely rule is systematically associated with retarded urban commerce."[22]

The *third* and clearly related milestone in the Rise of the West concerns the emergence of strong cities, and the associated demise of European feudalism. Beginning with medieval Magdeburg law, this process was marked by urban residents struggling to win for themselves broad sets of rights and privileges. The challenge to an emerging class of urban merchants was that success in their trade rested heavily on securing protection for horizontal commercial relations. To do so in an otherwise vertically organized society implied having to stand up to the feudal powers. The concessions that they won played an important role in successfully constraining the power of the monarchy. As Henri Pirenne notes, the emerging "middle class" was itself a privileged order: "It formed a distinct legal group and the special law it enjoyed isolated it from the mass of rural inhabitants which continued to make up the immense majority of the population."[23] The overall outcome, as inscribed in a series of German city charters, may be captured in the classic expression *Stadtluft macht Frei*, city air makes free. The literal meaning was that having been in residence for a year and a day, an escaped serf would enjoy full protection of the law.[24]

Again, Russia would produce no parallel to this important Western development. On the contrary, urban merchants long suffered from serfdom in much the same fashion as did the peasantry. Accounts of how merchants freely sold themselves into genuine slavery, simply to escape debt, provide sordid illustration of just how dreadful their existence must have been.[25] Everything that has been said and written about the absence in Russian tradition of a bourgeoisie, or of a middle class, must be viewed against precisely this background. Over the centuries, as Pipes puts it, "Moscow could not tolerate privileged sanctuaries from which a genuine urban civilization might have developed because they violated the kingdom's patrimonial constitution."[26]

---

[22] De Long, J. Bradford and Andrei Shleifer (1993), "Princes and Merchants: European City Growth before the Industrial Revolution," *Journal of Law and Economics*, vol. 36, no. 2, p. 674.

[23] Pirenne, Henri (1969), *Medieval Cities: Their Origins and the Revival of Trade*, Princeton, NJ: Princeton University Press, p. 213.

[24] Magdeburg law defined freedom as "the natural liberty of a man to do what he wants, unless prohibited by force of law" (Pipes, *Property and Freedom*, p. 109).

[25] Pipes, *Russia under the Old Regime*, p. 202.

[26] Ibid., p. 199.

Returning to the case of Novgorod, both it and the brother city Pskov produced city charters that established in great detail both rights and obligations.[27] Most important, the rulers of Novgorod managed to introduce what De Long and Shleifer hold up as the real key to economic success, namely, the security of property. In stark contrast to their Muscovite fellows, Novgorod merchants would not have to worry about "the possibility of arrest, ruin or execution at the command of the ruling prince or the possibility of ruinous taxation."[28]

The *fourth* and final of our milestones will have to be that of the Glorious Revolution in England and of the subsequent revolutions in America and in France. Recalling that the former inspired the Enlightenment, and that the latter were in turn inspired by the Enlightenment, we may conclude that we are faced here with vital mental transformations that proceeded in harmony with the formulation of increasingly complex formal rules of the game.

The main reason the English revolution could achieve such "glorious" results was that it occurred in the midst of an evolving intellectual tradition (Hobbes, Locke, Montesquieu, and the Scottish enlightenment) that was clearly supportive of the demands that were put forth. As North emphasizes, the outcome as such would have sweeping repercussions: "The incentive structure not only encouraged the evolution of a legal structure such as the law merchant, and the growth of science, but also the development of military technology that led ultimately to European hegemony."[29]

What makes the case so very special, and so relevant to the present account, is that the advances that were made in England following the Glorious Revolution would be so slow in spreading to the continent, and to date really have not been fully replicated in large parts of the remaining world. While economic theory would predict that entrepreneurs should be quick to copy the solutions of more successful competitors, the track record in large parts of Asia, Africa, and Latin America remains marred by failures of institutional transfer, or imitation, most notably in the crucial field of property rights enforcement.

Accepting North's further observation that the English case so "clearly separated the Western European experience from the rest of the world,"[30]

---

[27] In the case of Pskov, the text as a whole has survived, but in that of Novgorod only fragments remain. See further Kaiser, Daniel H. (ed. and transl.) (1992), *The Laws of Rus – Tenth to Fifteenth Centuries*, Salt Lake City, UT: Charles Schlacks Jr.

[28] De Long and Shleifer, "Princes and Merchants," p. 671.

[29] North, Douglass C. (1993a), "Institutions and Credible Commitment," *Journal of Institutional and Theoretical Economics*," vol. 149, no. 1, p. 17.

[30] Ibid., p. 19.

we may recall Greif's insistence that Venice and Genoa provide illustration of the *endogenous* emergence of self-enforcing institutions. In the twelfth century, there were no foreign models for them to emulate. Faced with striking opportunities for gain, they responded by evolving rules as well as norms that entailed a credible binding of the state to its commitment to act as a third party enforcer of contracts and property rights.

The important concluding point to be made here is that the four milestones that marked the emergence of the West, and to some extent also of Novgorod, must all be viewed as illustrations of the same, of how an endogenous process of responding to opportunity caused markets to develop in harmony with Mancur Olson's previously cited notion of "market-augmenting government."

It is for precisely these reasons that we may not identify an obvious starting point for any of the various processes that jointly created "the West." It is also here, in the context of dynamic interaction between state and market, that we may view most clearly why the contrast between the respective traditions of institution building in Russia and in the West must be seen as a clash if not of civilizations then at the very least of historical traditions.

The main message of the account as a whole is that observing a process of successful institution-building, and perhaps even succeeding in understanding what secured the success, can never be the same as also knowing how to transplant the solutions into other social and/or cultural settings. Lucas's warning about exhortations to "follow the Michael Jordan model" will drive this point home.

LIMITS TO POLICY INTERVENTION

Proceeding now to the core issue of what can be done to remedy problems of lacking development in the Third World, of unsuccessful transition in the Former Soviet Union, and of corporate greed on Wall Street, we may return to what has been said about the liberal economic tradition of laissez-faire. For as long as we remain within this tradition, it does lie close at hand to assume that if only markets can be freed up, and if only entrepreneurship can be allowed a free rein, good things will follow. This after all is the message that is contained in the combined Smithian and Olsonian images of invisible hands.

To understand why the results on the ground have often been so disappointing, despite at times well-intended ambitions to reform, it will be necessary to address not only the question of agency (how and by whom rules are made) but also the crucial role of self-interest (under what conditions and to what extent actors may be expected to opt for rule-abiding behavior). At the heart of the matter lies the question of whether individuals will passively adapt in accordance with changes in the rules, or if they will actively seek to improve their positions by breaking or bending the rules. Only by approaching this situation of strategic choice shall we be able to gain serious insights into the causes of systemic failures of the kinds repeatedly referred to above.

Beginning with the crucial role of self-interest, we may return to Adam Smith and agree with Emma Rothschild that the happy outcome of "the benevolence of the butcher, the brewer, or the baker" rests on how actors perceive their options: "The success of the invisible hand depends on whether people choose to pursue their own interests by political influence, by the use of force, or in other ways." Accepting that actors may at times behave in ways that corrupt the agency approach, some rather serious implications will follow: "It thus requires both good institutions and good norms, whereby individuals pursue their interests within the rules of well-defined games, and not by seeking to influence institutions or rules."[31]

While Rothschild's mention of "good institutions and good norms" does reflect the core of the matter at hand, the formulation as such also obscures the distinction that must be made between formal rules and mechanisms of enforcement, on the one hand, and internalized norms on the other. If actors are to be precluded from self-interest seeking that entails bending or corrupting the rules, with serious repercussions for the performance of the system as a whole, a more active role by the state and its various agencies must be assumed. The question is how this role should be devised.

Given the dangers that have been associated in previous chapters with use of the "invisible hand" as a carte blanche for unconstrained self-interest seeking, we may return again to Lionel Robbins and his warning that the pursuit of self-interest, unrestrained by suitable institutions, carries no guarantee of anything but chaos. His continued reasoning stresses that the Smithian invisible hand does not constitute God's finger, nor some power of nature that is external to man. On the contrary, and in line with what was just said, it is a question of the *visible hand* of the legislator, of a political

---

[31] Rothschild, Emma (1994), "Adam Smith and the Invisible Hand," *American Economic Review*, vol. 84, no. 2, p. 321.

process that seeks to withdraw from the sphere of the pursuit of self-interest such options that do not harmonize with the public good:

> There is absolutely no suggestion that the market can furnish everything; on the contrary, it can only begin to furnish anything when a whole host of other things have been furnished another way. It is not only the special services yielding indiscriminate benefit which fall outside its function, it is also the whole fabric of law without which it could not exist. Without Hume's theory of justice, or something very much like it, the Classical theory of self-interest and the market would remain completely in the air. Not only the good society, but the market itself is an artifact.[32]

The point is that "good institutions" will have to include so much more than simply the formal rules and enforcement mechanisms that jointly make up the "fabric of the law." Robbins's insistence that "the market itself is an artifact," based on Enlightenment ideals, recalls Geoffrey Hodgson's previously cited insistence that "the market itself is an institution [that] involves social norms and customs, instituted exchange relations, and information networks that themselves will have to be explained."[33]

Perhaps the most important insight that can be gained from a closer reading of Smith is that the liberal tradition of deregulation and laissez-faire that followed in his name has failed to appreciate the crucial interplay between visible and invisible hands. In line with Robbins's comment on the visible hand, Amartya Sen notes that the "most immediate failure of the market mechanism lies in the things that the market leaves _undone._" The whole point of the liberal idea is to allow and support the constructive efforts of self-interested behavior, while making sure that suitable intervention secures both the provision of public goods and safeguards against actions motivated by greed: "Smith rejects interventions that _exclude_ the market – but not interventions that include the market while aiming to do those important things that the market may leave undone."[34]

With these observations we have returned to the fundamental line of division between economics and sociology that has figured so prominently in the previous chapters. In his _History of Economic Analysis_, Joseph Schumpeter notes: "Economic analysis deals with the question how people behave at any time and what the economic effects are they produce by so behaving; economic sociology deals with the question how they came to behave as they do."[35]

[32] Robbins, Lionel (1952), _The Theory of Economic Policy in English Classical Political Economy_, London: Macmillan, pp. 56–57.
[33] Hodgson, Geoffrey M. (2004), _The Evolution of Institutional Economics: Agency, Structure and Darwinism in American Institutionalism_, London: Routledge, p. 20.
[34] Sen, Amartya (2009), "Capitalism beyond the Crisis," _New York Review of Books_, vol. 56, no. 5, p. 3 (cited from www.nybooks.com/articles/22490, accessed on May 14, 2009).
[35] Schumpeter, Joseph A. (1954), _History of Economic Analysis_, London: Allen & Unwin, p. 21.

Accepting that the core of the matter concerns our understanding of what guides and motivates human action, we may refer to Oliver Williamson's division of the landscape of neo-institutional economics into four different levels of analysis.[36] The bottom level is the territory of neoclassical theory. This is where actors behave as instrumentally rational "economic men," and where adjustment in consequence is continuous and instantaneous. Moving up one level, we will find theories of corporate governance that introduce competition between markets and hierarchies. At this level, heavily marked by Williamson's own research on governance, adjustment to changing circumstances is somewhat slower and less obvious. The third level houses theoretical approaches to the "institutional environment" that surrounds economic and political behavior, a subject that is associated with the works of Douglass North

What is mainly relevant for the purpose at hand, however, is Williamson's top level where we may find "social embeddedness." Associated with Karl Polanyi, this is a notion that captures a whole range of socially and culturally determined phenomena such as norms, customs, mores, traditions, and religion. Research about problems that are found at this level tends to become highly controversial, mainly because it touches on explanations that are rooted in cultural specificity.[37] Most economists, including most institutional economists, tend to view this level as more or less given and thus as less interesting.

While it must be intuitively obvious that human behavior is somehow influenced by factors such as those listed above, it remains immensely difficult to identify and explain more precisely by which mechanisms cultural specificity and differences in tradition may produce differences in current economic performance. All we can say, with some degree of certainty, is that change at this level will take place very slowly, if at all. Williamson mentions periods of hundreds or even thousands of years.

The theoretical problem that emerges here springs from the fact that whereas the economics approach is clean in the sense of securing causal clarity at the expense of realism, the sociological approach incorporates

---

[36] Williamson, Oliver E. (2000), "The New Institutional Economics: Taking Stock, Looking Ahead," *Journal of Economic Literature*, vol. 38, no. 3, pp. 596–600. His basic arguments may also be found in Williamson, Oliver (1998), "Transaction Cost Economics: How It Works; Where It Is Headed," *De Economist*, vol. 146, no. 1, pp. 23–58.

[37] As a few prominent examples of works that have not shied back from the challenges involved here we may note Banfield, Edward C. (1958), *The Moral Basis of a Backward Society*, Glencoe, IL: Free Press; Putnam, Robert (1993), *Making Democracy Work: Civic Traditions in Modern Italy*, Princeton, NJ: Princeton University Press; and Huntington, Samuel P. (1996), *The Clash of Civilizations and the Remaking of World Order*, New York: Simon & Schuster.

realism at the expense of being specific concerning what, more precisely, should be understood by notions such as that of "embeddedness." Different authors symptomatically pursue very different lines of approach.

While Mark Granovetter suggests that economic action is embedded in the social structure,[38] Ranjay Gulati and Martin Gargiulo take a broader approach that includes relational, structural, and positional embeddedness,[39] and Sharon Zukin and Paul DiMaggio take it even further, to cognitive, cultural, structural, and political embeddedness.[40] In the introduction to their *Handbook of Economic Sociology*, Neil Smelser and Richard Swedberg curtly conclude that "the concept of embeddedness remains in need of greater theoretical specification."[41]

The lack of a precise definition is important mainly because sociologists have so often used embeddedness as a way of substantiating a long-standing critique of methodological individualism. As we may recall from Chapter 2, the very notion of an "economic man" was subjected to sweeping condemnation by Thorstein Veblen at the outset of the twentieth century and was still referred to by James Coleman a near century later quite simply as "fiction."

The main problem with this line of attack, which is rooted in the tradition of hostility toward neoclassical economics that began with Auguste Comte and Émile Durkheim, is that it is so hard to see what is being proposed as an alternative. This is not to be taken as a partisan remark, but rather as concern that the social sciences still have not been able to complete the ambition of reintegrating the study of economy and society that was begun by Max Weber.

A closer reading of Polanyi's own works will reveal two interpretations of the core concept of "embeddedness." On the one hand, we have his famous critique of the emergence of a "self-regulating market" that makes up so much of the account in his main work, *The Great Transformation*,

---

[38] Granovetter, Mark (1985), "Economic Action and Social Structure: The Problem of Embeddedness," *American Journal of Sociology*, vol. 91, no. 3, pp. 481–510.

[39] Gulati, Ranjay and Martin Gargiulo (1999), "Where Do Interorganizational Networks Come From," *American Journal of Sociology*, vol. 104, no. 5, pp. 1439–93.

[40] Zukin, Sharon and Paul DiMaggio (1990), "Introduction," in Zukin and DiMaggio (eds.), *Structures of Capital: The Social Organization of the Economy*, New York: Cambridge University Press, pp. 14–23.

[41] Smelser, Neil J. and Richard Swedberg (1994), "The Sociological Perspective on the Economy," in Smelser and Swedberg (eds.), *The Handbook of Economic Sociology*, Princeton, NJ: Princeton University Press, p. 18.

and that may be worth citing here at some length, simply because it is so full of verve.[42]

The main idea is that the emergence of market economy represents a unique event. Never before in history had it been the case that markets were "more than accessories of economic life." In all of previous history, the economic system had been absorbed into the social system, based on household, reciprocity, and redistribution. Market self-regulation was the result of a "commodification" of land, labor, and money, which in the end threatens to result in "One Big Market."

Arguing that the "commodity description of land, labor, and money is entirely fictitious," Polanyi concludes that it is "with the help of this fiction that the actual markets for labor, land and money are organized." He also rails against use of the "commodity fiction" as a rationalization for not interfering in the free functioning of the market mechanism.

In sharp contrast to Smith's optimistic view of the invisible hand, he fears that the market mechanism will become the "sole director of the fate of human beings" and that in the end this will lead to "demolition of society" where "human beings would die from the effects of social exposure." As individuals will have to be "protected against the ravages of this satanic mill," a countermovement will be needed in the form of a protective response from society.[43]

Behind the harsh and sometimes amusing rhetoric, we may find a testable proposition on the crucial relation between economy and society. Arguing that market economy is possible only in a market society, Polanyi states that the self-regulating market mechanism "demands nothing less than the institutional separation of society into an economic and a political sphere." The core of the argument may thus be summarized as a process whereby the economy becomes "disembedded."[44]

This interpretation stands in sharp contrast to his other use of the notion of embeddedness, which may be captured in his equally famous dictum,

---

[42] Polanyi, Karl (1944), *The Great Transformation*, New York: Farrar & Rhinehart. The following citations have been culled from pp. 68–76.

[43] His notion of a "double movement" captures the essence of a nineteenth-century process whereby a proliferation of self-regulating markets caused a protective response of regulation by society: "Society protected itself against the perils inherent in a self-regulating market system – this was the one comprehensive feature in the history of the age" (ibid., p. 76).

[44] See further Lie, John (1991), "Embedding Polanyi's Market Society," *Sociological Perspectives*, vol. 34, no. 2, pp. 219–35. Arguments have been exchanged over whether this really was what Polanyi meant. Accepting that this question shall never receive a proper answer, we shall rest content here with noting that his critique against self-regulation is hard to reconcile with an understanding of the market as being embedded.

"The human economy, then, is embedded and enmeshed in institutions, economic and noneconomic."[45] What may be found here is an assault on the rationality and atomism of economic man. Polanyi's critique, in *The Great Transformation*, of the proliferation of market relations was continued in a 1947 piece titled "Our Obsolete Market Mentality," in which he castigates the "delusion of economic determinism as a general law for all human society."[46] It is, however, no longer a question of a testable proposition but of a fundamental holistic principle that economy and society may only be studied as a whole.

The main problem, as Kurtulus Gemici notes, is that one cannot really have it both ways. If it is the case that economic development has caused the economy to become institutionally separated from society, an idea that is in agreement with methodological individualism and the logic of economic man, then it makes little sense to argue the case for methodological holism, under which economy and society *cannot* be separated. At stake is the ability of economic sociology to present its own theory of the market: "Yet it should be recognized that embeddedness in this capacity falls short of providing a theoretical alternative to mainstream economics."[47]

The reason this must be viewed as so important is that when sociologists affiliated with Harvard University responded to the emergence of new institutional economics by launching their own "new economic sociology," the ambition as a whole was heavily centered on the notion of embeddedness, and it was a real trendsetter. According to Richard Swedberg, the birth of the field as such may be associated with the publication, in 1985, of Granovetter's previously cited "Economic Action and Social Structure."[48]

In this highly influential article, he resurrected Polanyi's notion of embeddedness and used it to criticize both the "oversocialized" understanding of social action, derived from Parsonian sociology, that views individuals as captives of internalized norms and values, and the

[45] Polanyi, Karl (1957), "The Economy as an Instituted Process," in Karl Polanyi, Conrad M. Arensberg, and Harry W. Pearson (eds.), *Trade and Markets in Early Empires: Economies in History and Theory*, Glencoe, IL: Free Press, p. 250.

[46] Polanyi, Karl (1947), "Our Obsolete Market Mentality," *Commentary*, vol. 3, February. Reprinted in George Dalton (ed.) (1968), *Primitive, Archaic, and Modern Economies: Essays of Karl Polanyi*, New York: Anchor Books, quote on p. 70.

[47] Gemici, Kurtulus (2007), "Karl Polanyi and the Antinomies of Embeddedness," *Socio-Economic Review*, vol. 6, no. 1, p. 26.

[48] Swedberg, Richard (1997), "New Economic Sociology: What Has Been Accomplished, What Is Ahead?," *Acta Sociologica*, vol. 40, p. 162. See also Guillén, Mauro F. et al. (eds.) (2002), *The New Economic Sociology: Developments in an Emerging Field*, New York: Russell Sage.

"undersocialized" approach of neoclassical economics that views social outcomes as simple aggregates of actions taken by isolated individuals. Arguing that both approaches are flawed, he suggested a middle course that focused instead on how social action is embedded in networks of social relations.[49]

In a comment that is sharply critical of the use of embeddedness as a paradigm for economic sociology, Greta Krippner claims that both Granovetter and his many followers have gotten it all wrong: "In attempting to steer an intermediate course between the twin perils of under- and oversocialized views of action, Granovetter has run the ship aground on a conception – common to both – that insists on a separate nature of economy and society."[50]

The main point of her assault is that in focusing on a single analytical aspect, such as that of networks of ongoing social relations, sociologists take the market itself for granted. Thus they essentially accept the separation of economy from the social, found also in parts of Polanyi's work, which they are so critical of. The fact that analysis of the market has tended to elude sociological researchers, from the time when the early sociologists ceded this area to economists, also marks the growing literature on "sociology of the market." In their efforts to "embed" the market, researchers resort to such high levels of abstraction that "social content is distilled away from the social structure." The outcome is that "economic sociology will find itself in the paradoxical position of propping up the asocial market model of neoclassical economics."[51]

Recalling the statements by Robbins that "the market itself is an artifact," and by Hodgson that "the market itself is an institution," we are left wondering whether new economic sociology is ready to help bridge the "cleavage" between economics and sociology into which so many of the crucial questions that have been asked here tend to disappear. Perhaps, as Gemici suggests, "a theoretical vacuum characterizes economic sociology."[52] Rather than pursue this internal debate among sociologists, we shall proceed now to a more detailed discussion of norm-driven behavior and of the associated risks that certain types of informal norms may impede economic progress.

[49] Granovetter, "Economic Action and Social Structure," p. 481.
[50] Krippner, Greta R. (2001), "The Elusive Market: Embeddedness and the Paradigm of Economic Sociology," *Theory and Society*, vol. 30, no. 6, p. 801.
[51] Ibid., pp. 797, 802.
[52] Gemici, "Karl Polanyi," p. 28.

NORM-DRIVEN BEHAVIOR

Let us begin by recalling what was said in our introductory chapter about greed as a mortal sin, and about the different practical manifestations of the same that have been played out on a variety of stages, ranging from Third World megacities, to the Moscow Kremlin and to New York's Wall Street. The main message is that greed, as portrayed by Dante and as traditionally condemned by the Christian Church, must be viewed as an inherent feature of the human personality. It may be unevenly distributed between individuals, and perhaps even between cultures, but it has surely been with us since time immemorial.

What does vary over time is the *leeway* for greed to result in behavior that is both socially and economically odious. As evidenced by the global financial crisis, this leeway can be only partly constrained by rules and regulations, and by designated oversight agencies. Far more important than such formal modes of intervention is the degree to which public culture will encourage or constrain self-interest seeking. If prevailing public norms are supportive of behavior that approaches or even degenerates into pure greed, and hostile toward intrusive state intervention in the freedom of markets to create wealth, then we have the preconditions in place for bad outcomes to follow.

Again it may be useful to emphasize that the dangers involved here have long been known and commented on. Recent political debates on an excessive drive toward risk-taking, associated with an alleged "culture" of financial market bonus schemes, may be easily led back to Adam Smith and his warning about lending to "prodigals and projectors." Smith's argument was that the state has a responsibility, via usury laws, to keep money out of the hands of those who are "most likely to waste and destroy it."[53] The historical parallel is explicitly drawn by Sen: "The implicit faith in the ability of the market economy to correct itself, which is largely responsible for the removal of established regulations in the United States, tended to ignore the activities of prodigals and projectors in a way that would have shocked Adam Smith."[54]

In further illustration of the crucial interplay between public policy and norms that influence individual action, we may advance the once so celebrated case of the Scandinavian welfare state. At the outset of this grand experiment in social engineering, when tax rates remained moderate and

---

[53] Smith, Adam (2000), *The Wealth of Nations*, New York: Modern Library, p. 388.
[54] Sen, "Capitalism beyond the Crisis," p. 4.

when there was a perception of returns to taxpayers from state-sponsored welfare programs, private norms were clearly supportive. While even in those days there were individuals who cheated the tax man, it remained a marginal phenomenon and it was definitely not something to be openly proud of.

The time when serious trouble started was when very high rates of marginal taxation began to afflict the middle class. As discontent over high tax pressure began to proliferate, two negative processes were set in motion. In the formal dimension, increasing incentives for legal tax *avoidance* not only caused a diversion of real resources into unproductive redistributive activities. By compounding the burden on enforcement, it also and more seriously caused the risk of detection to fall, thus adding an incentive for illegal tax *evasion*. A vicious spiral was in the making. Most important, the informal dimension was marked by shifting norms regarding the payment of taxes. A situation where cheating on taxes had been shameful was gradually transformed into one where the practice of tax avoidance and even tax fraud was becoming not only broadly acceptable but to some even an achievement to take pride in.

The main implication of the latter concerns the fragile relation between the formal rules of the game and the informal norms that provide legitimacy for those rules. Remaining with the Scandinavian case, the damage that was done by high marginal taxation would prove difficult to reverse even over the medium term. The reason is derived from a basic institutional asymmetry. While rising marginal tax rates caused a negative shift of supporting norms, bringing the tax rate back down was in no way sure to restore the previous set of norms.

The very same may be said with respect to the case of endemic Russian corruption. While there is a common understanding that corruption among professions such as the police or the customs service may be explained by low wages, perhaps even by low wages in combination with public acceptance that the officials in question will extort bribes, there is nothing to say that increased wages will reduce corruption in the short run. For this to happen, that is, for individuals to transform their norms regarding the morality of corruption, they will have to experience a steady stream of experience that is sufficient to overcome well-known threshold effects. The point is that while formal rules may be changed overnight, informal norms will change only gradually.

Proceeding to further qualify our understanding of informal constraints on individual action, we may begin with the simple cases of tradition, custom, and simple routine, that is, the ways in which we have always done things. While such institutions are important in the sense of economizing on the daily process of decision making, they have little relevance in cases where we are faced with broad societal transformation.

The same may be said with respect to conventions that have emerged to solve coordination problems, such as whether to drive on the left or on the right. The important point here is not the choice as such, which is inconsequential, but rather the need to reach an equilibrium that is known to all. A specific and for our purpose highly relevant problem with conventions is that both origins and functions may at times be poorly understood. Consider the universally accepted convention of extending an empty right hand in greeting. As Paul David suggests, this may originally have emerged as a way of showing a right hand that carried no weapon.[55] The main point, however, is that the convention as such remains powerful long after that (possible) explanation had lost all force. As will be shown later, this also applies to more complex cases of social norms.

The point where real complications begin is when we approach the more fundamental dimension of moral and social norms, which will be shown to act as serious constraints on the scope for deliberate policy intervention, and on institutional choice more generally. As a first step, we may return to our previous contrast between such instrumentally rational behavior that agrees with the agency approach, and the various types of norm-driven behavior that are associated with the structural approach.

Consider the case of a person walking in a park with the peel from a just eaten banana in one hand. Accepting that carrying this peel is associated with a certain cost in terms of discomfort, the rational course of action would be to simply drop it to the ground. The only cost from such action would be the aesthetic one of facing the consequences of littering. If the person does not look back, and is not likely to return to the same path any time soon, that cost may be assumed to be zero. The logical course of action would thus be clear.

What we have here is a version of the classic free rider dilemma. If all actors were to behave in the same instrumentally rational way, the costs in terms of littering would be compounded and all would be worse off. Reality, as we all know, offers plenty of similar illustrations.

Remaining with the case of the banana peel, there are two different ways of addressing the problem. The first agrees with the agency approach. By

[55] David, Paul A. (1994), "Why Are Institutions the 'Carriers of History?': Path Dependence and the Evolution of Conventions, Organizations and Institutions," *Structural Change and Economic Dynamics*, vol. 5, no. 2, p. 205.

introducing a prohibition against littering, and by associating this prohibition with a penalty, it will be possible for society to alter the individual calculus of cost and benefit. For as long as we remain within the framework of instrumentally rational forward-looking behavior, the course of action will hinge on the size of the penalty combined with the risk of detection. By ratcheting up one or both of these to sufficiently high levels, it will be technically possible for society to curb most if not all types of undesirable behavior.

Two factors, however, must be considered here. The first recognizes that the costs of enforcement, relative to the benefit derived from curbing the undesirable behavior, will in many cases be simply prohibitive, and the second that society will not accept penalties that are viewed, on grounds of fairness and morality, as out of proportion to the offense. Both of these combine to seriously constrain the ability of society to rely on modes of formal intervention.

The second option is different in the sense of relying on internalized norms to limit or completely rule out certain types of action. In a veiled reference to Veblen's critique of economic man, North underscores that the fundamental aim of ideology is "to energize groups to behave contrary to a simple, hedonistic, individual calculus of costs and benefits."[56] He also highlights the simple fact that in the absence of such norms, no organized society would be possible: "Indeed, a neoclassical world would be a jungle and no society would be viable."[57]

Let us assume that individuals can be motivated by moral norms, be they religious or ideological, to refrain from certain types of action that are harmful to the common good, or indeed to undertake certain other types of action that are helpful to the common good. If this could be achieved by deliberate intervention, then much would surely stand to be gained. Assume, for example, that the biblical Ten Commandments had been introduced to make the faithful abstain from committing murder, theft, and adultery, and from bearing false testimony. If it really had been within the reach of reformers to promote the evolution and internalization of norms against such behavior, then the reward would have been to greatly relieve the burden on enforcement. While the illustration as such is probably factually incorrect, in the sense of representing religious intervention based on instrumental rationality, it does bring home what is at stake here.

---

[56] North, Douglass C. (1981), *Structure and Change in Economic History*, New York: Norton, p. 53.
[57] Ibid., p. 11.

The fact that all societies make massive investments in nonspecialized education provides evidence of an ambition to communicate tacit knowledge that transcends professional skills: "The educational system in a society is simply not explicable in narrow neoclassical terms, since much of it is obviously directed at inculcating a set of values rather than investing in human capital."[58]

The same may be said about corporate investment in creating a "corporate culture." We may recall here Williamson's account of how the creation of hierarchies will be associated with the emergence of efficient codes of communication and with convergent expectations, all of which combine to create a special "atmosphere." In a similar vein, David suggests that organizations requiring particular channels for dealing with information will evolve or deliberately introduce specific codes that facilitate the filtering, coordination, and compression that is necessary to handle vast flows of information.[59]

The main question that arises here is why societies have not resorted fully to the promotion of such codes or cultures. An important part of the answer may be found if we consider the Soviet attempt to introduce "Soviet Man." If it had indeed proven possible to transform Soviet citizens into actors imbued on the private level with norms that corresponded to those broadcast on the public level, then command economy just might have been practicable after all. As it turned out, however, the attempt resulted in a serious disconnect between public and private worlds, leading not to rule-abiding but rather to extreme forms of rule-avoiding behavior. Perhaps the best account of the many absurdities that resulted may be found in the wildly funny satirical novel *Yawning Heights*, penned by the Soviet writer/philosopher Alexander Zinoviev.[60]

Returning to the case of the banana peel, we may note that individuals who are driven by *moral* norms will abstain from littering no matter what. (They will also honor speed limits on completely empty roads.) Since it is difficult to see how such norms can be transformed, in any meaningful way, by deliberate policy intervention, we shall have nothing more to say on this count. Individuals who in contrast are driven by *social* norms will abstain from littering only if someone else is watching. What makes this case so analytically interesting is that it assumes individual action to be conditioned by consideration not only of personal gain but also of how other people may react.

---

[58] Ibid., p. 54.
[59] David, "Why Are Institutions the 'Carriers of History?,'" pp. 212–13.
[60] Zinoviev, Alexander (1979), *The Yawning Heights*, New York: Random House.

Norm-driven behavior in general is different from instrumentally rational behavior in the sense that it is not outcome-oriented. A norm will prescribe that certain types of action should be taken, or not be taken, irrespective of the outcome. There may be conditionality involved, such that if A then do B, but it never involves rational action in the sense of if you want B then do A. The subcategory of social norms is special in that they must be shared by others and will be sustained by the approval or disapproval of others. Such norms have a powerful grip on the mind because of the strong emotions that their violation can trigger. Most individuals will quite simply be eager to win approval for their actions and fearful of the feelings of embarrassment, anxiety, guilt, and shame that are associated with anticipated disapproval.[61]

This is a complex matter: while actions driven by social norms will to a large extent be "blind, compulsive, mechanical or even unconscious," there will also be cases when there is considerable scope for skill, choice, interpretation, and manipulation. The very fact that we know so little both about both the origins and the functions of many social norms adds to the complications and prompts Elster to conclude that "following the lodestar of outcome-oriented rationality is easy compared with finding one's way in a jungle of social norms."[62]

Recalling our earlier discussion on the contrast, not to say conflict, between the methodological individualism of economics and the methodological holism of sociology, it is important to note that the distinction between rationality and social norms cannot be taken as a mere reflection of the same. It is, for example, Elster's firm conviction that social norms, defined as a "propensity to feel shame and to anticipate sanctions by others at the thought of behaving in a certain, forbidden way," may be fitted into a wholly individualist framework.[63] His point is that the presence of shared beliefs and common emotional reactions must not lead to thinking in terms of norms as supraindividual identities that somehow exist independently of their supports. While sociologists will maintain that the notion of "economic man" represents pure fiction, those who believe methodological individualism to be "trivially true"[64] will maintain that it is arguments on various forms of embeddedness that must be thrown out.

[61] See further Elster, Jon (1989b), *Nuts and Bolts for the Social Sciences*, Cambridge: Cambridge University Press, ch. 12.

[62] Elster, Jon (1989a), *The Cement of Society: A Study of Social Order*, Cambridge: Cambridge University Press, p. 100.

[63] Ibid., pp. 105–06.

[64] Elster, *Nuts and Bolts*, p. 13.

Before concluding our discussion of institutional choice and of limits to deliberate policy intervention, we shall return yet again to the agency approach. By far the greatest of all complications that will arise when we consider the role of norms in motivating human action emerges because so many of those transformations that are key to implementing broad societal reconstruction will come about only as by-products of other action, and often in fashions that again are not well understood.

From the account in our introductory chapter we may recall how Alexis de Tocqueville, in his classic study *Democracy in America*, maintained that the economic success of the United States was essentially a by-product of democratic institution-building. From a more theoretical perspective, Elster emphasizes that many desirable outcomes may simply not be within reach of deliberate policy: "Some mental and social states appear to have the property that they can only come about as the by-product of actions undertaken for other ends. They can never, that is, be brought about intelligently or intentionally, because the very attempt to do so precludes the state one is trying to bring about."[65]

The message here is that while we must remain focused on factors that drive individual action, consideration of such factors must, as we have argued, include the presence of a public culture, or of public norms, that will influence how decisions are made. While the personal motive of greed will always be there, its actual impact will be tempered by the type of public norms that are projected in public debates and are inherent in government policy. The scope for deliberate intervention must be viewed against this background.

Cases where it is obvious to most that overcoming free riding will be helpful to all, such as campaigns to "Keep America Clean," will be very different from cases where deeply engrained social norms prescribe actions that are clearly irrational. Putting an end to littering will pose less of a challenge than putting an end to vendetta and honor killings.

With specific respect to the Russian case, we have argued that ambitions to undertake marketizing reform have been impeded by a set of deeply engrained social norms that are distinctly market-contrary. In the words of Sergei Vasiliev, such norms include "the communal spirit (as opposed to individualism), contempt for commerce as an occupation, mistrust of the rich, especially the newly rich, and a grudge against prosperous neighbors."[66]

---

[65] Elster, Jon (1983), *Sour Grapes: Studies in the Subversion of Rationality*, Cambridge: Cambridge University Press, p. 43.

[66] Vasiliev, Sergei A. (1997), "Economic Reform in Russia: Social, Political and Institutional Aspects," in Anders Aslund (ed.), *Russia's Economic Transformation in the 1990s*, London: Pinter, p. 26.

In the somewhat broader terms that have been used in the this account, we may talk of a pronounced distrust in formal contracts and property rights, of a low degree of trust in government agencies and in individuals outside the network of personalized relations, of a propensity for self-interest seeking with guile, and of a general preference for nonmarket as opposed to market activities. A closer look at the experience of attempted systemic change will serve both to illustrate and to round off the discussion.

SYSTEMIC CHANGE

Accepting North's dictum that institutions are indeed "humanly devised," the general purpose of the present chapter has been to investigate the type of limitations that will constrain ambitions to introduce deliberate institutional change. Departing from the question posed by Greif, concerning what degree of choice individuals within a society will possess in selecting their institutions, we have presented the success story of the "Rise of the West" as a process of evolution, of incremental endogenous change where the introduction of formal rules has proceeded seamlessly in tandem with an ongoing transformation of informal norms. England's Glorious Revolution in particular was advanced as a case where change in the formal rules was successful because it fitted so well into a parallel cultural transformation.

In sharp contrast, we have presented the Russian case as one that is marked by repeated ambitions, often triggered by defeat in war, to introduce exogenous change from above. We have also argued that failures to achieve a corresponding transformation of informal norms have led to repeated reversals. Leaving the reasons behind the latter for discussion in the following chapter, here we shall conclude the argument on institutional choice by recalling again the image of Newton's "great clock."

Russia's most recent ambition to undertake systemic change may be viewed as a clear-cut case of deliberate institutional choice, to be implemented according to the belief in Newtonian mechanics. In consequence, it stands not only as an acid test of the belief in opportunity and self-interest seeking. More profoundly, what in reality amounted to a project of broad societal transformation and reconstruction also constituted a test of our earlier distinction between the agency approach of promoting change by introducing new rules and the evolutionary approach of emphasizing how actors will adapt to such change. For good measure, we may also recall here Schumpeter's distinction between the emphasis of economics on the choices people make and that of sociology on how they come to make those choices.

Beginning with the agency point of view, the policy recommendations that underpinned shock therapy were straightforward enough. Behind catchy slogans of liberalization, stabilization, and privatization, economists were busy formulating seemingly obvious laws and decrees that called for price deregulation, for a cessation of subsidies to state-owned enterprises, for the abolition of multiple exchange rates, and for the privatization of state property, to mention but a few of the items on the agenda. Overall, there was a firm belief that economic policy could and should be formulated without consideration of cultural specificity and/or of differences in historical legacy.

Looking back at the experience of the hyperdepression that followed, we are prompted to switch to the evolutionary perspective. How could deregulation and privatization *not* result in the sure efficiency gains that an application of neoclassical theory would have seemed to promise and that figured so prominently in the reform rhetoric? To be more specific, a successful outcome would have entailed a transformation of the monolithic hierarchy of central planning and its plethora of irrepressible markets into a set of socially contrived markets, based on "market-augmenting government." At the micro level, it would have been associated with the emergence of actors accepting constructive value-adding efforts, in accordance with the image of the invisible hand, as being consistent with self-interest. What did happen was very different – and predictably so. Faced with opportunity, self-interested actors overwhelmingly preferred redistributive over value-adding activities.

The collapse of central control triggered two types of adjustment. One led to the emergence of a set of loosely formed hierarchies that engaged in predatory schemes of asset grabbing and asset stripping. The other led to the emergence of an amorphous informal sector that consisted of actors striving to make a living outside what Hernando de Soto refers to as the "bell jar," that is, outside the realm of legally enforceable transactions on property rights.[67] The combined outcome was substantial "dead capital" and generally low value added. The parallel slump in global commodities markets could only serve to exacerbate these problems.

---

[67] Soto, Hernando de (2000), *The Mystery of Capital: Why Capitalism Triumphs in the West and Fails Everywhere Else*, New York: Basic Books. The quotation, which runs through his presentation, is taken from Fernand Braudel's portrayal of the early capitalist sector of society as living in a bell jar, cut off from and unable to expand and conquer the whole of society (Braudel, Fernand (1992), *Civilization and Capitalism: 15th – 18th Century, Vol. 2, The Wheels of Commerce*, Berkeley: University of California Press).

Recalling Williamson's discussion of the distribution of transactions, we again have a familiar case of unaccountability in government that is associated with a poorly functioning judiciary, and hence also with a bimodal distribution of transactions that remains inconsistent with a high-performance economy. It is symptomatic that much the same story could be told for other former Soviet republics, notably in Central Asia, that have a long heritage of being subjects of the Russian Empire, and that the only true exceptions to the rule may be found in the three Baltic republics.

Having a long-term history of being no more than Russian borderlands and a recent history of reasonably democratic rules-based market economies, the Baltics have been successful in reshaping "Western" identities that have supported the introduction of "market-augmenting" institutions. In line with what has been said, the introduction of new formal rules proceeded hand in hand with transformation or restoration of supporting informal norms. While some doubt may still remain as to just how robust this transformation has been, there can be little doubt about the contrast vis-à-vis Russia. The same will hold for several countries in Central Europe, where inclusion into the European Union has failed to be fully associated with the envisioned progress toward a functioning market economy.

In conclusion, we may note as a very special case the process of German unification, which did represent a very deliberate institutional choice. Over a period of four decades, the economy of the German Democratic Republic was locked into the "hierarchy of command." The outcome was a massive degradation of infrastructure and technology, as well as of physical capital in general. If this had been the end of the story, inclusion into the then still highly successful market economy of the Federal Republic and the associated allocation of massive investment should have led to a rapid turnaround and to equalization of living standards. It did not. Close to two decades later the economy of the eastern parts of the country remained a major headache.

Accepting that the two Germanies were populated by people with very similar long-term cultural and historical legacies, a tentative explanation must focus on the impact of a fairly brief postwar experience. Being locked into playing the games of command economy that have been laid out in detail, Germans in the GDR were subjected to a process of unlearning by doing, that is, to developing a set of skills, and human capital more generally, that was distinctly market-contrary. At the core of this process we may find exposure to a set of social norms that have been traced back to Muscovite times. The persisting troubles illustrate that the impact of the rather short-term exposure to the market-contrary social order of the GDR has outweighed the longer term heritage of the rules-based market economy. Perhaps this can be taken as evidence that corrupting the foundations of a sound market order is easier than to set things right again.

The time that it will take for the two Germanies to be united in a more profound sense will hinge critically on the prospects for two distinctively different sets of social norms to be harmonized and, one hopes, to converge on the ideal of support for democracy and a rules-based market economy. It is somehow symptomatic of the fragility of the institutional constituency of this ideal that two decades after formal unification, Germans on the two sides still talk about a *Mauer im Kopf,* a "wall in the head." Bearing these somber comments in mind, let us now look more closely at the argument for how culture and history may matter.

7

History Matters

To state that history matters is at once trivial and highly challenging. It is trivial in the sense that neither humans nor indeed organizations, or even states, can ever be assumed to live entirely in the present, and it is challenging in that it confronts us with a need to show causality. For it to be credible, an argument that history influences current affairs must entail more than simply mapping out striking historical parallels. The true challenge here lies in identifying processes whereby decisions taken in the past, even in the distant past, continue to exert non-trivial influence over decisions that are taken in the present.

In the following, we shall attempt to meet this challenge, and we shall do so by scrutinizing a set of very different approaches to establishing linkage between past and present. Given our overriding focus on the role of economics, it is only logical that economic approaches will be placed on center stage. We shall, however, also look at similar ambitions from scholars in sociology and in political science, all in line with our endeavor to outline how the role of history may be usefully incorporated into social science analysis more broadly.

Given the magnitude of this undertaking, the envisioned outline can be no more than tentative. Yet simply asking the right questions may take us a fair bit of the way toward resolving the multiplicity of problems that have been brought up in previous chapters.

To begin with an extreme illustration of when history clearly does *not* matter, we may consider the chess computer, which will never look back. Programmed to be perfectly rational and always forward looking, it will process all available information and compute an optimal move. In short, it will act in perfect conformity with the assumptions that underlie "economic man." While all would agree that no human action will ever be perfectly describable in such terms, the assumptions of the neoclassical economic tradition come close. Much of the critique that we have seen aimed at this tradition, from the times of Thorstein Veblen to those of James Coleman, has in consequence been focused mainly on the reduction of complex motivation for human action to formally elegant simplicity.

As we have also seen, ambitions to add realism have emphasized that humans will frequently act in accordance with the assumptions of bounded rationality. They will have to make decisions based on information that is incomplete and may be distorted. Their ability to process that information is constrained by a variety of factors, and they will at times be motivated to act with guile. Most important of all, however, they will indeed be prone to look back.

Similar things may be said with respect to firms, organizations, and states. While we may have different opinions on whether such non-human entities can be reasonably described as having a will, it should be quite clear that they all have collective or organizational memories and that they all do cultivate identities – ranging from corporate culture to national self-imagery – that are deliberately and intrinsically linked with events in history, real or fictional. The substantial efforts and resources that are devoted to maintaining and propagating such memories and identities will illustrate that we are faced here with important mechanisms of motivation and coordination.

The question that must now be approached concerns what, more specifically, actors see when they look back. The trivial dimension of the answer will include a whole range of features, from physical legacies of things that have been built to mental legacies of tradition and of course sheer inertia. None of this is unimportant. Matters such as the quality of existing infrastructure and of embodied technology will determine the leeway for economic policy choice, and memories of the way in which we have always done things will act as a drag on the potential for change.

Yet to meet the core of the challenge outlined previously we must add one further component. For it to be analytically important, historical influence must interfere with rational forward-looking utility or profit maximization. More specifically, history will matter in a non-trivial sense only when it can be shown to prevent market forces from weeding out inferior institutional solutions, in politics as well as in the economic marketplace.

To drive this point home, recall the previously outlined success story, which features a good deal of cumulative historical influence. In our presentation of an evolutionary process we may find an ongoing accumulation of experience, steadily enhanced technological prowess, incremental additions to physical capital, and the formation of supporting beliefs, expectations, and norms. All of these feed into and seamlessly support subsequent steps in the chain. How the process of endogenously driven success unfolded is an intriguing story in its own. It is, however, fundamentally different from what we are seeking to tell here.

There are good reasons that studying the causes of systemic failure will be more rewarding than simply trying to refine even further our knowledge of how successes have been achieved. Accepting the rather obvious need to address and alleviate the widespread social and economic costs of failure, we are faced here with serious shortcomings in social science theorizing. Not only do observations of failure go so clearly against the grain of the positive message of the liberal economic tradition and of the associated urge to abstain from intervening in markets. Even more so, in cases where the causes of failure in the present are rooted in the past, it becomes imperative to ensure that theorizing succeeds in capturing such influence. The latter constitutes the core of the challenge in this chapter.

The discussion here shall remain largely within the previous chapter's framework of contrasting the agency approach of economics against the structural approach of sociology. Arguing that history matters will in the agency approach depart from assumptions of instrumentally rational behavior, maintaining that past decisions have become embodied in investments that affect a calculus of costs and benefits. In the structural approach, actors will be viewed as captives of the past, in the extreme case as "mindless playthings" of private or collective memories. In both cases, we shall be looking at inferior institutional solutions that are stubbornly resistant to change – as theoretically superior solutions become available. Let us begin by looking at the role of history in economics.

HISTORY AND ECONOMICS

At a casual glance, it might be tempting to argue that there is a whole discipline of its own that deals with history and economics, namely, that of economic history. Although there are quite a few prominent scholars around, including some Nobel Prize laureates, who may be loosely grouped under this heading, the discipline as such is far from distinct and coherent.

As a field of learning, economic history grew up at the end of the nineteenth century. Its sources of inspiration were derived partly from the German historical school and partly "from the profuse use of historical illustrations by Adam Smith, Karl Marx, Alfred Marshall, and others as they expounded economic theory."[1] In the interwar years it became obvious

---

[1] Kindleberger, Charles P. (1990), *Historical Economics: Art or Science?*, New York: Harvester Wheatsheaf, p. 12.

that the discipline was destined for serious conflict over whether it should stand alone, with its own departments, teaching programs, and professional societies, or be integrated into economics or indeed into history. Over time, however, its affiliation with economics would become ever more pronounced, and with the birth, in the 1960s, of "new economic history," based on "cliometrics," the study of economic history had been firmly integrated into the neoclassical tradition.[2]

Although dissidents may be found, the generally increasing prominence of statistical and mathematical models is deeply symptomatic of just how far the modern discipline of economic history has been removed from German historicism. While it is certainly true that much valuable research has resulted from this new endeavor, it is also true that the de facto invasion of neoclassical economics into the realm of history has caused the former to effectively lose sight of the past.

As Graeme Snooks puts it, in a collection of papers on historical analysis in economics, the "most telling observation about modern economics is that the dimension of time has been lost." This, to his mind, is highly deplorable: "If the most important and pressing problems require a realistic analysis of the dynamics of human society, and if modern economics is unable to tell us much about this matter, then how seriously should society take this science?"[3] Others have phrased it even more to the point, notably Geoffrey Hodgson whose argument on how economics forgot history will figure prominently in our discussion.[4]

The Neoclassical Paradigm

The bottom line is that any ambition to introduce elements of historical and/or cultural specificity into the mainstream of economic analysis must begin by addressing the position of near-total hegemony that has been

---

[2] The origin of "cliometrics" is normally associated with the publication of Conrad, Alfred H. and John R. Meyer (1958), "The Economics of Slavery in the Ante-Bellum South," *Journal of Political Economy*, vol. 66, no. 2, pp. 95–130. A cliometric society was founded in 1983, and in 1993 Douglass North and Robert Fogel were awarded the Nobel Prize "for having renewed research in economic history by applying economic theory and quantitative methods in order to explain economic and institutional change." See also North, Douglass C. (1974), "Beyond the New Economic History," *Journal of Economic History*, vol. 34, no. 1, pp. 1–7.

[3] Snooks, Graeme D. (ed.) (1993a), *Historical Analysis in Economics*, London: Routledge, p. 1.

[4] Hodgson, Geoffrey M. (2001), *How Economics Forgot History: The Problem of Historical Specificity in Social Science*, London: Routledge.

achieved by the neoclassical tradition. As once noted by Thomas Kuhn, triumphant paradigms always revise the history of their fields.[5] In the case at hand, it is easy to be misled into believing that we are looking at a straight and unbroken tradition, stretching back to the publication, in 1890, of Alfred Marshall's classic *Principles of Economics*. This is problematic in the sense that rival traditions are perceived as theoretically less fit and thus best forgotten.

Although the influence of Marshall is hard to overstate, it is of equal importance to note that it would take decades for his introduction of marginal analysis, also known as the "marginal revolution," to win general acceptance. As Yuval Yonay points out in his exposition on the "struggle over the soul of economics," marginal analysis did gain wide acceptance at the end of the nineteenth century, and it did become part of the economic curriculum. Yet it was only one topic of many of equal importance: "It did not become the basic tool of economists until after World War II. Until then one could have been a successful economist without mastering or even knowing much about marginal analysis."[6]

Competing schools or traditions ranged from Marxism and German historicism to the emerging American institutionalism. Leaving Marxism aside, it is worth noting that for all his subsequent fame as "father" of the neoclassical tradition, which is fundamentally *deductive*, Marshall was no stranger to the *inductive*, that is, empirical, approaches of historicism and institutionalism.[7]

Perhaps most important, Marshall must not be dragooned into serving as a link between the ideal of laissez-faire that is associated with Adam Smith and the strong aversion to government intervention in the market that would mark the later neoclassical tradition. On the contrary, the early neoclassical economists shared with Smith great sensitivity to cases where private and public interests may not be in harmony, and where

---

[5] Kuhn's argument is that the emergence of a new "paradigm" will cause older schools to gradually disappear: "In part their disappearance is caused by the members' conversion to the new paradigm. But there are always some men who cling to one or another of the older views, and they are simply read out of the profession, which thereafter ignores their work" (Kuhn, Thomas S. (1962), *The Structure of Scientific Revolutions*, Chicago: University of Chicago Press, pp. 18–19). Although he speaks of "scientific revolutions" in the natural sciences, the Marshallian "marginal revolution" in economics would seem to qualify as a very similar case.

[6] Yonay, Yuval P. (1998), *The Struggle over the Soul of Economics: Institutionalist and Neoclassical Economists in America between the Wars*, Princeton, NJ: Princeton University Press, p. 31.

[7] Ibid., p. 32.

government intervention hence becomes necessary. The latter, as we may recall, would also constitute something of a raison d'être for the American institutionalists.

Summing up, Yonay reaches a conclusion that is very much in line with the argument pursued here, namely, that the leading school in British economics was well aware of the complexities of human nature and of the major role that institutions play in shaping human behavior: "It saw historical studies as an integral part of economic science and rejected the view that the economy was best left alone."[8] A century later, such insights would have been largely forgotten.

Accepting that the modern discipline of economics has been reduced to an essentially *ahistoric* venture in refined formal modeling, we shall proceed now to look at how the theory of "path dependence" was developed, to allow for a treatment of historical influence firmly *within* the neoclassical paradigm.

Path Dependence

Originating in works published by Paul David and Brian Arthur in the 1980s, the path dependence approach has presented a set of convincing arguments on how early random events may result in a path of development where inferior solutions survive. The chief implication for mainstream economic theory has been to show that early choices of technology may become locked in, proving highly resistant to change. Instead of one uniquely defined general equilibrium we must hence reckon with multiple equilibria, some of which are clearly inferior.

The first and still most frequently cited illustration, suggested by David in 1985, was that of the QWERTY typewriter keyboard.[9] Originally introduced

---

[8] Ibid., p. 35.

[9] David, Paul A. (1985), "Clio and the Economics of QWERTY," *American Economic Review*, vol. 75, no. 2, pp. 332–37. Other illustrations have ranged from the victory of VHS over Betamax as a standard for videocassette recorders, to the triumph of light-water nuclear reactors in the United States, the struggles between Microsoft and Macintosh computers, and competing standards for matters such as electrical current and railroad gauge. (See further, Puffert, Douglas J. (2003), "Path Dependence, Network Form, and Technological Change," in W. Sundstrom, T. Guinnane, and W. Whatley (eds.), *History Matters: Essays on Economic Growth, Technology, and Demographic Change*, Stanford, CA: Stanford University Press, pp. 80–88. For ample reference to studies of these various alternative cases, see also Mahoney, James (2000), "Path Dependence in Historical Sociology," *Theory and Society*, vol. 29, no. 4, p. 512, fn. 24.) While it should be recognized that some of these illustrations have been challenged on purely technical grounds, such debates are beside the point here.

by the arms maker Remington in 1873, for the simple reason that it allowed a salesperson to quickly type the words TYPE WRITER, subsequent studies would show that alternative arrangements of the keys allowed for greater speed in typing. Despite the availability of a clearly superior alternative, market forces would fail to weed out the inferior one.[10]

David offers three explanations for this puzzle, all of which are fairly straightforward. The first concerns technical *interrelatedness* between the hardware of the keyboard and the software that resides in the typist's memory. The second points at *system scale economies,* in the combined sense that employers will prefer to purchase hardware for which there is a ready supply of software, and that typists will seek to acquire those skills that are in highest demand. The market will hence converge on one standard. By historical chance this standard happened to be QWERTY, which initially had only a slender lead over competing designs. The third explanation is that while the costs of retraining typists did not come down, hardware conversion costs fell rapidly. In consequence, the software came to be marked by a *quasi-irreversibility of investments.*[11]

The compelling message of this illustration is threefold. *First,* historical accidents play a greater role in determining the growth paths and the technological development of various economies than is generally thought. *Second,* despite freedom of competition and free access to information, such growth paths may remain locked into inferior choices over an extended

---

[10] Particularly harsh critique against the theory of path dependence has been presented by Stanley Liebowitz and Stephen Margolis. Beginning by denying the technical validity of the QWERTY illustration, they proceeded to launch a broad assault on the relevance of the theory as such. (See Liebowitz, S. J. and Stephen E. Margolis (1990), "The Fable of the Keys," *Journal of Law and Economics,* vol. 33, no. 1, pp. 1–25; Liebowitz, S. J. and Stephen E. Margolis (1994), "Network Externality: An Uncommon Tragedy," *Journal of Economic Perspectives,* vol. 8, no. 2, pp. 133–50; Liebowitz, S. J. and Stephen E. Margolis (1995a), "Are Network Externalities a New Source of Market Failure?," *Research in Law and Economics,* vol. 17, no. 0, pp. 1–22; Liebowitz, S. J. and Stephen E. Margolis (1995b), "Path Dependence, Lock-in, and History," *Journal of Law, Economics, and Organization,* vol. 11, no. 1, pp. 205–26; Liebowitz, S. J. and Stephen E. Margolis (1995c), "Policy and Path Dependence: From QWERTY to Windows 95," *Regulation: The Cato Review of Business & Government,* vol. 3, pp. 33–41. For a rebuttal, see David, Paul (1997), "Path Dependence and the Quest for Historical Economics: One More Chorus of the Ballad of QWERTY," *Discussion Papers in Economic and Social History,* no. 20, November, available at http://www.nuffield.ox.ac.uk/economics/history/paper20/david3.pdf, accessed on November 9, 2009, and David, Paul A. (2001), "Path Dependence, Its Critics and the Quest for 'Historical Economics,'" in Pierre Garrouste and Stavros Ioannides (eds.), *Evolution and Path Dependence in Economic Ideas: Past and Present,* Cheltenham: Edward Elgar.

[11] David, "Clio and the Economics of QWERTY," pp. 332–36.

period of time, and, *third*, "irreversibilities due to learning and habituation" play an important role in the creation of such lock-in effects.[12]

Shortly after the publication of David's seminal article, Brian Arthur set out to explain and formally model how small random events in history can cause an economy to lock in to a technology that is inferior in development potential. Departing from a realization of the possible presence of positive feedback, or of increasing returns, which deviates from the traditional neoclassical assumption of diminishing returns on the margin, he identified four "generic sources" of self-reinforcing mechanisms that may combine to produce an outcome where the inferior technology wins out.[13]

The first is *large setup or fixed costs*, implying that unit costs will decrease as production expands. The second is *learning effects*, meaning that an increased prevalence of the product will lead to improved quality or lower cost. Third, *coordination effects* will arise from cooperation with economic agents who are involved in similar ventures, and fourth, *adaptive expectations* will ensure that increased prevalence on the market enhances consumer beliefs in further prevalence.

The final outcome will be marked by the following four properties: (a) there will be multiple equilibria, implying that the outcome of the process is indeterminate, (b) inefficient solutions are possible, so that an inferior technology may win out, (c) a lock-in can occur, which may prove difficult to break out of, and (d) there is path dependence, so that small and/or chance historical events may determine the chosen path.

In a later book-length contribution, Arthur emphasizes that the notion of multiple equilibria lies at the very core of what path dependence is about: "I became convinced that the key obstacle for economics in dealing with increasing returns was the indeterminacy introduced by the possibility of multiple equilibria." And the possibility of different equilibria in turn follows from the presence of increasing returns. What remains to ask is how to analyze the path that leads the system toward one or the other of these equilibria: "What was needed therefore was a method to handle the question of how one equilibrium, one solution, one structure, of the several possible came to be 'selected' in an increasing returns problem."[14]

[12] Ibid., p. 336.
[13] Arthur, W. Brian (1988), "Self-Reinforcing Mechanisms in Economics," in Philip W. Anderson, Kenneth J. Arrow, and David Pines (eds.), *The Economy as an Evolving Complex System*, Reading, MA: Addison-Wesley, p. 10 and *passim*. See also Arthur, W. Brian (1989), "Competing Technologies, Increasing Returns, and Lock-In by Historical Events," *Economic Journal*, vol. 99, March, pp. 116–31.
[14] Arthur, W. Brian (1994), *Increasing Returns and Path Dependence in the Economy*, Ann Arbor: University of Michigan Press, p. xv.

In a foreword to Arthur's book, Kenneth Arrow outlines the troubles generations of economists have had in coming to terms with the presence of increasing returns, which creates trouble for elegant theories that are based on assumptions of constant returns. He also compliments Arthur for contributing a solution: "It is in this context that Brian Arthur's precise and fully modeled papers caused us all to understand clearly and specifically what kinds of models have what kinds of implications."[15]

To sum up, the hallmark of the original theory of path dependence is that it does not stray far from the mainstream of neoclassical theory. The approaches of both David and Arthur are rooted in generally accepted theoretical formulations and are amenable to formal modeling. It is when we leave the highly distinct realm of technological choice that the waters begin to muddy. As we will show, the arguments listed previously can be transferred to explain how path dependence arises in historical development more generally. With respect to the crucial dimension of causality, however, the outcomes will be far less rigorously modeled.[16]

Before we proceed to look at such ambitions, pursued by scholars from across the social sciences, it will be useful to say a few more words about "dissidence" within the economics profession, expressed in terms of a plea for "historical economics."

Historical Economics

One of the foremost exponents of broadening the scope of economics was Charles Kindleberger, who died in 2003 at the age of ninety-two. A self-confessed "literary economist," he used his prestigious position as professor of economics at MIT as a lectern of sorts from which to issue unrelenting critique of the growing reliance of the profession on mathematics and on narrow models of rational human behavior. His best-known book, *Manias, Panics and Crashes*, which appeared in 1978, outlined how new discoveries have tended to result in expanded credit growth, causing a frenzy of speculation for short-term gain. As markets realize that a bubble is emerging, the initial mania is transformed into panic, and a crash becomes inevitable.[17]

---

[15] Ibid., pp. ix–x.
[16] While the original theory was based on self-reinforcing mechanisms that could be rigorously modeled, as the concept began to proliferate it often came to be loosely understood as an argument that history matters more generally, which is a wholly different proposition. As an illustration of just how broadly the concept has proliferated, note that a Google search for "path dependence" generated close to 2.5 million hits (on November 21, 2009).
[17] Kindleberger, Charles P. (1978), *Manias, Panics, and Crashes: A History of Financial Crises*, London: Macmillan.

Departing from the Dutch Tulip Bulb bubble in 1636, and the British South Sea bubble in 1720, Kindleberger's account demonstrated that the history of financial crises is interwoven with a number of common threads, all of which are of essential importance for a proper understanding of how government regulation should be devised. The implied argument was at loggerheads with the then prevailing efficient-market hypothesis, which essentially ruled out the possibility of bubbles in settings other than immature and fraud-prone markets.

In an obituary column, *The Economist* emphasized that Kindleberger had been fortunate in living long enough to see his views vindicated with a vengeance.[18] Following the stock market crash in 1987, the Asian meltdown of 1997–98, and the dotcom bubble that burst in 2001, studying bubbles became the rage in all of academia. Reprinted in 2000, Kindleberger's work also became essential reading on Wall Street. Given that all of this took place well before the collapse of Lehman Brothers and the ensuing global financial crisis, we may recall what was said in our introductory chapter, namely, that it is striking how little is actually learned and how much is so rapidly forgotten. The only thing we learn from history seems to be that we do not learn from history.

Kindleberger strove hard to change this, mainly by entering a plea for the profession to embrace an approach of "historical economics," which would be more encompassing than economic history. In *Historical Economics: Art or Science?* he set out by deploring that "economic history itself has bifurcated into cliometrics, manipulating statistics and models to try to prove contentions in history, or more generally disprove those of others, and traditional economic history, which is more inductive."[19] His own position was clearly stated:

I happen to profess historical economics, rather than economic history, using historical episodes to test economic models for their generality. Many economic models are plausible and will fit particular circumstances; the question is how general they are and how much one can rely on them to provide understanding and wisdom in particular circumstances.[20]

In a panel organized to honor the life and work of Charles Kindleberger, Ronald Findlay highlights as his "unique contribution to our discipline" the restoration of history as "an essential dimension of the economic analysis

---

[18] www.princeton.edu/~markus/research/papers/bubbles_crashes_media_mention_
July2003.pdf, accessed on November 21, 2009.

[19] Kindleberger, *Historical Economics*, p. 3.

[20] Ibid., pp. 3–4.

of international trade, business cycles, financial panics, economic development, or, indeed, of almost any economic phenomenon whatsoever." Concerning the man himself, Findlay notes that "he was an historical economist, a remarkable and inextricable blend of both economist and economic historian, rather than one or the other."[21]

The question that must now be asked concerns whether all of this simply reflects the qualities of one man, or if it can be taken to be reflective of a deeper need to develop an at least partially new discipline. Proceeding to address this question, we shall agree with Snooks that the argument is not that we should abandon what has been achieved by deductive economics. It is rather that "we should augment it with an historical analysis of both shortrun and longrun economic problems – problems that are an integral part of the dynamic processes of human society."[22]

For a more precise argument on how this may be achieved, we shall return to Paul David. In a later contribution, following his introduction of the formal theory of path dependence, he elaborates on a theme that is of great relevance to our understanding of the development of social science. Departing from the general belief in strict "laws of nature" that marked the eighteenth century, he shows how not only the natural but also the social sciences – notably economics – came to be profoundly influenced in the direction of indifference to the role of history.

From Adam Smith onward, economists have been drawn further and further into modeling where the influence of initial conditions is reduced to the point of insignificance. By assuming that social change, like that of nature in the world of Darwin, is always "slow, gradual and continuous," economics could be made amenable to analysis by mathematical techniques of infinitesimal calculus. In the end we are left with a situation where, as noted above, "much of modern economics remains essentially *ahistorical*."[23]

With reference to the growing interest that physicists and philosophers of physics had begun to show for matters of causation, that is, to ask not only *how* but also *why* things happen, David argues that the inattention by economists to matters of causal explanation "has impoverished modern economic theory." He then makes a plea for historical economics, which would be aimed at "understanding the reasons why particular sequences

---

[21] Findlay, Ronald (2005), "Kindleberger: Economics and History," *Atlantic Economic Journal*, vol. 33, no. 1, p. 19.

[22] Snooks, *Historical Analysis in Economics*, pp. 1–2.

[23] David, Paul (1993), "Historical Economics in the Long Run: Some Implications of Path Dependence," in Graeme D. Snooks (ed.), *Historical Analysis in Economics*, London: Routledge, p. 29.

of events in the past are capable of exerting persisting effects upon current conditions."[24]

While there are good reasons indeed to agree with these pleas for a new departure, which would make economics more sensitive to lasting influences of history, it remains that demonstrating a need is not exactly the same as providing a cure. The core question here concerns what it would take for modern economics to adjust and measure up to the challenge of introducing elements of history, not to mention culture, into the mainstream of analysis. In search for an answer, we shall proceed to the other end of the spectrum and look at calls for American institutionalism to be resurrected.

Resurrecting Old Institutionalism

The main line of the critique against how modern economics has been reduced to an ahistoric exercise in elegant modeling may be viewed as a continuation of the struggle between institutionalists and neoclassical economists that raged in the early decades of the twentieth century. As that struggle in turn could be led back to a seemingly unbridgeable methodological divide between deductive and inductive approaches to science, what we are dealing with here is the very nature of what we understand as science, and as acceptable scientific method. In the following, we have no ambition to grapple with these issues as such. We shall, however, use the debate over scientific method as a background against which to present the complexity of reintroducing history into the study of economic matters.

The fork in the road where classical political economy was set on a path that would lead to neoclassical economics, and to modern mathematical economics, may be dated back to the times of David Ricardo. As we noted, Adam Smith was both ready and able to combine deductive theory-building with empirical investigation and verification. It was Ricardo who, in the words of Snooks, "completely divorced economic model building from the experience of the past." It was he who "stripped economics of everything he considered superfluous to the economic problem under consideration, including history, sociology, philosophy, and the institutional setting."[25]

Considered quite unique at the time, Ricardo's ambition to simplify and generalize was not without critics. Thomas Malthus, for example, spoke of it

---

[24] Ibid.
[25] Snooks, Graeme D. (1993b), "The Lost Dimension: Limitations of a Timeless Economics," in Snooks (ed.), *Historical Analysis in Economics*, London: Routledge, p. 47.

as "precipitate," and retained for himself a more balanced ambition to combine deduction with elements of historical method.[26] Over time, as we know, the marginal revolution and the increasing reliance on sophisticated mathematics would cause the deductive method to become deeply entrenched. It would, however, remain controversial. In his previously cited attack on how modern economics has forgotten history, Hodgson quotes the following from a 1933 essay by Keynes: "If only Malthus, instead of Ricardo, had been the parent stem from which nineteenth century economics proceeded, what a much wiser and richer place the world would be today!"[27]

Given the fervor with which some scholars presently seek to rehabilitate the historical-inductive method, it is important to note that even the harshest critics of neoclassical economics will recognize that deductive theory has been extraordinarily successful: "The outstanding success story of the social sciences, particularly during the post-Second World War period, has been the rise of the discipline of economics."[28] Economics stands out as the only social science that is included in the illustrious circle of Nobel Prize awards. Its distinctly tribal culture and firmly enforced pecking order has also wielded such influence that neighboring tribes have responded with critique of "economic imperialism."[29]

Recognizing these advances, Snooks deplores the associated collateral damage, that is, that the "emergence of economics as a deductively-based discipline ... has led to the downgrading of the importance of applied economics in general and economic history in particular." The core of his argument is that "the discipline has been transformed from the practical empirical art of political economy to the abstract deductive science of economics."[30]

The main question to be asked here concerns whether the lost heritage from institutionalists and historicists really can be usefully incorporated into modern economics. It is one thing to note that "between the two World Wars the institutionalists themselves were the mainstream,"[31] and to recall Kuhn's observation on how "triumphant paradigms" always rewrite history.

---

[26] His full verdict was that "the principal cause of error, and of the differences which prevail at present among the scientific writers in political economy, appears to me to be a precipitate attempt to simplify and generalize" (cited in ibid., p. 48).

[27] Hodgson, *How Economics Forgot History*, p. 5.

[28] Snooks, "The Lost Dimension," p. 41.

[29] Granovetter, Mark (1992b), "Problems of Explanation in Economic Sociology," in Nitin Nohria and Robert G. Eccles (eds.), *Networks and Organizations: Structure, Form and Action*, Boston, MA: Harvard Business School Press, p. 33.

[30] Ibid., p. 42.

[31] Hodgson, *How Economics Forgot History*, p. 4.

Anyone arguing the case for rehabilitation must realize that the institution-alists did not constitute a "school," in the traditional understanding of hav-ing a unified and coherent common approach, and that in consequence they failed to develop a consistent theory of their own that could challenge the neoclassical paradigm.

The case for the defense is further weakened because the old institution-alists failed to hold their ground. The English historical school held out at the London School of Economics, protected by Sidney and Beatrice Webb, but was effectively pushed out via the appointments of John Hicks in 1926, of Lionel Robbins in 1929, and of Friedrich von Hayek in 1931.[32] Although the Americans held out a bit longer, they were far too divided to present effective resistance. While Thorstein Veblen and his followers wished to discard neoclassic theory as a whole, John Commons and Wesley Mitchell claimed to form part of the mainstream and argued merely for expanding the scope of economics.

The response from Yonay, one of the most ardent modern defenders of the old institutionalists, is that they did indeed have a theory, albeit of a different kind from the neoclassical one. Arguing that institutionalism con-stituted a "prospering, mighty and fertile school," he enters a strong plea for revisitation.[33] Based on a careful scrutiny of the early debates between institutionalists and neoclassicists, he advances three pivotal issues that separated the two camps and that still appear as main battle lines.[34]

The *first* concerns the core question of what constitutes proper science. Against the standard argument that historicism amounted to little more than an atheoretical collection of masses of data, the institutionalists retorted that economic systems cannot be viewed as mechanical systems, and that the mounting complexity of the social world placed economics in danger of being reduced to metaphysics. The lasting validity of this charge is reflected in Snooks's warning that economics remains in "very real dan-ger of becoming a branch of metaphysics and hence being irrelevant to the practical world of mankind."[35] While the neoclassicists on their side have conceded that parallels to the world of physics are imperfect, they remain insistent that deviations from rational and predictable behavior are suffi-ciently small to be ignored. The bottom line is that weighing simplicity of

[32] Snooks, "The Lost Dimension," p. 51. For a broader background, see also Hodgson, *How Economics Forgot History*, ch. 5.
[33] Yonay, *The Struggle over the Soul of Economics*, pp. 75–76.
[34] Ibid., ch. 4–5 and *passim*.
[35] Snooks, "The Lost Dimension," p. 43.

modeling against empirical vindication calls for a judgment to be made on the relative importance of aberrations.

The *second* point of disagreement is similar in nature. Focused on the assumptions of hedonism and rationality that underpin the notion of economic man, this debate has seen institutionalists joined by sociologists and other social scientists in condemning the gross lack of realism in such assumptions. Although once advanced in earnest, for example, by Stanley Jevons, later neoclassical economists have conceded that the associated view of human nature is indeed much too simple. Their line of defense has again been drawn at what is relevant. Maintaining that learning and adaptation constitute powerful correctives, the neoclassicists remain insistent that in the long run actors will abide by the laws of demand. Modeling may hence proceed "as if" the assumptions of economic man were justified. Which side is correct will thus again boil down to what we believe about the size and relevance of aberrations.

The *third* point is somewhat different. Pointing at structural complexities in the modern economy, the institutionalists challenged the assumption of perfect competition that was at the core of the neoclassical case. Listing imperfections that range from advertising and salesmanship, to environmental pollution, lacking occupational safety, overutilization of natural resources, and recurring depressions, a powerful case was made for intervention by the visible hand of the legislator. While many of these have since been incorporated into mainstream economics, under the label of "externalities," it remains debatable to what extent the full message of old institutionalism really has been absorbed.

In sharp contrast to the neoclassicists, the institutionalists were driven by ambitions to get their hands dirty, to approach and deal with mounting social problems in a rapidly changing world. They felt a need to emphasize the practical usefulness of their work and believed that this required inductive approaches. It also was in the area of social engineering that American institutionalism was the most influential, albeit differentially so.

The legacy of Wesley Mitchell is the least controversial. His contributions to the empirical and quantitative method laid much of the groundwork for economic forecasting that remains an important part of economic policy making. The role of John Commons was somewhat different. While his focus on welfare legislation contributed to the formulation of President Roosevelt's New Deal, his emphasis on the visible hand of the state has been overridden by the neo-liberal drive for minimal government, and his more encompassing definition of institutions has been largely forgotten. By far, however, the most controversial component of old institutionalism remains associated with Thorstein Veblen, who was the first of the institutionalists and whose vehement denunciation of neoclassicism served to burn many bridges. Can we usefully rescue something out of his emphasis on the role of psychology, and on the difference between making money and making goods? The neoclassical response will be largely negative, based on the understanding that only consistent deductive theory can render economic science truly useful.

The most vociferous opposition to this by now deeply ingrained attitude within mainstream economics emanates from Geoffrey Hodgson. In one of a long series of publications on institutions, evolution, historicism, and old institutionalism, he symbolically pays specific homage to Veblen: "It may take one hundred years from Veblen's death in 1929 for him to be recognized by social scientists as one of the leading social theorists of all time."[36] Driving the message home, he cites the following from Frank Hahn: "What the dead had to say, when of value, has long since been absorbed, and when we need to say it again we can generally say it better."[37] His own comment is that Hahn ignores the possibility that "much of value has simply been forgotten."[38]

An important dimension of Hodgson's critique concerns what he refers to as the "limits of explanatory unification in social science."[39] Earlier we charted the impact of Newtonian mechanics on the evolution of social science in general and on economics in particular. Speaking of the "lure of a general theory," Hodgson notes that there is nothing strange in this per se, that it lies in the nature of science to strive for general theories in an ambition to try to unify. As an extreme case he advances the search in physics for a TOE (Theory of Everything) or a GUT (Grand Unified Theory).

It is, however, imperative to note that there is a world of difference between the social and the natural or hard sciences: "A theory that every event is caused by the gods is an explanatory unification, but it is of little scientific significance. Likewise … a non-falsifiable general theory such as 'everyone is a utility maximizer' is also of little explanatory value."[40] While

[36] Hodgson, Geoffrey M. (2004), *The Evolution of Institutional Economics: Agency, Structure and Darwinism in American Institutionalism*, London: Routledge, p. 9. For a detailed exposition of "Veblenian institutionalism," see ibid., part III. On the broader background, see also Hodgson, Geoffrey M. (1999), *Evolution and Institutions: On Evolutionary Economics and the Evolution of Economics*, Cheltenham: Edward Elgar.

[37] Hahn, Frank (1992), "Autobiographical Notes with Reflections," in Michael Szenberg (ed.), *Eminent Economists: Their Life Philosophies*, Cambridge: Cambridge University Press, p. 165.

[38] Hodgson, *How Economics Forgot History*, p. xv.

[39] Ibid., p. 4.

[40] Ibid.

he is careful to note that the intention is not to discard deductive theory, he remains insistent that we must recognize the limits to its explanatory power. Given that utility maximization in particular can be made to fit *any* type of behavior, what it helps explain is dubious. We shall return to this in our final chapter.

Another and perhaps even more important strand in Hodgson's critique concerns "historical specificity," that is, the understanding that different socioeconomic phenomena may require theories that are in some respects different from each other: "An adequate theory of (say) the feudal system may differ from an adequate theory of (say) capitalism."[41] Once we recognize the presence of different types of socioeconomic systems, in time as well as in space, it follows that we can no longer subscribe to the common acceptance of one theory that fits all. Recognizing that such systems will share many common features, the challenge will be to identify significant underlying differences.

To the extent that such differences really can be identified, and particularistic theories built, we also have found an important factor that serves to demarcate the social from the physical sciences. As Hodgson notes, while socioeconomic systems have changed a great deal over the past few millennia, the laws of the physical world have not altered since the Big Bang: "This is one reason why economics should be closer to biology than to physics: biology has a problem of historical (or evolutionary) specificity."[42] With this plea for greater emphasis on evolutionary economics, we shall leave the problems of economics as such.

NEW INSTITUTIONALISMS

Turning now to developments within the neighboring disciplines, we may find approaches to the role of history that partly rival and partly complement those of economics. Agreeing with Paul David's view of institutions as "the carriers of history,"[43] we shall move here into the broader realm of what has come to be known as "new institutionalism."[44] In previous chapters we

[41] Ibid., p. xiii.

[42] Ibid., p. 26.

[43] David, Paul A. (1994), "Why Are Institutions the 'Carriers of History?': Path Dependence and the Evolution of Conventions, Organizations and Institutions," *Structural Change and Economic Dynamics*, vol. 5, no. 2, pp. 205–20.

[44] One of the seminal contributions to this field was March, James G. and Johan P. Olsen (1984), "The New Institutionalism: Organizational Factors in Political Life," *American Political Science Review*, vol. 78, no. 3, pp. 734–49. See also March, James G. and Johan P. Olsen (1989), *Rediscovering Institutions: The Organizational Basis of Politics*, New

have made frequent reference to the field of "new institutional economics." Here we shall add an account of contributions from the side of political science, and from sociology.

Recognizing that there is "considerable confusion" concerning what new institutionalism is and what it does, and that "it does not constitute a unified body of thought," Peter Hall and Rosemary Taylor identify three different strands that have emerged within this field, namely, rational choice institutionalism, historical institutionalism, and sociological institutionalism.[45] By and large, this agrees with our previous contrast between the agency view of economics and the structural view of sociology, only now with "historical institutionalism" inserted into the middle ground.

To what extent the gap between agency and structure, or between methodological individualism and methodological wholism or collectivism, really *can* be bridged is a core question that runs through the present text as a whole. It shall also be at the focus of our ambition, in the following chapter, to wrap up and close the argument. Whether historical institutionalism has the key, as implicitly suggested by Hall and Taylor, is a more specific question that we shall return to in a moment.

Retaining our focus on institutions as the carriers of history, we shall recapitulate very briefly the main steps in the argument as such. First and foremost we have the question of how institutions originate. Answers range from random events (path dependence), to incremental evolution,[46] intelligent design (agency or functionalism), by-products of other action (Tocqueville and Elster), and pure magic.[47] The second step is to ascertain

York: Free Press, and March, James G. and Johan P. Olsen (2008), "Elaborating the 'New Institutionalism,'" in R. A. W. Rhodes, Sarah A. Binder, and Bert A. Rockman (eds.), *The Oxford Handbook of Political Institutions*, Oxford: Oxford University Press. For other broad contributions, see also Brinton, Mary C. and Victor Nee (eds.) (1998), *The New Institutionalism in Sociology*, New York: Russell Sage Foundation; Peters, B. Guy (1999), *Institutional Theory in Political Science: The "New Institutionalism,"* London: Pinter: and Powell, Walter W. and Paul J. DiMaggio (eds.) (1991), *The New Institutionalism in Organizational Analysis*, Chicago: University of Chicago Press.

[45] Hall, Peter A. and Rosemary C. R. Taylor (1996), "Political Science and the Three New Institutionalisms," *Political Studies*, vol. 44, p. 936 and *passim*.

[46] Douglass North writes that institutions "evolve incrementally, connecting the past with the present and the future; history in consequence is largely a story of institutional evolution in which the historical performance of economies can only be understood as part of a sequential study" (North, Douglass C. (1991), "Institutions," *Journal of Economic Perspectives*, vol. 5, no. 1, p. 98).

[47] The latter was suggested very early on, in a 1938 book by Edward Sait: "When we examine political institutions, one after the other, they seem to have been erected, almost like coral reefs, without conscious design. There has been no pre-arranged plan, no architects' drawings and blue-prints; man has carried out the purposes of nature, we might say, acting

the impact of different institutions on individual action. Answers on this count (*homo economicus* versus *homo sociologicus*) have been suggested in previous chapters and will be further elaborated upon later. Step three, which is the main topic of this chapter, concerns how institutions are sustained over time, and step four, topic of the previous chapter, details to what extent institutions may be changed by deliberate action.

The various approaches to the role of history that are associated with the three different strands of new institutionalism will be outlined in the following sections, beginning with what Hall and Taylor refer to as rational choice institutionalism.

Rational Choice Institutionalism

The rational choice approach to the study of institutions within political science constitutes something of a bridge to economics in general, and to the new institutional economics in particular. Very much associated with Kenneth Shepsle and Barry Weingast, it arose from studies of American congressional behavior, drawing on tools from the "new economics of organization" that emphasize the importance of property rights, rent seeking, and transaction costs.[48]

Given this background, it is natural that rational choice institutionalism shares with neoclassical economics a number of fundamental assumptions regarding matters such as preference orderings, instrumentally rational maximizing behavior, strategic interaction, and a forward-looking orientation. Noting that "canonical" rational choice theory has been a staple in political science for four decades, Shepsle clearly emphasizes its affinity with the neoclassical tradition in economics:

[It] has become an engine of social scientific research, producing theoretical micro-foundations, an equilibrium orientation, deductively derived theorems and propositions about political activity, a comparative statics methodology yielding testable hypotheses, and an accumulation of tools and approaches that are routinely found in the curriculum of major graduate programs.[49]

blindly in response to her obscure commands" (Sait, Edward (1938), *Political Institutions – A Preface*, Boston: Appleton-Century-Crofts, p. 16, cited in Shepsle, Kenneth A. (1989), "Studying Institutions: Some Lessons from the Rational Choice Approach," *Journal of Theoretical Politics*, vol. 1, no. 2, p. 145).

[48] Hall and Taylor, "Political Science and the Three New Institutionalisms," p. 943 and further sources cited therein.

[49] Shepsle, Kenneth A. (2008), "Rational Choice Institutionalism," in R. A. W. Rhodes, Sarah A. Binder, and Bert A. Rockman (eds.), *The Oxford Handbook of Political Institutions*, Oxford: Oxford University Press, p. 23.

In an early article, published at the time when new institutional economics was emerging, he expressed surprise that there had been so little interaction across the fence between the two disciplines. Although the resurgence of interest in institutions from the side of economics followed in the wake of a long period of neglect, he found that "political studies have provided little of the inspiration or impetus." The latter was remarkable in the sense that "the study of institutions (together with the history of political thought) *was* political science." His explanation is that "little in the form of cumulative theory was produced," and the consequence that "the economists have gone ahead and invented the rigorous study of institutions *de nova*."[50]

Given how closely rational choice institutionalism follows in the tracks of the neoclassical economic tradition, one is wont to question to what extent it adds something that is genuinely novel, something that might warrant Shepsle's proud conclusion that "political science need no longer concede the study of institutions to the economists!"[51]

His own argument, presented in a brief but broad survey of the field, departs from a separation between interpretations that view institutions as exogenous constraints, or as the rules of the game, and those that focus on how rules are provided by the players themselves, that is, endogenously. While the former is rooted in traditional game theoretic terms, the latter represents "equilibrium ways of doing things." A further line is drawn between "structured" institutions that are robust over time, such as the U.S. Congress, and "unstructured" institutions that are amorphous and more fluid, such as norms, and other forms of motivation for cooperation, coordination, and collective action. Arguing that rational choice institutionalism has been highly successful in analyzing the structured institutions, Shepsle concludes by indicating a need to develop our understanding of the unstructured versions by delving into matters like bounded rationality, behavioral economics, transaction cost economics, and analytical narratives.[52]

Turning to Barry Weingast, we find an approach that is very similar. Setting out to "explain the comparative advantages of the rational choice perspective," he lists three categories of questions that are addressed. The first accepts institutions as exogenously given and proceeds to study the impact on rational actors. The second asks why institutions are necessary and emphasizes their role in helping to achieve gains from cooperation.

[50] Shepsle, "Studying Institutions," pp. 131–32.
[51] Ibid., p. 146.
[52] Shepsle, "Rational Choice Institutionalism," *passim*. See also Bates, Robert H. et al. (1998), *Analytic Narratives*, Princeton, NJ: Princeton University Press.

The third views institutions as endogenous and asks why certain forms emerge and others do not. The preconditions for credible commitments and for the emergence of self-enforcing institutions are of particular relevance here.[53]

Proceeding from political science to the side of sociology, where we have seen the most fundamental disagreements being formulated with regard to the neoclassical economic tradition, here as well we may find strands of rational choice theorizing that incorporates rather than· challenges economics. Departing from the argument that social organization and social institutions are missing from neoclassical economics, James Coleman outlines a rational choice perspective on economic sociology that essentially implies taking tools out of economics and modifying them with insights out of sociology.[54]

His first step is to outline four familiar economic cornerstones, namely, methodological individualism, maximizing behavior, social optimum, and system equilibrium. While rational choice sociology differs from economics in recognizing "social anomalies" in individual action, it also and more importantly differs from functionalism in sociology in denying that social optimum and social equilibrium are the same. The key to the latter is that due to collective action problems individual action may fail to achieve a Pareto optimal outcome.

The insights that are incorporated from the side of sociology also come in a set of four. One captures the presence of institutions, another the role of social capital, a third the social origin of rights, and a fourth the fact that individuals may sometimes stand to gain utility by giving up control. While the former two again come across as fairly well known, the third brings in important considerations of conflict and the distribution of power, and the fourth highlights a point of great relevance to the global financial crisis. Abandoning control and deciding to follow a leader may lead to unstable or even runaway systems that are marked by "fads, panics, crazes, fashions, 'bubbles,' and crashes."[55]

---

[53] Weingast, Barry (2002), "Rational Choice Institutionalism," in Ira Katznelson and Helen V. Milner (eds.), *Political Science: The State of the Discipline*, New York: Norton, p. 660 and *passim*. For a prior outline of much the same, see also Weingast, Barry (1996), "Political Institutions: Rational Choice Perspectives," in Robert E. Goodin and Hans-Dieter Klingemann (eds.), *A New Handbook of Political Science*, Oxford: Oxford University Press.

[54] Coleman, James (1994), "A Rational Choice Perspective on Economic Sociology," in Neil J. Smelser and Richard Swedberg (eds.), *The Handbook of Economic Sociology*, Princeton, NJ: Princeton University Press.

[55] Ibid., pp. 169–70.

By and large, however, the rational choice perspective in sociology bears a great deal of resemblance to that in political science. Above all, they are both heavily influenced by behavioral assumptions that have been derived from economics. While this does enhance the predictive power of the theoretical modeling, its emphasis on instrumental rationality also entails a functional view on the role and emergence of institutions, that is, that institutions are put into place to serve a purpose. Little if anything is in consequence said about how institutions are sustained over time, or indeed about problems that may arise in seeking to weed out inferior solutions. While rational choice institutionalism within sociology does attempt to blur the lines a bit, it remains beholden to the basic message. For a fundamentally different approach we shall have to cross the aisle and look at a more purely sociological approach.

Sociological Institutionalism

Compared to the other social sciences, sociology has by far the longest track record of institutional analysis. Harking back to Weber's theory on bureaucracy and Durkheim's portrayal of sociology as a "science of institutions," sociologists have produced a rich literature. Broadened in the 1950s to include Talcott Parsons's focus on functionalism it has not, however, always been clear how to draw a line between organizations and institutions. In diametrical contrast to economics, moreover, it has also been stronger at explaining how institutions are created than how they work.[56]

As was the case with rational choice institutionalism, which arose out of the economics of organization, the new institutionalism within sociology also has its roots within organization theory. The trigger for this new field to emerge was a growing dissatisfaction among some sociologists with the traditional approach of making a distinction between those parts of the social world that reflected formal means-ends rationality, typical of modern forms of organization, and those that were marked by practices of a "cultural" nature. From Weber onward, the means-ends approach had been viewed as driven by an inherent rationality in finding ever more efficient modes of organization of modern society. Culture, on the other hand, had been viewed as something entirely different.[57]

In a broad assault on rationalist approaches to organization, Frank Dobbin even speaks of an increasing "balkanization of social science,"

---

[56] Peters, *Institutional Theory in Political Science*, pp. 97–99 and ch. 6 *passim*.
[57] Hall and Taylor, "Political Science and the Three New Institutionalisms," p. 946.

whereby economists and recently also political scientists "organize their arguments about instrumentality around mathematical formulas that are thought to capture the asocial, acultural essence of universal economic laws." Anthropologists and sociologists in contrast "organize their arguments about culture around empirical evidence that is thought to capture the non-rational, historical essence of localized social practices."[58]

The main thrust of the new institutionalists' argument was to challenge the element of assumed rationality in the adoption of institutions. Many of the forms and procedures that are typical of modern organizations should rather be seen as culturally specific practices, as akin to the myths and ceremonies devised by societies as a result of processes that are associated with the transmission of cultural practices more generally. In consequence, even the most seemingly rational of Weberian bureaucratic practices would have to be explained in cultural terms.[59]

As presented by Hall and Taylor, three features render sociological institutionalism distinct from the other new institutionalisms.[60] The *first* is that sociological institutionalists tend to define institutions much more broadly than political scientists do. In addition to such formal rules, procedures, and norms that also figure in economic institutionalism, they expand to include symbol systems, cognitive scripts, and moral templates that provide frames of meaning to guide human action. As this effectively breaks down the conceptual divide between institutions and culture, it may be viewed as reflective of the "cognitive turn" within sociology, and as a challenge to the distinction between institutional (organizational structures) and cultural (shared attitudes and values) explanations that is common among political scientists.

The *second* feature concerns a distinctive understanding of the relations between institutions and individual action. In line with the cultural approach, it emphasizes how institutions provide the cognitive scripts, categories, and models that are indispensable for action. Reflecting influence from social constructivism, institutions are held to provide the very terms through which meaning is assigned in cultural life. Going beyond the

[58] Dobbin, Frank (1994), "Cultural Models of Organization: The Social Construction of Rational Organizing Principles," in Diane Crane (ed.), *The Sociology of Culture*, Oxford: Blackwell, p. 119.

[59] Hall and Taylor, "Political Science and the Three New Institutionalisms," pp. 946–47, and further references to a variety of case approaches. See also DiMaggio, Paul J. and Walter W. Powell (1991), "Introduction," in DiMaggio and Powell (eds.), *The New Institutionalism in Organizational Analysis*, Chicago: Chicago University Press.

[60] Hall and Taylor, "Political Science and the Three New Institutionalisms," pp. 947–50.

strategic calculation of rational actors, we are faced here with basic preferences and fundamental identities. The bottom line is not that actors are
not instrumentally rational, but that what an individual will see as "rational
action" will itself be socially constituted.

The *third* feature captures how institutional practices originate and
change. In contrast to the functionalist approach that explains institutions
in terms of the functions they are assigned to perform, sociological institutionalists argue that organizations embrace specific organizational forms
because the latter are widely valued within a broader cultural environment.
This will hold true even in cases when the institution may actually be dysfunctional in relation to achieving the formal goals of the organization.
The contrast is captured by John Campbell in terms of a "logic of social
appropriateness" versus a "logic of instrumentality."[61]

While all of this offers a view on the relation between institutions and
individual action that is very different from that of neoclassical economics,
and indeed also of rational choice institutionalism, it leaves unanswered the
question of how institutions develop and may be preserved over time. For
insights into this crucial matter, we shall turn to the third of the three new
institutionalisms, that of "historical institutionalism."

Historical Institutionalism

In his presentation of rational choice institutionalism, Shepsle offers a succinct characterization of how political science theorizing has been subjected to vital influence from the neighboring disciplines: "The behavioral
revolution in political science was a triumph of sociology and psychology.
The rational choice revolution, which came in the 1960s and 1970s and con-
tinues today, is a triumph of economics."[62] Proceeding now to the field of
"historical institutionalism" we shall find a third source of inspiration, one
that flows between what we have characterized as the agency and the structural approaches.[63]

The background to the emergence of this rapidly expanding subfield of
political science has a lot to do with the rise of behaviorism following the

[61] Campbell, John L. (1995), "Institutional Analysis and the Role of Ideas in Political
Economy," conference paper cited by Hall and Taylor, "Political Science and the Three
New Institutionalisms," p. 949.
[62] Shepsle, "Studying Institutions," p. 133.
[63] Credit for introducing the notion of "historical institutionalism" normally goes to Skocpol,
Theda (1979), *States and Social Revolutions: A Comparative Analysis of France, Russia and
China*, Cambridge: Cambridge University Press.

end of World War II.[64] In a somewhat belated parallel to the marginal revolution in economics, political scientists were increasingly drawn into survey research made possible by advances in computer technology. During the 1960s, the previous tradition of focus on the study of history and of institutional structures in consequence was largely abandoned. In the 1970s, however, such endeavors returned, and in the 1980s and 1990s they went into full bloom, taking on more analytical characteristics.

The driving force, as phrased by Elizabeth Sanders, was an "increasingly loud criticism" of institutions that had long been taken for granted. Democratic institutions long associated with stable economic growth came under attack, and scholars began to ask penetrating new questions. How had "the stable, adaptive path dependence of Western institutions come to experience operational crisis and undermined confidence in the ideas and processes on which they were founded?" The response was a new attention to ideas that could be viewed as "a rebellion of social scientists and historians against the individual centered behaviorism that had dominated political science ... and against its dominant paradigm, pluralism."[65]

While the rational choice approach became increasingly focused on the micromotives for individual action, undertaken within a set of stable institutional constraints, historical institutionalists turned their attention to the broader goals of such action, and to problems relating to various forms of interaction. While the former approach adopts an abstract and simplified attitude toward functions filled by market forces, the latter have a more normative and reformist bent that recalls the old American institutionalists. In condensed form, Sanders finds that while rational choice institutionalism takes preferences for granted, historical institutionalism is interested in "how ideas, interests, and positions generate preferences, and how (and why) they evolve over time."[66]

In an elaborate plea for the merits of this approach, which is held to "make visible and understandable the overarching contexts and interacting processes that shape and reshape states, politics, and public policymaking," Paul Pierson joins with Theda Skocpol in listing three main points of

---

[64] See further Thelen, Kathleen and Sven Steinmo (1992), "Historical Institutionalism in Comparative Politics," in Sven Steinmo, Kathleen Thelen, and Frank Longstreth (1992), *Structuring Politics: Historical Institutionalism in Comparative Analysis*, New York: Cambridge University Press, pp. 1–7.

[65] Sanders, Elizabeth (2008), "Historical Institutionalism," in R. A. W. Rhodes, Sarah A. Binder, and Bert A. Rockman (eds.), *The Oxford Handbook of Political Institutions*, Oxford: Oxford University Press, p. 41.

[66] Ibid, p. 43.

strength. The first is that historical institutionalists "address big, substantive questions that are inherently of interest to broad publics as well as to fellow scholars," the second that they "take time seriously," and the third that they "analyze macro contexts and hypothesize about the combined effects of institutions and processes."[67]

Over and above the ambition to deal with real-world questions and to "avoid academic navel gazing," the main importance for our purpose of this approach lies in its focus on tracing historical processes. Included here are matters of timing and sequencing that highlight "conjunctures," defined as interaction effects between distinct causal sequences, as well as the possible presence of path dependence, of which more will be said in a moment.

A recurrent theme in presentations of historical institutionalism is a strongly critical attitude toward rational choice and the implied functionalism.[68] Although recognizing that rational choice scholars have increasingly turned to historical case studies, Pierson and Skocpol view this mainly as "illustrative history." In contrast to the theory-driven rational choice approach, which is focused on the micro level, historical institutionalists move on the meso and macro levels, investigating the "rise and decline of institutions over time, probing the origins, impact and stability or instability of specific institutions as well as broader institutional configurations."[69]

Resembling the conflict between the old school of American institutionalism and the emerging neoclassical tradition, the argument between rational choice and historical institutionalism may be viewed as a trade-off between analytical rigor and a more encompassing approach that analyzes institutions in context. While the latter ambition is certainly laudable as such, it does not come without a price.

Pierson and Skocpol are quite convinced of the merits of their case: "Without historical institutionalism, our discipline would be shorn of much of its ability to tackle major agendas of concern to all political scientists. And without historical institutionalists, political science would have

---

[67] Pierson, Paul and Theda Skocpol (2002), "Historical Institutionalism in Contemporary Political Science," in Ira Katznelson and Helen V. Milner (eds.), *Political Science: The State of the Discipline*, New York: Norton, pp. 693–96 and *passim*.

[68] For a broad overview of the arguments of the respective sides, see Thelen, Kathleen (1999), "Historical Institutionalism in Comparative Politics," *Annual Review of Political Science*, vol. 2, no. 1, pp. 369–404.

[69] Pierson and Skocpol, "Historical Institutionalism," pp. 705–07. See also Thelen and Steinmo, "Historical Institutionalism in Comparative Politics," pp. 7–10.

much less to say about questions of great import to people beyond as well as within the ivory tower."[70]

The obvious counterargument is that historical institutionalism amounts to little more than storytelling, that case studies and small-n comparisons cannot generate valid knowledge, and that the approach as a whole is marred by intractable methodological problems. At the core of this debate lies by far the most controversial component of historical institutionalism, namely, its potential role as a bridge spanning the crucial methodological divide between structure and agency.

In a comment on the article by Hall and Taylor cited earlier, Colin Hay and Daniel Wincott argue that the respective approaches of rational choice and of sociological institutionalism are based on "mutually incompatible premises," and that any attempt to interpret historical institutionalism as made up of a combination of the two is tantamount to doing "a considerable disservice to this distinctive approach to institutional analysis."[71] Recalling Jon Elster's previously cited emphasis on a "persisting cleavage" within the social sciences, Hay and Wincott speak of an "intractable divide," and suggest that it is only by transcending this "unhelpful dualism" that historical institutionalism may be developed into a consistent and constructive approach in its own right.

In response, Hall and Taylor agree that the structure-agency problem is of fundamental importance, but they also make a crucial distinction. It is one thing to suggest that historical institutionalism has the potential to offer a novel approach, which may or may not be true. It is something altogether different to argue that this has already been achieved, which is clearly not the case. Pondering whether at some point it may indeed be achieved, they note that this represents a tall order indeed, one comparable to the search for an alchemist's stone. Although historical institutionalism is well placed to make progress, what Hay and Wincott have to offer is held to read "more like a wish list than a fully specified theory, though it is a good wish list."[72]

In conclusion, one is tempted here to resort to the old quip about being still confused, but at a much higher level. Perhaps the key to dispelling some of the confusion that surrounds structure versus agency lies in returning to the problematic of path dependence.

---

[70] Pierson and Skocpol, "Historical Institutionalism," p. 721.
[71] Hay, Colin and Daniel Wincott (1998), "Structure, Agency and Historical Institutionalism," *Political Studies*, vol. 46, p. 951.
[72] Hall, Peter A. and Rosemary C. R. Taylor (1998), "The Potential of Historical Institutionalism: A Response to Hay and Wincott," *Political Studies*, vol. 46, p. 960.

BACK TO PATH DEPENDENCE

In the preceding, we have presented the theory of path dependence as formulated by Paul David and Brian Arthur and based mainly on observations
concerning choices of technology. We have also indicated that scholars
from across the social sciences have picked up on this approach and sought
to demonstrate how social and political development can become more
broadly path dependent. Before we take a closer look at such endeavors, it
should be recognized that arguments on path dependence within economics have not been confined to technology alone. They have, on the contrary,
been applied in a broad range of contexts.

As emphasized by Paul Krugman, in a study of the emergence of the U.S.
"manufacturing belt," one of the most successful has been concerned with
the spatial location of production: "If there is one single area of economics
in which path dependence is unmistakable, it is in economic geography –
the location of production in space."[73] Numerous factors have combined to
produce zones or clusters of specialized economic activity that range from
the high-tech Silicon Valley to the fashion industry of northern Italy.

Other applications have been made to foreign trade theory and to endogenous growth theory, and the list could be made longer.[74] The bottom line,
however, is that all such endeavors remain firmly within the mainstream of
the neoclassical tradition, resting on the presence of increasing returns to
show how self-enforcing processes may cause path dependence to emerge.[75]
Proceeding now to look at cases that do *not* lend themselves as easily to elegant modeling, we shall return to Douglass North.

As we may recall from previous chapters, his theory on institutions and
institutional change aimed to expand the scope of the neoclassical tradition
while remaining firmly rooted in its main assumptions. Commenting on
the shift of focus from technological to institutional change, he points out

---

[73] Krugman, Paul (1991a), "History and Industry Location: The Case of the Manufacturing
Belt," *American Economic Review*, vol. 81, no. 2, p. 80. See also Krugman, Paul (1991b),
"Increasing Returns and Economic Geography," *Journal of Political Economy*, vol. 99, no.
3, pp. 483–99, and Arthur, W. Brian (1994), *Increasing Returns and Path Dependence in the
Economy*, Ann Arbor: University of Michigan Press, ch. 4.

[74] For example, Helpman, Elhanan and Paul Krugman (1985), *Market Structure and Foreign
Trade*, Cambridge, MA: MIT Press, and Romer, Paul M. (1986), "Increasing Returns and
Long-Run Growth," *Journal of Political Economy*, vol. 94, no. 5, pp. 1002–37.

[75] Kenneth Arrow departs from this pattern in arguing that due to irreversibilities of invest-
ment, path dependence can arise even under constant returns (Arrow, Kenneth J. (2004),
"Path Dependence and Competitive Equilibrium," in W. Sundstrom, T. Guinnane, and W.
Whatley (eds.), *History Matters: Essays on Economic Growth, Technology, and Demographic
Change*, Stanford, CA: Stanford University Press).

that in the latter case we have two forces that combine to form the path of change, namely, increasing returns and imperfect markets with significant transactions costs. With competitive markets and no increasing returns to institutions, institutions would simply not matter.

Allowing for increasing returns implies that all of the four self-reinforcing mechanisms outlined by Arthur will apply. Reflecting the preoccupation of rational choice institutionalism with U.S. congressional behavior, North illustrates with reference to the large setup costs of the U.S. Constitution, and the ensuing effects of learning, coordination, and adaptive expectations that have marked the development of the U.S. political system.

Increasing returns, however, constitute only part of the picture. For as long as markets are competitive, or even roughly approximate the zero-transactions-cost model, competition will ensure that inferior solutions are eliminated and that actors are forced to continually and correctly update their mental models. In consequence, the long-run path of development will be efficient. It is only when the latter assumptions are dropped that path inefficiency may emerge:

But if the markets are incomplete, the information feedback is fragmentary at best, and transaction costs are significant, then the subjective models of actors modified both by very imperfect feedback and by ideology will shape the path. Then, not only can both divergent paths and persistently poor performance prevail, the historically derived perceptions of the actors shape the choices that they make.[76]

The core of the argument is that history matters not only because increasing returns may influence the creation and preservation of specific institutional arrangements. More important, for our purpose, under conditions of imperfect competition, imperfect information, and high costs of transacting, actors may be locked into mental models of the world around them that profoundly influence future decision making. In short, a world of increasing returns to institutions is one where "the imperfect and fumbling efforts of the actors reflect the difficulties of deciphering a complex environment with the available mental constructs – ideas, theories, and ideologies."[77]

Recalling our main theme of structure versus agency, the former part of the argument comes across as very much in line with the rational choice approach, while the latter is less clear-cut. Invoking ideology and mental models might suggest a tilt toward the structural side, and thus a way of

---

[76] North, Douglass C. (1990a), *Institutions, Institutional Change and Economic Performance*, Cambridge: Cambridge University Press, pp. 95–96.
[77] Ibid., p. 96.

bridging the gap. Closer consideration, however, will show that we are still very much within the paradigm of rationality and functionalism.

Writing in other contexts, North has, inter alia, applied a transaction cost approach to the study of politics.[78] He has joined with Paul Milgrom and Barry Weingast in showing how medieval markets solved problems of trust and enforcement endogenously by developing the "law merchant,"[79] and with Weingast in emphasizing the role of credible commitments.[80] Pursuing the latter on his own,[81] he has also made reference to Shepsle.[82] All in all, we would thus indeed seem to be moving well within the confines of rational choice institutionalism.

Setting out to "explore the deficiencies of the rational choice approach, as it relates to institutions," North emphasizes aspects of motivation and of cognition.[83] The argument on the former count is derived from the role that is played by factors such as ideologies, altruism, and self-imposed standards of conduct. It remains, however, beholden to rational choice, arguing that there is a negative trade-off between wealth and such alternative values. The argument on cognition and mental models in turn goes back to matters of bounded rationality and thus constitutes a qualification rather than a challenge to rational choice.[84]

The main thrust of the argument as a whole is neatly formulated when North seeks to hedge against accusations of determinism: "At every step along the way there were choices – political and economic – that provided real alternatives. Path dependence is a way to narrow conceptually the choice set and link decision making through time. It is not a story of inevitability in which the past neatly predicts the future."[85] Recalling previously cited

[78] North, Douglass C. (1990b), "A Transaction Cost Theory of Politics," *Journal of Theoretical Politics*, vol. 2, no. 4, pp. 355–67.
[79] Milgrom, Paul R., Douglass C. North, and Barry R. Weingast (1990), "The Role of Institutions in the Revival of Trade: The Law Merchant, Private Judges, and the Champagne Fairs," *Economics and Politics*, vol. 2, no. 1, pp. 1–23.
[80] North, Douglass C. and Barry R. Weingast (1989), "Constitutions and Commitment: The Evolution of Institutions Governing Public Choice in Seventeenth Century England," *Journal of Economic History*, vol. 49, December, pp. 803–32.
[81] North, Douglass C. (1993a), "Institutions and Credible Commitment," *Journal of Institutional and Theoretical Economics*, vol. 149, no. 1, pp. 11–23.
[82] Shepsle, Kenneth A. (1991), "Discretion, Institutions and the Problem of Government Commitment," in Pierre Bourdieu and James Coleman (eds.), *Social Theory for a Changing Society*, Boulder, CO: Western Press.
[83] North, *Institutions, Institutional Change*, p. 20.
[84] The qualification brings into play approaches from cognitive psychology that we shall leave aside here. (See North, Douglass C. (2005), *Understanding the Process of Economic Change*, Princeton: Princeton University Press, and North, Douglass C. and Arthur T. Denzau (1994), "Shared Mental Models: Ideologies and Institutions," *Kyklos*, vol. 47, no. 3.)
[85] North, *Institutions, Institutional Change*, pp. 98–99.

quips about, for example, how economics is about the choices people make, and sociology about how they do not have any choices to make, North quite obviously remains at the economics end of the spectrum. His ambitions to account for the role of ideology similarly revolve largely around the role of transaction costs,[86] and around the functions filled by ideology in altering a calculus of cost and benefit.[87] The main challenge to this approach rests in recognizing the limits to functionalism. We shall return to this in a moment.

Leaving the narrowly defined realm of economics, we may return to Paul Pierson and the role of historical institutionalism. In something of a programmatic statement, he underscores the crucial importance of path dependent processes: "If path dependence arguments are indeed appropriate in substantial areas of political life, they will shake many subfields of political inquiry. This essay argues that they are."[88]

His argument as such is firmly rooted in Brian Arthur's presentation of the role of increasing returns, of timing and sequencing, of multiple equilibria, of critical junctures, and of the possibility that small contingent events can produce large consequences. Stepping across the divide between economics and political science, Pierson first lists four features that make increasing returns prevalent in politics, namely, the central role of collective action, the high density of institutions, the use of political authority to enhance asymmetries of power, and the intrinsic complexity and opacity of politics. He then adds three features that make increasing returns processes in politics particularly intense, as compared to the economic sphere, namely, the absence or weakness of efficiency-enhancing competition and learning, the shorter time horizons of political actors, and the strong bias toward the status quo that is inherent in politics.[89]

Presenting detailed and credible arguments on all seven counts, he concludes that an "awareness of increasing returns processes can change not only the questions we ask but also the answers we provide." Of particular importance here is that increasing returns arguments "provide a plausible counter to functionalist explanations in political science, which often go unchallenged."[90] In line with previous claims concerning the merits

---

[86] North, Douglass C. (1988), "Ideology and Political/Economic Institutions," *Cato Journal*, vol. 8, no. 1, pp. 15–28.

[87] North, Douglass C. (1981), *Structure and Change in Economic History*, New York: Norton, ch. 5.

[88] Pierson, Paul (2000), "Increasing Returns, Path Dependence, and the Study of Politics," *American Political Science Review*, vol. 94, no. 2, p. 251.

[89] Ibid., p. 257 and *passim*.

[90] Ibid., p. 263.

of historical institutionalism, Pierson argues that the recognition of path dependence derived from increasing returns constitutes a challenge to the profession's "lofty aspirations about developing a science of politics, rooted in parsimony and generalization and capable of great predictive power."[91]

In a pointed critique of what he refers to as "actor-centered functionalism," viewed here as distinct from "societal functionalism," Pierson also lists a set of important limitations that have great implications for the rational choice approach as a whole. The *first* is that while actors may be both instrumental and farsighted, they may have such multiple and diverse goals that outcomes may not be easily derived from the preferences of designers. The *second* questions to what extent actors really do behave instrumentally, and the *third* adds that even if they are instrumental they may not be sufficiently farsighted. *Fourth*, and perhaps most important, is the possibility that even if actors are farsighted and do have a single instrumental goal, major institutional effects may be unintended. *Finally*, changes in the broader social environment and in the character of the actors themselves may blur the link between intentions and outcomes.[92]

For a considerably different approach to the same problem, we shall turn to the field of historical sociology, which in a similar vein is held by its practitioners to "offer tools of analysis especially well suited for the study of path dependence."[93] Echoing claims by historical institutionalists to have a broader understanding of what institutions are, historical sociologists reach beyond the "utilitarian" approach that is derived from the neoclassical economic tradition. Departing from the familiar emphasis on contingency and critical junctures as explanations of how path dependence may arise, the broadened scope relates to the question of institutional reproduction.

James Mahoney illustrates by noting that applying different types of sociological explanations will generate different understandings both of institutional reproduction and of possible sources of reversal. The key here is to focus on the prominent role of potential path inefficiency, which is "an interesting outcome only in relation to the utilitarian theoretical framework of neoclassical economics."[94] Mahoney's suggestion, "loosely derived" from Randall Collins's presentation of four sociological traditions,[95] is that

---

[91] Ibid., p. 266.
[92] Pierson, Paul (2004), *Politics in Time: History, Institutions, and Social Analysis*, Princeton, NJ: Princeton University Press, pp. 108–22.
[93] Mahoney, James (2000), "Path Dependence in Historical Sociology," *Theory and Society*, vol. 29, no. 4, p. 507.
[94] Ibid., p. 516.
[95] Collins, Randall (1994), *Four Sociological Traditions*, New York: Oxford University Press.

the utilitarian explanation must be complemented with explanations that focus, respectively, on function, power, and legitimation.[96]

The benchmark *utilitarian* approach views actors as being driven by rational calculations of cost and benefit. Inefficient solutions may emerge and become locked in simply because the costs of switching or reversal outweigh potential benefits. For as long as we remain within a traditional market setting, the message will be an optimistic one, assuming that competitive pressures together with learning effects will eventually alter the calculus in favor of an optimal outcome. What historical sociologists may add, together with historical institutionalists, is that such utilitarian mechanisms of correction will be less salient in the social and political world. In consequence, there are "good reasons to believe that path dependent institutions supported by utilitarian mechanisms will be especially enduring outside of the marketplace."[97]

Turning to the *functional* explanation, an institution is generally assumed to be introduced and reproduced simply because it serves a function within the overall system. In cases of path dependence, where contingency will explain the origin of an institution, reproduction over time may follow a path that is less functional than available alternative solutions. While this is similar to the case of inefficiency in the utilitarian explanation, it lacks the corrective mechanisms associated with the market logic. Once a self-reinforcing process has been set in motion, reversal will be possible only following an exogenous shock to the system in which the institution is embedded.

Explanations of self-reinforcing processes that focus on *power* are similar to the utilitarian ones in that actors are assumed to be driven by a calculus of costs and benefits. The difference lies in recognizing that institutions may serve to produce an uneven distribution of outcomes, and that actors with different endowments may have conflicting interests with regard to institutional reproduction. An institutional solution may thus persist even when most individuals or groups would prefer change. While this approach has little if anything to say about origin, it relies on power dynamics to explain reproduction and views change as possible only due to a weakening of the power elite. Arguments on path dependence that follow the approach of emphasizing power and conflict may hence be helpful in explaining both long-term stability and sudden drastic transformations.

---

[96] The argument is summarized in Mahoney, "Path Dependence in Historical Sociology," pp. 515–26.

[97] Ibid., p. 519.

The fourth and final approach is fundamentally different in the sense of focusing on *legitimation*, that is, on institutional reproduction that is driven by actors' subjective beliefs about what is morally just or appropriate. While the former three explanations are all in various ways derived from rational calculations of utility, functionality, and power, here we are faced with norms that establish the right thing to do. Self-reinforcement will arise due to increasing legitimation of an institution that initially emerges as a moral standard. Given that path dependence may be associated with active approval as well as passive acquiescence, it follows that we are faced here with complex problems of cognition and with dangers of emerging gaps between private values and official policy. Simply put, we have been returned yet again to the "persisting cleavage" between structure and agency.

On this note, we shall move to wrap up and conclude the argument as a whole, which will be the task of the following chapter, and to indicate what implications may be seen for social science theorizing, a task to be approached in Chapter 9.

8

Concluding Discussion

We began the present journey in the world of financial markets, detailing how the sudden onset of the global financial crisis raised the specter of a return to the Great Depression of the 1930s. Deeply shaken by the collapse of the venerable investment bank Lehman Brothers, markets were gripped by fear that rapidly spilled over into the public and political spheres. As investors stampeded for the door, seeking to sell whatever could be sold, and as bankers refused to lend, the real side of the economy went into tailspin and outraged members of the general public began fielding accusations of inveterate corporate greed.

Caught in the midst of the turmoil, governments faced a dual challenge. On the one hand, it was viewed as clearly necessary to take swift action to stem a rising tide of panic that just *might* have caused a global depression. On the other, it was viewed as equally necessary to show political resolve in curbing the various manifestations of greed that were held by so many to constitute the main cause of the crisis. While it was easy enough to be caught by the high drama of the ensuing events, it is important to remember that they form only part of an overall and far more complex picture.

The main reason we have chosen to place so much emphasis on the role of financial markets is that what happens there may in a sense be likened to the tip of an iceberg. This is surely not to belittle in any sense the gravity of the matters at hand. As recent events have brought home, and as the historical track record shows, financial crises may impact quite severely the real side of the economy and may thus inflict serious hardship on the population at large.

Retaining our focus on systemic failure, however, it is equally important to note that it was not the tip of the iceberg that sank the Titanic. The real dangers, to shipping as well as to economic systems, will always lie below the surface. The very fact that "manias, panics and crashes," for example, constitute such an integral part of the history of the market economy is highly symptomatic. It illustrates that we are faced here with problems that are deeply embedded in the institutional structures surrounding economic transactions. Previous chapters have attempted to shed light on these problems from a variety of directions. Here we shall sum up the main arguments, leaving our final chapter to discuss what implications may be seen for social science theorizing.

The chapter is divided into three sections. The first recapitulates what lessons may be learned from the financial crisis of 2008–9, and from the ensuing European turmoil that erupted in the spring of 2010, triggered by fears of a Greek sovereign default. The second deals with the long term and the role of invisible hands, and the third returns to the Russian experience, as further illustration of arguments on embeddedness.

GREED AND FINANCIAL CRISES

Looking back at how governments and central banks responded to the subprime mortgage crisis and to the ensuing freeze of global financial markets, it seems fair to say that – following a slow start – decisive action *was* taken that mitigated what could otherwise have turned into a very serious global depression. There is value judgment involved here, and many would surely beg to disagree. On the whole, however, one is left with the impression that although the pain was very unevenly distributed, the world economy did escape the crisis with limited damage. Initial fears of a broad return to the 1930s did not materialize.

This said, there are good reasons to contemplate what lessons may and should be learned. First, we have the slow initial reaction, which allowed matters to deteriorate even further than might have needed be the case. It was striking that despite the fairly recent experience of the Asian financial crisis and of the dotcom bubble, the response from markets as well as governments was marked by a drawn-out reluctance to appreciate and accept the full gravity of the matters at hand. The U.S. case also was particular in the sense that warning voices urging decisive government intervention could be countered by raising the specter of a pending nationalization of banks.

The initial response from the U.S. government was to undertake a series of ad hoc interventions that included bailouts and government-brokered sales of investment banks like Bear Stearns and Merrill Lynch, as well as de facto taking over the mortgage giants Fannie Mae and Freddie Mac. Only following the collapse of Lehman Brothers and the rescue, within days, of insurance giant AIG did the realization dawn that the situation was untenable and that a program of massive financial support would have to be launched.

Backed by Federal Reserve Chairman Ben Bernanke, in mid-September 2008 Treasury Secretary Henry M. Paulson proposed the introduction of a "Troubled Asset Relief Program," commonly known as TARP. Approved by Congress in early October, it set aside an unprecedented total of $700 billion to support the financial system as a whole.[1]

Although highly controversial at the time, a year later most analysts would agree that the intervention, paralleled by similar interventions from the European Union (EU) and other governments, had been successful. Acting with support from central banks that cut interest rates and injected massive amounts of liquidity, governments finally got their acts together. It was certainly not without cost. Massive deficit financing produced unprecedented borrowing requirements that wreaked havoc on government finance in many countries. Yet the bottom line remains: there was no repetition of the 1930s. By early 2010, signs were emerging that the worst of the crisis was over. Then the Greek crisis struck, of which we shall say more in a moment.

Turning to the second part of the challenge – curbing the inherent driving force of greed and hence also ensuring that there would be no repeat performance – the story turned out very differently. When the dust has finally settled and the books may be closed, the conclusion will likely be that while governments did succeed in treating the symptoms, they failed to address the underlying causes.

At first it looked as though the political climate was ripe for undertaking serious financial market reform, including the rules of the game as well

---

[1] Although the plan was backed not only by President George Bush but also by both presidential candidates and by the Democratic Party leadership in Congress, it was opposed by most Republicans. Approved on a second attempt, when markets were in free fall, the TARP allowed the Treasury to disburse over the remainder of the year a first installment of $350 billion. Abandoning his initially stated objective to ease the burden on bank balance sheets by buying toxic mortgage-backed securities at a premium, Secretary Paulson opted instead for major capital injections. The first round saw nine major banks receive no less than $25 billion each. The last big disbursement went to automakers Chrysler and GM. (For a long and detailed list of the variety of entities that received support from the TARP, see http://projects.nytimes.com/creditcrisis/recipients/table, accessed on January 18, 2010.) The flat refusal by the administration to use TARP funds to prevent mortgage foreclosures, which constituted the main burden on the population at large, added further to the public sense of outrage. (For more details on the TARP, see http://topics.nytimes.com/top/reference/timestopics/subjects/c/credit_crisis/bailout_plan/index.html?inline=nyt-classifier, accessed on December 26, 2009.)

as the role of oversight agencies. On the U.S. side, the main instrument was linked to the TARP, specifying that financial and other institutions that received taxpayer dollars in support would have to abide by strict regulations on executive remunerations. Other governments followed suit, albeit to varying degrees.

If this pressure had been kept up and if temporary regulations had been transformed into permanent legislation, as many argued was imperative, a process of fundamental institutional change might have been set in motion, including a transformation of informal norms regarding financial market ethics. As it turned out, however, the system was stirred but not shaken. Despite continuing public outrage, the underlying culture of executive perks and financial market bonus schemes would prove to be highly resilient, not only in the United States but also in the European Union.

Having worked closely with the Bush administration, the incoming Obama administration inherited responsibility for continued crisis management and for deciding what to do with the second half of the TARP. Following a "stress test" of banks that had received financial support, in June 2009 it was decided that ten of the large banks would be allowed to return their cash injections to the government and thus also to escape associated restrictions on executive remuneration schemes. A case of particular importance occurred in December, when Bank of America was allowed to return $25 billion. Given that the bank was in the process of recruiting a new CEO, ending government restrictions on executive pay was held to be imperative.[2]

Needless to say, these latter developments could not help but further aggravate the general public's sense of outrage. In the absence of government support, many of the large banks would most likely have simply collapsed. Helped out by the taxpayers they not only survived. They actually proceeded to make such profits that within a year they were able to return the TARP funds and thus also to return to the old mode of handing out perks and bonuses.

Suggesting that the history of bubbles and crises will simply keep repeating itself, the reasons that produced this unfortunate outcome may be usefully divided into the superficial and the more fundamental. In the superficial we may advance traditional imagery of how both politics and financial markets are characterized by short memory spans, such that even nasty shocks will soon enough be followed by business as usual. While this view of cyclical

---

[2]   http://www.nytimes.com/2009/12/03/business/03bank.html, accessed on January 18, 2010.

systemic failure does contradict basic economics assumptions on learning and adaptation, it adds little to our understanding of root causes.

Accepting that risk-taking is a necessary component in the operation of financial markets, regulators will face a task that in a purely neoclassical world would be simply impossible. Assuming that profit and utility maximization constitute the main driving forces for economic actors more generally, and that such hedonistic behavior will be particularly pronounced in the very short-term context of financial market operations, discriminating among legitimate risk-taking, an excessive appetite for risk, and a readiness to resort to outright fraud will clearly not be possible to achieve with regulation alone.

Fine-tuning may certainly be undertaken. It is possible to introduce rules to put a time lag on the payment of bonuses and to ensure that such payments factor in the consequences of short-term risk-taking. It is possible to increase capital requirements for banks, thus reducing their scope for adventurous lending, and it may even be possible to formally separate traditional banking operations from those that are purely speculative. To be very specific, reinstatement of Glass-Steagall (of which more will be said in the final chapter) and the introduction of similar regulations in other Western countries would go a long way toward preventing the "too big to fail" situation from being repeated. The core issue, however, is that even if such formal interventions could be helpful indeed, they would not, in and of themselves, transform temptations for behavior that is unduly speculative or even fraudulent. Even if quite draconian penalties were to be introduced, previously cited arguments on enforcement swamping and on moral objections to disproportionate punishment would render the situation untenable.

The saving grace that prevents a broad slide down the slippery slope will have to be found in internalized norms. In our previous discussion we have emphasized the role of visible versus invisible hands and pointed at the responsibility of government to effectively remove from the choice set of actors such options that are clearly detrimental to the public good. Although, as we have just argued, this will not be achievable by direct regulatory intervention alone, it will have to remain a fact that the ambitions and spirit of public policy *will* influence the formation of public culture, and thus also of private norms.

The problem from a social science perspective is that we are faced here with analytical asymmetry. While we are able to explain within the box how ill-advised public policy may erode such norms that have, say, supported orderly payment of taxes and prevented greed from being perceived as "good," seeking to demonstrate how a formal policy reset might be associated with a restoration also of previous sets of informal norms and cultural values regarding trust and honesty represents a whole different type of challenge.

It is here that we must seriously consider structural arguments on embeddedness, perhaps even to the point of recalling Thorstein Veblen's emphasis on psychology and on the need to distinguish between entrepreneurship that is focused on making goods and that which is bent simply on making money. We shall have reason to return to these issues in our discussion on implications for social science theorizing.

Before proceeding to look at the long term and the role of invisible hands, we shall have to make a few brief comments also on the Greek turmoil. When realization suddenly dawned that the Greek government had built up a 13 percent budget deficit for 2009 and was unlikely to be able to meet debt service requirements for 2010, three factors combined to aggravate matters.

The *first* was that the crisis emerged in a situation when many European governments had been forced into heavy bailout spending that had resulted in massive budget deficits and a rapid buildup on sovereign debt. This implied that there was little room in financial markets to accommodate a Greek rescue operation.

The *second* factor was linked to the realization that in its efforts to evade common rules on the size of the budget deficit, the Greek government had received valuable assistance from financial market operators, coming up with "instruments" that were sufficiently opaque to prevent a broad realization of what was going on. This realization made it politically even more difficult for governments to provide assistance, without calling for creditors to take their share of the loss.

The *third* and clearly decisive factor was that failing to provide a rescue might cause the whole project of a common European currency to collapse. Faced with the combined prospects of a massive loss of political prestige and an equally massive mess trying to reconstruct national currencies, Euro zone leaders were quite literally held hostage by Greece. On May 10, fully cognizant that they were breaking their own rules, they in consequence agreed to provide a package of nearly $1 trillion USD, in an effort to keep the Greek debt crisis from spreading to other indebted EU members.[3]

---

[3]   http://www.csmonitor.com/Money/new-economy/2010/0510/EU-rescue-plan-buys-
time-to-defuse-Greek-debt-crisis, accessed on June 13, 2010.

Whether or not the common currency had been dealt a fatal blow, implying that its eventual demise is now only a matter of time, is a question that will not be pursued here. Let us instead look at problems in dealing not with short-term speculative crises, but rather with patterns of long-term inability to achieve development. This shift of focus will call for serious reconsideration of previously advanced arguments on the role of invisible hands, both in the Smithian sense of self-interested individual action being guided in the direction of the common good and in the Olsonian one of states perceiving market-augmenting government to be in their best interests.

DEALING WITH THE LONG TERM

In previous chapters we have repeatedly returned to the core question of what causes long-term divergence in economic performance, between countries as well as between regions of the world economy. We have also asked why only *some* poor countries have been able to break out of poverty and to achieve sustained development. Seeking to broaden the analytical approach, we shall add here a perspective that is somewhat different from that of how a long process of institutional evolution produced the "Rise of the West."

As a point of departure we shall take Vincent Ostrom's observation that "the twentieth century has been marked by revolutionary aspirations for an array of great experiments in the constitution of order in human societies," and his argument that all such "great experiments" have been "subject to potential sources of failure and breakdown."[4] The examples that he advances represent cases of substantial transformation of the social order, ranging from the historical English, American, French, and Russian revolutions to the more recent attempts to build new nations in Africa and Asia. A common denominator is that a new central authority proceeds to introduce a new set of formal rules, with constitutional dignity. In cases where failure results, this may be explained by an overestimation of the ability to make sure that the new rules do produce the anticipated changes in behavior.

Although Ostrom does not formulate the problem in this way, the core of the issue concerns the first and second conditions of social order, that is, to achieve coordination and cooperation. Under the by now familiar standard assumptions of hedonism and instrumentally rational profit and utility

---

[4] Ostrom, Vincent (2004), "Great Experiments and the Welfare State: Basic Paradigmatic Changes," in M. M. Sankhder and Sahrda Jain (eds.), *Social Security, Welfare and Polity*, New Delhi: Deep & Deep, pp. 49, 66.

maximization, undertaken on the basis of perfect information, neither of these presents an analytical problem. Yet, recognizing that we are faced in surrounding reality with massive and repeated cases of systemic failure, the causes of which remain poorly understood, it follows that there must be something wrong with the theoretical approach. The question is what.

In their repeatedly cited account of *The Rise of the Western World*, Douglass North and Robert Thomas open with the following program-matic statement: "Efficient organization is the key to growth; the develop-ment of an efficient economic organization in Western Europe accounts for the rise of the West."[5] This understanding is well in line with the rational choice approach of neoclassical economic orthodoxy, where the objective is to optimize via marginal fine-tuning of the formal rules. For as long as we remain within its own realm, there is nothing essentially wrong in this approach. Yet it does not really explain very much that is of relevance to the issues at hand.[6]

Reconstructing how efficient organization served to produce economic achievement will enhance our understanding of what components are *nec-essary* for success, but it will have little to say about what may also be *suf-ficient* for good economic performance to result. Most important, it leaves open the crucial question of whether the experiences of recorded success are at all transferable. Historical evidence indicates that the answer has been largely negative, and that surely calls for explanation.

Part of that explanation will have to address the conditions under which we will be helped by, say, "getting the property rights right." Economic research has established strong correlations between economic perfor-mance and the security of property rights. This link has been proven in rigorous theoretical modeling, and it has been confirmed with econometric evidence. As Avner Greif points out, however, it leaves open the question of *how* rights to property are rendered more or less secure: "Understanding how property is secured requires knowing why those who are physically able to abuse rights refrain from doing so."[7]

It is rather sobering to note, for example, that when Russia set out to privatize its economy, after the collapse of the centrally planned economy

[5] North, Douglass C. and Robert Paul Thomas (1973), *The Rise of the Western World: A New Economic History*, Cambridge: Cambridge University Press, p. 1.

[6] For a study of the development of capitalism that emphasizes the role of ideas and val-ues, see Appleby, Joyce (2010), *The Relentless Revolution: A History of Capitalism*, New York: Norton.

[7] Greif, Avner (2006), *Institutions and the Path to the Modern Economy: Lessons from Medieval Trade*, Cambridge: Cambridge University Press, p. 7.

of the USSR, none of the well-published knowledge about property rights would be of much use. What began as an exercise in ideological triumphalism, supported by the IMF and the World Bank, soon turned into a nightmarish bonanza of mass looting that would end in the financial meltdown in 1998. Faced with a choice between value-adding and predatory types of entrepreneurship, actors overwhelmingly preferred the latter, and the state was seemingly happy to play along.[8] Something was very clearly missing, something that cannot be explained within the realm of the rational choice approach alone.

The main thrust of Ostrom's argument follows precisely this line of thought, albeit implicitly so. As illustration, he devotes much of his attention to one of the successful cases, namely, the American Revolution, and he builds much of his case on Alexis de Tocqueville's previously cited study *Democracy in America*, from which the notion of a "great experiment" has also been scalped: "In that land the great experiment of the attempt to construct society upon a new basis was to be made by civilized man; and it was there, for the first time, that theories hitherto unknown, or deemed impracticable, were to exhibit a spectacle for which the world had not been prepared by the history of the past."[9]

Before we proceed to grapple with Tocqueville and the American "great experiment" it may be useful to say a few added words also about the Glorious Revolution that was played out in England in 1688–89. The triumph that was then scored by the English Parliament against the king is viewed by North as a "crucial watershed in development," the reason being that it marked the beginning of a constitutional process whereby subjects began looking for ways of formally binding or constraining kings and governments. It was important most of all in that it represented a successful "shackling of the arbitrary behavior of government with respect to property rights."[10]

Remaining within our previous framework of interaction between a new set of formal rules and the parallel evolution of supportive norms, it follows

---

[8] The actual outcome of Russian privatization is perceptively described by Joel Hellman as a "partial reform equilibrium," where the initial insider winners succeeded in securing a steady flow of rents by blocking further reform. The conclusion is that policy should have been aimed not so much at insulating the state from the short-term losers but rather at restraining the short-term winners. Given that the latter were in all likelihood operating in cahoots with the state, it is hard to see how that could have been achieved (Hellman, Joel S. (1998), "Winners Take All: The Politics of Partial Reform in Postcommunist Transitions," *World Politics*, vol. 50, no. 2, pp. 203–34).

[9] Tocqueville, Alexis de (1945), *Democracy in America*, New York: Alfred A. Knopf, p. 25.

[10] North, Douglass C. (1993a), "Institutions and Credible Commitment," *Journal of Institutional and Theoretical Economics*," vol. 149, no. 1, p. 19.

that such shackling could not have been successful if undertaken only in terms of imposing a new set of formal rules. Unless backed by a set of shared mental models that supported the contract between king and Parliament, it would have remained a mere formality, of little practical consequence. As North specifically underlines, the real key to success was that the mental models of the actors at the time were "equally context specific."[11]

We may take a step back here, to note that the context in sixteenth- and seventeenth-century Europe was rather similar across the board. Monarchies were locked in battle with nobles, with independent cities, and with a variety of ecclesiastical authorities. The outcome of the Glorious Revolution in England was that the monarchy came up short. In consequence, it was forced to accept constitutional constraints on its exercise of power, which in time turned into the foundations for modern parliamentary democracy. In France, it was the monarchy that prevailed, thus setting in motion a long-term process of centralizing authority around the absolute power of the French state.[12]

Commenting on this vital contrast, Francis Fukuyama notes that the consequences for the further development of the political culture of the respective countries would be far-reaching:

> The centralization of political authority in France undermined the autonomy of voluntary associations and made the French more dependent on centralized authority in later generations, whether that authority was monarchical or republican. In England, by contrast, society became far more self-organizing because people were not dependent on centralized authority to adjudicate their differences, a habit that was carried over by the English settlers to the new world.[13]

Returning to North, we may recall his previously cited account of the main reason the English "revolution" could achieve such "glorious" results, namely, that it occurred in the midst of an evolving intellectual tradition (Hobbes, Locke, Montesquieu, and the Scottish enlightenment) that was clearly supportive of the demands put forth from the side of Parliament. The outcome, as we know, was very tangible. It encouraged

---

[11] Ibid., p. 17.

[12] The contrast between the divergent paths of England and France may, as I am reminded by Tom Owen, be dated back to the High Middle Ages, when the Magna Carta of 1215 ended absolute power in England, whereas in 1302 the French monarchy under Philip the Fair emerged with increased power, having defeated Pope Boniface VIII with the support of the essentially consultative assembly of churchmen, nobles, and townsmen that eventually would becomes the Estates General. England's Glorious Revolution may in this perspective be viewed as a continuation of a longer historical trend.

[13] Fukuyama, Francis (1995), *Trust: The Social Virtues and the Creation of Prosperity*, New York: Free Press, p. 39.

the evolution of a legal structure, promoted the growth of science, and entailed the development of military technology that led ultimately to European hegemony.

While the positive example that was set by England was special in the sense that it failed to be replicated in Spain, in Africa, China, or Latin America, it would be successfully transplanted into the colonial world in North America, where it would prosper beyond imagination. The following is Tocqueville's enthusiastic verdict: "The emigrants who colonized the shores of America in the beginning of the seventeenth century somehow separated the democratic principle from all the principles that it had to contend with in the old communities of Europe, and transplanted it alone to the New World."[14]

We are faced here with important empirical illustrations of our previous theoretical discussion concerning the origins of institutions. According to the agency and functionalist approaches, sets of formal rules are deliberately introduced to promote good outcomes. It is also implicit that such sets of rules may be copied from more successful competitors. In the present account, we not only have a whole range of cases where institutional transfer or emulation fails to take place, in some cases even over the long term. It is also questionable to what extent the original success of the Glorious Revolution may be explained solely within the realm of functionalism, ignoring the structural argument on a parallel transformation of embedded norms and values.

Viewed within the context that we have sought to establish in previous chapters, the success of the American Revolution may be explained largely as a set of by-products. By launching a constitutional process that called for broad participation and that invited open debate on a range of fundamental issues, notably so in the *Federalist Papers*, both experts and the citizenry at large were exposed to formal processes of constitution and state-building that caused them to evolve strong supportive norms.

An important reason that Tocqueville's account has remained a classic is that he places emphasis on the side effects of the introduction of democratic government: "This ceaseless agitation which democratic government has introduced into the political world influences all social intercourse. I am not sure that, on the whole, this is not the greatest advantage of democracy; and I am less inclined to applaud it for what it does than for what it causes to be done."[15]

[14] Tocqueville, *Democracy in America*, p. 13.
[15] Ibid., p. 251.

The main point is that the social system that would come to be known as "Western" emerged not as a result of deliberate action but rather as a set of positive by-products of other actions: "I have no doubt that the democratic institutions of the United States, joined to the physical constitution of the country, are the cause (*not the direct, as is so often asserted, but the indirect cause*) of the prodigious commercial activity of the inhabitants."[16]

What we have here is a powerful endorsement of the need to consider the informal dimension of a country's institutional matrix, that is, the structural argument on embeddedness. In Ostrom's brief summary, Tocqueville clearly believed that "the customs and mores of the American people reflected in their habits of the heart and mind were the most important factors, that the institutional arrangements were of the second order of importance, and that the environing and material conditions of the country were of the third order of importance."[17]

It is not surprising that Jon Elster has shown similar interest, deducing that the "advantages of democracies, in other words, are mainly and essentially by-products." While democracy is normally viewed as a good system of government, Tocqueville argues that viewed purely as a decision-making apparatus it is inferior to aristocracy. Yet, "the very activity of governing democratically has as a byproduct a certain energy and restlessness that benefits industry and generates prosperity."[18]

The message is that the rational choice approach of emphasizing self-interested instrumentally rational behavior must be complemented with consideration of arguments regarding forces of motivation that are embedded in social structures. Accepting this message, a crucial point will concern the prospects for successfully introducing democracy in countries – like Russia or indeed Iraq – that have no previous experience of enjoying the fruits of this system of government. Can a project of democratic institution-building really be initiated on the assumption of having a tabula rasa, a clean slate upon which the new design may be outlined, for all to follow?

This question was very much at the heart of contemplation and discussion among the founding fathers of the American republic. In the opening paragraph of the first essay of *The Federalist*, Alexander Hamilton dwelled on the intellectual and experimental significance of work devoted to formulating a Constitution for the United States:

---

[16] Ibid., Emphasis added.
[17] Ostrom, "Great Experiments and the Welfare State," pp. 52–53.
[18] Elster, Jon (1983), *Sour Grapes: Studies in the Subversion of Rationality*, Cambridge: Cambridge University Press, pp. 95–96.

It has been frequently remarked that it seems to have been reserved to the people of this country, by their conduct and example, to decide the important question, whether societies of men are really capable or not of establishing good government from reflection and choice, or whether they are forever destined to depend for their political constitutions on accident and force.[19]

The outcome of the "great experiment" that was undertaken by this fairly small group of men has left an indelible imprint not only on the evolution of political and constitutional systems. It also has provided much of the empirical input for modern rational choice theorizing. The question that is left suspended, however, concerns the crucial role of deeply embedded norms and values. To what extent may the previously described intellectual tradition that stretches from Hobbes and Locke, via the Scottish enlightenment and the French *philosophes* to the American founding fathers be viewed as generally applicable? Does it really represent universal values, or is it merely a special case, able to thrive only in its own fertile humus?

The core of this question recalls what was said in Chapter 6 about the contrast between institutional change and institutional choice. By initiating a "great experiment," those in charge may certainly be correct in anticipating change to result, but will it really be change of the anticipated kind? The answer will hinge critically on what we assume about the reach of deliberate action, that is, the extent to which desired outcomes really are within the realm of what can be achieved via direct action.

There is an intriguing "Catch-22" of sorts here. If democracy has positive effects that are by-products, and if you inform people that they should get involved in democratic institution-building not for the cause as such but to promote some hazy secondary effects, will it then not have to be self-defeating? As Elster puts it, there needs to be another point of the exercise, since "if the system has no inherent advantages in terms of justice or efficiency, one cannot coherently and publicly advocate its introduction because of the side effects that would follow in its wake."[20]

Tocqueville presents a similar argument with respect to the American system of trial by jury: "I do not know whether the jury is useful to those who have lawsuits, but I am certain it is highly beneficial to those who judge them; and I look upon it as one of the most efficacious means for the education of the people which society can employ."[21] Again we have a situation where the main feature of the system is a by-product, and where that

---

[19] Cited from Ostrom, "Great Experiments and the Welfare State," p. 50.
[20] Ibid., p. 96.
[21] Tocqueville, *Democracy in America*, p. 285.

by-product would not arise if participants could not be otherwise motivated to take part: "A necessary condition for the jury system to have the
educational effects on the jurors for which Tocqueville recommended it is
their belief that they are doing something that is worth while and important, beyond their own personal development."[22]

If we may conclude that both democracy and the rule of law, and by
implication also market economy, have been successfully built on foundations that to some considerable extent are essentially by-products of other
action and activity, where does that leave us? How far will we then get with
"archaeological" work that is designed simply to uncover how those *formal*
institutions were built that produced the Rise of the West? Is it really sufficient to know that secure property rights promote good economic performance? Is it not the case that we shall have to know also under what
conditions those who are in a position to violate rights to property, ranging
from the state to criminal gangs and unscrupulous business partners, will
refrain from doing so? And will the latter not have to be viewed as an essentially "cultural" thing that is somehow embedded and that varies both over
time and across nations?

We may usefully recall here how Hernando de Soto chose to illustrate his
account of the informal sector in the Third World, and the massive amounts
of "dead capital" associated therewith, by referring to Fernand Braudel's
portrayal of the early capitalist sector of society as existing in a "bell jar," cut
off from and unable to expand into and conquer the whole of society. The
very fact that such a long parallel may be usefully drawn reflects that despite
the presence of both opportunity and self-interest, the metaphorical invisible hands have clearly not been universally successful in fulfilling the functions ascribed to them by the story script of the liberal economic tradition.

The implications are as clear as they are provocative. If the notion of invisible hands, used in the singular or the plural tenses, is to have any meaning at all, over and above the purely magical, that meaning will have to be
understood as a reflection of norms and values that are embedded in social
structures, at times even deeply so. In some cases, such informal institutions will promote behavior that is well in line with the liberal free market
tradition; in others they will prompt actors – including governments – to
take action that is clearly against the common good.

The core of the challenge to social science theorizing is that our understanding of what factors determine in which direction such action will
be pushed is so poorly developed, and that in consequence our ability to

22 Elster, *Sour Grapes*, p. 96.

prescribe corrective action will also be seriously circumscribed. We shall have reason to return to these important issues in our concluding chapter.

Returning to Ostrom's perspective of "great experiments" that are destined for failure, the stunning economic successes of the Anglo-American case will be viewed here as an exception that confirms and in a sense highlights the rule. What we really need to grapple with is not the stories of success but rather the broad experiences of systemic failure that have left large parts of the Third World in abject poverty and have caused the ambitions to achieve a rapid transition to democracy and a rules-based market economy in countries like Russia to fall so short. How much of this can we explain within the framework of the agency or rational choice approach?

In a thought-provoking article about the failure of many generations of Icelanders to develop a specialized fishing industry, Thráinn Eggertsson makes an important contribution toward enhancing our understanding of why opportunity and self-interest alone may not be sufficient for good outcomes to result. Based on opportunity and instrumental rationality, mainstream economics would certainly not have predicted an outcome where actors living under harsh natural conditions would give priority to farming and attend only part-time "to one of the world's most valuable fisheries that surrounded their country."[23]

The fact that the latter would remain true for such a long period of time, from the Middle Ages until the nineteenth century, does call for an explanation. Eggertsson suggests that from a "long-run perspective, economic stagnation has political and social roots and reveals failures of cooperation, coordination and organization." With explicit reference to Ostrom's "great experiments," he asks if there may perhaps even be cases of "pathological institutions," whereby societies are locked into inferior positions for extended periods of time: "However, long-run economic failures may also reflect an inability to experiment at all – a social paralysis where institutions thwart economic progress and trap communities at levels of low income."[24]

In a later contribution, he ponders the experience of the attempted Russian transition to a market economy and arrives at an even more provocative suggestion. Is it perhaps even the case that there may be instances of "pathological path dependence," which would come close indeed to pure determinism:

[23] Eggertsson, Thráinn (1996), "No Experiments, Monumental Disasters: Why It Took a Thousand Years to Develop a Specialized Fishing Industry in Iceland," *Journal of Economic Behavior and Organization*, vol. 30, no. 1, p. 2.

[24] Ibid.

The strong version of path dependence (which is still controversial) can be compared to the discovery of debilitating genes in specific human groups, and the implications for structural policy are devastating. The new institutionalism does not appear to propose any instruments or measures for manipulating models at this level, which indicates a new type of policy determinacy and calls for more research.[25]

Russia is certainly not alone in exhibiting a track record that may be construed as long-term systemic failure. In our previous account we have asked how it could be that China and the Islamic world, both of which were once far ahead of Europe in development, could be transformed from leaders to laggards, and we have noted how the Latin part of America fell far behind the northern part. Most of all, we have emphasized how decolonization failed to result in endogenously driven economic development in Africa and many other parts of the Third World.

What does make Russia so special, and thus so analytically challenging, is not the persistent pattern of economic backwardness as such, nor the fact that colonialism does not enter into the equation. It is rather that Russia is geographically situated in Europe, and that for centuries Russian intellectual discourse has been embroiled in a seemingly intractable conflict between ambitions to modernize and to westernize. While the former may be taken as reflective of the agency approach of promoting institutional change, with an aim to achieve improved governance and economic efficiency, the latter reflects the presence of deeply embedded norms and value systems – religious and otherwise – that have effectively prevented westernization.

If there is to be any sense at all in a notion such as that of pathological path dependence, short of unacceptable determinism, it must be taken as reflective of how deeply such norms and values may be embedded that prevent "great experiments" from achieving the intended results. The Russian case, to which we shall now return, provides vital illustration of this argument.

BACK TO THE RUSSIAN EXPERIENCE

In our previous account of the Russian experience, we followed rather closely the approach of the "continuity theory," aiming to illustrate a pattern of persistent institutional reproduction over time. Placed at the core of this approach was Richard Hellie's notion of repeated "service class revolutions." In his presentation, it is the "repetition of service class revolutions and the

---

[25] Eggertsson, Thráinn (1997), "Rethinking the Theory of Economic Policy: Some Implications of the New Institutionalism," in Joan M. Nelson, Charles Tilly, and Lee Walker (eds.), *Transforming Post-Communist Economies*, Washington, DC: National Academy Press, p. 75.

channeling of resources into a garrison state" that drives development and forms "perhaps the most striking pattern in modern Russian history."[26]

There can be little doubt that the Russian experience does constitute an analytically challenging contrast to what has been said earlier about successful institutional development. One of the most striking facts in the whole of Russian history is that following the first "time of trouble," conventionally dated to 1598–1613, which represented a complete collapse of Muscovy, when the boyars finally got together to elect a new tsar, they did not call for a Magna Carta or seek to undertake a Glorious Revolution.

Given that the new tsar – Mikhail Romanov – was chosen from one of the lesser families, there can be little doubt that had the leading families so wished they could have simply imposed on him a set of conditions regarding rights and obligations, similar to the set of twenty-three "Heads of Grievances" that were presented to William before he accepted the throne of England. The fact that they opted instead for a fully fledged reconstitution of the autocracy of Ivan the Terrible must hence be viewed as a deliberate choice, reflecting the presence of a common understanding that the outcome was indeed in their common best interest. Can this really be made to agree with the emphasis on opportunity and self-interest that marks the rational choice approach?

It is of course possible to argue that every type of action actually undertaken is consistent with utility maximization and may thus be viewed as fully rational. As noted by Geoffrey Hodgson in the previous chapter, however, a theory that explains everything in practice explains nothing. The crucial challenge rests in identifying when and how informal norms that are somehow embedded will interfere with instrumentally rational behavior.

In the following we shall return briefly to the Russian experience, not to rehash arguments on institutional reproduction but rather to look more closely at those "great experiments" that were undertaken with the aim of breaking out of the cyclical pattern of institutional erosion and reproduction. Departing from Hellie's emphasis on the service class revolutions of Ivan the Terrible, Peter the Great, and Joseph Stalin, we shall look first at the institutional matrix that emerged as a result of the first instance, proceed to re-examine developments in the post-Petrine era, and conclude with the events that preceded Vladimir Putin's restoration. The main point will be to contrast agency against structural explanations, and to demonstrate the tenacity of deeply embedded norms.

---

[26] Hellie, Richard (2005), "The Structure of Russian Imperial History," *History and Theory*, Theme issue 44, December, p. 89.

In our previous account of the emergence of a distinct Muscovite institutional matrix we emphasized the agency approach. Given the poor resources
that were available to counter the challenges of the time, introducing features such as autocracy and conditional property rights could be explained
as instrumentally rational, and the same holds for the process of adjustment
by individual actors to the new rules of the game that were thus laid down.

In one of his favored illustrations, North emphasizes that if the payoff
matrix in a society rewards negative behavior, then rational actors will have
an incentive to invest in becoming better at such behavior: "The kinds of
skills and knowledge that will pay off will be a function of the incentive
structure inherent in the institutional matrix. If the highest rates of return
in a society are piracy then organizations will invest in knowledge and skills
that will make them better pirates."[27]

To the boyars of Muscovy, the choice was an easy one. As Robert
Crummey puts it, "Muscovy offered an ambitious man no other options."
In theory, he could decide to simply opt out and remain at his estate, but
in practice that was not an option, and not only because it probably would
not have been allowed in the first place. Given the formidable centralization of control over resource allocation that marked the Muscovite order,
being away from Moscow would mean fading into oblivion and thus into
poverty. The latter effect was reinforced by the fact that the private estates
were still practicing subdivision of the land between heirs into ever smaller
parcels. The only real counterweight to such poverty-inducing fragmentation was the granting of new lands that went with service. There was of
course also the possibility of collecting bribes and fees, but the land question was the one that really tied the boyars to service.[28]

While the agency approach may thus take us quite far in explaining
how the Muscovite matrix emerged, we shall maintain that by far the most
important dimension of the process rested not in the formal dimension of
instrumentally rational choice but rather in the informal one of rationalization. It was the latter that produced what North would refer to as a distinct
set of mental models conditioning individual action.

An important reason for the boyars to think twice before opting out of
service was linked to their heavy investments into the self-enforced system of maintaining rank, known as *mestnichestvo*. Their well-documented

[27] North, Douglass C. (1993b), "Toward a Theory of Institutional Change," in W. A. Barnett,
      M. J. Hinich, and N. J. Scofield (eds.), *Political Economy*, Cambridge, MA: Cambridge
      University Press, p. 62.
[28] Crummey, Robert O. (1983), *Aristocrats and Servitors: The Boyar Elite in Russia, 1613–
      1689*, Princeton, NJ: Princeton University Press, p. 35.

obsession with receiving correct "places" (*mesta*) in the pecking order reflected not only the rewards that would be derived from climbing. It also and more importantly would feed into norm systems, offering vital increases in status and "honor" (*chest*). By the early seventeenth century, as Crummey puts it, "the Russian nobility wore the harness of service like a well-trained horse."[29]

The end result would greatly surprise outside observers: "Most Europeans simply could not believe that the Russians possessed an ethos in which service to the tsar was the honorable obligation of every subject."[30] In the mental universe that was evolving among the Muscovites, however, service to the tsar "was precisely the condition that preserved their freedom and dignity." They would look upon a man without a master as "a poor creature indeed, for he was subject to the violence and insults that predatory humans were so wont to inflict on their fellow men. But a man in service – particularly in service of the tsar – was protected by the strength of his master and shared in his lord's dignity."[31]

Introduced under Ivan the Great and Ivan the Terrible in the fifteenth and sixteenth centuries, this system reached its apogee under Peter the Great. As detailed in Chapter 4, his service class revolution was highly successful in overcoming the dislocations that had been caused by the terror under Ivan the Terrible and by the "great schism" over church reform that well-nigh tore both church and state asunder. Mainly relevant for our purpose, however, are the events that were played out in the post-Petrine era, when Russia had been transformed into an empire and when the old way of forced mobilization could no longer be viewed as necessary for external security.

In contrast to our previous account of how Russia failed to break out of the Muscovite mold, here we look more closely at those components that make up the contrary view, namely, the understanding of a process of steady westernization begun under Peter the Great and derailed by the Bolsheviks. To emphasize the shift in focus, we may recall Martin Malia's argument that "the economic dimension of the process is the one least relevant to deciding modern Russia's fate: ideology has been much more crucial."[32] While we do know that Russia failed to achieve a sustained

---

[29] Ibid., p. 34.

[30] Poe, Marshall T. (2000), *"A People Born to Slavery," Russia in Early Modern European Ethnography, 1476–1748*, Ithaca, NY: Cornell University Press, p. 223.

[31] Ibid., pp. 223–24.

[32] Malia, Martin (1999), *Russia under Western Eyes: From the Bronze Horseman to the Lenin Mausoleum*, Cambridge, MA: Harvard University Press, pp. 13–14.

transformation of the formal dimension of the institutional matrix, substantial controversy remains over the informal dimension and over its impact on the ambitions to reform.

At stake here is not only the impact of informal norms on the degree to which actors will actually honor and abide by changes in the formal rules. While fundamentally important to the institutional approach as a whole, understanding this nexus calls also for an understanding of the link between public ideology and private norm formation. That public Russian discourse, as well as Western perceptions thereof, did convey impressions of growing westernization can in no way be construed as conclusive evidence that private norms were marked by a similar process of transformation. The absence of a sustained change in the path of economic development, away from the cyclical pattern of reform and reaction, should make us wary of drawing such conclusions.

The most important feature of the early post-Petrine era was the gradual erosion of the service obligation. From a perspective of opportunity and self-interest, one would have predicted that this should have led boyars to form their own ventures, and that in consequence an economic system should have emerged based on plurality, competition, and initiative from below. The actual outcome was that they overwhelmingly preferred to remain in service, likely for a combination of reasons that included rational considerations of comparative advantage and an adherence to the "service ethos."

Following the complete removal of the formal service obligation, the early post-Petrine era also witnessed a brief but fundamentally important exposure of Russian elites to Enlightenment ideals and discourse. Catherine the Great not only befriended and corresponded with the *philosophes*. She also allowed their works to be both imported and translated, and thus to influence the project of reform. Her legislative commission in consequence introduced notions of division of powers and a rules-based economy, and her introduction of the Charter of the Nobility confirmed formal rights to property and due process.

Recalling Alexander Hamilton's question regarding "whether societies of men are really capable or not of establishing good government from reflection and choice," one might perhaps have expected Russia to emulate the parallel American example of creating a constitutional order, to serve as the foundation for a rules-based market economy. The conclusive answer, however, was negative, at the very least in the short term. As outlined in our previous account, retrenchment had set in already in the later part of Catherine's rule, followed by vacillation under Alexander I and culminating in a fully repressive regime under Nikolai I. The latter's Criminal Code in particular was deeply reflective of the nature and scope of the restoration.[33]

Behind the repressive façade, however, as argued by Malia and others, the ideological universe was indeed being transformed. Even within Nikolai's personal chancellery were sections charged with thinking about questions of legal reform and of abolishing serfdom.

The second stage of the post-Petrine era was introduced by Alexander II, whose celebrated Great Reforms may be rightly viewed as a "great experiment," in the sense suggested by Tocqueville and Ostrom. His abolition of serfdom paved the way for improved efficiency in agriculture and thus for a market-based transfer of resources into the secondary manufacturing sector. His introduction of judicial reform reconnected with the Enlightenment ideals of Catherine and suggested the possibility of an independent judiciary. His reform of local administration, finally, in the form of the zemstvo movement, opened the way for self-determination and greater initiative from below.

Again recalling the question posed by Hamilton, one might have speculated that the outcome should have been replacement of autocracy and state tutelage over all economic activity with division of power and a rules-based economy. The outcome, as again we may recall, was the opposite. Following the assassination of Alexander II, the rule of Alexander III would be marked by reaction and restoration, seeking, in the previously cited words of Konstantin Pobedonostsev, to correct the "criminal error" of the previous regime.

The third and final stage of the post-Petrine era was what we have referred to as the "democratic parenthesis" of the early twentieth century. Triggered by the violent events of 1905, which caused the autocracy to retreat and to allow substantial concessions, it featured significant formal steps toward democratic institution-building, including elections to a popular assembly and the introduction of a Basic Law that secured a broad catalogue of rights. It also added to the economic upswing of the final decade of the nineteenth century by introducing important land reform. The outcome, yet again, was reaction and restoration. Following the horrors of the Great War and the introduction of Bolshevik rule, by the end of the 1920s Joseph Stalin would have completed Russia's third service class revolution.

---

[33] Richard Pipes argues that one "is justified in saying, therefore, that Chapters Three and Four of the Russian Criminal Code of 1845 are to totalitarianism what the Magna Carta is to liberty" (Pipes, Richard (1974), *Russia under the Old Regime*, New York: Charles Scribner's Sons, p. 295).

Looking back at this more than two centuries long sweep of post-Petrine developments, we may return to what was said about the link between public discourse and private norms. While a powerful case can be made to suggest an ongoing process of westernization of Russian elites, and while we have repeated cases of agency interventions to introduce the formal components of democracy and a rules-based market economy, the cyclical record of reform and reaction shows that something was conspicuously missing. That something may be politically construed as powerful vested interests within the bureaucracy, but it may also be seen as the presence of deeply embedded norms, supportive of autocracy and market-contrary governance, that simply would not budge. It was highly symptomatic that even to the liberal Alexander II considering an assembly of nobles was anathema.

Although writing in a different context, Elster has an important point when he suggests that "the variation in corruption across countries is explained largely by the degree of public-spiritedness of their officials, not by the cleverness of institutional design." The point is that we must be wary of believing that changes in the formal rules of the game will by themselves produce the desired outcomes: "Morality and social norms seem to count for more than enlightened self-interest. Desires matter more than opportunities."[34] Whether we choose to refer to such factors as "trust" or "social capital," or indeed as embedded norms, it will remain that we are faced with obstacles to deliberate institutional change that we do not really know how to approach.

Perhaps the most fundamental difference that we may observe between Russia and the western parts of Europe lies in the absence of Russian exposure to those deep legal and mental transformations that resulted from the emergence of a distinctly European urban culture. The consequence was a failure to evolve the distinctive "middle class" that would make up the foundation of European development, following the revival of trade in the tenth century.[35] As illustration of the importance of this point, we may recall the previously cited study by Bradford De Long and Andrei Shleifer, analyzing links between urban commerce and type of political rule.

Concluding that strong princely rule was detrimental to commerce, they produced findings that are eerily similar to our account of the Muscovite

---

[34] Elster, Jon (1989b), *Nuts and Bolts for the Social Sciences*, Cambridge: Cambridge University Press, p. 158.

[35] Pirenne, Henri (1969), *Medieval Cities: Their Origins and the Revival of Trade*, Princeton, NJ: Princeton University Press, ch. 4 and *passim*.

heritage. Ruling princes "saw the legal order as an instrument of control rather than as a constraint on their actions." They lived in "parasite cities" that were "centers of neither trade nor urban industry but instead the homes of bureaucrats and the favored dwelling places of landlords." And under their rule, property was always legally insecure: "Subjects do not have rights; they have privileges, which endure for only as long as the prince wishes."[36]

Viewed from the latter perspective, the formation of Muscovy as a centralized state under strong princely rule may not have been the best thing that could happen to the Russians: "The rise of an absolutist government and the establishment of princely authority are, from a perspective that values economic growth, events to be mourned and not celebrated."[37] Yet, recalling what was said earlier about keeping score in different games, we may at the very least speculate that over the centuries the special Russian path of development would come to be associated with powerful mechanisms of rationalization, reinforced by observation that every attempt at deviation would be associated with dislocation and loss of prestige. Perceptions of economic backwardness may from this perspective have been viewed as secondary to more deeply embedded beliefs and expectations concerning the merits of the chosen path.

Our previous depiction of the Soviet era as a reconstitution in modernized garb of the tried and tested components of the Muscovite institutional matrix may be fitted nicely into this model of interpretation. Taken to the point even of casting the Communist Party in a role similar to that of the Orthodox Church, and of holding up images of surrounding enemies to rationalize forced mobilization of resources, Stalin's service class revolution represented a broad repression of all those advances toward westernization that had been recorded in the post-Petrine era. Significantly, it also entailed imposing a new mental universe on the subjects, aiming to eradicate all possibly remaining vestiges of Enlightenment ideals and aspirations. While the associated repression of markets and heavy focus on resource mobilization did cause mounting relative technological backwardness, from the Kremlin's perspective this may well have been viewed as a price worth paying. Increased intensity in resource mobilization could after all always compensate for decreased efficiency in resource use.

---

[36] De Long, J. Bradford and Andrei Shleifer (1993), "Princes and Merchants: European City Growth before the Industrial Revolution," *Journal of Law and Economics*, vol. 36, no. 2, pp. 673, 675, 679.

[37] Ibid., p. 700.

The program of post-Soviet reconstruction that was introduced by Boris Yeltsin may in turn serve as broad confirmation of our main points about agency versus structural explanations. From an agency perspective there was little indeed left to be desired. All the main components of formal democratic institution-building were put into place, including a constitution accepted by referendum, and the same holds for the formal fundamentals of a rules-based market economy. As an antithesis of sorts to the mental universe of the Soviet order, moreover, ideological westernization was taken to the point of seeking to be holier than the pope.

The outcome may be seen as a reflection of North's Nobel Prize speech observation that "since it is the norms that provide 'legitimacy' to a set of rules, revolutionary change is never as revolutionary as its supporters desire, and performance will be different than anticipated."[38] In lieu of adjusting to the new formal rules of liberal democracy and market economy, actors overwhelmingly preferred to remain with coping strategies of blat and networking, accepting fuzzy property rights as a license to engage in predation, and demonstrating much tolerance for the autocratic ambitions of the president. The price to be paid in terms of economic hyperdepression and associated social ills was devastating.

With the coming to power of Vladimir Putin, yet another phase of reaction and restoration was set in motion. Whether it merits the label of a fourth service class revolution, as suggested by Hellie, is a matter of taste, but there can be little doubt that to many Russians it represented a much-desired conclusion to the "time of trouble" under Yeltsin. As we have noted, early opinion polls showed broad support for Putin's authoritarian agenda.

The main message of the account as a whole is that instead of debating whether during Yeltsin's regime Russia had indeed finally "become" a market economy,[39] we should maintain in focus that a good outcome will hinge critically on whether actors view abiding by sets of new rules as being consistent with self-interested behavior. Recall how the emergence of Venice and Genoa, and indeed also of Novgorod, as economic success stories was associated with an endogenous evolution of institutions that included "market-augmenting" government and supportive invisible

---

[38]   North, Douglass, C. (1994), "Economic Performance through Time," *American Economic Review*, vol. 84, no. 3, p. 366.

[39]   For a critical assessment of this proposition, see Hedlund, Stefan (2008), "Such a Beautiful Dream: How Russia Did *Not* Become a Market Economy," *Russian Review*, vol. 67, no. 2, pp. 187–208.

hands embedded in social structures. The Muscovite case has demonstrated the contrary, namely, a persistent reliance on agency to achieve not only changes in the formal rules but also transformations of mental models that are essentially by-products and hence located outside the realm of deliberate policy intervention.

Let us proceed now to sum up what implications we may identify from the account as a whole for social science theorizing.

Implications for Social Science

In our introductory chapter, we cited Douglass North's apprehension over the growing trend of divergence within the family of social sciences. Noting that the "human environment is a human construct of rules, norms, conventions, and ways of doing things that define the framework of human interaction," he deplored the division by social scientists of this environment into discrete disciplines. The problem was that the latter "artificial categories" do not coincide with the constructions that the human mind produces to make sense out of the human environment.[1]

The reason this problem is so relevant to the present purpose is that many of the pressing problems of our time are located in an area where economics, sociology, and political science meet, and where at a now distant time in history they did have a common approach. Using a parallel from astronomy, one might even speak here of an expanding scholarly universe where over time a proliferating number of subdisciplines within the family of social science have increased their respective distances to neighboring disciplines, leaving behind in the middle an analytical no man's land. Whether this barren space really can be filled, or even bridged, by approaches from within new institutionalism still remains to be seen.

The following concluding account is divided into four sections. The first sums up and reflects on our understanding of financial crises, viewed as short-term systemic failures. The second digests what has been said about the causes and implications of path dependence, representing long-term systemic failures. The third approaches the core dimensions of the institutional context of transactions, which is where the roots of the problem must

---

[1] North, Douglass C. (2005), *Understanding the Process of Economic Change*, Princeton: Princeton University Press, p. 11.

be sought, and the fourth presents the scaffolding for a new departure in social science research.

The overall aim is to show how in cases where things go massively wrong modern social science fails to achieve a full understanding of the motivation for human action, and how the search for solutions to problems of systemic failure in consequence remains locked into a field of gravity and tension between agency and structural approaches.

UNDERSTANDING FINANCIAL CRISES

Returning yet again to the controversial matters of greed and financial market operations, we may note that a rational choice-based approach will be most helpful in explaining the profound transformation of modern capitalism over recent decades. We may show how the traditional focus on productive long-term investment, geared into building value-adding industrial structures and into the promotion of technological advancement, has been increasingly supplanted by an emphasis on short-term and highly footloose investment, geared into a financial industry that is becoming increasingly separated from the real side of the economy.

With those same tools we may also explain how the associated mode of entrepreneurship has been transformed, how the traditional "captains of industry" have been replaced by venture capitalists, corporate raiders, and actors that in general focus more on short-term profit (including bonuses) than on long-term viability and on contributions to value.

Where we come up short is in prescribing how to deal with those new forms of moral hazard that are so obviously linked to the problematic present-day cohabitation of the real and the financial sectors of the economy. Considering what has happened over the past few years, it may perhaps even be time to question how much of modern-day financial activity is in any sense productively linked to the original purpose of such markets, that is, to serve as an intermediary between savers and investors. Might it be possible to simply discard some of the purely and grossly speculative activities that cause so much harm, without in any way impairing the fundamental purpose?

It may be tempting here to listen to Nobel Laureate and former World Bank Chief Economist Joseph Stiglitz when he launches an assault on the effects of the TARP bailout program as a system where "you socialize the losses and privatize the gains," claiming that the U.S. economy has been transformed into a type of "ersatz capitalism."[2] While such critique

---

[2] http://www.cnbc.com/id/34921639, accessed on February 4, 2010.

is effective in fueling anger at those allegedly responsible for the financial mess, it is less so in adding to an understanding of how a repeat performance may be prevented.

It is surely correct that policies of deregulation, such as repealing the previously mentioned (Glass-Steagall) Banking Act of 1933, which was originally introduced to curb speculation, did contribute to the seriousness of the global financial crisis.[3] Such formal rule changes cannot, however, by themselves be held up as causes of crises. The core of the question again must be viewed as a reflection of structural arguments on embeddedness.

Stiglitz was considerably more to the point when, in an earlier contribution, he lashed out at the role of neoliberal economic policies in creating the preconditions for financial market deregulation and for the associated spread of beliefs that greed was somehow inherently good:

The world has not been kind to neo-liberalism, that grab-bag of ideas based on the fundamentalist notion that markets are self-correcting, allocate resources efficiently, and serve the public interest well. It was this market fundamentalism that underlay Thatcherism, Reaganomics, and the so-called "Washington Consensus" in favor of privatization, liberalization, and independent central banks focusing single-mindedly on inflation.[4]

Recalling Tocqueville's emphasis on "habits of the heart and mind" we shall argue that the line of causation must be drawn from a politically driven shift in public culture, entailing ever greater emphasis on self-enrichment, to decisions on financial market deregulation, and to consequences in terms of renewed "manias, panics and crashes." Recalling further our previous argument on an asymmetric relation between policies that cause an erosion of norms supporting a rules-based market economy, and policies that aim to achieve a reset of previous norms and values, we have here an outline of the essential dilemma that emerges in relation to financial market crises. While we can explain how and why they erupt, we have insufficient theoretical grounds on which to suggest how repetition may be prevented.[5]

---

[3]   The central provision of the Banking Act, namely, prohibiting a bank holding company from owning other financial companies, was repealed on November 12, 1999, by the "Gramm-Leach-Bliley Act." Thus the sluice gates were opened for the major banks to begin trading in fanciful new financial market products such as "mortgage-backed securities," "collateralized debt obligations," and "structured investment vehicles," that is, those very components that would cause the subprime mortgage crisis to erupt.

[4]   http://www.project-syndicate.org/commentary/stiglitz101, accessed on January 29, 2010.

[5]   On July 15, 2010, President Obama finally won Senate approval for a broad package of financial regulatory reform, to be known as the "Dodd-Frank Act," that in the words of the president would "organize protection of the American consumer the most efficient in the history of the United States and put an end to rescue of big banks with taxpayers' money"

In our subsequent remarks on the core of the problems at hand, we shall return to Veblen's distinction between making goods and making money, and suggest a need to focus more on psychology. Before doing so, we shall, however, take a brief second look also at our understanding of problems of path dependence and of historical influence more generally.

PROBLEMS OF PATH DEPENDENCE

In the previous chapter, we explored the emergence of ambitions to integrate history into social science analysis, taking the forms of historical economics, of historical sociology, and of historical institutionalism more broadly. At the heart of these ambitions we could find the controversial notion of path dependence. While most would probably agree that matters such as technological choice, spatial location of production, and the formulation of endogenous growth theory do exhibit patterns of increasing returns, and of positive feedback processes that generate path dependence, even here we may find sources of controversy.

By far the harshest attacks on the original formulations by Paul David have been fielded by Stanley Liebowitz and Stephen Margolis. We have referred to the ensuing debate in passing and will return here mostly to highlight one of its main dimensions, namely, that of remediable versus non-remediable path dependence.[6] The main point of contention concerns what type of information was available at the point of origin. Three possibilities emerge, referred to as first, second, and third degree path dependence. In the first case, a choice is made that subsequently gets locked in. Although based on incomplete information, as it turns out that the choice was after all an optimal one there is no problem. The second case represents a choice made on incomplete information that gets locked in and is subsequently regretted. As it is non-remediable, it too is unproblematic. The true problem, namely, that of *remediable* path dependence, arises in the case of third degree path dependence. Here a choice is made that is subsequently

---

(http://news.spreadit.org/wall-street-reform-passed-senate-obama-financial-regulatory-reform/, accessed on July 17, 2010). The act was signed into law by the president on July 21. While from an agency perspective this represented a major milestone, from a structural perspective of embeddedness it must remain debatable if it alone will have much impact on financial market norms and ethics.

6 See especially Liebowitz, S. J. and Stephen E. Margolis (1995b), "Path Dependence, Lock-in, and History," *Journal of Law, Economics, and Organization*, vol. 11, no. 1, pp. 205–26.

regretted despite the fact that complete information was available at the outset. If market forces fail to achieve correction, based on competition and self-interest, then we are faced with a case of serious market failure that challenges neoclassical orthodoxy. Maintaining that this type of market failure would be a very rare occurrence, Liebowitz and Margolis conclude that neoclassical economic theory remains unfazed.

In a forceful defense of the analytical importance of theories on path dependence, Paul Pierson makes two crucial points. It is, to begin with, inappropriate to dismiss non-remediable path dependence. While such dismissal may be appropriate for policy reasons, where it makes little sense to address impossibility, once we seek to understand why societies move in directions that are clearly inefficient, understanding causation is of paramount importance. Second, with respect to remediable path dependence, it is questionable how much faith should be placed in the corrective forces of learning and competition within the market context. Once we turn our eyes to politics, such forces are greatly diminished and problems of path dependence consequently enhanced.[7]

The main point to recognize is that while economic approaches to path dependence are firmly rooted in the neoclassical paradigm and applied to highly specific problems, once we move into neighboring disciplines we encounter what Peter Hall and Rosemary Taylor referred to as "considerable confusion." Much as one should encourage ambitions from within economics to sensitize economists to the role of history, one should look with appreciation at the "cognitive turn" within sociology and at the ambitions of historical institutionalists to "take time seriously" and to focus on "how ideas, interests, and positions generate preferences." This said, those who pursue such approaches share with the proponents of "historical economics" and of "historical specificity" a need to confront the unquestionable neatness and analytical power of deductive as compared to inductive theory.

While recognizing that the fundamental assumption on rationality has served economists (and other social scientists) well for a limited range of issues in micro theory, North argues that there has also been great damage: "Indeed the uncritical acceptance of the rationality assumption is devastating for most of the major issues confronting social scientists and is

---

[7]   Pierson, Paul (2000), "Increasing Returns, Path Dependence, and the Study of Politics," *American Political Science Review*, vol. 94, no. 2, pp. 256–57. See also Puffert, Douglas J. (2003), "Path Dependence, Network Form, and Technological Change," in W. Sundstrom, T. Guinnane, and W. Whatley (eds.), *History Matters: Essays on Economic Growth, Technology, and Demographic Change*, Stanford, CA: Stanford University Press, pp. 66–68.

a major stumbling block in the path of future progress."[8] His own focus, however, on the "imperfect and fumbling efforts" of actors to decode their environment does not take us much further than to bounded rationality and problems of cognition.

A real breakthrough would have to bridge the gap between a "logic of instrumentality" that agrees with functionalism and the rational choice approach, and a "logic of social appropriateness" that would integrate consideration of "culturally specific practices." Recalling the critique that was presented in Chapter 6 against the ambitions of economic sociology to present a viable alternative to mainstream economics, alleging that "a theoretical vacuum characterizes economic sociology," there would seem to remain some way yet to go before social constructivism can be brought into peaceful and constructive coexistence with rational choice. It is also symptomatic that Hall and Taylor refer to claims of historical institutionalism to be able to bridge the gap between agency and structural approaches as "more like a wish list than a fully specified theory."

None of this, however, should be taken as dismissal of the stated ambitions to integrate history and cultural specificity into modern social science. Even short of raising the specter of economics being transformed into a form of metaphysics, it should be clear that these represent fundamental challenges.

Looking more closely at the methodological complications that will arise, we may carry with us what the French historian Fernand Braudel has written not only about capitalism in the "bell jar," but also and even more important about *la longue durée*. In his masterpiece about the Mediterranean world under Philip II, he writes, "Civilizations are transformed only over very long periods of time, by imperceptible processes, for all their apparent changeability."[9] A pivotal notion in this context is the formation of distinctive mental models, referred to as *mentalité*. The link to structural approaches and embeddedness is obvious.

THE CORE OF THE PROBLEM

Having arrived at the end of a long series of arguments on causes of systemic failure, it is time to address the core of the problem, namely, to what extent

---

[8] North, *Understanding the Process of Economic Change*, p. 5.

[9] Braudel, Fernand (1976), *The Mediterranean and the Mediterranean World in the Age of Philip II*, Vol. 2, New York: Harper Colophon Books, p. 773. In his seminal article on the topic, published in 1958, he notes that in the *longue durée* of economic history, beyond, or beneath, the cycles and structural crises, lie "old attitudes of thought and action, resistant frameworks dying hard, *at times against all logic*." (Emphasis added. Cited from http://en.wikipedia.org/wiki/Longue_dur%C3%A9e, accessed on February 11, 2010.)

we may hope for such improvements in understanding that we may also prescribe successful remedial action. As a point of departure we may again take Lionel Robbins's insight that the pursuit of self-interest, unrestrained by suitable institutions, carries no guarantee of anything but chaos.

While the previous chapters have provided ample illustration that calls for Smithian laissez-faire and deregulation will not always bring about the hoped-for outcomes, and while we have been insistent that from Smith onward non-ideologically inclined scholars have been well aware of the dangers involved in allowing a free rein for self-enrichment, we have been less specific in suggesting what should be understood by "suitable institutions."

An important reason for this ambiguity is linked to the striking absence of a common understanding of the very notion of "institutions." The literature on new institutionalism is replete with comments on this fact, with some trying to introduce definitions of their own and others remaining content with expressing regret. And it is not a new problem.

Beginning with the early American institutionalists, Thorstein Veblen introduced a definition that was rooted in human culture and in prevalent spiritual attitudes: "The institutions are, in substance, prevalent habits of thought with respect to particular relations and particular functions of the individual and of the community." In later work he focused on how such attitudes become embedded, viewing an institution as "the nature of a usage which has become axiomatic and indispensable by habituation and general acceptance."[10]

John Commons in contrast was more focused on the instrumental function of institutions as enabling rather than as merely constraining, arguing that "we may define an institution as collective action in control, liberation and expansion of individual action." Collective action as such, moreover, was defined as "a liberation of individual action from coercion, duress, discrimination, or unfair competition by other individuals."[11]

Proceeding to the more recent contributions that were cited in Chapter 5, linking institutions specifically to the market, we may again contrast Oliver Williamson's (admittedly rhetorical) statement that "in the beginning there were markets," with Geoffrey Hodgson's argument that "the market itself is an institution," and Lionel Robbins's insistence that "not only the good society, but the market itself is an artifact."

---

[10] See further Waller, William T. Jr. (1982), "The Evolution of the Veblenian Dichotomy: Veblen, Hamilton, Ayres, and Foster," *Journal of Economic Issues*, vol. 16, no. 3, p. 759.

[11] Commons, John R. (1931), "Institutional Economics," *American Economic Review*, vol. 21, no. 4, pp. 649, 651.

The ambition of these scholars to expand the focus from a narrow agency view of institutions as the rules of the game, to an encompassing structural view that includes social and cultural context, is certainly laudable. However, it immediately calls attention to another equally striking absence of common understanding: "It is a peculiar fact that the literature on economics and economic history contains so little discussion of the central institution that underlies neoclassical economics – the market."[12]

While economists have in general proceeded "as if" there were no problems here, sociologists have been handicapped by their surrender very early of study of the market to economics. Although the literature has since been filled by virulent attacks on markets and market mentalities, notably but not exclusively from the side of Karl Polanyi and his followers, ambitions within economic sociology to produce its own theory of the market have not been overly successful. As noted in Chapter 6, harsh critique has been advanced to suggest that the use of embeddedness for this purpose falls short of providing a theoretical alternative to mainstream economics.

The lack of a common understanding of what constitutes a market is problematic not only in theoretical terms. As Hodgson notes, it has ramifications also for the design of policy to achieve economic development, ramifications that recall arguments holding that culture matters: "Understanding the institutional nature of markets is also vital in the context of economic development. This process involves a deeply embedded cultural and moral fabric, involving the behavioral norms that are necessary for the market to function."[13]

The challenge in finding "suitable institutions" may be usefully approached from North's triadic perspective of formal rules, informal norms, and enforcement mechanisms. For as long as we remain within the domain of formal rules, agency and rational choice approaches will do just nicely. The only real complications will arise in how we understand rules versus constraints, and whether organizations should be viewed as players or as institutions. This we may leave aside.[14]

It is when we turn to the side of informal norms that serious problems emerge. Here we are faced not only with a conflict between methodological individualism and methodological holism, yet again recalling Elster's

---

[12] North, Douglass C. (1977), "Markets and Other Allocation Systems in History: The Challenge of Karl Polanyi," *Journal of Economic History*, vol. 6, p. 710, pp. 703–16.

[13] Hodgson, Geoffrey M. (2001), *How Economics Forgot History: The Problem of Historical Specificity in Social Science*, London: Routledge, p. 254.

[14] For a detailed argument, see Hodgson, Geoffrey M. (2006), "What Are Institutions?," *Journal of Economic Issues*, vol. 40, no. 1, pp. 2–5.

emphasis on a persisting cleavage within the social sciences. We also face a need to incorporate history, which under any type of consideration will have to appear as the carrier of norms, values, beliefs, and expectations. In a pure neoclassical world of forward looking rational actors there would be no room for any consideration of such legacies.

Adding to the complications, the role of the latter will be prominent also in relation to the third part of the triad: enforcement. While questions regarding third party enforcement by the state have figured prominently in the rational choice literature on credible commitment, it has not been without problems. Writing about a desirable shackling of a ruler's discretionary power, Barry Weingast notes that this requires not only "institutions that limit and define the legitimate boundaries of state action." To be successful, it will also require a "set of shared beliefs among citizens who react against the state when the latter attempts to transgress the boundaries defined by those institutions."[15]

North clearly recognizes what is at stake here: "The key to success is the establishment of a viable polity that will support and enforce such institutional constraints and at this stage in our knowledge we know very little about such an institutional framework."[16]

Agreeing that only shared concepts will make rules meaningful, Hodgson suggests that we should "define institutions broadly as durable systems of established and embedded social rules that structure social interactions." A "social structure" is in consequence defined as "a set of significant relations between individuals that can lead to causal interactions."[17]

This focus on interpersonal relations brings us into another classic minefield, namely, whether society should be viewed as something more than a collection of individuals or simply as the sum of its members. The collection of individuals constitutes the main message of methodological holism or collectivism, where action is constrained by embedded norms and where the legitimacy of government hinges on actors' subjective beliefs on what is morally just or appropriate.[18] The Russian experience provides clear illustration of how remedial action that would be prescribed by rational choice

[15] Weingast, Barry R. (1993), "Constitutions as Governance Structures: The Political Foundations of Secure Markets," *Journal of Institutional and Theoretical Economics*, vol. 149, no. 1, p. 305.

[16] North, Douglass C. (1993a), "Institutions and Credible Commitment," *Journal of Institutional and Theoretical Economics*, vol. 149, no. 1, p. 21.

[17] Hodgson, Geoffrey M. (2004), *The Evolution of Institutional Economics: Agency, Structure and Darwinism in American Institutionalism*, London: Routledge, pp. 12, 14.

[18] For a brief discussion of the problems of methodological collectivism, see ibid., pp. 23–28.

is blocked by embedded beliefs concerning the appropriateness of the system as such.[19] Powerful moral and/or ideological objections to individualism, to private property, and to market relations in general – or indeed advocacy thereof – also qualify under this heading.

Irrespective of what significance we assign to such factors, in the final analysis action is taken by individuals. To Elster, who believes methodological individualism to be "trivially true," it is obvious that institutions cannot be viewed as "monolithic entities," which may be counted on to transmit and then carry out decisions from the top: "Talk about institutions is just shorthand for talk about individuals who interact with one another and with people outside the institutions. Whatever the outcome of the interaction, it must be explained in terms of the motives and the opportunities of these individuals."[20]

The implication is that we are back at individual choice, albeit perhaps no longer necessarily in the shape of rational choice.

Under a strict assumption of methodological individualism, the context of individual decision making will be taken for granted (namely, the assumptions of game theory). While this enhances predictive power, it is also tantamount to ignoring factors that jointly make up the famed invisible hands that guide individual action in at times unpredictable directions. States, organizations, and firms may for convenience be viewed as actors, but it will again be only as shorthand for individuals acting with at times conflicting interests.

The crux of the matter is that hierarchies in various forms will serve as repositories for features of organizational "culture" that may be inherited

---

[19] The powerful norms of collectivism that permeated the Soviet era as a whole have roots that may be traced to times long before the Bolsheviks. Associated with powerful resentment of self-enrichment by way of mercantile activity, such norms had a strongly negative impact on efforts to promote commerce and an urban culture of the kind so typical of Western Europe. While the functional origins are surrounded by great controversy, one may easily document how communal rural institutions such as the *mir* and the *obshchina* have been romanticized and viewed as something of the essence of what is Russian. It was also symptomatic of this heritage that following the Bolsheviks' takeover of power, poor peasants took matters into their own hands and forcefully put an end to the ambition, begun under Prime Minister Stolypin in 1906, to allow households that so desired to set themselves up as private farmers, with legal rights to their share of the communal property. The Soviet model of collective agriculture developed out of this spontaneous movement among the peasantry (Hedlund, Stefan (1984), *Crisis in Soviet Agriculture*, London: Croom Helm; Hedlund, Stefan (1989), *Private Agriculture in the Soviet Union*, London: Routledge).

[20] Elster, Jon (1989b), *Nuts and Bolts for the Social Sciences*, Cambridge: Cambridge University Press, p. 158.

but may also be deliberately introduced and manipulated. Living and acting within the confines of such hierarchies, individuals will face continual exposure to elements of public culture that may or may not agree with private norms.

Understanding how individuals cope with the gap between private and public norms and morality, and with associated expectations regarding how others will cope with the same, constitutes by far the most important challenge to the social sciences. The bottom line, as Hodgson suggests, is that "individuals nevertheless remain to be explained."[21] This is a task that economics in particular has long ignored. As illustration of how economics has chosen to shun problems of human motivation, Hodgson cites Friedrich von Hayek: "If conscious action can be 'explained,' this is a task for psychology not for economics ... or any other social science."[22]

Our repeated reference to Veblen's distinction between making money and making goods has served to illustrate how different socioeconomic contexts will give rise to different types of norms regarding individual versus collective best interest. Even if we assume that the motive of greed is eternal, the scope for greedy behavior will be determined not only by formal rules but even more so by informal norms of restraint that reside in private as well as in public culture.

Illustrating the true complexity of the matter, while actions driven by social norms will to a large extent be blind, compulsive, mechanical, or even unconscious, there will also be cases where there is considerable scope for skill, choice, interpretation, and manipulation. We know little about the origins and functions of many social norms, adding to the complications and prompting Elster to conclude that "following the lodestar of outcome-oriented rationality is easy compared with finding one's way in a jungle of social norms."[23]

Perhaps the most damaging of all forms of critique against agency and functionalist approaches lies in Elster's identification of two important classes of fallacy. One is the *moral fallacy* of by-products, a self-defeating form of instrumental rationality aiming to bring about desirable outcomes that can only arise as consequences of other actions. Ambitions to undertake radical systemic change would fall into this category. The other is the *intellectual fallacy* of by-products, the urge to explain an observable and

---

[21] Hodgson, *The Evolution of Institutional Economics*, p. 6.
[22] Ibid., p. 38.
[23] Elster, Jon (1989a), *The Cement of Society: A Study of Social Order*, Cambridge: Cambridge University Press, p. 100.

desirable state as the consequence of action designed to bring it about, even when no causality can be shown.[24] Illustrations here will include politicians' and governments' readiness to claim credit for positive events without seeking to learn what may really have caused those events to come about.

Viewed from a perspective of public policy formulation, these are observations that not only should give pause to beliefs in the corrective powers of the market, in the economy as well as in politics, but they should also cause reflection over the scope for deliberate intervention to result in the aimed-for outcomes. Recognizing that the "social sciences are light years away from the stage at which it will be possible to formulate general-law-like regularities about human behavior," Elster suggests that perhaps we should concentrate instead on "specifying small and medium-sized mechanisms for human action and interaction."[25]

Agreeing on a definition of mechanisms as "plausible, frequently observed ways in which things will happen," Pierson adds a suggestion that social science should focus more on "social mechanisms that have a strong temporal dimension."[26] It is also against this background that we should view his previously cited caution concerning "lofty aspirations about developing a science of politics, rooted in parsimony and generalization and capable of great predictive power."[27]

SCAFFOLDING FOR A NEW DEPARTURE

So, then, where does this all leave us? First, it should be noted that little if anything of what has been said in preceding chapters is of much relevance to routine situations or marginal change, where actors have adequate information and where most if not all of the parameters that define a situation of choice are well known. The social sciences have over recent decades strived hard to refine methods that are designed to address precisely such situations, and there can be no question that great progress has been made. When we proceed now to present the scaffolding for a new departure in social science research, it is important to bear this in mind.

As stated at the outset of the preface, what we have been concerned with here is fundamentally different. Over and above cases where path

---

[24] Elster, Jon (1983), *Sour Grapes: Studies in the Subversion of Rationality*, Cambridge: Cambridge University Press, p. 43.

[25] Elster, Jon (1989c), *Solomonic Judgments*, Cambridge: Cambridge University Press, p. viii.

[26] Pierson, Paul (2004), *Politics in Time: History, Institutions, and Social Analysis*, Princeton, NJ: Princeton University Press, p. 6.

[27] Pierson, "Increasing Returns," p. 266.

dependence prevents intended change, we have focused on non-routine situations of extra-marginal change taking place on multiple margins, under conditions of great uncertainty and of substantial disconnect from prevailing sets of norms, beliefs, and expectations. The latter form of cases may arise endogenously, such as when "manias and panics" result in financial crashes, and they may be triggered exogenously by system managers seeking to undertake "great experiments" that range from postcommunist transition to the introduction of democracy in Iraq and Afghanistan, and to attempts to escape Third World poverty traps. The common denominator is that under such conditions social science will be faced with challenges that to date it has fallen far short of meeting.

Again, this is said not to question the value of the tradition of deductive model building that has become the mainstay of modern social science. However, accepting, Elster's argument that the social sciences are light years away from being able to formulate laws on human behavior, we do have grounds for arguing that the increasingly narrow focus on deduction constitutes part of the problem rather than of the solution. While there can be no getting around Karl Popper's insistence on falsifiability as the main criterion of acceptable science, we also must recognize that there is a trade-off of sorts between neatly formulated hypotheses that are amenable to rigorous testing and more broadly formulated questions that are of relevance to the serious real-life problems that surround us.[28]

We may usefully listen here to what Mancur Olson once said about preferring to approach the really big issues: "Many researchers have … an instinct for the capillaries and there is some work in the journals that, even when right, is hardly worth bothering about. Just as the great fighter is looking for the jugular, so the great scientist is looking for areas where there can be a breakthrough – for areas where strong statements are in order."[29]

---

[28]   At the time of the collapse of the Soviet order there was a large group of area specialists, known at the time as "Sovietologists," some of whom were Russian émigrés. Within their ranks, they possessed a great deal of profound understanding of how the system worked. Alec Nove in particular deserves mentioning here. Although in retrospect it seems fairly clear that this pool of knowledge could have added much needed realism to the ambitions of undertaking radical systemic change, at the time it was striking how easily it could be brushed aside as being simply obsolete. The winning theme, symptomatically, was that of deductive general modeling.

[29]   Words cited by Charles Cadwell, in his foreword to Olson, Mancur (2000), *Power and Prosperity: Outgrowing Communist and Capitalist Dictatorships*, New York: Basic Books, p. xv.

Accepting, in consequence, the argument of historical institutionalism in general that we must focus more on the big issues, and of Pierson in particular that we must be wary of "lofty aspirations," it follows that we also have strong grounds on which to plead for a reintegration that would bring us back to the approach of "economy *and* society" that was championed by Max Weber. Given that the core of such an ambition must depart from Hodgson's statement that individuals remain to be explained, and from our repeated emphasis on the role of government in shaping public culture, the only way forward must be to resurrect some of the heritage of the tradition of inductive science.

While this might seem heretical to Harvard economists residing in Widener Hall, across the River Charles we may find colleagues at the Harvard Business School (HBS) who have a long tradition of practicing a "case method," developed at the Harvard Law School in the nineteenth century, which rests on induction. The rationale offered by the HBS for this approach to learning, that is, to promote leadership and decision making under conditions of limited or even insufficient information, may be found also at the Kennedy School of Government.[30]

Transplanted into the mainstream of economics and sociology, an ambition to complement the tradition of deductive modeling with insights gained from inductive case studies would in practice amount to a call for such genuinely interdisciplinary efforts of explanation and theorizing that could be found with Adam Smith but have since been largely forgotten. Once we accept that the invisible hand is no more than shorthand for embedded norms, beliefs, and expectations that allow uncoordinated actions by many individuals to result in coherent and even effective outcomes, it follows that the key to bridging the gap between agency and structural approaches must lie in Hodgson's call for "explaining individuals."

Case studies of events that are played out at times of great experiments and other forms of systemic shocks will be helpful in providing a better understanding of how and why actual behavior may deviate from predictions based on such narrow and partly contradictory assumptions that are associated with *homo economicus, homo sociologicus,* and *homo politicus.* The reason this is so has been captured by Robert Bates et al. Recognizing that rational choice theory has been successful in analyzing political outcomes in stable institutional settings, they also note that "in moments of

[30] For further outlines, see the respective websites of the HBS (http://www.hbs.edu/learning/case.html) and the KSG (http://www.ksgcase.harvard.edu/content/Teaching_Resources/Using_the_Case_Method.html).

transition, rules are ill defined, and symbols, emotions, and rhetoric seem to count for more than do interests, calculations and guile."[31] Similarly, Adam Przeworski notes that moments of transition constitute moments of maximal uncertainty, implying that at such times people may simply not know where their interests lie.[32]

An endeavor to investigate the relative importance, at times of great dislocation, of hard-nosed interests as opposed to softer and more deeply rooted or embedded informal norms will have to entail a return to the original formulations of self-interest and of invisible hands. Although Adam Smith has come to be most immediately associated with the belief in a spontaneous order, whereby uncoordinated actions by many individuals produce outcomes that are to the benefit of all, he was far from alone. Similar views could be found with contemporaries like David Hume and Adam Ferguson,[33] and if we broaden the perspective, the implicit notion of an invisible hand may be traced back to Enlightenment philosophers who preceded the Scots.[34]

A case in point is Immanuel Kant, whose *Universal Natural History and Theory of the Heavens*, published in 1755, contains formulations that are eerily similar to those subsequently made famous by Smith:

Individual men and even entire nations little imagine that, while they are pursuing their own ends, each in his own way and often in opposition to others, they are unwittingly guided in their advance along a course intended by nature. They are unconsciously promoting an end which, even if they knew what it was, would scarcely arouse their interest.[35]

Prior to Kant, Bernard Mandeville had expanded on the same theme, albeit to a somewhat different tune. In *The Fable of the Bees: or, Private Vices, Publick Benefits*, published in 1715, he made the same arguments

---

[31] Bates, Robert H., Rui J. P. de Figueiredo Jr., and Barry R. Weingast (1998), "The Politics of Interpretation: Rationality, Culture, and Transition," *Politics & Society*, vol. 26, no. 2, p. 222.

[32] Ibid., citing Przeworski, Adam (1991), *Democracy and the Market: Political and Economic Reforms in Eastern Europe and Latin America*, Cambridge: Cambridge University Press.

[33] Ferguson, Adam (1996), *An Essay on the History of Civil Society*, New York: Cambridge University Press, and Hume, David (1969), *A Treatise of Human Nature*, edited with an introduction by Ernest C. Mossner, Harmondsworth: Penguin. See also Herman, Arthur (2001), *The Scottish Enlightenment: How the Scots Invented the Modern World*, London: Fourth Estate.

[34] I am indebted to Jukka Gronow for drawing my attention to this prior history of thought.

[35] Cited from Reiss, H. S. (ed.) (1991), *Kant: Political Writings*, Cambridge: Cambridge University Press, p. 41. The German original was titled *Allgemeine Naturgeschichte und Theorie des Himmels*.

about actions of the many leading to effects that in the end would benefit all. What made the book so famous, or perhaps infamous, was that he drew an explicit line between private vices and public virtues. Driven by vicious greed, in the form of the basest and vilest of behaviors, even libertines will produce positive economic effects, simply because their actions will create a demand for other actions to be performed. Long before Wall Street sharps began to proclaim that greed is good, it could thus be argued that rapaciousness and violence of base passions will in the end benefit society in general.[36]

While we may in consequence conclude that Smith's conceptualization of the invisible hand was well in line with general philosophical thinking of the time, it is important to add that there were differences of opinion concerning the underlying dimension of morality. While Kant, for example, viewed actions as driven by something akin to a force of nature, Mandeville was explicit in calling for intervention by politicians. Long before Lionel Robbins would emphasize the need for a "visible hand" of the legislator, he understood that the passions of men would result in public benefit only if properly channeled.

The main question here concerns the interplay between the social order and what Jean-Philippe Platteau refers to as "generalized morality." In his *Treatise of Human Nature*, published in 1740, David Hume took a profoundly optimistic view of the evolution of the institutions of market economy. Arguing that the public good cannot be established unless individuals are driven not by selfish passions alone but also by a moral sense, he was confident that rational considerations would promote moral behavior. Property, law, and government could therefore be viewed as the outcome of the evolution of human society. In sharp contrast, Edmund Burke would argue that the expansion of commerce depended in itself on the prior existence of suitable norms. In *Reflections on the Revolution in France*, published in 1790, he spoke of "manners" and "civilization" and of "natural protecting principles" grounded in the "spirit of a gentleman" and the "spirit of religion."[37]

What is at stake here is whether market economy can be expected to gradually and unconsciously generate the social conditions upon which its viable existence depends. As we may recall from our previous discussion,

[36] The text is reprinted in Mandeville, Bernard (1988), *The Fable of the Bees: or, Private Vices, Publick Benefits*, Indianapolis: Liberty Classics.

[37] Cited from Platteau, Jean-Philippe (1994), "Behind the Market Stage Where Real Societies Exist – Part II: The Role of Moral Norms," *Journal of Development Studies*, vol. 30, no. 3, pp. 777–80.

Smith comes across as ambivalent. On the one hand, the opening chapter of *The Theory of Moral Sentiment* clearly states, "How selfish soever man may be supposed, there are evidently some principles in his nature, which interest him in the fortune of others, and render their happiness necessary to him, though he derives nothing from it, except the pleasure of seeing it."[38] On the other, *The Wealth of Nations* contains ample warnings about the implications of human selfishness and rapaciousness.

The challenge to social science theorizing that is implied here concerns the fundamental need to model morality, and norms more generally. As Platteau points out, we still have a fair way to go: "Now, to have a theory of norms, we should know how they arise, how they are maintained, how they change over time (how they vanish and how they are displaced by other norms), and whether and how they can be manipulated, all questions which are essentially unanswered to this date."[39]

In his classic study of commercial expansion and the competition between passions and interests, Albert Hirschman traces the optimistic view of how commerce may promote the evolution of good supporting norms back to the *philosophes*. In *De l'esprit des lois*, Montesquieu maintains that democracy can survive only when wealth is not too abundant or too unequally distributed, but then goes on to make an exception for "a democracy that is based on commerce." The reason is that the spread of commerce brings in its wake a sense of "gentleness" (*douceur*) that promotes a positive spirit of commerce.[40] This view of commerce as a powerful moralizing agent may be found also with Hume and Smith, and it provides fuel for the assumptions of neoclassical economic theory that we may safely ignore the dimension of culture and associated norms.[41]

Others have over time presented contrary interpretations, emphasizing how the spread of commercial and capitalist relations erodes and corrodes the very foundations of civilized society. To previously cited accounts from Karl Marx, Karl Polanyi, and Joseph Schumpeter, we may add the somewhat more ambivalent view of Georg Simmel, whose powerful account of the alienating role of money was tempered by a positive assessment of com-

---

[38] Smith, Adam (1976), *The Theory of Moral Sentiments*, Indianapolis: Liberty Classics, p. 9.
[39] Platteau, "Behind the Market Stage," p. 777.
[40] Hirschman, Albert O. (1977), *The Passions and the Interests: Political Arguments for Capitalism before Its Triumph*, Princeton: Princeton University Press, pp. 70–71.
[41] For an account of the virtues that are enumerated by Hume and Smith, see Rosenberg, Nathan (1964), "Neglected Dimensions in the Analysis of Economic Change," *Oxford Bulletin of Economics and Statistics*, vol. 26, no. 1, pp. 62–66.

petition as an institution that "fosters empathy and the building of strong social ties."[42]

It is in this long tradition of fundamental differences in opinion and interpretation of the motivations for human action that we may find good cause not only to argue that institutions matter, but even more so to agree with Platteau that a theory of norms is badly needed, a theory that captures origins as well as the driving forces of change and the scope for manipulation. In making this argument, it is important to note that statements on the importance of culture and history, as the repositories of embedded norms, have been backed up by substantial hard evidence, suggesting correlations between historical legacies and present-day performance.

As a case in point, we may refer to a study by Rafael La Porta et al. that investigates empirically the determinants of the quality of governments in a large cross-section of countries. Their findings are, inter alia, that countries that have a heritage of French or socialist law, or have high proportions of Catholics or Muslims, exhibit inferior government performance. The rationale in the former case is that while the tradition of common law that emerged in England was associated with an ambition to constrain government, the rival traditions of civil law that emerged in France, and of socialist law that emerged in the Soviet Union, were designed to support government ambitions of state-building and of extending control over society. Similarly, the negative impact of the religious factor is ascribed to the hierarchical nature of Catholicism and Islam.[43]

While the correlations as such are powerful enough, as is the case with, for example, previous studies of correlations between religion and corruption and religion and economic performance, we are still left with the question of how institutional reproduction over time takes place.[44]

Recognizing that new institutionalists in economics have built a lively research program around the assumption that institutions matter in

[42] Hirschman, Albert O. (1982), "Rival Interpretations of Market Society: Civilizing, Destructive, or Feeble?," *Journal of Economic Literature*, vol. 20, no. 4, p. 1472, citing Simmel, Georg (1955), *Conflict and the Web of Group Affiliations*, Glencoe, IL: Free Press, pp. 61–63. See also Hirschman, Albert O. (1992), *Rival Views of Market Society and Other Recent Essays*, Cambridge, MA: Harvard University Press.

[43] La Porta, Rafael, Florencio Lopez-de-Silanes, Andrei Shleifer, and Robert Vishny (1999), "The Quality of Government," *Journal of Law, Economics and Organization*, vol. 15, no 1, pp. 222–80.

[44] Inglehart, Ronald (2000), "Culture and Democracy," in Lawrence E. Harrison and Samuel P. Huntington (eds.), *Culture Matters: How Values Shape Human Progress*, New York: Basic Books.

determining performance in organizations and economies, Victor Nee and Paul Ingram conclude, "Without a theory of the origin of norms and the mechanisms through which institutions shape individual behavior, however, new institutionalists in economics cannot develop a satisfactory explanation for variation in economic performance."[45]

With respect to the "mechanisms" in question, La Porta et al. suggest that "cultural theories can work through politics," implying that political heritage may matter more than the cultural counterpart. The main point is that a political interpretation of religious variables may be more appropriate, in the sense that the use of religion for political purposes "may have shaped policies in a way that ended up being quite hostile to market development." Similarly, it is suggested that the transformation of such norms of intolerance and xenophobia that marked Tokugawa Japan into the more Western beliefs that were associated with Meiji Japan may be explained by a shift from controlling domestic threats under the Shoguns to addressing external threats under the Meiji reformers: "In short, culture appears to be quite often shaped by politics."[46]

The latter observation in particular is of great relevance to our main argument on the role of public culture in influencing private norms. Before proceeding to this issue, we shall, however, have to say a few words more about the need to model and understand the formation and transformation of norms that influence and condition economic performance. Whether we choose for this purpose to argue a direct link to religious beliefs, or a roundabout one that proceeds via politics conditioned by religion, we shall still be left with the same basic questions. Can we assume, for example, that the spread of commerce will have a positive or a negative impact on norms of trust, honesty, and civicness in general?

Going back to Max Weber, we may find, in his classic account of the Protestant ethic and the spirit of capitalism, an argument that is well in line with the optimistic view of Montesquieu, namely, that "the universal diffusion of unscrupulousness in the pursuit of self-interest was far more common in precapitalist societies than in their more competitive capitalist counterparts."[47] Although he was a sociologist, Weber's "institutional theory drew liberally from economics," and his "conception of the market was

---

[45] Nee, Victor and Paul Ingram (2001), "Embeddedness and Beyond: Institutions, Exchange, and Social Structure," in Mary C. Brinton and Victor Nee (eds.), *The New Institutionalism in Sociology*, Stanford, CA: Stanford University Press, pp. 40–41.

[46] La Porta et al., "The Quality of Government," pp. 230, 264.

[47] Cited from Platteau, "Behind the Market Stage," p. 769

virtually indistinguishable from that of neoclassical economists."[48] Given what we have argued at length about a cleavage between sociology and economics, these are interesting observations. As evidenced by the following excerpt, they may be used to place Weber partly but not wholly in the camp of methodological individualism: "Not ideas, but material and ideal interests, directly govern men's conduct. Yet very frequently the 'world images' that have been created by 'ideas' have, like switchmen, determined the tracks along which action has been pushed by the dynamic of interest."[49]

The famous metaphor of the "switchmen" points us straight into the analytical void where, as argued earlier, answers to the major questions of social science theory and methodology must be sought. Accepting our previous metaphor of social science as an expanding universe, it follows that it is only by bringing together perspectives from economics, sociology, and anthropology, in focused studies of actual developments at times of great dislocation, that we may increase our understanding of human motivation. Accepting further North's observation of the paucity of discussion on the central institution that underlies neoclassical economics, namely, the market itself, we have added support for the need to arrive at a better understanding of the origins and functions of such institutions that jointly make up this elusive concept. There are, however, good reasons that this has remained to date a challenge that is hard to live up to.

In his previously cited account of rival views on market society, Hirschman notes as rather striking that those who praise the capitalist system should have an interest in keeping alive the thought that "multiple acts of buying and selling characteristic of advanced market societies forge all sorts of social ties of trust, friendliness, sociability, and thus help keep society together." What is so striking is that "in actual fact, this sort of reasoning is conspicuously absent from the professional economics literature." The reason goes to the core of what has been said in previous chapters about the neoclassical tradition, namely, "Economists who wish the market well have been unable, or rather have tied their own hands and denied themselves the opportunity, to exploit the argument about the integrative effect of markets.

---

[48] Nee, Victor (2001), "Sources of the New Institutionalism," in Mary C. Brinton and Victor Nee (eds.), *The New Institutionalism in Sociology*, Stanford, CA: Stanford University Press, pp. 5–6, citing Collins, Randall (1980), "Weber's Last Theory of Capitalism: A Systematization," *American Sociological Review*, vol. 45, no. 6, p. 928.

[49] Weber, Max (1946a), "The Social Psychology of the World Religions," in H. H. Gerth and C. Wright Mills (trans. and eds.), *From Max Weber: Essays in Sociology*, New York: Oxford University Press, p. 280.

This is so because the argument cannot be made for the ideal market with perfect competition."[50]

There is a good deal of realization that norms of trust, honesty, and transparency will have an impact on economic behavior. Echoing Arrow's previously cited emphasis on the role of ethics, Thráinn Eggertsson states, "There is no doubt that one of the most important and difficult tasks that the new institutionalism must grapple with in years to come is to explain what Arrow refers to as commercial morality."[51] The problem, as noted by Hirschman, is that getting such realizations into the equations has proven to be immensely difficult, and the consequences have been rather negative: "In this manner, [the economists] endeavored to endow the market with economic legitimacy. But, by the same token, they sacrificed the sociological legitimacy that could rightfully have been claimed for the way, so unlike the perfect-competition model, most markets function in the real world."[52]

The structural absence of a genuine willingness on the part of many economists to listen, and to consider the arguments raised by sociologists, has prompted a colleague who generously offered to read and comment on a draft of this volume to note that "economics has now become more scientific than physics." Yet, "there is such a thing as applied physics but no applied economics. How can sociologists communicate with an autistic discipline?"[53]

The main reason behind this lack of communication, and of a genuine ambition to arrive at a common understanding of how to model and understand the role and adaptability of informal norms, may be traced back to seemingly irreconcilable views on methodological individualism and methodological holism. The understanding of the latter, that the social order cannot be reduced to the behavior of individual social actors, is a legacy from Émile Durkheim that has served to cement the line of separation. As emphasized by Victor Nee:

Methodological holism in sociology has been an obstacle to acceptance of the choice theoretic approach underlying the new institutionalist paradigm. A consequence of

[50]   Hirschman, "Rival Interpretations of Market Society," p. 1473.
[51]   Eggertsson, Thráinn (1993), "Mental Models and Social Values: North's Institutions and Credible Commitment," *Journal of Institutional and Theoretical Economics*, vol. 149, no. 1, p. 25, citing Arrow, Kenneth J. (1990), "Kenneth Arrow," in Richard Swedberg (ed.), *Economics and Sociology. Redefining Their Boundaries: Conversations with Economists and Sociologists*, Princeton: Princeton University Press, p. 139.
[52]   Hirschman, "Rival Interpretations of Market Society," pp. 1473–74.
[53]   The colleague in question desires to be identified as a "well known British public policy expert." Identity will be revealed upon oral request only.

this impasse has been sociology's growing isolation from allied social science disci-pline at a time when rapid progress is being made in understanding and explaining the social order.[54]

While economists remain insistent on methodological individualism, to the point even of a form of normative individualism, an assumption that there can be no such thing as a separate corporate, communal, or national welfare interest that is anything more or less than the sum of the welfare or interests of the individual persons involved, sociologists remain uncon-vinced. The tradition of new economic sociology that emerged in response to new institutionalism in economics is founded on an understanding of embeddedness that explicitly recognizes the role of social structure and that castigates the way in which "new economic imperialism attempts to erect an enormous superstructure on a narrow and fragile base."[55]

In response to Granovetter's argument on embeddedness, Oliver Williamson maintains that with some small exception "the entire argument is consistent with, and much of it has been anticipated by, transaction cost reasoning. Transaction cost economics and embeddedness reasoning are evidently complimentary in many respects." Adding to this positive inter-pretation, he also expresses a belief that previous disrespectful relations have been replaced by engagement and "healthy tension."[56] Close to two decades later, however, we remain mired in a lack of common understand-ing on how we should model and understand the role of informal norms, whether viewed as embedded or not, in determining individual as well as collective action.

Perhaps the most important challenge that still lies before us rests in seek-ing to understand the scope for consciously or subconsciously manipulat-ing norms, be it from an exogenous agency perspective of deliberate policy intervention or from an endogenous structural perspective of individual adaptation aiming to reduce cognitive dissonance. Perhaps cross-cultural and interdisciplinary comparisons of the impact of different historical leg-acies on such processes, at time of great dislocations, would be helpful in advancing social science theorizing more generally.

Going down this path would entail not only a return to the ideals of the Enlightenment thinkers, notably to the happy coexistence of political

---

[54] Nee, "Sources of the New Institutionalism," p. 11.

[55] Granovetter, Mark (1992a), "Economic Institutions as Social Constructions: A Framework for Analysis," *Acta Sociologica*, vol. 35, no. 3, p. 4.

[56] Williamson, Oliver E. (1994), "Transaction Cost Economics and Organization Theory," in Smelser and Swedberg (eds.), *The Handbook of Economic Sociology*, Princeton, NJ: Princeton University Press, pp. 77, 85.

economy and moral philosophy that was once so distinctive not only of Adam Smith but also of contemporaries like Adam Ferguson and David Hume. It would also imply an at least partial resurrection and reconsideration of the heritage of German historicism and of old American institutionalism. Perhaps in the end we might even arrive at a point where Hodgson is proven right in his anticipation that Thorstein Veblen will be recognized as one of the great names in the tradition of social science.

The prospects for any of this to happen, however, must be viewed as regrettably slim. On the positive side, it should be recognized that many good things have been said regarding the shortcomings of functionalism and of the agency approach, and that much effort has been devoted to sensitizing modern social scientists to the importance of cultural specificity and of such embedded beliefs, expectations, and norms that are carried forward by the progression of history.[57] Although we have cited many leading names from across the social sciences who argue for a new and more encompassing approach, we cannot ignore that their voices remain a small minority.[58]

A closer look at any of the subdisciplines of modern social science will bring home what has also been argued, namely, that over recent decades the trend toward increasingly narrow intra-disciplinary specialization has become strongly path dependent. It is entrenched in undergraduate textbooks and curricula, in rational choices of graduate thesis work, in coordinated expectations regarding what may be publishable in leading journals, and of course in assessing the prospects for winning tenured academic positions. Self-reinforcement arises from heavy investment in relevant skills, and from internalization of narrow disciplinary cultures and identities that are associated with maintaining external as well as internal pecking orders.

What makes this all so regrettable is that the problems of systemic failure that call for our attention remain overwhelming, and we are still not even remotely within sight of a successful formal deductive modeling of motives for individual action that would achieve the analytical and predictive powers of deductive natural science. To the "bottom billion" in particular, but also to those affected by financial crises, by failed transitions, and by botched attempts to introduce democracy by outside agency, this is not a happy outlook.

---

[57] For a recent set of case studies, see Harrison, Lawrence E. and Peter L. Berger (eds.) (2006), *Developing Cultures: Case Studies*, New York: Routledge.

[58] For a recent ambition to integrate considerations of history and culture that introduces the notion of a "cultural entrepreneur" and explicitly recognizes the Weberian "switchmen," see Zweynert, Joachim (2009), "Interests versus Culture in the Theory of Institutional Change," *Journal of Institutional Economics*, vol. 5, no. 3, pp. 339–60.

It is tempting to conclude the account as a whole by returning to Axel Leijonhufvud's humorous piece on the Econ, penned back in 1973, which he chose to end on a rather somber note: "It is true that virtually all Econographers agree that the present modl-making has reached aesthetic heights not heretofore attained. But it is doubtful that this gives cause for much optimism."[59] At the time of writing these final lines, close to four decades have passed during which the social sciences have reached levels of aesthetic refinement that are even more impressive. Yet we have perhaps even stronger reasons today to be doubtful if this gives cause for much optimism.

Last two chapters — repetitive

---

[59] Leijonhufvud, Axel (1973), "Life among the Econ," *Western Economic Journal*, vol. 11, no. 3, p. 337.

Bibliography

Appleby, Joyce (2010), *The Relentless Revolution: A History of Capitalism*, New York: Norton.

Aquinas, Thomas Saint (1981), *Summa Theologica: Complete English Edition in Five Volumes*, London: Sheed & Ward.

Arrow, Kenneth J. (1973), *Information and Economic Behavior*, Stockholm: Federation of Swedish Industries.

   (1990), "Kenneth Arrow," in Richard Swedberg (ed.), *Economics and Sociology. Redefining Their Boundaries: Conversations with Economists and Sociologists*, Princeton, NJ: Princeton University Press, pp. 133–51.

   (1994), "Methodological Individualism and Social Knowledge," *American Economic Review*, vol. 84, no. 2, pp. 1–9.

   (2004), "Path Dependence and Competitive Equilibrium," in W. Sundstrom, T. Guinnane, and W. Whatley (eds.), *History Matters: Essays on Economic Growth, Technology, and Demographic Change*, Stanford, CA: Stanford University Press, pp. 23–35.

Arrow, Kenneth and Gérard Debreu (1954), "The Existence of an Equilibrium for a Competitive Economy," *Econometrica*, vol. 22, no. 3, pp. 265–90.

Arthur, W. Brian (1988), "Self-Reinforcing Mechanisms in Economics," in Philip W. Anderson, Kenneth J. Arrow, and David Pines (eds.), *The Economy as an Evolving Complex System*, Reading, MA: Addison-Wesley, pp. 9–27.

   (1989), "Competing Technologies, Increasing Returns, and Lock-In by Historical Events," *Economic Journal*, vol. 99, March, pp. 116–31.

   (1994), *Increasing Returns and Path Dependence in the Economy*, Ann Arbor: University of Michigan Press.

Banfield, Edward C. (1958), *The Moral Basis of a Backward Society*, Glencoe, IL: Free Press.

Baran, Paul A. and Paul M. Sweezy (1966), *Monopoly Capital: An Essay on the American Economic and Social Order*, New York: Monthly Review Press.

Barber, Bernard (1995), "All Economies Are 'Embedded': The Career of a Concept, and Beyond," *Social Research*, vol. 62, no. 2, pp. 387–413.

Barkai, Haim (1977), *Growth Patterns of the Kibbutz Economy*, Amsterdam: North-Holland.

Barone, Enrico (1908), "Il Ministro della Produzione nello Stato Collettivista," *Giornale degli Economisti*, September/October, 2, pp. 267–293, translated as Barone, Enrico

(1935), "The Ministry of Production in the Collectivist State," in Friedrich A. Hayek (ed.), *Collectivist Economic Planning: Critical Studies on the Possibilities of Socialism*, London: G. Routledge, pp. 245–90.

Bates, Robert H., Rui J.P. de Figueiredo Jr., and Barry R. Weingast (1998), "The Politics of Interpretation: Rationality, Culture, and Transition," *Politics & Society*, vol. 26, no. 2, pp. 221–56.

Bates, Robert H. et al. (1998), *Analytic Narratives*, Princeton, NJ: Princeton University Press.

Beccaria, Cesare, Marchese di (2006), *An Essay on Crimes and Punishments*, Clark, NJ: Lawbook Exchange. (Original published in 1764.)

Bergson, Abram (1967), "Market Socialism Revisited," *Journal of Political Economy*, vol. 75, no. 5, pp. 655–73.

Berry, Lloyd E. and Robert O. Crummey (eds.) (1968), *Rude and Barbarous Kingdom: Russia in the Accounts of Sixteenth-Century English Voyagers*, Madison: University of Wisconsin Press.

Billington, James H. (1970), *The Icon and the Axe: An Interpretive History of Russian Culture,* New York: Vintage.

Birnbaum, Henrik (1996), *Novgorod in Focus: Selected Essays by Henrik Birnbaum*, Columbus, Oh: Slavica.

Blum, Jerome (1964), *Lord and Peasant in Russia: From the Ninth to the Nineteenth Century*, New York: Atheneum.

Brabant, Jozef M. van (1998), *The Political Economy of Transition: Coming to Grips with History and Methodology*, London: Routledge.

Braudel, Fernand (1976), *The Mediterranean and the Mediterranean World in the Age of Philip II*, Vol. 2, New York: Harper Colophon Books. (First published in 1949.)

(1992), *Civilization and Capitalism: 15th – 18th Century, Vol. 2, The Wheels of Commerce*, Berkeley: University of California Press.

Brinton, Mary C. and Victor Nee (eds.) (1998), *The New Institutionalism in Sociology*, New York: Russell Sage Foundation.

Brown, A. H. [Archie] (1975), "Adam Smith's First Russian Followers," in Andrew S. Skinner and Thomas Wilson (eds.), *Essays on Adam Smith*, Oxford: Clarendon Press, pp. 247–73.

Brown, Archie (2006), "Cultural Change and Continuity in the Transition from Communism," in: Lawrence E. Harrison and Peter L. Berger (eds.), *Developing Cultures: Case Studies*, New York: Routledge, pp. 387–405.

(2007), *Seven Years that Changed the World: Perestroika in Perspective*, Oxford: Oxford University Press.

(2009), *The Rise and Fall of Communism*, London: Vintage Books.

Buchanan, James M. (1975), *The Limits of Liberty – Between Anarchy and Leviathan*, Chicago: Chicago University Press.

(1979), "An Economist's Approach to 'Scientific Politics,'" in Buchanan (ed.), *What Should Economists Do?,* Indianapolis, IN: Liberty Press, pp. 143–59.

Cairnes, John (1873), "M. Comte and Political Economy," in Cairnes, *Essays in Political Economy: Theoretical and Applied*, London: Macmillan, pp. 265–311.

Cardoso, Fernando Henrique and Enzo Faletto (1979), *Dependency and Development in Latin America*, Berkeley: University of California Press.

Carlyle, Thomas (1837), *The French Revolution: A History*, Vols. 1–3, London: Chapman and Hall.

(1853), *Occasional Discourse on the Nigger Question*, London: Bosworth.

Clark, Gregory (2007), *A Farewell to Alms: A Brief Economic History of the World*, Princeton, NJ: Princeton University Press.

Colson, Elizabeth (1974), *Tradition and Contract: The Problem of Order*, Chicago: Adeline.

Coase, Ronald H. (1937), "The Nature of the Firm," *Economica*, vol. 4, no. 16, pp. 386–405.

(1984), "The New Institutional Economics," *Journal of Institutional and Theoretical Economics*, vol. 140, no. 1, pp. 229–31.

(1992), "The Institutional Structure of Production," *American Economic Review*, vol. 82, no. 4, pp. 713–19.

Coleman, James S. (1990), *Foundations of Social Theory*, Cambridge, MA: Belknap Press of Harvard University Press.

Coleman, James (1994), "A Rational Choice Perspective on Economic Sociology," in Neil J. Smelser and Richard Swedberg (eds.), *The Handbook of Economic Sociology*, Princeton, NJ: Princeton University Press, pp. 166–80.

Collier, Paul (2008), *The Bottom Billion: Why the Poorest Countries Are Failing and What Can Be Done About It*, Oxford: Oxford University Press.

Collins, Randall (1980), "Weber's Last Theory of Capitalism: A Systematization," *American Sociological Review*, vol. 45, no. 6, pp. 925–42.

(1994), *Four Sociological Traditions*, New York: Oxford University Press.

Commons, John R. (1924), *Legal Foundations of Capitalism*, New York: Macmillan.

(1931), "Institutional Economics," *American Economic Review*, vol. 21, no. 4, pp. 648–57.

(1934a), *Institutional Economics: Its Place in Political Economy*, New York: Macmillan.

(1934b), *Myself*, New York: Macmillan.

Comte, Auguste (1830–42), *Cours de philosophie positive*, Vols. 1–6, Paris: Bachelier.

(1869), *Cours de philosophie positive*, 3d ed., Vol. 4, Paris: Ballière.

(1883), *Opuscules de Philosophie Sociale, 1819–1828*, Paris: E. Leroux.

Conquest, Robert (1968), *The Great Terror: Stalin's Purge of the Thirties*, London: Macmillan.

(1986), *The Harvest of Sorrow: Soviet Collectivization and the Terror-famine*, New York: Oxford University Press.

(1990), *The Great Terror: A Reassessment*, Oxford: Oxford University Press.

Conrad, Alfred H. and John R. Meyer (1958), "The Economics of Slavery in the Ante-Bellum South," *Journal of Political Economy*, vol. 66, no. 2, pp. 95–130.

Cooper, Julian M. (2006), "Can Russia Compete in the Global Economy?," *Eurasian Geography and Economics*, vol. 47, no 4, pp. 407–25.

Cross, Samuel H. (ed. and transl.) (1953), *The Russian Primary Chronicle*, Cambridge, MA.

Crummey, Robert O. (1983), *Aristocrats and Servitors: The Boyar Elite in Russia, 1613–1689*, Princeton, NJ: Princeton University Press.

Custine, Astolphe, Marquis de (1989), *Empire of the Czar: A Journey through Eternal Russia*, New York: Doubleday. (Original published in 1843.)

David, Paul A. (1985), "Clio and the Economics of QWERTY," *American Economic Review*, vol. 75, no. 2, pp. 332–37.

(1993), "Historical Economics in the Long Run: Some Implications of Path Dependence," in Graeme D. Snooks (ed.), *Historical Analysis in Economics*, London: Routledge, pp. 29–40.

(1994), "Why Are Institutions the 'Carriers of History?': Path Dependence and the Evolution of Conventions, Organizations and Institutions," *Structural Change and Economic Dynamics*, vol. 5, no. 2, pp. 205–20.

(1997), "Path Dependence and the Quest for Historical Economics: One More Chorus of the Ballad of QWERTY," *Discussion Papers in Economic and Social History*, no. 20, November, pp. 1–47, http://www.nuffield.ox.ac.uk/economics/history/paper20/david3.pdf, accessed on November 9, 2009.

(2001), "Path Dependence, Its Critics and the Quest for 'Historical Economics,'" in Pierre Garrouste and Stavros Ioannides (eds.), *Evolution and Path Dependence in Economic Ideas: Past and Present*, Cheltenham: Edward Elgar, pp. 15–40.

Debreu, Gérard (1956), *Theory of Value*, New York: Wiley.

De Long, J. Bradford and Andrei Shleifer (1993), "Princes and Merchants: European City Growth before the Industrial Revolution," *Journal of Law and Economics*, vol. 36, no. 2, pp. 671–702.

Desai, Raj M. and Itzhak Goldberg (eds.) (2008), *Can Russia Compete?*, Washington, DC: Brookings Institution.

Dewey, Horace W. (1987), "Political Poruka in Muscovite Rus," *Russian Review*, vol. 46, no. 2, pp. 117–34.

Dewey, Horace W. and Ann M. Kleimola (1984), "Russian Collective Consciousness: The Kievan Roots," *Slavonic and East European Review*, vol. 62, no. 2, pp. 180–91.

Diamond, Jared and James A. Robinson (eds.) (2010), *Natural Experiments of History*, Cambridge, MA: Belknap Press of Harvard University Press.

DiMaggio, Paul J. and Walter W. Powell (1991), "Introduction," in Paul J. DiMaggio and Walter W. Powell (eds.), *The New Institutionalism in Organizational Analysis*, Chicago: Chicago University Press, pp. 1–40.

Djankov, Simeon, Edward Glaeser, Rafael La Porta, Florencio Lopez-de-Silanes, and Andrei Shleifer (2003), "The New Comparative Economics," *Journal of Comparative Economics*, vol. 31, no. 4, pp. 595–619.

Dobb, Maurice (1933), "Economic Theory and the Problem of a Socialist Economy," *Economic Journal*, vol. 43, no. 172, pp. 588–98.

Dobbin, Frank (1994), "Cultural Models of Organization: The Social Construction of Rational Organizing Principles," in Diane Crane (ed.), *The Sociology of Culture*, Oxford: Blackwell, pp. 117–53.

Durkheim, Émile (1888), "Cours de science sociale: Leçon d'ouverture," *Revue internationale d'enseignement*, Vol. 15, pp. 23–48.

(1909), "Sociologie et sciences sociales," in H. Bouasse et al., *De la méthode dans les sciences*, Paris: F. Alcan, pp. 259–85.

(1978), *On Institutional Analysis*, Chicago: University of Chicago Press.

Eberstadt, Nicholas (2005), "Russia, The Sick Man of Europe," *The Public Interest*, winter, http://www.nationalaffairs.com/public_interest/detail/russia-the-sick-man-of-europe, accessed on February 9, 2010.

Eggertsson, Thráinn (1990), *Economic Behavior and Institutions*, Cambridge: Cambridge University Press.

(1996), "No Experiments, Monumental Disasters: Why It Took a Thousand Years to Develop a Specialized Fishing Industry in Iceland," *Journal of Economic Behavior and Organization*, vol. 30, no. 1, pp. 1–23.

(1997), "Rethinking the Theory of Economic Policy: Some Implications of the New Institutionalism," in Joan M. Nelson, Charles Tilly, and Lee Walker (eds.), *Transforming Post-Communist Economies*, Washington, DC: National Academy Press, pp. 61–79.

Eklof, Ben, John Bushnell, and Larissa Zakharova (eds.) (1994), *Russia's Great Reforms, 1855–1881*, Bloomington: Indiana University Press.

Elster, Jon (1974), *The Empiricists*, Garden City, NY: Anchor Books, .

Elster, Jon (1983), *Sour Grapes: Studies in the Subversion of Rationality*, Cambridge: Cambridge University Press.

(ed.) (1986), *Rational Choice*, New York: New York University Press.

(1989a), *The Cement of Society: A Study of Social Order*, Cambridge: Cambridge University Press.

(1989b), *Nuts and Bolts for the Social Sciences*, Cambridge: Cambridge University Press.

(1989c), *Solomonic Judgments*, Cambridge: Cambridge University Press.

Ferguson, Adam (1996), *An Essay on the History of Civil Society*, New York: Cambridge University Press. (Original published in 1767.)

Findlay, Ronald (2005), "Kindleberger: Economics and History," *Atlantic Economic Journal*, vol. 33, no. 1, pp. 19–21.

Frank, A. G. (1998), *ReOrient: Global Economy in the Asian Age*, Berkeley: University of California Press.

Friedland, Roger and A. F. Robertson (1990), "Beyond the Market Place," in Friedland and Robertson (eds.), *Beyond the Market Place: Rethinking Economy and Society*, New York: Aldine de Gruyter, pp. 3–49.

Fukuyama, Francis (1989), "The End of History?," *The National Interest*, no. 16, summer, pp. 3–18.

(1992), *The End of History and the Last Man*, New York: Free Press.

(1995), *Trust: The Social Virtues and the Creation of Prosperity*, New York: Free Press.

Furubotn, Eirik G. and Rudolf Richter (eds.) (1991), *The New Institutional Economics: A Collection of Articles from the Journal of Institutional and Theoretical Economics*, College Station: Texas A & M University Press.

(1998), *Institutions and Economic Theory: The Contribution of the New Institutional Economics*, Ann Arbor: University of Michigan Press.

Gemici, Kurtulus (2007), "Karl Polanyi and the Antinomies of Embeddedness," *Socio-Economic Review*, vol. 6, no. 1, pp. 5–33.

Gerschenkron, Alexander (1962), *Economic Backwardness in Historical Perspective*, Cambridge, MA: Harvard University Press.

Goldman, Emma (1923), *My Disillusionment in Russia*, Garden City, NY: Doubleday, Page.

Goldman, Marshall (1994), *Lost Opportunity: What Has Made Economic Reform in Russia so Difficult?*, New York: Norton.

(2003), *The Piratization of Russia: Russian Reform Goes Awry*, London: Routledge.

Gossen, H. H. (1854), *Entwicklung der Gesetze des menschlichen Verkehrs und der daraus fließenden Regeln für menschliches Handeln*, Braunschweig: Vieweg.

Granovetter, Mark (1985), "Economic Action and Social Structure: The Problem of Embeddedness," *American Journal of Sociology*, vol. 91, no. 3, pp. 481–510.

(1990), "The Old and the New Economic Sociology: A History and an Agenda," in Roger Friedland and A. F. Robertson (eds.), *Beyond the Market Place: Rethinking Economy and Society*, New York: Aldine de Gruyter, pp. 89–112.

(1992a), "Economic Institutions as Social Constructions: A Framework for Analysis," *Acta Sociologica*, vol. 35, no. 3, pp. 3–11.

(1992b), "Problems of Explanation in Economic Sociology", in Nitin Nohria and Robert G. Eccles (eds.), *Networks and Organizations: Structure, Form and Action*, Boston, MA: Harvard Business School Press, pp. 25–56.

Greenfield, Sidney M., Arnold Strickton, and Robert T. Aubey (eds.) (1979), *Entrepreneurs in Cultural Context*, Albuquerque: University of New Mexico Press.

Greenspan, Alan (1997), "Remarks by Chairman Alan Greenspan," at http://www.federalreserve.gov/boarddocs/speeches/1997/19970610.htm, accessed on January 19, 2010.

(2008), *The Age of Turbulence: Adventures in a New World*, New York: Penguin.

Gregory, Paul R. and Robert C. Stuart (1974), *Soviet Economic Structure and Performance*, New York: Harper & Row.

Greif, Avner (1993), "Contract Enforceability and Economic Institutions in Early Trade: The Maghrebi Traders' Coalition," *American Economic Review*, vol. 83, no. 3, pp. 525–48.

(1994a), "Cultural Beliefs and the Organization of Society: A Historical and Theoretical Reflection on Collectivist and Individualist Societies," *Journal of Political Economy*, vol. 102, no. 5, pp. 912–50.

(1994b), "On the Political Foundations of the Late Medieval Commercial Revolution: Genoa during the Twelfth and Thirteenth Centuries," *Journal of Economic History*, vol. 54, no. 4, pp. 271–87.

(1995), "Political Organizations, Social Structure, and Institutional Success: Reflections from Genoa and Venice during the Commercial Revolution," *Journal of Institutional and Theoretical Economics*, vol. 151, no. 4, pp. 734–40.

(2006), *Institutions and the Path to the Modern Economy: Lessons from Medieval Trade*, Cambridge: Cambridge University Press.

Grossman, Gregory (1963), "Notes for a Theory of the Command Economy," *Soviet Studies*, vol. 15, no. 2, pp. 101–23.

Guillén, Mauro F. et al. (eds.) (2002), *The New Economic Sociology: Developments in an Emerging Field*, New York: Russell Sage.

Gulati, Ranjay and Martin Gargiulo (1999), "Where Do Interorganizational Networks Come From?," *American Journal of Sociology*, vol. 104, no. 5, pp. 1439–93.

Hahn, Frank (1992), "Autobiographical Notes with Reflections," in Michael Szenberg (ed.), *Eminent Economists: Their Life Philosophies*, Cambridge: Cambridge University Press, pp. 160–66.

Haitani, Kanji (1986), *Comparative Economic Systems: Organizational and Managerial Perspectives*, Englewood Cliffs, NJ: Prentice-Hall.

Hall, Peter A. and Rosemary C. R. Taylor (1996), "Political Science and the Three New Institutionalisms," *Political Studies*, vol. 44, pp. 936–57.

(1998), "The Potential of Historical Institutionalism: A Response to Hay and Wincott," *Political Studies*, vol. 46, pp. 958–62.

Hall, Peter A. and David Soskice (2001), "An Introduction to Varieties of Capitalism," in Hall and Soskice (eds.), *Varieties of Capitalism: The Institutional Foundations of Comparative Advantage*, Oxford: Oxford University Press, pp. 1–70.

Haller, Markus (2004), "Mixing Economics and Ethics: Carl Menger vs Gustav von Schmoller," *Social Science Information*, vol. 43, no. 5, pp. 5–33.

Hanson, Philip (2002), "Barriers to Long-Run Growth in Russia," *Economy and Society*, vol. 31, no. 1, pp. 62–84.

(2003), *The Rise and Fall of the Soviet Economy: An Economic History of the USSR from 1945*, London: Longman

Harrison, Lawrence E. (2000a), *Underdevelopment Is a State of Mind: The Latin American Case*, Lanham: Madison Books.

(2000b), "Why Culture Matters," in Lawrence E. Harrison and Samuel P. Huntington (eds.), *Culture Matters: How Values Shape Human Progress*, New York: Basic Books, pp. xvii–xxxiv.

Harrison, Lawrence E. and Peter L. Berger (eds.) (2006), *Developing Cultures: Case Studies*, New York: Routledge.

Hay, Colin and Daniel Wincott (1998), "Structure, Agency and Historical Institutionalism," *Political Studies*, vol. 46, pp. 951–57.

Hayek, Friedrich A. von (1935), *Collectivist Economic Planning: Critical Studies on the Possibilities of Socialism*, London: G. Routledge.

(1944), *The Road to Serfdom*, Chicago: University of Chicago Press.

Hedlund, Stefan (1984), *Crisis in Soviet Agriculture*, London: Croom Helm.

(1989), *Private Agriculture in the Soviet Union*, London: Routledge.

(1999), *Russia's "Market" Economy: A Bad Case of Predatory Capitalism*, London: UCL Press.

(2001), "Russia and the IMF: A Sordid Tale of Moral Hazard," *Demokratizatsiya*, vol. 9, no. 1, pp. 104–36.

(2005), *Russian Path Dependence*, London: Routledge.

(2006), "Vladimir the Great, Grand Prince of Muscovy: Resurrecting the Russian Service State," *Europe-Asia Studies*, vol. 58, no. 5, pp. 781–85.

(2008), "Such a Beautiful Dream: How Russia Did *Not* Become a Market Economy," *Russian Review*, vol. 67, no. 2, pp. 187–208.

Hedlund, Stefan and Niclas Sundström (1996), "Does Palermo Represent the Future for Moscow?" *Journal of Public Policy*, vol. 16, no. 2, pp. 113–55.

Hellie, Richard (1977), "The Structure of Modern Russian History: Toward a Dynamic Model," *Russian History*, vol. 4, no. 1, pp. 1–7.

(2005), "The Structure of Russian Imperial History," *History and Theory*, Theme issue 44, December, pp. 88–112.

Hellman, Joel S. (1998), "Winners Take All: The Politics of Partial Reform in Postcommunist Transitions," *World Politics*, vol. 50, no. 2, pp. 203–34.

Helpman, Elhanan and Paul Krugman (1985), *Market Structure and Foreign Trade*, Cambridge, MA: MIT Press.

Herman, Arthur (2001), *The Scottish Enlightenment: How the Scots Invented the Modern World*, London: Fourth Estate.

Hirschman, Albert O. (1977), *The Passions and the Interests: Political Arguments for Capitalism before Its Triumph*, Princeton, NJ: Princeton University Press.

(1982), "Rival Interpretations of Market Society: Civilizing, Destructive, or Feeble?," *Journal of Economic Literature*, vol. 20, no. 4, pp. 1463–84.

(1992), *Rival Views of Market Society and Other Recent Essays*, Cambridge, MA: Harvard University Press.

Hobbes, Thomas (1968), *Leviathan*, Harmondsworth: Pelican. (Original published in 1651.)

Hodgson, Geoffrey M. (1999), *Evolution and Institutions: On Evolutionary Economics and the Evolution of Economics*, Cheltenham: Edward Elgar.

(2001), *How Economics Forgot History: The Problem of Historical Specificity in Social Science*, London: Routledge.

(2004), *The Evolution of Institutional Economics: Agency, Structure and Darwinism in American Institutionalism*, London: Routledge.

(2006), "What Are Institutions?," *Journal of Economic Issues*, vol. 40, no. 1, pp. 1–25.

Hollander, Paul (1981), *Political Pilgrims: Travels of Western Intellectuals to the Soviet Union, China, and Cuba, 1928–1978*, New York: Oxford University Press.

(1998), *Political Pilgrims: Western Intellectuals in Search of the Good Society*, New Brunswick, NJ: Transaction.

Hosking, Geoffrey (2001), *Russia and the Russians: A History from Rus to the Russian Federation*, Harmondsworth: Penguin Press.

Hume, David (1969), *A Treatise of Human Nature*, edited with an introduction by Ernest C. Mossner, Harmondsworth: Penguin. (Original published in three volumes in 1739–40.)

Hunter, Holland and Janusz M. Szyrmer (1992), *Faulty Foundations: Soviet Economic Policies, 1928–1940*, Princeton, NJ: Princeton University Press.

Huntington, Samuel P. (1993), "The Clash of Civilizations," *Foreign Affairs*, vol. 72, no. 3, pp. 22–49.

(1996), *The Clash of Civilizations and the Remaking of World Order*, New York: Simon and Schuster.

Hutchison, Terence W. (1984), "Institutionalist Economics Old and New," *Journal of Institutional and Theoretical Economics*, vol. 140, no. 1, pp. 20–29.

Inglehart, Ronald (2000), "Culture and Democracy," in Lawrence E. Harrison and Samuel P. Huntington (eds.), *Culture Matters: How Values Shape Human Progress*, New York: Basic Books, pp. 80–97.

Jevons, W. Stanley (1866), "Brief Account of a General Mathematical Theory of Political Economy," *Journal of the Royal Statistical Society*, vol. 29, June, pp. 282–87.

(1871), *Theory of Political Economy*, London: Macmillan.

Johnson, Juliet Ellen (1994), "The Russian Banking System: Institutional Responses to the Market Transition," *Europe-Asia Studies*, vol. 46, no. 6, pp. 971–95.

Kaiser, Daniel H. (ed. and transl.) (1992), *The Laws of Rus – Tenth to Fifteenth Centuries*, Salt Lake City, UT: Charles Schlacks Jr.

Katsenelinboigen, Aron (1977), "Colored Markets in the Soviet Union," *Soviet Studies*, vol. 29, no. 1, pp. 62–85.

Kantorovich, Leonid (1968), *The Best Use of Resources*, New York: Macmillan.

Keegan, William (1993), *The Specter of Capitalism: The Future of the World Economy after the Fall of Communism*, London: Vintage.

Keenan, Edward (1986), "Muscovite Political Folkways," *Russian Review*, vol. 45, no. 2, pp. 115–81.

Kennan, George F. ["X"] (1947), "The Sources of Soviet Conduct," *Foreign Affairs*, vol. 25, no. 4, pp. 566–82.

(1971), *The Marquis de Custine and His Russia in 1839*, Princeton, NJ: Princeton University Press.

Keynes, John Maynard (1936), *The General Theory of Employment, Interest and Money*, New York: Harcourt, Brace.

Keynes, John Neville (1917), *The Scope and Method of Political Economy*, 4th ed., London: Macmillan. (First edition published in 1890.)

Kindleberger, Charles P. (1978), *Manias, Panics, and Crashes: A History of Financial Crises*, London: Macmillan.

(1990), *Historical Economics: Art or Science?* New York: Harvester Wheatsheaf.

Kleimola, Ann M. (1972), "The Duty to Denounce in Muscovite Russia," *Slavic Review*, vol. 31, no. 4, pp. 759–79.

Kluchevsky, V. O. (1911), *A History of Russia*, Vol. 1, London: J. M. Dent & Sons.

(1912), *A History of Russia*, Vol. 2, London: J.M. Dent & Sons.

Kochan, Lionel and Richard Abraham (1990), *The Making of Modern Russia*, Harmondsworth: Penguin.

Koopmans, Tjalling C. and Michael Montias (1971), "On the Description and Comparison of Economic Systems," in A. Eckstein (ed.), *Comparison of Economic Systems*, Berkeley: University of California Press, pp. 27–78.

Kornai, János (1992), *The Socialist System: The Political Economy of Communism*, Oxford: Clarendon Press.

Krippner, Greta R. (2001), "The Elusive Market: Embeddedness and the Paradigm of Economic Sociology," *Theory and Society*, vol. 30, no. 6, pp. 775–810.

Krugman, Paul (1991a), "History and Industry Location: The Case of the Manufacturing Belt," *American Economic Review*, vol. 81, no. 2, pp. 80–83.

(1991b), "Increasing Returns and Economic Geography," *Journal of Political Economy*, vol. 99, no. 3, pp. 483–99.

(1994), "The Myth of Asia's Miracle," *Foreign Affairs*, vol. 73, no. 6, pp. 62–78.

(2003), *The Great Unraveling: Losing Our Way in the New Century*, New York: Norton.

Kuczynski, Marguerite and Ronald L. Meek (eds.) (1972), *Quesnay's Tableau économique*, London: Macmillan.

Kuhn, Thomas S. (1962), *The Structure of Scientific Revolutions*, Chicago: University of Chicago Press.

La Porta, Rafael, Florencio Lopez-de-Silanes, Andrei Shleifer, and Robert Vishny (1999), "The Quality of Government," *Journal of Law, Economics and Organization*, vol. 15, no 1, pp. 222–80.

Landes, David S. (1969), *The Unbound Prometheus: Technological Change and Industrial Development in Western Europe from 1750 to the Present*, Cambridge: Cambridge University Press.

(1990), "Why Are We So Rich and They So Poor?," *American Economic Review*, vol. 80, no. 2, pp. 1–13.

(1999), *The Wealth and Poverty of Nations: Why Some Are so Rich and Some so Poor*, New York: Norton.

Lange, Oskar (1936), "On the Economic Theory of Socialism: Part One," *Review of Economic Studies*, vol. 4, no. 1, pp. 53–71.

(1937), "On the Economic Theory of Socialism: Part Two," *Review of Economic Studies*, vol. 4, no. 2, pp. 123–142.

Layard, Richard and John Parker (1996), *The Coming Russian Boom: A Guide to New Markets and Politics*, New York: Free Press.

Ledeneva, Alena V. (1998), *Russia's Economy of Favors: Blat, Networking and Informal Exchange*, Cambridge: Cambridge University Press.

(2006), *How Russia Really Works: The Informal Practices that Shaped Post-Soviet Politics and Business*, Ithaca: Cornell University Press.

Leijonhufvud, Axel (1973), "Life among the Econ," *Western Economic Journal*, vol. 11, no. 3, pp. 327–37. (Reprinted in Joshua S. Gans (ed.) (2000), *Publishing Economics*, Cheltenham: Edward Elgar, pp. 3–13.)

Lenin, V.I. (1976), *The State and Revolution*, Peking: Foreign Languages Press.

Leonardi, Robert (1995), "Regional Development in Italy: Social Capital and the Mezzogiorno," *Oxford Review of Economic Policy*, vol. 2, no. 2, pp. 165–79.

Lewis, Archibald R. (1951), *Naval Power and Trade in the Mediterranean, A.D. 500–1100*, Princeton, NJ: Princeton University Press.

Lie, John (1991), "Embedding Polanyi's Market Society," *Sociological Perspectives*, vol. 34, no. 2, pp. 219–35.

Liebowitz, S. J. and Stephen E. Margolis (1990), "The Fable of the Keys," *Journal of Law and Economics*, vol. 33, no. 1, pp. 1–25.

(1994), "Network Externality: An Uncommon Tragedy," *Journal of Economic Perspectives*, vol. 8, no. 2, pp. 133–50.

(1995a), "Are Network Externalities a New Source of Market Failure?," *Research in Law and Economics*, vol. 17, no. 0, pp. 1–22.

(1995b), "Path Dependence, Lock-in, and History," *Journal of Law, Economics, and Organization*, vol. 11, no. 1, pp. 205–26.

(1995c), "Policy and Path Dependence: From QWERTY to Windows 95," *Regulation: The Cato Review of Business & Government*, vol. 3. pp. 33–41.

Lippincott, Benjamin (ed.) (1938), *On the Economic Theory of Socialism*, Minneapolis: University of Minnesota Press.

Locke, John (1821), *Two Treatises on Government*, London: R. Butler. (Original published in 1689.)

(1975), *An Essay concerning Human Understanding*, Oxford: Clarendon Press. (Original published in 1690.)

Lotman, Yurii M. and Boris A. Uspenskii (1984), "The Role of Dual Models in the Dynamics of Russian Culture (Up to the End of the Eighteenth Century)," in A. Shukman (ed.), *The Semiotics of Russian Culture*, Ann Arbor: University of Michigan, pp. 3–35.

Loury, Glenn C. (1977), "A Dynamic Theory of Racial Income Differences," in Phyllis A. Wallace and Annette M. La Mond (eds.), *Women, Minorities and Employment Discrimination*, Lexington, MA: Lexington Books, pp. 153–86.

Lucas, Robert E. (1993), "Making a Miracle," *Econometrica*, vol. 61, no. 2, pp. 251–72.

Macfie, A. L. (1967), *The Individual in Society: Papers on Adam Smith*, London: Allen & Unwin.

Maddison, Angus (1995), *Monitoring the World Economy 1820–1992*, Paris: OECD Development Centre.

(2001), *The World Economy: A Millennial Perspective*, Paris: OECD.

Mahoney, James (2000), "Path Dependence in Historical Sociology," *Theory and Society*, vol. 29, no. 4, pp. 507–48.

Malia, Martin (1999), *Russia under Western Eyes: From the Bronze Horseman to the Lenin Mausoleum*, Cambridge, MA: Harvard University Press.

Malthus, Thomas (1798), *An Essay on the Principle of Population, as It Affects the Future Improvement of Society*, London: J. Johnson.

Mandeville, Bernard (1988), *The Fable of the Bees: or, Private Vices, Publick Benefits*, Indianapolis: Liberty Classics. (The original was published in a first edition 1714 and in an expanded edition in 1723.)

March, James G. and Johan P. Olsen (1984), "The New Institutionalism: Organizational Factors in Political Life," *American Political Science Review*, vol. 78, no. 3, pp. 734–49.

(1989), *Rediscovering Institutions: The Organizational Basis of Politics*, New York: Free Press.

(2008), "Elaborating the 'New Institutionalism,'" in R. A. W. Rhodes, Sarah A. Binder, and Bert A. Rockman (eds.), *The Oxford Handbook of Political Institutions*, Oxford: Oxford University Press, pp. 3–20.

Marshall, Alfred (1885), *The Present Condition of Economics*, London: Macmillan.

(1890), *Principles of Economics*, London: Macmillan.

Marshall, Gordon (1982), *In Search of the Spirit of Capitalism: An Essay on Max Weber's Protestant Ethics Thesis*, London: Hutchison.

Martin, David (1990), *Tongues of Fire: The Explosion of Protestantism in Latin America*, Oxford: Blackwell.

Matthews, R. C. O. (1986), "The Economics of Institutions and the Sources of Growth," *Economic Journal*, vol. 96, no. 384, pp. 903–18.

McDaniel, Tim (1996), *The Agony of the Russian Idea*, Princeton, NJ: Princeton University Press.

McMillan, John (2002), *Reinventing the Bazaar: A Natural History of Markets*, New York: Norton.

McNeill William H. (1963), *The Rise of the West: A History of the Human Community*, Chicago: University of Chicago Press.

Ménard, Claude (ed.) (2000), *Institutions, Contracts and Organizations: Perspectives from New Institutional Economics*, Cheltenham: Edward Elgar.

Ménard, Claude and Mary M. Shirley (eds.) (2005), *Handbook of New Institutional Economics*, Dordrecht: Springer.

Menger, Carl (1871), *Grundsätze der Volkswirtschaftslehre*, Wien: W. Braumüller.

(1883), *Untersuchungen über die Methode der Socialwissenschaften: und der politischen Ökonomie insbesondere*, Leipzig: Duncker & Humblot.

(1884), *Die Irrthümer des Historismus in der deutschen Nationalökonomie*, Wien: A. Hölder.

Mielants, Eric H. (2007), *The Origins of Capitalism and the "Rise of the West,"* Philadelphia, PA: Temple University Press.

Milford, Karl (1995), "Roscher's Epistemological and Methodological Position: Its Importance for the *Methodenstreit*," *Journal of Economic Studies*, vol. 22, nos. 3/4/5, pp. 26–52.

Milgrom, Paul R., Douglass C. North, and Barry R. Weingast (1990), "The Role of Institutions in the Revival of Trade: The Law Merchant, Private Judges, and the Champagne Fairs," *Economics and Politics*, vol. 2, no. 1, pp. 1–23.

Mill, John Stuart (1844), *Essays on Some Unsettled Questions of Political Economy*, London: J. W. Parker.

(1865), *Auguste Comte and Positivism*, London: Trübner.

Mises, Ludwig von (1920), "Die Wirtschaftsrechnung im sozialistischen Gemeinwesen," *Archiv für Sozialwissenschaften*, vol. 47, pp. 86–121.

Mitchell, Wesley (1935), "Commons on Institutional Economics," *American Economic Review*, vol. 25, no. 4, pp. 635–52.

Mokyr, Joel (1990), *The Lever of Riches: Technological Creativity and Economic Progress*, New York: Oxford University Press.

Montchrestien, Antoine de (1999), *Traicté de l'oeconomie politique*, Genève: Droz.

Montesquieu, Charles de Secondat, Baron de (2002), *The Spirit of Laws*, Amherst, NY: Prometheus Books. (Original published in 1748.)

   (1900), *The Spirit of Laws*, London: Colonial Press. (Original published in 1748.)

Moore, Henry L. (1914), *Economic Cycles: Their Law and Cause*, New York: Macmillan.

Nash, E. Gee (1929), *The Hansa: Its History and Romance*, New York: Dodd, Mead.

NBER (1960), *Demographic and Economic Change in Developed Countries: A Conference of the Universities-National Bureau Committee for Economic Research*, Princeton, NJ: Princeton University Press.

Nee, Victor (2001), "Sources of the New Institutionalism," in Mary C. Brinton and Victor Nee (eds.), *The New Institutionalism in Sociology*, Stanford, CA: Stanford University Press, pp. 1–16.

Nee, Victor and Paul Ingram (2001), "Embeddedness and Beyond: Institutions, Exchange, and Social Structure," in Mary C. Brinton and Victor Nee (eds.), *The New Institutionalism in Sociology*, Stanford, CA: Stanford University Press, pp. 19–45.

North, Douglass C. (1974), "Beyond the New Economic History," *Journal of Economic History*, vol. 34, no. 1, pp. 1–7.

   (1977), "Markets and Other Allocation Systems in History: The Challenge of Karl Polanyi," *Journal of Economic History*, vol. 6, winter, pp. 703–16.

   (1981), *Structure and Change in Economic History*, New York: Norton.

   (1986), "The New Institutional Economics," *Journal of Institutional and Theoretical Economics*, vol. 142, no. 1, pp. 230–37.

   (1988), "Ideology and Political/Economic Institutions," *Cato Journal*, vol. 8, no. 1, pp. 15–28.

   (1990a), *Institutions, Institutional Change and Economic Performance*, Cambridge: Cambridge University Press.

   (1990b), "A Transaction Cost Theory of Politics," *Journal of Theoretical Politics*, vol. 2, no. 4, pp. 355–67.

   (1991), "Institutions," *Journal of Economic Perspectives*, vol. 5, no. 1, pp. 97–112.

   (1993a), "Institutions and Credible Commitment," *Journal of Institutional and Theoretical Economics*," vol. 149, no. 1, pp. 11–23.

   (1993b), "Toward a Theory of Institutional Change," in W. A. Barnett, M. J. Hinich, and N. J. Scofield (eds.), *Political Economy*, Cambridge: Cambridge University Press, pp. 61–69.

   (1994), "Economic Performance through Time," *American Economic Review*, vol. 84, no. 3, pp. 359–68.

   (2005), *Understanding the Process of Economic Change*, Princeton, NJ: Princeton University Press.

North, Douglass C. and Arthur T. Denzau (1994), "Shared Mental Models: Ideologies and Institutions," *Kyklos*, vol. 47, no. 3, pp. 3–30.

North, Douglass C. and Robert Paul Thomas (1973), *The Rise of the Western World: A New Economic History*, Cambridge: Cambridge University Press.

North, Douglass C. and Barry R. Weingast (1989), "Constitutions and Commitment: The Evolution of Institutions Governing Public Choice in Seventeenth Century England," *Journal of Economic History*, vol. 49, December, pp. 803–32.

Nove, Alec (1977), *The Soviet Economic System*, Boston: Allen & Unwin.

(1982), *An Economic History of the USSR*, Harmondsworth: Pelican.

(1983), *The Economics of Feasible Socialism*, London: George Allen & Unwin.

OECD (2006), *Economic Survey of the Russian Federation 2006*, Paris: OECD.

Olson, Mancur (1995), "Why the Transition from Communism Is so Difficult," *Eastern Economic Journal*, vol. 21, no. 4, pp. 437–61.

(1996), "Big Bills Left on the Sidewalk: Why Some Nations Are Rich and Others Poor," *Journal of Economic Perspectives*, vol. 10, no. 2, pp. 3–24.

(1997), "The New Institutional Economics: The Collective Choice Approach to Economic Development," in Christopher Clague (ed.), *Growth and Governance in Less-Developed and Post-Socialist Countries*, Baltimore: Johns Hopkins University Press, pp. 37–64.

(2000), *Power and Prosperity: Outgrowing Communist and Capitalist Dictatorships*, New York: Basic Books.

Ostrom, Elinor (1990), *Governing the Commons: The Evolution of Institutions for Collective Action*, Cambridge: Cambridge University Press.

Ostrom, Vincent (2004), "Great Experiments and the Welfare State: Basic Paradigmatic Changes," in M. M. Sankhder and Sahrda Jain (eds.), *Social Security, Welfare and Polity*, New Delhi: Deep & Deep, pp. 46–83.

Pareto, Vilfredo (1896), *Cours d'économie politique professé à l'Université de Lausanne*, Lausanne: F. Rouge.

(1916), *Trattato di sociologia generale*, Firenze: G. Barbèra.

Parsons, Talcott (1937), *The Structure of Social Action: A Study in Social Theory with Special Reference to a Group of Recent European Writers*, New York: McGraw Hill.

Parsons, Talcott and Neil J. Smelser (1956), *Economy and Society: A Study in the Integration of Economic and Social Theory*, Glencoe, IL: Free Press.

Peters, B. Guy (1999), *Institutional Theory in Political Science: The "New Institutionalism,"* London: Pinter.

Pierson, Paul (2000), "Increasing Returns, Path Dependence, and the Study of Politics," *American Political Science Review*, vol. 94, no. 2, pp. 251–67.

(2004), *Politics in Time: History, Institutions, and Social Analysis*, Princeton, NJ: Princeton University Press.

Pierson, Paul and Theda Skocpol (2002), "Historical Institutionalism in Contemporary Political Science," in Ira Katznelson and Helen V. Milner (eds.), *Political Science: The State of the Discipline*, New York: Norton, pp. 693–721.

Pipes, Richard (1974), *Russia under the Old Regime*, New York: Charles Scribner's Sons.

(1996), "Russia's Past, Russia's Future," *Commentary*, June, pp. 30–38.

(1999), *Property and Freedom*, New York: Alfred A. Knopf.

(2004), "Flight from Freedom: What Russians Think and Want," *Foreign Affairs*, vol. 83, no. 3, pp. 9–15.

Pirenne, Henri (1969), *Medieval Cities: Their Origins and the Revival of Trade*, Princeton, NJ: Princeton University Press. (Original published in 1929.)

Platteau, Jean-Philippe (1994), "Behind the Market Stage Where Real Societies Exist – Part II: The Role of Moral Norms," *Journal of Development Studies*, vol. 30, no. 3, pp. 753–817.

Poe, Marshall T. (2000), *"A People Born to Slavery." Russia in Early Modern European Ethnography, 1476–1748*, Ithaca, NY: Cornell University Press.

  (2001), "Moscow the Third Rome: The Origins and Transformation of a 'Pivotal Moment,'" *Jahrbücher für Geschichte Osteuropas*, vol. 49, no. 3, pp. 412–29.

  (2003), *The Russian Moment in World History*, Princeton, NJ: Princeton University Press.

Polanyi, Karl (1944), *The Great Transformation*, New York: Farrar & Rhinehart.

  (1947), "Our Obsolete Market Mentality," *Commentary*, vol. 3, February, pp. 109–17. Reprinted in George Dalton (ed.) (1968), *Primitive, Archaic, and Modern Economies: Essays of Karl Polanyi*, New York: Anchor Books, pp. 59–77.

  (1957), "The Economy as an Instituted Process," in Karl Polanyi, Conrad M. Arensberg, and Harry W. Pearson (eds.), *Trade and Markets in Early Empires: Economies in History and Theory*, Glencoe, IL: Free Press, pp. 243–70.

Powell, Walter W. and Paul J. DiMaggio (eds.) (1991), *The New Institutionalism in Organizational Analysis*, Chicago: University of Chicago Press.

Przeworski, Adam (1991), *Democracy and the Market: Political and Economic Reforms in Eastern Europe and Latin America*, Cambridge: Cambridge University Press.

Puffert, Douglas J. (2003), "Path Dependence, Network Form, and Technological Change," in W. Sundstrom, T. Guinnane, and W. Whatley (eds.), *History Matters: Essays on Economic Growth, Technology, and Demographic Change*, Stanford, CA: Stanford University Press, pp. 63–95.

Putnam, Robert (1993), *Making Democracy Work: Civic Traditions in Modern Italy*, Princeton, NJ: Princeton University Press.

Quesnay, Francois (1980), *Tableau Économique*, Tokyo: Bibliothèque de la Faculté des sciences économiques, Université Nihon. (Original published in 1759.)

Raeff, Marc (1976), "Imperial Russia: Peter I to Nicholas I," in Robert Auty and Dimitri Obolensky (eds.), *An Introduction to Russian History*, Cambridge: Cambridge University Press, pp. 121–95.

Raphael, D. D. (1975), "The Impartial Spectator," in Andrew S. Skinner and Thomas Wilson (eds.), *Essays on Adam Smith*, Oxford: Clarendon Press, pp. 83–99.

Reiss, H.S. (ed.) (1991), *Kant: Political Writings*, Cambridge: Cambridge University Press.

Ricardo, David (1817), *On the Principles of Political Economy and Taxation*, London: John Murray.

Robbins, Lionel (1952), *The Theory of Economic Policy in English Classical Political Economy*, London: Macmillan.

Roland, Gérard (2000), *Transition and Economics: Politics, Markets, and Firms*, Cambridge, MA: MIT Press.

Romer, Paul M. (1986), "Increasing Returns and Long-Run Growth," *Journal of Political Economy*, vol. 94, no. 5, pp. 1002–37.

Roscher, Wilhelm G. F. (1843), *Grundriss zu Vorlesungen über die Staatswirtschaft: nach geschichtlicher Methode*, Göttingen: Dieterich.

Rose, Richard (1999), "Living in an Anti-Modern Society," *East European Constitutional Review*, vol. 8, nos. 1–2, pp. 68–75.

Rose, Richard and Ian McAllister (1996), "Is Money the Measure of Welfare in Russia?," *Review of Income and Wealth*, vol. 42, no. 1, pp. 75–90.

Rosefielde, Steven (1998), *Efficiency and Russia's Economic Recovery Potential to the Year 2000 and Beyond*, Aldershot: Ashgate.

(2002), *Comparative Economic Systems: Culture, Wealth, and Power in the 21st Century*, Malden, MA: Blackwell.

(2009), *Red Holocaust*, London: Routledge.

Rosenberg, Nathan (1964), "Neglected Dimensions in the Analysis of Economic Change," *Oxford Bulletin of Economics and Statistics*, vol. 26, no. 1, pp. 59–77.

Rosenberg, Nathan and L. E. Birdzell, Jr. (1986), *How the West Grew Rich: The Economic Transformation of the Industrial World*, New York: Basic Books.

Rothschild, Emma (1994), "Adam Smith and the Invisible Hand," *American Economic Review*, vol. 84, no. 2, pp. 319–22.

(2001), *Economic Sentiments: Adam Smith, Condorcet, and the Enlightenment*, Cambridge, MA: Harvard University Press.

Rousseau, Jean-Jacques (1911), *Émile, ou de l'éducation*, Paris: E. Flammarion. (Original published in 1762.)

(1993), *The Social Contract and the Discourses*, New York: Alfred A. Knopf.

Samuelson, Paul (1947), *Foundations of Economic Analysis*, Cambridge, MA: Harvard University Press.

Sanders, Elizabeth (2008), "Historical Institutionalism," in R. A. W. Rhodes, Sarah A. Binder, and Bert A. Rockman (eds.), *The Oxford Handbook of Political Institutions*, Oxford: Oxford University Press, pp. 39–55.

Sait, Edward (1938), *Political Institutions – A Preface*, Boston: Appleton-Century-Crofts.

Schmoller, Gustav von (1883), "Zur Methodologie der Staats- und Sozial-Wissenschaften," *Schmoller's Jahrbuch*, vol. 7, no. 3, pp. 975–94.

Schumpeter, Joseph A. (1908), *Das Wesen und der Hauptinhalt der theoretischen Nationalökonomie*, Leipzig, Duncker & Humblot.

(1942), *Capitalism, Socialism, and Democracy*, New York: Harper & Brothers.

(1950), "The March into Socialism," *American Economic Review*, vol. 40, no. 2, May, pp. 446–56.

(1951), "Vilfredo Pareto, 1848–1923," in Schumpeter, *Ten Great Economists: From Marx to Keynes*, New York: Oxford University Press, pp. 110–42.

(1954), *History of Economic Analysis*, London: Allen & Unwin.

Schwoerer, Lois G. (1981), *The Declaration of Rights, 1689*, Baltimore: Johns Hopkins University Press.

Scruton, Roger (2002), *The West and the Rest: Globalization and the Terrorist Threat*, Wilmington, DE: ISI Books.

Sen, Amartya (2009), "Capitalism beyond the Crisis," *New York Review of Books*, vol. 56, no. 5, p. 3, www.nybooks.com/articles/22490, accessed on May 14, 2009.

Senik-Leygonie, Claudia and Gordon Hughes (1992), "Industrial Profitability and Trade among the Former Soviet Republics," *Economic Policy*, vol. 7, no. 2, pp. 354–86.

Shepsle, Kenneth A. (1989), "Studying Institutions: Some Lessons from the Rational Choice Approach," *Journal of Theoretical Politics*, vol. 1, no. 2, pp. 131–47.

(1991), "Discretion, Institutions and the Problem of Government Commitment," in Pierre Bourdieu and James Coleman (eds.), *Social Theory for a Changing Society*, Boulder, CO: Western Press.

(2008), "Rational Choice Institutionalism," in R. A. W. Rhodes, Sarah A. Binder, and Bert A. Rockman (eds.), *The Oxford Handbook of Political Institutions*, Oxford: Oxford University Press, pp. 23–38.

Shleifer, Andrei and Robert Vishny (1998), *The Grabbing Hand: Government Pathologies and Their Cures*, Cambridge, MA: Harvard University Press.

Simmel, Georg (1955), *Conflict and the Web of Group Affiliations*, Glencoe, IL: Free Press.

Simon, Herbert (1957), *Models of Man*, New York: Wiley.

(1991), "Organizations and Markets," *Journal of Economic Perspectives*, vol. 5, pp. 25–44.

Skocpol, Theda (1979), *States and Social Revolutions: A Comparative Analysis of France, Russia and China*, Cambridge: Cambridge University Press.

Small, Albion W. (1907), *Adam Smith and Modern Sociology: A Study in the Methodology of the Social Sciences*, Chicago: University of Chicago Press.

Smelser, Neil J. and Richard Swedberg (1994), "The Sociological Perspective on the Economy," in Smelser and Swedberg (eds.), *The Handbook of Economic Sociology*, Princeton, NJ: Princeton University Press, pp. 3–26.

Smith, Adam (1976), *The Theory of Moral Sentiments*, Indianapolis: Liberty Classics. (The original was published in a first edition 1759 and in a sixth and last edition in 1790, only weeks before the author's death.)

(2000), *The Wealth of Nations*, New York: Modern Library. (The original was published in 1776, under the somewhat more elaborate title *An Inquiry into the Nature and Causes of the Wealth of Nations*.)

Snooks, Graeme D. (ed.) (1993a), *Historical Analysis in Economics*, London: Routledge.

Snooks, Graeme D. (1993b), "The Lost Dimension: Limitations of a Timeless Economics," in Snooks (ed.), *Historical Analysis in Economics*, London: Routledge, pp. 41–66.

Solow, Robert (1985), "Economic History and Economics," *American Economic Review*, vol. 75, no. 2, pp. 328–31.

Soto, Hernando de (2000), *The Mystery of Capital: Why Capitalism Triumphs in the West and Fails Everywhere Else*, New York: Basic Books.

Steffens, Lincoln (1931), *The Autobiography of Lincoln Steffens*, New York: Literary Guild.

Stiglitz, Joseph E. (1999), "Whither Reform? Ten Years of the Transition," http://siteresources.worldbank.org/INTABCDEWASHINGTON1999/Resources/stiglitz.pdf, accessed on October 1, 2009.

Sutela, Pekka (1984), *Socialism, Planning and Optimality: A Study in Soviet Economic Thought*, Helsinki: Finnish Society of Sciences and Letters.

Swedberg, Richard (1987), "Economic Sociology: Past and Present," *Current Sociology*, vol. 35, no. 1, pp. 1–221.

(1990), *Economics and Sociology: Redefining Their Boundaries: Conversations with Economists and Sociologists*, Princeton, NJ: Princeton University Press.

(1997), "New Economic Sociology: What Has Been Accomplished, What Is Ahead?," *Acta Sociologica*, vol. 40, pp. 161–82.

Szamuely, László (1974), *First Models of the Socialist Economic Systems: Principles and Theories*, Budapest: Akademiai Kiadó.

Thelen, Kathleen and Sven Steinmo (1992), "Historical Institutionalism in Comparative Politics," in Sven Steinmo, Kathleen Thelen, and Frank Longstreth (1992), *Structuring Politics: Historical Institutionalism in Comparative Analysis*, New York: Cambridge University Press, pp. 1–32.

Thelen, Kathleen (1999), "Historical Institutionalism in Comparative Politics," *Annual Review of Political Science*, vol. 2, no. 1, pp. 369–404.

Thompson, William (1963), *An Inquiry into the Principles of the Distribution of Wealth, Most Conducive to Human Happiness*, New York: Augustus M. Kelley.

Tinbergen, Jan (1961), "Do Communist and Free Economies Show a Converging Pattern?," *Soviet Studies*, vol. 12, no. 4, pp. 333–41.

Tiner, John H. (1975), *Isaac Newton: The True Story of His Life as Inventor, Scientist and Teacher*, Milford, MI: Mott Media.

Tocqueville, Alexis de (1945), *Democracy in America*, New York: Alfred A. Knopf. (The French original was published in two volumes, in 1835 and 1840, under the title *De la Démocracie en Amérique*.)

Vallance, Edward (2006), *The Glorious Revolution, 1688: Britain's Fight for Liberty*, London: Little, Brown.

Vasiliev, Sergei A. (1997), "Economic Reform in Russia: Social, Political and Institutional Aspects," in Anders Aslund (ed.), *Russia's Economic Transformation in the 1990s*, London: Pinter, pp. 25–37.

Veblen, Thorstein (1898), "Why Is Economics Not an Evolutionary Science?," *Quarterly Journal of Economics*, vol. 12, no. 4, pp. 373–97.

(1899), *The Theory of the Leisure Class: An Economic Study in the Evolution of Institutions*, New York: Macmillan.

(1917), *An Inquiry into the Nature of Peace and the Terms of its Perpetuation*, New York: Macmillan.

Volin, Lazar (1970), *A Century of Russian Agriculture: From Alexander II to Khrushchev*, Cambridge, MA: Harvard University Press.

Voltaire (2000), *Treatise on Tolerance*, New York: Cambridge University Press. (Translated by Brian Masters; translated and edited by Simon Harvey. Original published in 1763.)

Voslensky, Michael (1984), *Nomenklatura: The Soviet Ruling Class*, Garden City, NY: Doubleday.

Waller, William T. Jr. (1982), "The Evolution of the Veblenian Dichotomy: Veblen, Hamilton, Ayres, and Foster," *Journal of Economic Issues*, vol. 16, no. 3, pp. 757–71.

Wallis, John J. and Douglass C. North (1986), "Measuring the Transaction Sector in the American Economy," in Stanley Engerman and Robert E. Gallman (eds.), *Long-Term Factors in American Growth*, Chicago: University of Chicago Press, pp. 95–161.

Walras, Léon (1874), *Éléments d'économie politique pure ou Théorie de la richesse sociale*, Lausanne: Imprimerie L. Corbaz & Cie.

Webb, Sidney and Beatrice (1935), *Soviet Communism: A New Civilisation?*, London: Longmans, Green.

Weber, Max (1904/05), "Die protestantische Ethik und der Geist des Kapitalismus," *Archiv für Sozialwissenschaften und Sozialpolitik*, vol. 20, no. 1, pp. 1–54, vol. 21, no. 1, pp. 1–110.

(1922), *Wirtschaft und Gesellschaft*, Tübingen: J. C. B. Mohr (P. Siebeck).

(1946a), "The Social Psychology of the World Religions," in H. H. Gerth and C. Wright Mills (trans. and eds.), *From Max Weber: Essays in Sociology*, New York: Oxford University Press, pp. 267–301.

(1946b), "The Protestant Sects and the Spirit of Capitalism," in H. H. Gerth and C. Wright Mills (trans. and eds.), *From Max Weber: Essays in Sociology*, New York: Oxford University Press, pp. 302–22.

(1961), *General Economic History*, New York: Collier Books.

(2001), *The Protestant Ethic and the Spirit of* Capitalism, London: Routledge. (Original published in 1904/05.)

Wedel, Janine R. (1998), *Collision and Collusion: The Strange Case of Western Aid to Eastern Europe 1989–98*, New York: St. Martin's.

(2000), "Tainted Transactions: Harvard, the Chubais Clan and Russia's Ruin," *The National Interest*, no. 59, spring, pp. 23–34.

Weingast, Barry R. (1993), "Constitutions as Governance Structures: The Political Foundations of Secure Markets," *Journal of Institutional and Theoretical Economics*, vol. 149, no. 1, pp. 286–311.

Weingast, Barry (1996), "Political Institutions: Rational Choice Perspectives," in Robert E. Goodin and Hans-Dieter Klingemann (eds.), *A New Handbook of Political Science*, Oxford: Oxford University Press, pp. 167–90.

(2002), "Rational Choice Institutionalism," in Ira Katznelson and Helen V. Milner (eds.), *Political Science: The State of the Discipline*, New York: Norton, pp. 660–92.

Weitzman, Martin (1974), "Prices versus Quantities," *Review of Economic Studies*, vol. 41, no. 4, pp. 477–91.

White, Harrison (1981), "Where Do Markets Come From?," *American Journal of Sociology*, vol. 87, no. 3, pp. 517–47.

Williamson, John (ed.) (1990), *Latin American Adjustment: How Much Has Happened?* Washington, DC: Institute for International Economics.

Williamson, John (1993), "Democracy and the 'Washington Consensus,'" *World Development*, vol. 21, no. 8, pp. 1329–36.

Williamson, Oliver E. (1975), *Markets and Hierarchies: Analysis and Antitrust Implications*, New York: Free Press.

(1985a), *The Economic Institutions of Capitalism*, New York: Free Press.

(1985b), "Reflections on the New Institutional Economics," *Journal of Institutional and Theoretical Economics*, vol. 141, no. 1, pp. 187–95.

(1994), "Transaction Cost Economics and Organization Theory," in Smelser and Swedberg (eds.), *The Handbook of Economic Sociology*, Princeton, NJ: Princeton University Press, pp. 77–107.

(1995), "The Institutions and Governance of Economic Development," *Proceedings of the World Bank Annual Conference on Development Economics 1994*, Washington, DC: World Bank, pp. 171–97.

(1996), *The Mechanisms of Governance*, New York: Oxford University Press.

(1998), "Transaction Cost Economics: How It Works; Where It Is Headed," *De Economist*, vol. 146, no. 1, pp. 23–58.

(2000), "The New Institutional Economics: Taking Stock, Looking Ahead," *Journal of Economic Literature*, vol. 38, no. 3, pp. 595–613.

Winter, Ella (1933), *Red Virtue: Human Relationships in the New Russia*, New York: Harcourt, Brace.

Yakovlev, Alexander M. (1995), "The Rule-of-Law Ideal and Russian Reality," in Stanislaw Frankowski and Paul B. Stephan III (eds.), *Legal Reform in Post-Communist Europe: The View from Within*, Dordrecht: Martinus Nijhoff, pp. 5–19.

Yanov, Alexander (1981), *The Origins of Autocracy: Ivan the Terrible in Russian History*, Berkeley: University of California Press.

(1984), *The Drama of the Soviet 1960s: A Lost Reform*, Berkeley: CA: Institute of International Studies.

Yonay, Yuval P. (1998), *The Struggle over the Soul of Economics: Institutionalist and Neoclassical Economists in America between the Wars*, Princeton, NJ: Princeton University Press.

Zinoviev, Alexander (1979), *The Yawning Heights*, New York: Random House.

Zukin, Sharon and Paul DiMaggio (1990), "Introduction," in Zukin and DiMaggio (eds.), *Structures of Capital: The Social Organization of the Economy*, New York: Cambridge University Press, pp. 1–36.

Zweynert, Joachim (2009), "Interests versus Culture in the Theory of Institutional Change," *Journal of Institutional Economics*, vol. 5, no. 3, pp. 339–60.

Index